THE
RELIGION TOOLKIT

John Morreall and Tamara Sonn

THE
RELIGION TOOLKIT

A Complete Guide to Religious Studies

WILEY-BLACKWELL

A John Wiley & Sons, Ltd., Publication

This edition first published 2012
© 2012 John Morreall and Tamara Sonn

Blackwell Publishing was acquired by John Wiley & Sons in February 2007. Blackwell's publishing
program has been merged with Wiley's global Scientific, Technical, and Medical business to form
Wiley-Blackwell.

Registered Office
John Wiley & Sons Ltd, The Atrium, Southern Gate, Chichester, West Sussex,
PO19 8SQ, United Kingdom

Editorial Offices
350 Main Street, Malden, MA 02148-5020, USA
9600 Garsington Road, Oxford, OX4 2DQ, UK
The Atrium, Southern Gate, Chichester, West Sussex, PO19 8SQ, UK

For details of our global editorial offices, for customer services, and for information about how
to apply for permission to reuse the copyright material in this book please see our website at
www.wiley.com/wiley-blackwell.

The right of John Morreall and Tamara Sonn to be identified as the authors of this work been asserted
in accordance with the UK Copyright, Designs and Patents Act 1988.

Library of Congress Cataloging-in-Publication Data

Morreall, John.
  The religion toolkit: a complete guide to religious studies / John Morreall, Tamara Sonn.
    p.   cm.
  Includes bibliographical references and index.
  ISBN 978-1-4051-8247-8 (hardback) – ISBN 978-1-4051-8246-1 (paperback)
1. Religion—Study and teaching.   2. Religion—Research.   I. Sonn, Tamara.   II. Title.
BL41.M625 2011
200—dc22

                                        2011010576

A catalogue record for this book is available from the British Library.

This book is published in the following electronic formats: ePDFs 9781444343700;
mobi 9781444343724; ePub 9781444343717

Set in 10/13pt Minion by SPi Publisher Services, Pondicherry, India

Printed and bound in Singapore by Markono Print Media Pte Ltd

1   2012

Wherever we are,
whatever the tune,
we dance in the light
of the very same moon.

BRIEF CONTENTS

List of Figures and Maps xiii

Timeline xvi

Acknowledgments xxii

Credits xxiii

1 Introduction: Prepare to Be Surprised 2

PART I THE TOOLS 15

2 An Overview of Religion: Making Sense of Life 16

3 The Early Development of Religious Studies 44

4 Religious Studies in the 20th Century 76

PART II USING THE TOOLS: SURVEYING WORLD RELIGIONS 103

5 Early Traditions 104

6 The Family of Western Monotheisms: Jewish, Christian, and Islamic Traditions 124

   UNIT I Judaism 126

   UNIT II Christianity 151

   UNIT III Islam 167

   UNIT IV The Impact of Religious Studies on the Western Monotheisms 183

7 330 Million Gods – or None: Two Traditions from India 206

8 Balancing and Blending: Confucianism, Taoism, and Buddhism in China 246

9 Zoroastrianism, Shinto, Baha'i, Scientology, Wicca, and
Seneca Traditions: What Makes a "World Religion"? 274

10 Closing Questions 308

Glossary 338

Index 344

CONTENTS

List of Figures and Maps xiii
Timeline xvi
Acknowledgments xxii
Credits xxiii

1   **Introduction: Prepare to Be Surprised** 2

PART I THE TOOLS 15

2   **An Overview of Religion: Making Sense of Life** 16

Explaining Suffering and Evil 18

Explaining Death 22
Ghosts 23
Resurrection 24
Souls 25
Reincarnation 26

The Importance of Order 26
Order Out of Chaos 27
Order and Predictability: Eschatology, Prophecy, Divination 27
Social Order 30
Group Identity 31
Ethics/Morality and Law 34
Authority and Power 37

The Role of Ritual 39

Conclusion 41

3   **The Early Development of Religious Studies** 44

Philosophy, Theology, and Religious Studies 47
The Relationship between Philosophy and Theology 48
Two Kinds of Christian Theology 50

Scriptural (Biblical) Studies and the Impact of the Printing Press 52
Baruch Spinoza (d. 1677): The Beginnings of Source Criticism 53
William Robertson Smith (d. 1894): Historical Criticism 54

The Rise of Modernity and New Academic Disciplines: Oriental Studies, Anthropology, Sociology, and Psychology 55
Max Müller (d. 1900): Oriental Studies and Religion 57
Edward Burnett Tylor (d. 1917): Anthropology and Religion 58
James Frazer (d. 1941): Evolution and Religion 61

Negative Views of Religion 65
Karl Marx (d. 1883): Religion as the Opiate of the Masses 65
Sigmund Freud (d. 1939): Religion as Neurosis 68

Sociology of Religion 71
Emile Durkheim (d. 1917): Modernization Theory 71

Max Weber (d. 1920): The Protestant Ethic and the Secularization Thesis 72

Conclusion 74

4 Religious Studies in the 20th Century 76

Back to Philosophy 80
  Analytic Philosophy: Antony Flew (d. 2010) 81
  Phenomenology and Religious Studies 82
    Rudolf Otto (d. 1937) 82
    Mircea Eliade (d. 1986) 83

Philosophy of Religion 85
  John Hick (b. 1922) 85
  William Lane Craig (b. 1949) 87

Anthropology of Religion 89
  Clifford Geertz (d. 2006) 89
  Mary Douglas (d. 2007) 91

Sociology of Religion 94
  Peter L. Berger (b. 1929) 94
  Robert N. Bellah (b. 1927) 95

Psychology of Religion 96
  William James (d. 1910) 96
  Carl Jung (d. 1961) 98

Conclusion: Theories and Methods 99
  Philosophical Theories 99
  Genetic/Historical Theories 100
  Functionalist Theories 100

PART II USING THE TOOLS: SURVEYING WORLD RELIGIONS 103

5 Early Traditions 104

Prehistoric Religions? 107
  Animism and Anthropomorphism 108
  Death Rituals 112

Fertility Goddesses 113
Hunting Rituals 114
Shamans 114
Ancient Traditions, Oral Traditions, and Religion 115

The Neolithic Revolution and the Rise of Historic Religions 118

Conclusion 121

6 The Family of Western Monotheisms: Jewish, Christian, and Islamic Traditions 124

UNIT I Judaism 126

The Torah, the Hebrew Bible, the Old Testament 127

The History and Teachings of Judaism 135
  The First Five Centuries 135
  The Middle Ages (500–1500 CE) 137
  The Modern Period (1750 to the present) 141
    The Enlightenment 141
    The Development of Reform Judaism 142
    Conservative Judaism 148
    Reconstructionist Judaism 148

The Rituals of Judaism 149

Judaism Today 150

UNIT II Christianity 151

The History and Teachings of Christianity 151
  Origins 151
  The Development of Christian Doctrine 154
    The Institutionalization and Politicization of Christianity 157
    Eastern and Western Christians 159
      The Western/Roman Church 160
      The Eastern Orthodox Churches 163
  The Protestant Reformation 164

Christian Rituals 166

Christianity Today 166

UNIT III Islam 167

The History and Teachings of Islam 167
    Core Teachings 167
    Early History: The Life of Muhammad
      and the Rashidun Caliphs 174
    The Dynastic Caliphates 176
    The Modern Period: Reform
      and Recovery 179

Islamic Rituals 180

Major Divisions Today 182

UNIT IV The Impact of Religious
Studies on the Western
Monotheisms 183

Biblical Studies 184
    Rudolf Bultmann (d. 1976):
      "Demythologizing" Scripture 185
    John Dominic Crossan (b. 1934):
      The Historicity of Scripture 186

Theology 192
    Liberation Theology 192
      Gustavo Gutierrez (b. 1928) 192
      Farid Esack (b. 1959) 194
    Feminist Theology 196
      Judith Plaskow (b. 1947) 198
      Rosemary Radford Ruether
        (b. 1936) 199
      Amina Wadud (b. 1952) 201

Conclusion 203

7 **330 Million Gods – or None: Two
Traditions from India** 206

Hinduism and Buddhism 208

Hinduism 209
    History and Teachings of Hinduism 211
      *Indus Valley Civilization
        (3000–1500 BCE)* 211

*The Aryans and the Vedas
   (1500–600 BCE)* 211
*The Mystical Worldview of the
   Upanishads* 213
*Classical Hinduism (3rd century BCE–7th
   century CE)* 216
   The Ramayana 216
   The Mahabharata 217
   The Puranas 221
   The Laws of Manu 223
Hinduism Today 226
Rituals 226

Buddhism 229
    History and Teachings of Buddhism 230
      *Understanding the Four Noble
        Truths* 233
      The Ethics of "Awakening" 235
      The Core of All Buddhist Traditions 235
      *The Development of the Three Main
        Traditions* 237
        Theravada (Hinayana) 238
        Mahayana 238
        Vajrayana 240
    Buddhism Today 242
    Rituals 243

Conclusion: Religious Studies and Indian
    Traditions 244

8 **Balancing and Blending:
Confucianism, Taoism, and
Buddhism in China** 246

The Tao, Yin and Yang 248

The History of Chinese Religious Thought 251
    The Shang Period (18th–11th
      centuries BCE) 251
    The Zhou Period (11th–3rd centuries BCE) 253

Confucius (551–479 BCE) 255

Taoism 258

Buddhism in China 260
    Pure Land Buddhism 262
    Chan (Zen) Buddhism 262

Chinese Folk Traditions 265

Rituals in Chinese Traditions 266
    Weddings 267
    Funerals 267

Chinese Traditions Today 269

Conclusion: Religious Studies and the
    Traditions of China 271

**9 Zoroastrianism, Shinto, Baha'i,
Scientology, Wicca, and Seneca
Traditions: What Makes a "World
Religion"?** 274

What Makes a "World Religion"? 276

Zoroastrianism 278
    History and Teachings of Zoroastrianism 278
    Zoroastrian Rituals 281

Shinto 283
    History and Teachings of Shinto 283
    Shinto Rituals 285

Baha'i 287
    History and Teachings of Baha'i 287
    Baha'i Rituals 289

Scientology 291
    History and Teachings of Scientology 291
    Scientology Practices 292
    Scientology Rituals 293

Wicca 294
    History and Teachings of Wicca 294
    Wiccan Rituals 296

The Traditions of the Seneca 298
    History and Teachings of the
        Seneca 298
    Seneca Rituals 302

Conclusion: To Be or Not to Be a
    Religion? 304

10 Closing Questions 308

Can We Define Religion? 310

Secularization? 311
    Contemporary Atheist Views 311
    Contemporary Opposition to Secularization
        Theory 313
        Resurgent Islam 313
        Resurgent Religion in the U.S.? 315
        Secularization in Europe 318
    Religion Revisited 319

Other Issues 322
    The Range of Research Areas in the
        American Academy of Religion 322
    Medical Science and Religion 326
        Religion and Physical Health 327
        Religion and Mental Health 329
        Does Prayer Work? 330
        *Brain Science and Mystical Experience:
          Neurotheology* 330
Conclusion: Another Surprise? 335

Glossary 338
Index 344

FIGURES AND MAPS

Figures

1.1 "That's what they all say, honey" 2
1.2 A temple of Ganesha 8
1.3 *Ostara, Goddess of the Dawn* 9
1.4 Slave 11
1.5 Pope John Paul II 13
2.1 "Actually, I preferred 'Heaven' too, but then the marketing guys got a hold of it" 16
2.2 Luca Signorelli (1450–1523), *The Resurrection of the Dead* 25
2.3 Victor Vasnetsov, *Four Horsemen of the Apocalypse (War, Famine, Pestilence and Death)*, 1887 28
2.4 Hammurabi before a god 38
2.5 Prayer for the auto industry 40
3.1 "Theologian? You guys are always fun" 44
3.2 Aristotle 49
3.3 Baruch Spinoza 53
3.4 Max Müller 57
3.5 Edward Burnett Tylor 59
3.6 Cargo cults 63
3.7 Karl Marx 66
3.8 Sigmund Freud 68
4.1 "I had a nice chat with my trainer today about Allah" 76
4.2 Mircea Eliade 83
4.3 Rangda the Witch, mask, Bali 90
4.4 Rats at Karni Mata, "Rat Temple," in Rajasthan, India 92
4.5 William James 97
5.1 "Couldn't be a man. Must be a god!" 104
5.2 Caves in Lascaux, France 108
5.3 Face in rock – Mars 109
5.4 Nun Bun, Tennessee 1996 110
5.5 The Makapansgat cobble/pebble 110
5.6 Rock person, Morocco 111
5.7 Venus of Willendorf 113
5.8 Image from a cave in Ariège, France, of a man/stag, painted and engraved about 13,000 BCE 115
5.9 Photo of shaman 116
5.10 Wall carving from the Temple of Horus at Edfu in Egypt 121
6.1 "I'm calling it 'Genesis.' It's part of a five-book contract" 124
6.2 Clay figure of Asherah 132

6.3 Yochanan Ben Zakai Synagogue in Jerusalem's Old City 136
6.4 First page of the Babylonian Talmud 139
6.5 Rebbe Menachem Schneerson 142
6.6 Moses Mendelssohn 147
6.7 At his Bar Mitzvah ceremony, a young man holds the Torah Scrolls 149
6.8 Statue of Jesus Christ the Redeemer above Rio de Janiero, Brazil 152
6.9 Woman baptized in the Jordan River 156
6.10 *In hoc signo vinces* 157
6.11 Greek Orthodox priests, Palm Sunday procession 164
6.12 Indian Muslims praying 168
6.13 A page from a 14th-century Qur'an 169
6.14 Mevlevis, known as Whirling Dervishes for their spinning spiritual dance, are followers of Rumi 178
6.15 Pilgrims walking around the Kaaba in Mecca during the Hajj 182
6.16 Rudolf Bultmann 185
6.17 Sculpture of Romulus and Remus suckling under a wolf 188
6.18 The Creation Museum in Petersburg, Kentucky 191
6.19 Farid Esack 195
6.20 Rosemary Radford Ruether 200
6.21 Amina Wadud 202
7.1 "I imagine serenity's pretty much the same, one season to the next?" 206
7.2 Men conduct ritual for Durga, who is worshipped during Navaratri 210
7.3 Arjuna and Krishna 217
7.4 Woman bending backwards – hatha yoga 219
7.5 Statue of Sarasvati outside music college in Puttaparthi 220
7.6 Shiva as Lord of the Dance 222
7.7 Shaivite with marks on forehead 222
7.8 Vaishnavite with marks on forehead 223
7.9 Dalits, Untouchables, at an anti-government rally, 2006 224
7.10 Carvings on the outside of Khajuraho temple 225
7.11 Students celebrating Holi 227
7.12 Mohandas Gandhi 228
7.13 Sculpture of the Buddha near starvation 231
7.14 The Great Stupa at Sanchi, Madhya Pradesh in India 233
7.15 Buddhist laypeople putting food into the bowls of monks 237
7.16 Statue of the Bodhisattva Kannon with blue sky 239
7.17 Tenzin Gyatso, the 14th Dalai Lama, is the best known representative of Vajrayana Buddhism 241
8.1 "Nothing happens next. This is it" 246
8.2 Help one another, for we are all in the same boat – old Chinese saying 248
8.3 Part of a giant traditional Chinese landscape painting: A Trip to Hills and Lakes in Spring by Chen Minglou 249
8.4 Yin–yang 250
8.5 An oracle bone with writing on it 252
8.6 Lao Tzu, riding his legendary "green" buffalo, Chinese, 18th century 258
8.7 A painting of Confucius, Lao Tzu, and the Buddha together by Kano Masonobu, 1480 261
8.8 Meditating frog, painting by Sengai 264
8.9 Traditional Chinese wedding 268
8.10 Mao Zedong 269
9.1 "Put up with thy neighbor" 274
9.2 Wiccan Beltane Fire Festival, Edinburgh, spring 2008 277

FIGURES AND MAPS

9.3   Freddie Mercury 280

9.4   A Zoroastrian priest starts a fire as part of Sadeh, the ancient feast celebrating the creation of fire 282

9.5   *Kami kaze* – "the wind of the kami" or "divine wind" 284

9.6   A Shinto shrine with a torii gate 286

9.7   Dizzy Gillespie 289

9.8   Baha'i temple in Wilmette, Illinois, in the U.S. 290

9.9   The Hubbard Professional Mark Super VII E-Meter 293

9.10   Calling the elements (earth, air, fire, water, and aether) – part of a Wiccan ritual of handfasting (marriage) 295

9.11   The Wiccan pentagram 296

9.12   Dancers from the Allegany and Cattaraugus Reservations of the Seneca Nation of Indians perform at St. Bonaventure University's first Native American Heritage Celebration in 2008 299

9.13   Portrait of Red Jacket by John Lee Mathies, oil on canvas, 1828 301

10.1   "I guess this is where we part ways" 308

10.2   A megachurch service, Katedral Mesias, Jakarta 315

10.3   Pilgrims visiting the grotto at Lourdes, France 327

10.4   A mystic in India 333

Maps

6.1   Map of the Ancient Near East 130

6.2   Map of the Roman Empire – East and West 160

6.3   Spread of Islam in the 1st century 172

TIMELINE

3000–1500 BCE	Cities are built in the Indus Valley.
c.2100 BCE	Abraham is called by God.
c.2000 BCE	Jacob, a descendant of Abraham through his son Isaac, is born; later he is called Israel. Thus the descendants of Abraham through this line are called the people of Israel (or Israelites).
c.1900 BCE	Joseph, a son of Jacob, is sold into slavery in Egypt. The Israelites eventually become captives there.
c.1766–1046 BCE	The Shang Dynasty.
c.1440 BCE	Led by Moses, the Israelites leave Egypt and after 40 years settle in the land of Canaan. During the trip, the Exodus, God describes himself to Moses as Yahweh.
1200–900 BCE	Early Vedic Period – the first Vedas are compiled.
c.1046–256 BCE	The Zhou Dynasty.
c.1010 BCE	David becomes king of the Israelites, and makes Jerusalem his capital.
c.970 BCE	David's son Solomon becomes king and later builds a temple in Jerusalem to honor the God of Israel.
930 BCE	After Solomon's death, his kingdom is divided into a northern kingdom led by the tribes of Israel and a southern kingdom led by the tribe of Judah.
900–600 BCE	Late Vedic period – the religion of the Brahmins emphasizes sacrifice and social obligation.
800–300 BCE	The 11 major Upanishads are written; they include the ideas of reincarnation and karma.
722 BCE	The kingdom of Israel is destroyed by the Assyrians.
612 BCE	The Babylonians conquer the Assyrians.
c.604 BCE	Lao Tzu is born.
586 BCE	The Babylonians defeat the kingdom of Judah, capture Jerusalem, and destroy Solomon's temple. Many members of the kingdom of Judah are taken into captivity in Babylon (the Exile).
c.566–486 BCE	Siddhartha Gautama is born, becomes enlightened, and preaches in India.
551–479 BCE	Confucius lives.
c.538 BCE	Many of the exiled members of the tribe of Judah return to Jerusalem, and begin the rebuilding of the temple.

c.486 BCE	The first Buddhist council meets.
c.383 BCE	The second Buddhist council meets, leading to divisions in the community.
371–289 BCE	Mencius lives.
369–286 BCE	Zhuang Tzu lives.
c.330 BCE	The Jews (as the descendants of the tribe of Judah are called) are conquered by Alexander the Great. Greek culture – Hellenism – starts to influence Jewish culture.
c.300 BCE	Buddhism spreads to Southeast Asia.
c.269–232 BCE	Indian emperor Ashoka the Great converts to Buddhism and rules over most of the Indian subcontinent. He sends missionaries to Sri Lanka.
c.250 BCE	The work of translating the Bible from Hebrew into Greek begins. This Greek Bible is called the Septuagint.
c.200 BCE–200 CE	The Laws of Manu are compiled.
1st century BCE	Buddhism enters China and Southeast Asia.
c.100 BCE	The *Bhagavad Gita* is composed.
63 BCE	Roman rulers defeat the Greeks, beginning 700 years of Roman rule of the land they name Palestine.
c.5 BCE	Jesus of Nazareth is born.
c.30 CE	Jesus begins teaching a new interpretation of the law of God to his fellow Jews.
c.32	Jesus is executed by the Roman rulers of Palestine.
c.48	The followers of Jesus hold a meeting in Jerusalem and accept Gentiles (non-Jews) into their community.
70	A Jewish rebellion against the Roman rulers ends with the destruction of the temple in Jerusalem.
c.70	The first Gospel is written – Mark.
c.80–90	The Gospels of Matthew and Luke are written.
c.90–100	The Book of Revelation and the Gospel of John are written.
c.150–250	Nagarjuna develops his Doctrine of Emptiness.
161–180	Under the Roman emperor Marcus Aurelius, there is widespread persecution of Christians.
175	The Five Classics, carved in stone, are displayed in China's capital.
c.200	The Mishnah is compiled and committed to writing.
c.250	The third Buddhist council leads to split between Theravada and Mahayana Buddhism.

312	The Roman emperor Constantine defeats his rival, Maxentius, after having his soldiers paint a Christian symbol on their equipment.
313	Constantine issues the Edict of Milan, making Christianity legal in the Roman empire.
325	Constantine holds a meeting of Christian leaders ("ecumenical council"), at Nicea, to overcome disagreement in their interpretations. They agree on a list of beliefs known as the Nicene Creed.
350–650	The Gupta Dynasty rules in India. Buddhist philosophy and art flourish.
367	Saint Athanasius compiles a list of the 27 books now known as the New Testament.
381	At an ecumenical council at Constantinople, Christian leaders continue their debates and revise the Nicene creed to its current form.
4th century	Vajrayana Buddhism begins.
c.400	The Palestinian Talmud is completed.
	Buddhism enters Korea.
431	Christian leaders meet at Chalcedon, and declare Mary, the mother of Jesus, to be Theotokos, "God-bearer," "Mother of God."
449	Pope Leo asserts the supremacy of the Bishop of Rome over other bishops.
520	The Buddhist missionary Bodhidharma arrives in China.
527	Korea accepts Buddhism.
552	Buddhism enters Japan from Korea.
c.570	Muhammad is born in Mecca.
572–621	Prince Shotoku sponsors Buddhism in Japan.
c.589	Chinese Buddhist commentaries are written.
6th century	Burma accepts Theravada Buddhism.
600	The Babylonian Talmud is completed.
600s	Mahayana Buddhism is adopted in Indonesia.
c.600–650	Buddhism enters and spreads in Tibet.
c.600–1600	Devotional Hinduism becomes popular.
610	Muhammad receives his first revelation from God and begins to teach a new interpretation of the will of God.
618–907	T'ang Dynasty, the golden age of Buddhism in China.
	Pure Land and Chan Buddhism develop.
622	Muhammad and his followers complete their emigration (*hijra*) from Mecca to Medina, marked as the beginning of the Islamic calendar.

630	Muhammad gains control over Mecca, and rededicates its shrine – the Kaaba – to the one God/Allah.
632	Muhammad dies. His close companion Abu Bakr is recognized by the majority as "Leader of the Believers."
	Muhammad's companion Umar succeeds Abu Bakr as Leader of the Believers, and begins the process of expanding Muslim rule throughout the region.
638	Muslim forces defeat the Romans and take control of Jerusalem.
644	Muslims complete their defeat of Persian forces.
c.650	God's revelation through Muhammad, known as the Qur'an, is committed to writing.
661	The Ummayads take control of the Islamic empire, establishing their capital at Damascus and continuing expansion of Islamic sovereignty.
700s	Buddhism becomes the state religion of Japan.
711	The Umayyads establish control of part of Spain.
732	Muslim westward expansion is halted at the Battle of Tours.
740	Mahayana Buddhism is established in Tibet.
750	The Umayyad dynasty ("caliphate") is replaced by the Abbasids, who will establish Baghdad as their capital.
c.792–794	Indian Mahayana Buddhism is chosen as the form of Buddhism for Tibet.
800	Charlemagne is crowned Emperor of the Holy Roman Empire by Pope Leo III.
845	Chinese emperor Wu Tsang persecutes Buddhists.
early 900s	Korea institutes a Buddhist constitution.
1054	The Eastern Orthodox and the Western Catholic churches split.
1095	Pope Urban II authorizes the first Crusade to recover the "Holy Land" from Muslims.
1099	European Christian "Crusaders" capture Jerusalem.
c.1150	Buddhism is almost extinct in India.
1185–1333	Kamakura period in Japan.
	Rinzai, Soto Zen, Pure Land, True Pure Land, and Nichiren Buddhism.
1187	Jerusalem is recaptured by a Muslim army led by Salah al-Din (Saladin).
1231–1259	Mongols invade Korea and destroy Buddhist scriptures.
1253	Mongolian leader Kublai Khan accepts Tibetan Buddhism.
1258	The Mongols destroy Baghdad and end Abbasid rule.
1360	Theravada Buddhism becomes the state religion of Thailand.
1392	Confucianism is made the state religion of Korea.

14th century	Theravada Buddhism comes into Laos.
1453	The Ottoman Turks conquer Constantinople and change its name to Istanbul.
1492	The king and queen of Spain expel Muslims and Jews.
1498	Europeans enter southern Asia with the arrival of Vasco da Gama.
15th century	Theravada Buddhism spreads in Cambodia.
1517	Martin Luther writes his 95 Theses in Wittenberg, Germany, beginning the Protestant Reformation.
	The Ottomans claim leadership of the Muslim world.
1526	The Mughal Empire begins in India.
1534	The Act of Supremacy is passed – King Henry VIII becomes head of the English Church.
1536	John Calvin publishes his *Institutes of the Christian Religion*.
1545–1563	The Catholic Council of Trent meets to respond to the Protestant Reformation.
1578	The first Dalai Lama is recognized.
1617–1682	Dalai Lamas begin to rule Tibet.
1618–1648	Protestants and Catholics fight the Thirty Years War in Germany.
c.1700	The British East India Company is formed.
1722	The Saffavid Dynasty is established in Persia.
1730–1760	The "Great Awakening" – a revival movement among Protestants in the United States.
1757	British rule is established in Calcutta.
1828	The French take control of Algeria.
1844	The first Buddhist text is published in the United States, translated by Henry David Thoreau.
1857	The British take control of India.
	The unsuccessful National War of Independence is launched by Indians against the British.
1876	Queen Victoria of England is declared Empress of India.
1895	The Vedanta Society is founded by Vivekananda, to promote Hinduism as a world religion and India as a single nation.
1897	The World Zionist Organization is formed in Basel, Switzerland, advocating emigration to Palestine and creation of a homeland for Jews in response to ongoing discrimination and persistent persecution of Jews in Europe.
1882	The British take control of Egypt.
1910–1945	Reformations of Korean and Chinese Buddhism.
1919	The British take control of Palestine and Mesopotamia (Iraq), and the French take control of Syria and Lebanon, betraying promises of independence made to Arabs in return for their assistance in defeating Turkey and Germany in World War I.

1920	Mohandas (Mahatma) Gandhi starts non-violent campaign against British rule of India.
1931	Zen Buddhist Society is formed in New York.
1939–1945	World War II; culmination of persecution of Jews in Europe in the Holocaust/Shoah, leading to rapid escalation of emigration of European Jews to Palestine and, in turn, conflict with local inhabitants of Palestine.
1945	Religious freedom introduced in Japan.
1947	Britain partitions India into independent states for Hindus and Muslims. The Muslim sections are named East and West Pakistan, separated by over 1,000 miles. Both India and Pakistan are declared independent of Britain.
1948	The United Nations partitions Palestine into Jewish and Arab sections, against the will of local Arab inhabitants. Israel declares itself an independent Jewish state; the Arabs declare war.
	Gandhi is assassinated.
	The World Council of Churches is formed.
1949	The Chinese communist government begins suppressing religions.
1950	Tenzin Gyatso becomes the 14th Dalai Lama.
	China invades Tibet and suppresses Buddhism.
1959	The Dalai Lama goes into exile.
1960–1965	The Roman Catholic Church is modernized by the Second Vatican Council.
1966–1976	The Cultural Revolution suppresses religion, traditional culture in China.
1971	Civil war results in the separation of East Pakistan from West Pakistan. East Pakistan becomes the independent country of Bangladesh.
1976	Death of Mao Zedong.
1989	The International Network of Engaged Buddhists is founded.
1995	The U.K. Association of Buddhist Studies is formed.

ACKNOWLEDGMENTS

WE WOULD LIKE TO THANK OUR COLLEAGUES RAVI GUPTA AND KEVIN VOSE for their careful reading and valuable advice concerning our treatment of Hinduism and Buddhism. Continued gratitude, too, to friends and mentors John Esposito and John Voll for their unfailing inspiration and guidance.

We would also like to express deep appreciation for our William & Mary students; they demand and deserve nothing but the best from their teachers.

Most importantly, our publisher Rebecca Harkin deserves credit for this unique book. It was her idea and she encouraged us every step in the process of giving it life. Any blame due belongs to us alone.

JM
TS

CREDITS

The authors and publisher gratefully acknowledge the permission granted to reproduce the copyright material in this book.

9.10 photo Paul Gapper/www.worldreligions.co.uk.

9.12 photo Tom Donahue.

9.13 Memorial Art Gallery of the University of Rochester, lent by the estate of John W. Brown.

10.1 cartoon © Alex Gregory 2007/The New Yorker Collection/www.cartoonbank.com.

10.2 photo © Enny Nuraheni/Reuters/Corbis.

10.3 photo Mike Blenkinsop/Alamy.

10.4 photo Around the World in a Viewfinder/Alamy.

Every effort has been made to trace copyright holders and to obtain their permission for the use of copyright material. The publisher apologizes for any errors or omissions in the above list and would be grateful if notified of any corrections that should be incorporated in future reprints or editions of this book.

THE
RELIGION TOOLKIT

INTRODUCTION
Prepare to Be Surprised

"That's what they all say, honey."

FIGURE 1.1 © Tom Cheney 1996/The New Yorker Collection/www.cartoonbank.com.

The Religion Toolkit: A Complete Guide to Religious Studies, First Edition. John Morreall and Tamara Sonn.
© 2012 John Morreall and Tamara Sonn. Published 2012 by Blackwell Publishing Ltd.

> *When the missionaries came to Africa, they had the Bible and we had the land. They said, "Let us pray." We closed our eyes. When we opened them, we had the Bible and they had the land.*
>
> **BISHOP DESMOND TUTU**

1

Religion is found around the world and may well be as old as the human race. Some of the earliest evidence of human life found by archaeologists seems to involve religious **ritual**. And throughout history human beings have developed a mind-boggling multiplicity of beliefs and practices that scholars recognize as religious. Today there are over 10,000 distinct traditions identified as religions, and many of these are divided into smaller groups called denominations and sects. According to the *World Christian Encyclopedia*, Christianity alone includes over 9,000 denominations and over 34,000 sects. The diversity within some traditions is so extensive that some scholars do not even use terms like "Judaism" or "Christianity." Instead, they speak of "Judaisms" and "Christianities."

The sheer number of religious groups is only one of the surprises awaiting students of religion. Many are also surprised to discover how different *learning about* religion is from *learning* a religion. The goals and methods of the academic study of religion are quite distinct from those found in the *devotional* or *normative* study of religion. These are terms that describe the approach most people follow when they are taught their own religion. The scholarly approach to learning about religion is so different, in fact, that it is usually called Religious Studies, to distinguish it from the devotional or normative study of religion.

In learning a religion, people are trained to follow it. When people give children lessons in religion, these lessons are about their own religion (or denomination or sect or

What is a Cult?

In ordinary conversation, we may say simply that some people belong to certain religions and other people belong to other religions. But in Religious Studies we make finer distinctions. Scholars have developed several terms to deal with the divisions and subdivisions within religions.

According to the standard vocabulary, a *church* is a religious group that exists in harmony with its social environment, and is sufficiently institutionalized to be passed on from one generation to the next. The term "church" is technically appropriate only for Christianity; people of other religions have different terms for their groups and houses of worship. But "church" is used generically here, so that even Judaism, Islam, and Buddhism count as churches.

A *denomination* is a subset of a church – also existing in harmony within its church and among other denominations, and institutionalized enough to be passed on through the generations. Again, scholars use the term "denomination" for subsets within all religions so that, for example, Reform Judaism is a denomination of Judaism, and Shi'ism is a denomination of Islam.

A *sect* is a subset of a church that does not exist in harmony within its environment or church, although it may eventually come to be accepted within its church and develop institutions to survive generational changes, thus achieving the status of a denomination. An example is The Society of St. Pius X, started in 1970 by French Archbishop Marcel Lefebvre in opposition to recent reforms within the Roman Catholic Church. Archbishop Lefebvre was excommunicated from the Catholic Church when he took upon himself the right to consecrate bishops – a right reserved for the pope. That was in 1988. But in 2009, the Church revoked the excommunication and started a process to integrate members of the Society of St. Pius X back into the Church.

A *cult* is a religious movement that develops outside an established church structure and often exists in tension with socially accepted religious institutions. Scientology is considered by some authorities to be a cult, since it originated outside an established church structure. However, followers of Scientology have organized themselves sufficiently to survive and prosper since their beginning in 1953, and they refer to themselves as members of the Church of Scientology.

While many scholars use these terms as defined above, some reject them as imposing concepts from Christianity onto other religions.

cult). This approach to religion is a kind of initiation into one tradition. Students are taught what their tradition considers true, so that they will be able to distinguish between that and what is false. And they are taught what their tradition considers right and wrong, so that they may do the one and avoid the other. They may learn some of the history of their group, but will probably spend more time learning stories, rituals, and prayers. If, in the process of being trained, they learn about other religions, it is often so that they will understand why their own tradition is right, and what is wrong with the teachings and practices of other traditions.

In Religious Studies, on the other hand, we are not trying to determine what is true or false or right or wrong about any religion's teachings or practices. Our goal is to understand religious traditions, not be trained in them. In doing this, we examine many traditions that are identified as religions without judging any of them. We do study what certain traditions teach is right and wrong, and true and false, and why they teach what they do. But whether we agree with those teachings or not is not part of Religious Studies. When we study the teachings of a single tradition, we may well learn how they changed over time. There, too, we do not judge the truth or rightness of either the old or the new teachings. In other words, in Religious Studies we learn about diversity, both among and within religious traditions, but our goals and methods are like those of scientists rather than those of preachers.

A second goal of Religious Studies is to understand what religion is in the first place. And this holds still more surprises about the field. When you take a course in Accounting, you know that you will be studying how to manipulate numbers for specific purposes. When you sign up for Chemistry 101, you know you will be introduced to the tiny particles that make up the world we see around us. But when you sign up to study a religion other than your own, you may find yourself studying things that you were not aware could be considered religious.

If you think of your own religion as consisting of certain beliefs, rituals, and values, you might expect to study the beliefs, rituals, and values of the other religion. So it often comes as a surprise to students in Religious Studies courses that they may be studying history, anthropology, sociology, psychology, philosophy, and even economics. In Religious Studies we study these things, and more, because many traditions do not confine themselves to beliefs, rituals, and neatly identified values. Some traditions consider themselves simply a way of life, so that everything in life is subject to religious teaching.

Similarly, you may have grown up with the idea that religion is about what is holy or sacred, as opposed to what is worldly or secular. And so you may expect to find that distinction in other traditions. But, as just mentioned, many traditions consider all of life as the domain of religion, and so they do not use the distinction between sacred and secular.

Because the study of religion gets into so many areas, it is necessarily multi-disciplinary. Experts in Religious Studies may have their primary training in any of the fields mentioned above, or others such as Art History and Classics. And this wide-ranging approach to the subject matter of Religious Studies is also why there is so much debate within the field regarding what "religion" is.

The 19th-century German scholar who introduced the term Religious Studies (*Religionswissenschaft*), Max Müller (*see* Chapter 3), is often credited with saying "He who knows one, knows none." His idea is that people who know only their own religion cannot understand the nature of religion itself, just as people who know only one language are not qualified to explain the nature of language itself. Asking someone who knows only one religion what religion is would be like asking a fish what water is. "Compared to what?" would be a reasonable answer. Not until we have at least two examples of something can we try to describe the category to which the two specimens belong.

As we shall see, trying to figure out just what religion is began as soon as scholars started trying to identify religions other than their own. Should tribal practices associated with healing in pre-modern societies be considered religious? In modern industrialized societies we generally leave healing to science, not religion. Should practices designed to influence the thoughts or feelings of someone far away be categorized as religion, or should they be called magic or superstition? Should stories about events that modern science says could not have happened be included in religion, or should they be dismissed as holdovers from a pre-scientific era? Is it even possible to distinguish religious stories from myths, or religion from superstition or magic?

This quest, to understand what religion is, is made even harder by the fact that many languages have no word that means the same thing as "religion" in English. Scholars are not even sure where the term "religion" came from. We know that its root is Latin, but what did it mean in early Latin? The 1st-century BCE philosopher Cicero traces the term to *legere*, to read, so that "religion" would mean to re-read (*re-legere*), but the 4th- to 5th-century CE Christian thinker Augustine traces the term to *ligare*, meaning "to connect or bind" (the same root as the English word "ligament"), so that "religion" would mean "to bind again" or "to reconnect." Many modern theologians favor this etymology, seeing religion as something that binds a community together. However, *A Latin Dictionary* by Lewis and Short traces our modern meaning, "reverence for God or the gods, careful pondering of divine things, [or] piety," only to the 13th century CE. So what word might earlier Christians have used for what modern Christians think of as religion?

To complicate things further, the term that the **sacred** texts of Judaism and Islam use for "religion" means something quite different from any of the Latin roots for "religion." This term is *din*. (It might also be counted as a surprise that in both Hebrew and Arabic, the languages of Judaic and Islamic **scriptures**, the term is the same. Hebrew and Arabic are closely related Semitic languages, and Judaism and Islam are very similar traditions.) *Din* can mean "judgment," as in "Day of *din*" or "Court of *din*." It can also mean "way of life." What is more, the same term is used in modern Persian, but that usage is traced to Zoroastrian (the ancient religion of Persia) texts, where it means "eternal law" or "duty." Similarly, the term from Buddhist texts that sometimes is translated as "religion" is *dharma*. But dharma does not mean what "religion" means in English. Dharma means "cosmic truth" or "the way the world is." It also means the teachings of the Buddha, and "duty," too. *Dharma* is used in Hinduism to mean both "ultimate reality" and human beings' duties.

Scholars may not agree on exactly what "religion" means, but they generally agree that the term is too narrow to refer to all the phenomena that are examined in Religious Studies. As a result, many scholars use the term **tradition** rather than "religion." This may be not only surprising, but confusing. By "tradition" Religious Studies scholars do not mean simply something that people do because it has always been done that way. We use the term "tradition" to refer to the amalgam of a group's beliefs, rules, and customs insofar as they are associated with that group's ultimate concerns, values, and ideas about the meaning of life.

Because of its interest in understanding what "religion" is in general, Religious Studies includes both historic and comparative elements. Religious Studies scholars examine traditions not just as they are now but as they have developed over time. This aspect of

Religious Studies is known as **History of Religions**. The comparative elements of Religious Studies may involve looking at a single religious tradition in various historic periods, tracing any changes that developed. As well, it may involve studying a number of religious traditions within a single historical period. It may also involve comparing and contrasting the ways several religious traditions deal with a certain topic, such as salvation or war. This approach to Religious Studies is called **Comparative Religions**.

The historical and comparative approaches to the study of religious traditions lead to a number of other surprises for the new student. People who are used to religions that revolve around a single God may be surprised to find that some traditions involve many gods and some do not even require belief in a god. In Hinduism, for example, there are countless **deities** (gods) – 330,000,000 is the traditional number given. Some people worship one of them, such as Shiva or Vishnu, some worship several, and others turn to specific deities for assistance, depending upon the need at hand. The deities of some traditions may have a number of personas. The Indian god Vishnu, for example, can be worshipped as Vishnu, or as Rama, Krishna, the Buddha, or any of several other personalities. These diverse **avatars** are considered manifestations of the one god. Moreover, people who are used to conceiving of God in spiritual or non-material terms may be surprised to find gods that are quite physical. A popular god in India is Ganesha, who has the head of an elephant, with one broken tusk, and is variously depicted with two to sixteen arms.

In Western religions such as Judaism, Christianity, and Islam, a central idea is that God has revealed himself and certain truths to human beings, often through messengers called **prophets**. People who believe in divine revelation typically believe that the information transmitted in this way – or at least the most important parts of it – could not have been obtained in any other way. They also consider the written records ("scripture") of that revelation to be extremely special ("sacred" or **holy**) and, in fact, perfect and absolutely true (**inerrant**, without error). However, if we assume that religions must include divine revelation, we have another surprise coming. Many traditions have texts that they consider sacred, even though these texts come from human sources. The Hindu **Upanishads** and Zoroastrian **Avestas** are examples. Moreover, other traditions, those of some Native Americans, for instance, have no sacred texts; they transmit their wisdom in oral form from one generation to the next. The Anishinaabe teachings shared by the Algonquin, Ojibwa, and other tribes of the United States and Canada hold regular meetings to recount, explain, and pass along their Midewiwin teachings in traditional stories (called *aadizookaanan*) to the next generations.

On a related theme, people who are used to **orthodoxy** – the idea that there is a single set of truths – will be surprised as well to find that in traditions such as Hinduism it is considered perfectly normal for some people to believe in one God, while others believe in several gods, and some believe in no god at all. Another way to put that is that, while some traditions are **exclusivist** – believing there is only one true religion, others are pluralist – believing that different people have different traditions and that each of them is legitimate. Religious **pluralism** can even extend to a single person. **Monotheists** – people who believe in one God – tend to think of each person as belonging either to one religion or to none, but in Japan, for instance, most people follow both Buddhism and Shinto – an ancient set of Japanese traditions. When Japanese people want to get married, they may go to a Shinto priest; to arrange a funeral they may go to a Buddhist priest. The same temple may house

FIGURE 1.2 A temple of Ganesha, one of the five most popular gods in India. He is worshipped as the Remover of Obstacles, and also as the Lord of Success. Ganesha is a god of knowledge and wisdom, and so a patron of the arts and sciences. Stuart Forster/Alamy.

both of them. In China and Taiwan, people participate in Buddhist rituals, Taoist rituals, and rituals dedicated to local gods, and they also visit temples dedicated to Confucius.

As Religious Studies explores how various traditions have developed their worldviews, rituals, and rules, more surprises come to light. For example, we often find that a belief or practice we thought was unique within our own tradition is actually shared by a number of

INTRODUCTION: PREPARE TO BE SURPRISED

Who Was Easter?

FIGURE 1.3 *Ostara, Goddess of the Dawn*, by Johannes Gehrts, 1884, from Felix and Therese Dahn, *Walhall: Germanische Gotter und Heldensagen…*, 1901.
SLUB Dresden/Deutsche Fotothek.

The *Oxford English Dictionary* tells us that the word "Easter" – the name of the most sacred day in the Christian calendar, the day commemorating Jesus' resurrection from death – is derived from "Eostre," the name of an ancient goddess of spring. According to *Compton's Encyclopedia*, "Our name Easter comes from Eostre, an ancient Anglo-Saxon goddess, originally of the dawn. In pagan times an annual spring festival was held in her honor." So Eostre was a pre-Christian goddess venerated at the vernal equinox (beginning of spring). The Easter Bunny and the colored eggs at Easter also come from pre-Christian rituals to promote fertility. The *Encyclopaedia Britannica* tells us, "The egg as a symbol of fertility and of renewal of life goes back to the ancient Egyptians and Persians, who had also the custom of coloring and eating eggs during their spring festival."

traditions. Christian students, for example, are often surprised to find that Muslims revere Jesus as a great prophet, and honor his mother Mary with an entire chapter of the **Qur'an** (Islamic scripture) named for her. Islam also shares with Judaism and Christianity the story of Adam and Eve in the Garden of Eden, and the history of prophets from the time of Abraham forward.

It is potentially even more stunning, especially for those from religions with divinely revealed scriptures, that a number of their beliefs are found in texts that pre-date those of Judaism, Christianity, and Islam. Scholars trace the story of Noah and the Flood that appears in the Book of Genesis of the Hebrew Bible (Christian **Old Testament**) and Qur'an, for example, to the Gilgamesh Epic of **Mesopotamia**. In that story, the gods flood the earth, one man is told to build a huge boat, and he brings many kinds of animals on board.

Religious Studies also includes careful (or "critical") study of scripture that often reveals how people's understanding of their own texts has changed. For example, students are often surprised to find that the Hebrew Bible (Christian Old Testament) speaks of a time when there was more than one god, the gods intermarried with humans, and the babies they had were giants:

> When mankind began to increase and to spread all over the earth and daughters were born to them, the sons of the gods saw that the daughters of men were beautiful; so they took for themselves such women as they chose…. In those days, when the sons of the gods mated with the daughters of men and got children by them, the Nephilim [Giants] were on earth. They were the heroes of old, men of renown. (Genesis 6:1–4)

Not only does religious people's understanding of what happened in history change, but their understanding of morality does too. To take a contemporary example, millions of Jews and Christians now work and shop on the **Sabbath** without giving it a second thought, but the Hebrew Bible (Christian Old Testament) condemns work and commerce on the Sabbath. Exodus 31:15 says that "[w]hoever does any work on the Sabbath day must be put to death." In fact, many Jews and Christians took the Sabbath seriously until just a few decades ago, and did not work, or buy or sell things on that day.

Another issue that shows how a tradition can change over time is the morality of war. A book by John Driver is aptly titled *How Christians Made Peace with War*. He explains how, for the first three centuries, Christians followed Jesus' injunction "Do not resist the evildoer. But if someone strikes you on the right cheek, turn to him the other as well…. Love your enemies, and pray for those who persecute you" (Matthew 5:39–44). In the Roman Empire, Christians were well known for their pacifism, and they did not accept soldiers into their group. But then in the fourth century, Christianity became the state religion of the Roman Empire, and soon Christian leaders were talking about "just wars." The 4th- to 5th-century Christian thinker Augustine developed a rationale for wars in order to justify attacking the Donatists, a group of fellow Christians who disagreed with him on some theological issues, and since then Christian scholars have elaborated justifications for war under certain conditions. Similarly, there is lively debate among modern Muslim scholars over whether war may be legally declared at all, and if so, under what conditions.

Is Slavery Wrong?

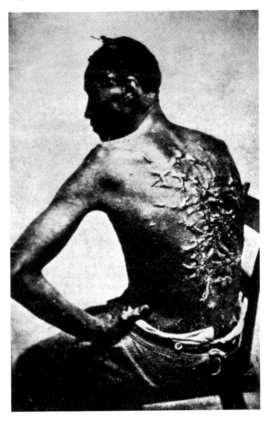

FIGURE 1.4 Slave.
MPI/Getty Images.

All major traditions, including Christianity, now condemn slavery and consider it immoral, but before 1770 none did. John Newton (1725–1807), the Anglican priest who wrote the hymn "Amazing Grace," had earlier been the captain of a ship that transported newly enslaved Africans to slave markets in the Americas. He thought that the job of slave ship captain was spiritually enriching because of the long periods at sea. There was, he wrote, no profession that provided "greater advantages to an awakened mind, for promoting the life of God in the soul."

In the Bible, God not only permits slavery but regulates it. In Exodus 21, right after God gives Moses the Ten Commandments, he says, "When a man sells his daughter as a slave, she shall not go free [after seven years] as male slaves do." In the Christian New Testament, too, Paul says, "Slaves, obey your earthly masters with respect and fear, and with sincerity of heart, just as you would obey Christ" (Ephesians 6:5).

Actually, the whole history of religious traditions includes a lot of killing. Five hundred years ago, the rituals of the Aztecs included the sacrifice of thousands of people, followed by the eating of the corpses. Most of those killed were captives taken in battle. Here is anthropologist Marvin Harris' account of an Aztec religious ritual:

> Forced to ascend the flat-topped pyramids that dominated the city's ceremonial precincts, the victim was seized by four priests, one for each limb, and bent backward face up, over a stone altar. A fifth priest then opened the victim's chest with an obsidian knife, wrenched out the heart, and while it was still beating, smeared it over the nearby statue of the presiding deity. Attendants then rolled the body down the steps. Other attendants cut off the head, pushed a wooden shaft through it from side to side, and placed it on a tall latticework structure or skull rack alongside the heads of previous victims. (Harris 1989, 432)

After they had decapitated the corpse, they cut up the body and distributed it for eating. If these rituals seem brutal, consider the treatment of religious heretics and suspected witches in Europe at the same time: burning at the stake. Again, the point is that in Religious Studies we study not just what people currently believe and practice but also how beliefs and practices change over time.

As these examples show, Religious Studies is about far more than right and wrong, true and false – which are the main concerns when people learn about their own religions. Religious Studies also looks at what people actually do, and so it is not just about the holy and the noble. It is about religion as it is lived, including "The Good, the Bad, and the Ugly." In 1978, for example, a religious group of over 900 people from the United States who had established themselves in Jonestown, Guyana, committed mass suicide at the insistence of their founder, Jim Jones. In an article that has become widely known, leading Religious Studies scholar Jonathan Z. Smith criticized those who felt that Mr. Jones was too far out of the norm to require serious scholarly attention. Some even refused to talk about the event, Smith claimed derisively, "because it revealed what had been concealed from public, academic discussion for a century – that religion has rarely been a positive, liberal force. Religion is not nice; it has been responsible for more death and suffering than any other human activity" (Smith 1982, 104).

Some students taking their first course in Religious Studies may find this objective approach disturbing at first. They may feel that it is too relativistic because it treats every tradition as equally valid. Just as a zoology course might compare lions, tigers, and leopards, say, without asking "Which is best?" a major university offers a course called "God/s: a Cross-Cultural Gallery" that compares Yahweh, the God of the Bible, with dozens of other gods, without ranking them. Similarly, the British Library has an online gallery of sacred texts in which the Bible appears alongside dozens of other scriptures: http://www.bl.uk/onlinegallery/features/sacred/homepage.html. While it is perfectly natural to feel uneasy when you first see your own religion treated as one among many, it is important to remember that Religious Studies does not preclude the belief that there is really only one true religion. Religious Studies only precludes *teaching* that any given religious tradition is the correct or incorrect one. These are personal convictions that may be described in the classroom, but not advocated in the classroom.

FIGURE 1.5 Pope John Paul II. © Rene Leveque/Sygma/Corbis.

The major lesson of this chapter, then, is that studying religions is like studying any other subject – with one exception. As with the study of any other subject, we have to be willing to look at surprising facts. We have to be ready to imagine what the world looks like to people who think quite differently from the way we do. The 19th-century English poet Samuel Taylor Coleridge once said that appreciating some literature required a "willing suspension of disbelief." One could say that understanding other people's religions requires a temporary suspension of belief – our own beliefs. This certainly does not mean that scholars of religion must abandon their own beliefs. It only means that we must not make them the standards by which to judge others' beliefs and practices. As one of the greatest scholars of religion in the 20th century, Wilfred Cantwell Smith, said,

We have not understood any action or any saying in another century or another culture until we have realized that we ourselves, had we been in that situation, might well have done or said exactly that. Not that we would have done it; that would mean denying human freedom. We must simply appreciate, must feel and make our readers feel, that of the various possibilities open to us at that point, this particular thought or move or comment would have seemed attractive to us, and perceive the reasons why that would be so. (Smith, unpublished paper)

But note that Smith does not use the word "religion" here. He speaks of people's actions and words; that is what we are really trying to understand in the study of religions. And that is the "one exception." Unlike the study of other subjects, in the study of religion we are not sure exactly what the topic is. We are still trying to understand what religion is – a question to which we shall return in the final chapter.

REFERENCES

Marvin Harris, *Our Kind*. New York: Harper & Row, 1989.
Jonathan Z. Smith, "The Devil in Mr. Jones," in *Imagining Religion: From Babylon to Jonestown.* Chicago: University of Chicago Press, 1982.
Wilfred Cantwell Smith, "The Christ of History and the Jesus of the Historians," unpublished paper.

FURTHER READING

Talal Asad, *Formation of the Secular: Christianity, Islam, Modernity.* Palo Alto: Stanford University Press, 2003.
Wilfred Cantwell Smith, *The Meaning and End of Religion.* Philadelphia, Fortress Press, 1991.
Rodney Stark and William Simms Bainbridge, "Of Churches, Sects, and Cults: Preliminary Concepts for a Theory of Religious Movements," *Journal for the Scientific Study of Religion* 18 (June 1979).
J. Milton Yinger, *The Scientific Study of Religion.* New York: Macmillan, 1970.

PART I
THE TOOLS

AN OVERVIEW OF RELIGION

Making Sense of Life

"Actually, I preferred 'Heaven' too, but then the marketing guys got a hold of it."

FIGURE 2.1 Published in the *New Yorker*, December 15, 1997. © Lee Lorenz 1997/The New Yorker Collection/www.cartoonbank.com

The Religion Toolkit: A Complete Guide to Religious Studies, First Edition. John Morreall and Tamara Sonn.
© 2012 John Morreall and Tamara Sonn. Published 2012 by Blackwell Publishing Ltd.

If there were no God, it would have been necessary to invent him.
VOLTAIRE

Overview

Humans are the only religious animals. Some scholars think that this is because they are the only ones who have self-awareness, especially of the fact that they suffer and are going to die. Religious traditions help people make sense of suffering and death.

The **Problem of Evil** is a philosophical puzzle based on standard Western ideas about God. How can there be evil in the world if God is all-powerful and all-good?

- A theodicy is an explanation for how there can be evil in a world created by an all-powerful, all-good God.

- The Punishment Theodicy says that human suffering is God's punishment for sin.

- The Warning Theodicy says that human suffering is God's warning to people to live as he wants them to live.

- The Free Will Theodicy says that God had to allow for the possibility that humans would do evil in order to give them Free Will.

- Soul-Building Theodicy says that by suffering humans grow in goodness and strength of character.

- The Best Possible World Theodicy says that any complex world would have some evil in it, and that the world we have has a minimum amount of evil.

- The Contrast Theodicy says that without evil "good" would be meaningless.

Explaining Suffering and Evil

Explaining Death
   Ghosts
   Resurrection
   Souls
   Reincarnation

The Importance of Order
   Order Out of Chaos
   Order and Predictability:
      Eschatology, Prophecy, Divination
   Social Order

The Role of Ritual

Conclusion

Another way to explain suffering is to attribute it to an evil force other than God.

Religious traditions explain death, and often make it seem less frightening. This is usually done by saying that death is not the permanent end of human existence.

Four standard ideas about humans surviving death are that they do so as ghosts, as resurrected persons, as non-physical souls, and as reincarnated persons.

Religious traditions are concerned with order and chaos.

- They usually portray order as good and chaos as evil.
- Some traditions foresee an apocalypse – a cataclysmic end to this world, followed by a good and orderly world.
- Some traditions practice divination to reveal future events or hidden aspects of the world.
- Religious traditions are especially concerned with social order. To foster social order, they provide a sense of group identity, rules to live by, and a system of governance.

Religious traditions also make sense of life through their rituals – actions, often symbolic, that are repeated systematically for specific purposes.

Explaining Suffering and Evil

Scholars may not agree on a definition of religion, but they are pretty sure that only human beings are religious. Other animals share many features with human beings. Some have even developed complex social patterns, including communication. However, none appears to have developed anything similar to what humans call religion. Essayist Arthur Koestler (d. 1983) wondered why. He suggested that it is because only human beings have consciousness. Like other animals, he argued, human beings suffer and die, but unlike other animals humans know that they suffer and die. They think about it and worry about it. Religion developed as a way of dealing with our major fears. Or, more simply, "I worry, therefore I am religious."

Religious Studies scholars agree that dealing with suffering – our own or that of others – is a significant aspect of religion. According to American theologian Forrest Church, "Religion is the human response to being alive and having to die."

The challenge of suffering and death is often associated with "the problem of evil." For religions based on belief in a God who is both all-powerful ("omnipotent") and all-good, the existence of evil can be particularly vexing. If God is all-good and all-powerful, then where does evil come from? Either God cannot stop evil and so is not all-powerful, or God could stop evil but does not, in which case God is not all-good. Neither alternative is attractive to most believers, so many thinkers in Judaism, Christianity, and Islam have come up with explanations for how God can be both all-powerful and all-good, and there can be evil at the same time. These explanations are called *theodicies*, and they can be quite sophisticated, as we shall see. The fact that people need to explain suffering and death in such detail shows that, as a species, we want to understand what happens to us. We want there to be reasons for things. We want to make sense of our lives. Religions help us do that.

Theodicy and the Problem of Evil

Theodicy is a term used by monotheists – people who believe in one God – to discuss the challenge of reconciling divine benevolence and justice. It is more specific than the problem of suffering. Suffering of various kinds can be explained without having to justify it as somehow part of a divine plan. Theodicies try to explain evil in terms of divine justice. The term is taken from the Greek words *theos*, meaning god, and *dikaios*, just. Many of them take human free will into consideration. People sometimes commit evil deeds, and God has promised punishment for such acts. But if God is all-powerful and all-good, then why did not God just prevent the evil deed in the first place? A **theodicy** is an answer to a question like this.

Here are some common theodicies.

- *Punishment Theodicy*. Evil was not part of God's original creation, but came into being when the first humans disobeyed God. Human suffering is God's punishment for the Original Sin of Adam and Eve.

- *Warning Theodicy*. Natural disasters such as earthquakes are God's warning to people that they are not living the way he wants them to live.

- *Free Will Theodicy*. To make a universe without evil, God would have to make it impossible for human beings to do evil. But if God did that, there would be no free will. Humans would be like the lower animals, doing only what they were caused to do by outside forces and by their instincts. But God wanted humans to be a higher kind of creature than that. He wanted them to respond freely to him. So God gave humans free will – the ability to do evil as well as good – and they often choose evil. However, a world in which humans sometimes freely choose evil is a better world than one in which no creature has free will. (Associated with the Christian thinker Augustine of Hippo; d. 430.)

Some thinkers try to explain suffering independently from sin. For example:

- *"Soul-Building" Theodicy*. God set up the universe so that we can learn from our experience and grow in goodness and strength of character. If we never faced setbacks, we would remain childishly shallow. The suffering and difficulties we face are opportunities to become more patient, courageous, and loving – to "build our souls." (Suggested by the Christian thinker Irenaeus; d. 202.)

- *The Best Possible World Theodicy*. Any possible universe of any complexity would eventually have some evil in it. In any world where animals move around, for example, some of them are going to bump into others and hurt them, if only accidentally. God – being all-good – chose the possible world in which the happiness of creatures is maximized and their suffering is minimized. So this is the best of all possible worlds. (Attributed to the German philosopher and mathematician Gottfried Leibniz; d. 1716.)

- *The Contrast Theodicy*. Evil and *good* are contrasting terms, like *pain* and *pleasure*. We learn each word as the opposite of the other one. If there were no suffering and other evil to experience, we would not be able to understand what pleasure and other kinds of good were.

The "Punishment" Theodicy Today

A contemporary example of the theodicy that suffering is punishment for sin was given in January 2010 in response to the devastating earthquake in Haiti. American Evangelical Christian preacher Pat Robertson explained that the earthquake, resulting in an estimated 200,000 deaths and massive property destruction, was God's punishment for the Haitians' sins. They had "made a pact with the devil" when they were trying to free themselves from French colonial control. They said, " 'We will serve you if you will get us free from the French'... so the devil said, 'OK, it's a deal' and they kicked the French out. The Haitians revolted and got themselves free but ever since they have been cursed by one thing after the other."

One ancient and still popular theodicy is that suffering is punishment for sin. This explanation is particularly common in the **Abrahamic religions** – those that trace their heritage to the patriarch Abraham: Judaism, Christianity, and Islam. It is expressed most starkly in the Christian teaching called Original Sin. This is an interpretation of the story told in the first book of the Hebrew Bible (the Christian Old Testament) and in the Qur'an, explaining that when the first human beings disobeyed God's first command, God punished them. He expelled them from the Garden of Eden and changed human life from pleasant to painful. Evicted from paradise, humans since Adam have lived in a "vale of tears." According to this explanation, the pain of childbirth, the need to work hard, disease, and death at the end of the whole ordeal are God's way of punishing Adam and Eve for disobeying him, and all their descendants as well.

Another common way to explain suffering is to attribute it to an evil force external to God. A good example is found in Zoroastrianism, the ancient religion of Persia (called Iran since the 1930s). (Today most Zoroastrians live outside Iran; Indian Zoroastrians are known as Parsees.) According to Zoroastrian teaching, there is a single eternal and transcendent god, **Ahura Mazda**, who created the world and to whom all creation will return at the end of time. Ahura Mazda created a beautiful and orderly universe. The principle of order or truth is known as *asha* and, as we shall see in Chapter 9, human beings' duty is to think, speak, and act well in order to preserve order. If they think, speak, or act badly, the result is evil, which is an affront to all that is good and true. Evil is represented by **Angra Mainyu**, also known as Ahriman, an evil spirit independent of the great creator Ahura Mazda. All of history is characterized by the conflict between good and evil, but in the end Ahura Mazda will triumph over all evil. However, Ahura Mazda did not create evil. Variously described as the destructive force of untruth and "nothing," Angra Mainyu is nevertheless considered the manifestation of all that is evil, and its source. But even so, Zoroastrian teaching leaves unanswered the ultimate question of evil. It does not account for why evil has to persist until the end of the world as we know it.

The problematic nature of suffering within the monotheistic worldview is probably nowhere better laid out than in the Book of Job from the **Hebrew Bible**. Job is described as a morally upright man of whom God was proud. In fact, God boasts to Satan (described here as an angel who reports to God, rather than as "the Devil") that "there is no one on earth like him: a man of perfect integrity, who fears God and avoids evil." However, Satan points out that it is easy for Job to be faithful to God, since Job is rich and successful and has a wonderful family. But if Job lost his wealth and his family, Satan says, "He would curse you to your face." Taking up this challenge, God lets Satan destroy Job's possessions and kill his children, to see how he will react. However, after Job has lost most of his family and his possessions, he continues to worship God. Then, creating a new bet, Satan points out that Job still has his health, whereupon God lets Satan cover Job with horrible sores all over his body. Job finally asks why a just God would allow a perfectly good man to suffer so. Three of Job's friends present the standard theodicy that suffering is a punishment for sin, and say that either Job or his children must have done something wrong. Job rejects this explanation, and ultimately dismisses his friends sarcastically. "Oh, how kind you all have been to me! How considerate of my pain! What would I do without you and the good advice you have given?"

Then Job takes his case directly to God, who responds, not with an explanation of why Job is suffering, but with a flurry of confusing questions such as, "Where were you when I planned the earth? Tell me if you are so wise." Instead of answering Job's question about justice, God reminds Job that he is the sovereign creator. The overall impression left is that questions about "the problem of suffering" are not answerable. At the end of the book, God says to one of Job's friends, "I am very angry at you and your two friends, because you have not spoken the truth about me, as my servant Job has." Then God instructs them to ask Job to pray on their behalf, and God forgives them because of Job's intercession. God then gives Job back double his lost possessions and gives him new children, the point having been made: bad things just happen.

Traditions based on belief in a god who is not all-powerful have an easier time explaining evil. In this story from the Native American Comanche tribe, the Great Spirit who created the Comanche banished the evil demon, but it still is able to inflict suffering:

One day the Great Spirit collected swirls of dust from the four directions in order to create the Comanche people. These people formed from the earth had the strength of mighty storms. Unfortunately, a shape-shifting demon was also created and began to torment the people. The Great Spirit cast the demon into a bottomless pit. To get revenge, the demon took refuge in the fangs and stingers of poisonous creatures and continues to harm people every chance it gets.

Traditions that are not based on a single god in control of the entire world have other ways of explaining suffering. Indian traditions, both Hindu and Buddhist (see Chapter 7), claim that suffering results from our own deluded attachment to material things. In fact, evil and suffering are not ultimately real; we perceive evil and suffering in the world only because we do not see things correctly. In this worldview, only minds and ideas are real; the material world has no objective reality. Our ordinary experience of a material world in which there is evil is illusory. To the person who sees the world correctly, there is no evil or suffering. So the answer to the question of suffering and apparent evil is to adopt a higher, truer perspective.

Explaining Death

Of all the problematic aspects of life, the most challenging is that it comes to an end. The desire to understand its meaning is perhaps most acute when babies or mothers die in childbirth, or when the lives of children and other innocents become "collateral damage" in war, or are taken in natural disasters. Sometimes people die slowly or more "naturally," as when an elderly person dies in her sleep. But even then death raises profound questions. When the people who are close to us die, can they be gone completely and forever? The presence of deceased loved ones often seems so real; it sometimes seems impossible that they no longer exist. And the inevitability of our own deaths is – at the very least – disturbing. How can it be that, after all the struggles of life, it just ends? After all the efforts to face the challenges of life, to overcome adversity, to make the hard choices and do the right thing, can my life just be over? Can one even imagine the end of one's own existence? As 17th-century French pundit François de La Rochefoucauld said, "Death and the sun are not to be looked at steadily." As *Star Trek's* Mr. Spock would say, "It does not compute."

One of the strongest statements about the enigma of death is found in the biblical Book of Ecclesiastes. The announced author of this book is "a king in Jerusalem" (some commentators say it was Solomon) who had everything he desired. Unlike Job, he was not afflicted with loss of family, illness, and pain. But still he complains that there is no apparent design to his life or to anyone else's, and that it all ends in a few decades. "Man is a creature of chance and the beasts are creatures of chance, and one mischance awaits them all: death comes to both alike." (3:19) To die is to be destroyed. "The dead know nothing; they have no more reward, and even the memory of them is lost. Their love and their hate and their envy have already perished; never again will they have any share in all that happens under the sun." (9:5–6) And when people die, he continues, someone else inherits all their hard-earned possessions. All one's efforts have come to nothing. So life is futile and meaningless. "God has so ordered it that man should not be able to discover what is happening here under the sun. However hard a man may try, he will not find out." (8:17)

If we are going to make sense of life, we must refute the idea in Ecclesiastes that death makes life meaningless. Among the most common ways that religions do that is by saying that death is not the end. Many teach that death is not the permanent end of a person, and that something happens after death that makes life worthwhile.

We can identify four basic explanations of how people might live after they die:

- as ghosts,
- as persons resurrected at the end of the world,
- as non-physical souls, and
- as persons reincarnated in new bodies.

Ghosts

As we shall see in Chapter 5, the idea of ghosts is probably the oldest idea about life after death, and the most widespread. A ghost looks like the person who died and may talk like them, too. But ghosts are not solid like living persons, and are not subject to the laws of physics. They may pass through doors and walls, for example, and may travel thousands of miles effortlessly in seconds. Belief in ghosts is popular around the world, even among people whose religions rule out such belief, such as Christians and Jews. According to a recent poll, 34% of Americans believe in ghosts, with 23% saying that they have seen a ghost or felt its presence; 58% of Britons believe in ghosts – 4% more than believe in God.

Unlike the other three concepts of life after death on our list, surviving death as a ghost is not something that people look forward to as making life worthwhile. In most cultures, ghosts are thought of as unhappy, lonely, even angry. As a result, they may cause trouble for living people, as by haunting a house, which explains why many people are afraid of ghosts.

Spiritualism

One modern religion based on belief in ghosts is Spiritualism. It got started in Hydesville, New York, near Rochester, in 1848 when Kate and Margaret Fox, ages 12 and 15, claimed that spirits of the dead were causing "rappings" and other noises in their home, which had a reputation for being haunted. Kate snapped her fingers and challenged the spirit to repeat the sound. The spirit did, she said. Kate and Margaret asked the spirit to rap out their ages, which it did. In the days that followed, they got lots of attention from neighbors, and they worked out a code for the spirit to signify Yes or No, and to signify letters to spell out words. They quickly became famous and in 1850 they travelled to New York City to conduct public séances with spirits. Soon people around the U.S. and the U.K. were holding séances and claiming that they had contacted spirits, usually of their dead relatives. Peaking at eight million followers, Spiritualism stayed popular into the 1920s. Mary Todd Lincoln, wife of the American President, was said to have held séances in the White House to contact her dead sons.

In 1888, Margaret Fox explained how the "rappings" had started forty years before:

> When we went to bed at night we used to tie an apple to a string and move the string up and down, causing the apple to bump on the floor, or we would drop the apple on the floor, making a strange noise every time it would rebound. Mother listened to this for a time. She would not understand it and did not suspect us as being capable of a trick because we were so young.

Resurrection

The second idea of life after death is something that people do look forward to, particularly in the monotheisms – Zoroastrianism, Judaism, Christianity, Islam, and Baha'i. It is that after they die, they will be resurrected, that is, brought back to life at the end of the world. In Zoroastrian texts we are told that once evil is vanquished, a savior will renovate the world to a beautiful condition and the dead will be resurrected to live without a trace of evil. In the Abrahamic traditions, resurrection is mentioned late in the Hebrew Bible (Christian Old Testament), and became important in the Christian New Testament and the Qur'an (Islamic scripture), as we shall see in Chapter 6.

In most of the Hebrew Bible, there is no mention of life after death. It is simply assumed that at death a person becomes a corpse in *she'ol*, the hole in the ground in which a person is buried. The dead are not conscious, are not with God, and are not being rewarded or punished. As the Hebrew Bible puts it, they are "asleep in the dust." The writer of **Psalm** 6:5 asks God to spare his life, arguing, "No one remembers you when he is dead. Who praises you from the grave?"

The idea that death destroys the person dominates early biblical texts, but then the writers of the books of Isaiah and Daniel had prophetic visions about the end of the world in which some of the dead would be resurrected. Isaiah envisions a day when God will vindicate the people of Israel by bringing them back to life while leaving their enemies dead.

> The dead do not live; shades do not rise – because you have punished and destroyed them, and wiped out all memory of them….
>
> Your dead shall live, their corpses shall rise. Awake and sing for joy, you who lie in the dust! (Isaiah 26:14, 19)

The writer of Daniel is more cryptic:

> There shall be a time of anguish…. But at that time your people shall be delivered, everyone who is found written in the book. Many of those who sleep in the dust of the earth shall awake; some to everlasting life, and some to shame and everlasting contempt. (Daniel 12:1–3)

In more than 1,000 pages of the Hebrew Bible, these late, prophetic visions are the only passages that mention life after death. Some scholars think that these passages were written at a time when the Jews were being persecuted by Greeks, and they were being killed precisely for staying faithful to God. This raised the question of justice. They were remaining faithful to God because that was God's demand. Should they not be rewarded for their loyalty? If they are destroyed forever, then their fate is the same as those who disobey God. This leaves little incentive for obeying God. The writers of Isaiah and Daniel offer hope to such martyrs: the oppressors may triumph for now, but in the future God will bring his faithful people back to life. Thus, belief in divine justice is maintained; it will simply happen in the future, not necessarily on earth. And life's suffering maintains meaning.

The idea of the resurrection of the dead and the serving of justice in an "afterlife" came to be accepted by many Jews, including Jesus. However, Jesus taught that everyone – bad and

FIGURE 2.2 Luca Signorelli (1450–1523), *The Resurrection of the Dead*. © Sandro Vannini/Corbis.

good – will be resurrected and judged and then rewarded or punished. This view of resurrection and final judgment is also found in some Zoroastrian texts, although without the emphasis on reuniting with a body. Moreover, it was reiterated in the Qur'an and is accepted by Muslims.

Souls

The first Christians believed that the resurrection of the dead would happen at the end of the world. Before the resurrection, they thought, those who have died are simply "asleep in the dust" – dead and buried. Missing from this worldview was the later Christian idea that people are made up of two parts – physical and nonphysical or spiritual. The Hebrew Bible (Old Testament) and the Qur'an reflect a holistic view of the human person. A person (a "self") is one thing. At death the physical body is destroyed and goes into the ground, but it can be brought back to life by the same Creator who made it in the first place.

The region in which early Christians and Muslims lived, however, had a number of influences – primarily Greek, Roman, and Persian. In the worldviews of those cultures, persons are composed of an immaterial soul or spirit that was embedded in a material body at birth. The material body perishes, but the soul – being immaterial – is not subject to the wounds of the flesh. This **dualist** view of human beings was eventually adopted into the perspectives of Christians and Muslims. Thus they came to think of a person as an immortal soul living in a mortal body.

Adopting the dualist perspective entails an interpretation of death that is different from that held by people who see the human being as an integrated whole. In the dualist view, instead of the entire person dying, only the body dies. The soul, being non-physical, is unable to die. As we shall see in Chapter 6, some monotheistic traditions teach that the soul survives in the ground until the end of the world. According to others, particularly worthy souls go to heaven while particularly guilty souls go to hell; either way, they will eventually be reunited with their resurrected bodies. And some traditions allow for the soul to inhabit earthly regions.

The dualist perspective also implies a reorientation toward personal identity. The body ceases to be essential to an individual's identity. It will perish but the soul, bearing all the personal characteristics developed during the individual's lifetime, including merit for good deeds and guilt for misdeeds, lives on.

Despite the disconnect between the idea of the resurrection of the person and the idea that we survive death as immortal souls, the two beliefs serve a similar purpose. They both make sense of death by saying that after death good people will be rewarded and bad people will be punished.

Reincarnation

Many religious traditions in Africa, Asia, and Australia have taught that each of us has been reborn countless times and may be reborn countless times in the future. This belief was common in ancient Greece. (Even in early Christianity, there were discussions of the idea. Some scholars see the idea of bodily resurrection as a kind of limited **reincarnation**.) Clearly, belief in reincarnation allows people to see the death of a loved one in a less tragic light than if this were the person's only life.

Today, in many traditions of India, death is treated not as a tragic end at all. Instead, it is a transition to a new life. In this perspective, physical life is part of a long learning process, the goal of which is to recognize that physical life is illusory at best – a punishment, at worst – and that people's true identities are as part of a much greater non-physical whole. Until individuals reach this awareness, they are born again and again – that is, "put into a body again" or "reincarnated." In Buddhism, the goal is different. Instead of recognizing one's true identity, the epitome of awareness is recognizing that there is no such thing as a true individual identity. But either way, people generally must go through many lifetimes before reaching this awareness and being released from the cycle of rebirths.

The Importance of Order

So religion helps people deal with their ultimate concerns, such as suffering and death. These are problematic for obvious reasons: they cause us enormous pain and so far human beings have found no way to avoid them. They are inevitable. As we shall see in Chapter 7, the Buddha said that life is characterized by suffering. This is the first "Noble Truth," and understanding it is the first step toward dealing effectively with it. However, there is something else about these inevitable difficulties that causes us discomfort – the fact that we do not know just when they are going to come. In fact, we know very little about the future except that it will involve suffering and death at some point. (Yes, and taxes.)

Again we are confronted with Koestler's theory about the role of consciousness in religion. We are concerned about the future because we know that there have been difficult challenges in the past and it is unlikely that they will be the only ones in our lives. Not knowing what will happen next makes us feel vulnerable. Knowing what the future is going to bring would provide great comfort. It would allow us to prepare for it, and give us a sense of control, a feeling that there is order in the world. This concern for order is clearly reflected in many religious traditions.

Order Out of Chaos

Many traditions explain the beginning of the world as "bringing order out of chaos." In the ancient **Babylonian** tradition of Mesopotamia (present-day Iraq), the text **Enuma Elish** describes the feats of the great god **Marduk**, who killed his grandmother **Tiamat** and made the world out of her body. Tiamat is described as the great, raging sea; scholars see her as the personification of primeval, terrifying chaos. So the great god created an orderly world out of chaos. Tiamat/chaos is evil, and order is seen as a very good thing.

Interestingly, the Hebrew Bible (Old Testament) uses a similar term for the out-of-control raging primordial waters. At the beginning of the first book, Genesis, we are told that "the earth was without form… and darkness was upon the face of the deep" before "the spirit of God moved upon the face of the waters." Then God created light and separated it from darkness, and separated the waters of the sky from those of the sea. He then gathered the waters into one place, "let[ting] the dry land appear." The Hebrew term for those raging, abysmal waters is *tehum*, a cognate of the Akkadian (the language of the Enuma Elish) *tiamat*. So again, God brought order out of chaos, "and God saw that it was good."

In Zoroastrian scriptures, the Avestas, the term for what is true and right and good, is **asha**. As we saw, asha also means "order" or "proper functioning." Its opposite, **druj**, means "lie" and "chaos" or "disorder." At the end of time, disorder will be ended and life will return to its original, beautiful, and good order.

Even in contemporary popular culture we see evidence of the correlation between chaos and evil. In the 1990s video game Sonic the Hedgehog, one of the evil characters is called Chaos. In the 2008 movie *Get Smart* (and the 1960s television series it was based on), the evil organization that the hero Max has to combat is called KAOS, and the good guys belong to the secret intelligence agency CONTROL. The Dutch techno musician Danny Masseling (aka Angerfist) titled one of his 2007 hits "Chaos and Evil." And, in a slight linguistic variation, the American group System of a Down raged against "Disorder" in their brilliant 2001 album *Toxicity*.

Order and Predictability: Eschatology, Prophecy, Divination

Religions address the human desire for order and predictability in life in a number of ways. Some include predictions of the future in their formal teachings, often making them central to the tradition's worldview. The Abrahamic traditions of Judaism, Christianity, and Islam,

FIGURE 2.3 Victor Vasnetsov, *Four Horsemen of the Apocalypse (War, Famine, Pestilence and Death)*, 1887. Museum of Religion and Atheism, St. Petersburg, Russia/The Bridgeman Art Library.

for example, envision a time when God will destroy the world as we know it, will judge everyone, and will reward or punish them. This time is called the *eschaton*, which means the last thing, and its defining characteristics are described in detail in Judaic, Christian, and Islamic scripture.

In the Book of Daniel of the Hebrew Bible, for example, we are told of the coming of four great beasts, the last one of which will be really terrible. It has ten horns and crushes the entire earth and then eats it. But believers do not have to worry; as we saw above, Daniel tells us, "Many of those who sleep in the dust of the earth will awake, some to everlasting life, some to shame and everlasting contempt." (12:2)

Christian scriptures refer to the Book of Daniel and reiterate that the "end times" will be marked by "abomination of desolation" and the coming of "great tribulation such as has not been seen since the beginning of the world." (Mt. 24:15–22; Mark 13:14–20) The Gospel of Luke provides more detailed indicators or "signs" so that readers will be able to prepare themselves and (literally) head for the hills: "There shall be signs in the sun, and in the moon, and in the stars; and upon the earth distress of nations, with perplexity; the sea and the waves roaring." (21:2–33) Evil chaos will return, but the righteous can take comfort; they will be rescued.

The last book of the Christian Bible provides even more detailed descriptions of the "end times." Often called the Book of Revelation, the book was originally known as *The Apocalypse of John* ("apocalypse" means "revelation"), and as a result the dramatic events accompanying the end the world as described in Revelation are often referred to simply as the **apocalypse**. Here we are told of the "book with seven seals." With the opening of the first four seals, four riders appear, one each on a white, red, black, and "pale" horse – the "four horsemen of the apocalypse." Opening the fifth seal reveals a vision of those who were slain for their loyalty

Apocalyptic Visions Today

For decades the idea that God will soon end the world has been popular among Evangelical Christians in the U.S. This can be seen in the sales figures of over 65,000,000 for the *Left Behind* series of books written by Tim LaHaye and Jerry B. Jenkins. Seven of the sixteen books have reached No.1 on the bestseller lists for the *New York Times*, *USA Today*, and *Publishers Weekly*. In the stories about the "End Times," the good Christians in the "Tribulation Force" are battling the "Global Community" and its leader, Nicolae Carpathia, who is the Antichrist. These books have been made into three action thriller movies and two PC games.

to the "word of God." The sixth seal releases a great earthquake, "and the sun became black as hair sackcloth, and the whole moon became as blood, and the stars of heaven fell upon the earth … and the heaven was removed as a scroll rolled up, and every mountain and island were removed out of their places." This is described as "the great day of wrath." (Revelation 6)

The Qur'an's descriptions of the end times are similarly striking:

[T]he sun will be darkened, when the stars will be thrown down, when the mountains will be set in motion, when the pregnant camels will be abandoned, when the savage beasts are herded together, when the seas boil over, when the souls are sorted into classes, when baby girl buried alive is asked for what sin she was killed, when the record of deeds are spread open, when the sky is stripped away, when Hell is made to blaze, when Paradise brought near, then every soul will know what it has brought about. (81:1–14)

Clearly, there will be no mistaking the coming of the end of the world. We shall be able to get ready.

Many fundamentalist Christians and Muslims interpret the descriptions of the end times literally. Scholars, on the other hand, generally see in apocalyptic literature reflections of the anxieties of the times in which it was produced. Many scholars think that the apocalyptic passages in the books of Daniel and Isaiah were written while the Jews were being persecuted by the Greeks, and that the Book of Revelation was written after Jerusalem was attacked by the Romans, the temple destroyed, and Jews evicted (70 CE). The popularity of apocalyptic texts and their "doomsday scenarios" in our own time suggests that, like the people in the age of Daniel, we are experiencing a heightened sense of insecurity and angst.

However, not all religious traditions have a linear view of history, with a beginning, a middle, and an end. The traditions of India, for example, see the world as going through very long cycles of birth, growth, decline, and renewal, eternally. There is, therefore, little need for concern about "end times." But these traditions still reflect people's concern for knowing what the future holds. Astrology is a highly developed art in these traditions.

Astrology, the art of predicting events based on the positions of stars, planets, and moons, is an integral part of most Asian traditions, in fact. Its focus is on the individual, based on the belief that one's destiny can be discerned by the positions of celestial orbs at the time of one's birth. Astrology can also be used to predict important events in a community's life, especially catastrophic events such as natural disasters and wars. However, it can also deal with more mundane things such as political and financial developments. Thus, people consult astrologers to determine when to begin an important undertaking. They want to find out when the celestial bodies will be aligned in such a way as to indicate success of something undertaken under their alignment.

The term for such a time is "auspicious." It comes from a Latin term meaning someone who can determine the future based on patterns observed in the flight of birds. This was one ancient approach to **divination** – the effort to read the future, and it was common in both ancient Rome and Greece. Another popular form of ancient divination was to inspect patterns in the internal organs of sacrificed animals. These ancient methods of reading the future were generally superseded by later developments in European cultures, but astrology remains popular. In India today, it is still common even for members of traditions that do not recognize astrology to consult an astrologer before planning an important event such as a wedding.

In the traditions of the **Yoruba** people of western Africa, and traditions developed by Yorubas who came to the Americas as slaves, such as Santeria and Vodou, divination is a responsibility of religious authorities (generically known as priests and priestesses). It may be used for solving a current problem or obtaining advice on future undertakings. Known as Ifa, Yoruba divination is practiced only by those who have reached the highest level of learning and are able to "receive" Orunmila, the god of wisdom and knowledge or destiny. It may be accomplished through a variety of instruments, including reading the patterns in a group of cowry shells or palm nuts or a special divining chain. The petitioner (the person who has brought a problem to the priest or priestess) is then given advice that often includes offering a sacrifice to the god whose efforts would be most helpful with the issue at hand.

Social Order

Many religious traditions deal with another kind of order, one that stems from the fact that human beings are intensely social. Some have observed that we are reluctantly so. The 4th- to 3rd-century BCE Chinese philosopher Hsun Tzu (Xun Tzu) wrote a chapter titled "Human Dispositions Are Detestable." In it he argued that we are naturally selfish and so we must be controlled by society or else sink into chaos. English philosopher Thomas Hobbes (d. 1679) agreed. He wrote in his book *Leviathan* that, due to inherent selfishness, human beings would be fighting constantly, living lives that were "solitary, poor, nasty, brutish, and short," if it were not for the control imposed by government. Whether we are naturally beastly and so must be controlled or, as Hsun Tzu's near contemporary Mencius (Meng Tzu) argued, naturally good but easily perverted by society, there is general agreement that human beings are social and that societies need order.

We need communities in order to survive. More than any other animals, human beings must rely on others to meet their needs. We are born virtually helpless and require years of nurturing before we can meet even our most basic needs on our own. And from our earliest moments we learn to interact with and depend upon others. Ideally, we learn to cooperate. The more cooperatively a social group interacts, the better are its chances of survival. Religions play fundamental roles in fostering effective, orderly social interaction.

Group Identity

A major component of the social function of religions is that they provide us with an identity. Religions help us understand who we are – as individuals and as members of communities – and how we must treat other members of our group in order to ensure both our own survival and that of the community. Religions also tell us how to deal with those who threaten the order that ensures our survival – and sometimes religions even identify just who those "others" are.

The stories that describe who we are typically explain where we came from, or how we came to exist in the first place. These stories are called "creation **myths**." The use of the term "myth" here does not mean that the stories are not true; Religious Studies scholars use "myth" to refer to explanatory stories. Myths are explanations of things in ways that help us understand and navigate life. They both give meaning to and help order or regulate our lives.

In Western culture, the most familiar creation myths are found in Genesis, the first book of the Hebrew Bible. "Genesis" in Greek means "origin," and this book explains the origin of the world and of human beings. As we saw above, the story begins:

> In the beginning when God created the heavens and the earth, the earth was a formless void and darkness covered the face of the deep, while a wind from God swept over the face of the waters. Then God said, "Let there be light;" and there was light. And God saw that the light was good; and God separated the light from the darkness. God called the light Day, and the darkness he called Night. And there was evening and there was morning, the first day. (Genesis 1:1–5)

Over the next four days, God created the sky, plants, the sun and moon, and fish and birds.

> And God said, "Let the earth bring forth living creatures of every kind: cattle and creeping things and wild animals of the earth of every kind." And it was so. God made the wild animals of the earth of every kind, and the cattle of every kind, and everything that creeps upon the ground of every kind. And God saw that it was good. Then God said, "Let us make humankind in our image, according to our likeness; and let them have dominion over the fish of the sea, and over the birds of the air, and over the cattle, and over all the wild animals of the earth, and over every creeping thing that creeps upon the earth."

> So God created humankind in his image, in the image of God he created them; male and female he created them. God blessed them, and God said to them, "Be fruitful and multiply, and fill the earth and subdue it; and have dominion over the fish of the sea and over the birds of the air and over every living thing that moves upon the earth." (Genesis 1: 24–28)

Creation does not have to have been at the hands of a god. Here is another creation myth, from an aboriginal tribe of Australia:

> In the beginning the earth was a bare plain. All was dark. There was no life, no death. The sun, the moon, and the stars slept beneath the earth. All the eternal ancestors slept there, too, until at last they woke themselves out of their own eternity and broke through to the surface.
>
> When the eternal ancestors arose, in the Dreamtime, they wandered the earth, sometimes in animal form – as kangaroos, or emus, or lizards – sometimes in human shape, sometimes part animal and human, sometimes as part human and plant.
>
> Two such beings, self-created out of nothing, were the Ungambikula. Wandering the world, they found half-made human beings. They were made of animals and plants, but were shapeless bundles, lying higgledy-piggledy, near where water holes and salt lakes could be created. The people were all doubled over into balls, vague and unfinished, without limbs or features.
>
> With their great stone knives, the Ungambikula carved heads, bodies, legs, and arms out of the bundles. They made the faces, and the hands and feet. At last the human beings were finished.
>
> Thus every man and woman was transformed from nature and owes allegiance to the totem [symbol] of the animal or the plant that made the bundle they were created from – such as the plum tree, the grass seed, the large and small lizards, the parakeet, or the rat.
>
> This work done, the ancestors went back to sleep. Some of them returned to underground homes, others became rocks and trees. (http://www.crystalinks.com/australiacreation.html)

In this story there is no single Creator, nor does the story account for the creation of the earth. But it does describe the creation of a particular group – those whose story it is. They were created by their ancestors, providing a solid basis for strong group identity and social solidarity.

We see the same pattern in this story from the Iroquois tribes in North America:

> Long, long ago, one of the Spirits of the Sky World came down and looked at the earth. As he traveled over it, he found it beautiful, and so he created people to live on it. Before returning to the sky, he gave them names, called the people all together, and spoke his parting words:
>
> "To the Mohawks, I give corn," he said. "To the patient Oneidas, I give the nuts and the fruit of many trees. To the industrious Senecas, I give beans. To the friendly Cayugas, I give the roots of plants to be eaten. To the wise and eloquent Onondagas, I give grapes and squashes to eat and tobacco to smoke at the camp fires."

Many other things he told the new people. Then he wrapped himself in a bright cloud and went like a swift arrow to the Sun. There his return caused his Brother Sky Spirits to rejoice. (http://www.shannonthunderbird.com/creation_stories.htm)

Even in traditions based on cyclical generation and destruction of the universe, stories explaining social identities and order are critical. The sacred **Rig Veda** of the Hindu tradition explains how society came to be comprised of four hierarchically ordered groups of people. The explanation is found in one of the many stories told about Purusha, "Cosmic Man."

The Hymn to Purusha

One of the most influential parts of the Rig Veda is the Hymn to Purusha, the Cosmic Man. It recounts how the universe itself came out of a sacrifice in which the Cosmic Man was offered by the gods. This hymn is still sung today, 3,000 years after it was composed.

The Man has a thousand heads, a thousand eyes, a thousand feet. He pervaded the earth on all sides and extended beyond it as far as ten fingers…

It is the Man who is all this, whatever has been and whatever will be…

Such is his greatness, and the Man is yet more than this. All creatures are a quarter of him; three quarters are what is immortal in heaven…

When the gods spread the sacrifice with the Man as the offering, spring was the clarified butter, summer the fuel, autumn the oblation…

From that sacrifice in which everything was offered, the melted fat was collected, and he made it into those beasts who live in the air, in the forest, and in villages…

Horses were born from it, and those other animals that have two rows of teeth; cows were born from it, and from it goats and sheep were born.

When they divided the Man, into how many parts did they apportion him? What do they call his mouth, his two arms and thighs and feet?

His mouth became the Brahmin; his arms were made into the warrior, his thighs the People, and from his feet the Servants were born.

The moon was born from his mind; from his eye the sun was born… and from his vital breath the Wind was born.

From his navel the middle realm of space arose; from his head the sky evolved. From his two feet came the earth, and from his ears the four directions. Thus they set the worlds in order.

Rig Veda 10.90

Purusha was split apart. The elite priestly Brahmins were created from his mouth; the royal warrior Kshatriyas were created from Purusha's mighty arms; the hard-working merchants and traders – the Vaishyas – came from his thighs; and the peasant Shudras came from the soles of his feet. These four **varnas** form the foundation for social structure in Indian tradition.

Ethics/Morality and Law

In the process of telling us who we are and why we exist, foundational myths often lay out fundamental norms or rules to regulate the community's life. In India, for example, the **Laws of Manu**, dating from between the 2nd century BCE and the 2nd century CE, explain in detail how to protect the purity of the upper three social groups, *varnas* (Brahmins, Kshatriyas, and Vaishyas), from pollution by the impure Shudras (and women). The upper three varnas are known as *aryan*, or "noble;" they are *dvija*, or "twice born," meaning they have behaved well in previous lives and therefore have been reborn into their higher social stations. The Shudra are not twice born. They must recognize that their only hope for rebirth in a higher varna is in serving the Brahmins, Kshatriyas, and Vaishyas. Thus, if a Shudra insults a "twice born," then he must have his tongue cut out, according to the laws of Manu. If he even mentions their names insultingly, then he must either have a red-hot iron nail put into his mouth or go live in the forest. (Women are assumed to be even lower than the Shudras. In order to achieve a higher birth next time, they must subject themselves at all times to men. We shall see more in Chapter 7.)

In the Western traditions of Judaism, Christianity, and Islam, with their vision of resurrection to an eternal reward or punishment, the rules typically deal with assuring the orderly working of the society. They do this by regulating the aspects of life most critical to group survival: successful procreation, maturing into adulthood and carrying out adult responsibilities, and death. Moreover, they are often developed by the community into more complex regulations, accompanied by methods of enforcement. The group must be protected from those who violate the regulations and so threaten the social order and perhaps even the survival of the group.

Judaism, Christianity, and Islam, for example, all have stringent regulations for assuring that anyone born of the group will be properly incorporated into the group. This process begins with making sure that sex – viewed strictly in terms of its function in procreation – happens only between a woman and a man who has pledged to take care of her and any offspring. In some cases, sex is only supposed to take place when a woman is capable of getting pregnant. Judaic and Islamic laws prohibit sex during a woman's menstrual period, explaining that it is impure or uncomfortable.

Many traditions require men to support their families, and for all people to contribute to the support of those members of the community who need help. Many traditions also require that people contribute to the support of institutions, especially those that train teachers so that the tradition can be passed on to the next generation. As well, it is common for religious traditions to require that parents ensure that their children are educated and trained within the tradition. In fact, many religions prohibit marriage with someone outside the tradition. Those traditions that allow "inter-marriage" generally require that, if any children are born, they must be brought up within the religion.

Laws prohibiting theft, personal injury, and murder have obvious connections to social order.

Condemning Terrorism: Law and Order in Islam

Islamic law provides an interesting example of concern for social order. Like all legal systems, Islamic law prohibits theft and murder. But there are certain kinds of crimes that are considered particularly egregious, so much so that capital punishment is mandated if they are committed. The category of such grievous offenses is *hiraba*. It is described as murder committed randomly. Murder committed as a result of a grievance is an entirely different category from hiraba, and the family of the deceased may agree to allow the murderer to pay compensation rather than be subjected to capital punishment. Classical Islamic law explains that the reason for the severe penalty for hiraba is that this crime, because it is committed against random victims, makes everyone else afraid that they could be next. Hiraba "sows terror" in the community. Making everyone feel unsafe, hiraba crimes violate the security that is supposed to characterize Islamic society. They create chaos. Hiraba is therefore the Islamic term for terrorism, considered a heinous crime in Islamic law.

In short, laws meant to ensure the orderly functioning of society are also standard components of religious traditions. These regulations describe not simply what is legal and illegal, in the contemporary sense of those terms. Many people recognize that certain things are "illegal" or "prohibited" but they do not necessarily consider doing them to be immoral or unethical. For example, many religious traditions involve dietary regulations. Jews and Muslims may not eat pork, for example; Jews may not eat shellfish; Hindus may not eat beef; Buddhists are advised to avoid eating meat. But it is not uncommon for people to violate these laws without feeling that they have behaved immorally or unethically. Actions that are considered moral or ethical often reflect a deeper concern for the wellbeing of the individual and the group.

Not all traditions have written codes of law, of course, since many remain oral, but we would be hard pressed to find a tradition without fundamental concepts of what constitutes right and wrong, moral and immoral, ethical and unethical behavior. Nevertheless, the world's religions display a wide variety of approaches to what is moral or ethical.

In the Hebrew Bible, for example, after God creates human beings, he gives them commands and some prohibitions. Adam and his wife are to take charge of things but they are not to eat of the fruit of a certain tree. They are not told why they should not eat from that tree, but they are expected to obey God's command. We see this again in the biblical story of Abraham, the common ancestor of Jews, Christians, and Muslims. Abraham and his wife were an elderly couple who had given up hope of having a child. But then God spoke to Abraham and promised him offspring. Abraham's wife was at first skeptical but in fact she did conceive and bear a son. The parents were delighted and the child thrived. Then, when the son was about twelve years old, God told Abraham to kill him. He was not told why; he was just expected to obey. He therefore prepared to kill his son. But God intervened at the last minute and told Abraham he did not really have to kill him. And for Jews, Christians, and Muslims, Abraham's willingness to obey God at all costs, even the life of his son, is seen as a model of good behavior.

This understanding of morality is called **Divine Command Ethics**. Under Divine Command Ethics, something is moral or immoral, right or wrong, simply because God commanded or prohibited it. So if God gives different commands to different people, the same action can be right for some of them and wrong for others. Killing your child, for example, is normally bad, because God forbids murder in the Ten Commandments. But when God tells Abraham to kill his son, it becomes the right thing for Abraham to do.

Related to ideas about morality are ideas about punishment and recompense. In the Ancient Near East, violating the king's commands was often punished by a fine, so breaking a law created a debt owed to the king. Monotheistic traditions apply this idea to breaking God's laws. Thus, sin – violating God's rules – creates a debt that the sinner must pay. The standard payment in the Hebrew Bible is a sacrifice – the destruction of something valuable, usually an animal. In ancient Judaism, the debts owed for small sins were paid with the sacrifice of small animals such as doves, and larger sins were paid by killing larger animals such as rams.

The understanding of sin and recompense as based on debt and payment is evident in Christianity and Islam, as well. Jesus' death on the cross, according to most Christian churches, was the sacrifice required to make up for human sinfulness. And in both traditions, people must pay their debt for sins through suffering in the afterlife. The Qur'an frequently warns people to obey God now because they will find out what they have "earned" in the afterlife. We are told, "The earners of sin shall be recompensed for what they have earned." (6:120)

While Divine Command Ethics may seem obvious to those who have grown up with the Bible or the Qur'an, there are other ways of understanding questions of right and wrong or good and evil. In Zoroastrianism, as well as in Indian and Chinese traditions, right actions are those that reflect the inherent order of the universe, and wrong actions are misguided attempts to violate that order.

As we saw above, the Zoroastrian principle of order in the universe is known as *asha*. Asha is seen as the inherent law of the universe, at once balanced, equitable, and, above all, orderly. It applies equally to all. Attempts to go against the law are doomed to failure. As such, asha is also truth and righteousness. Violations of asha are druj: falsehood, disorder, evil.

Asha is etymologically related to the Sanskrit term **rita**, which carries the same range of meanings. In Hindu scripture, rita is the cosmic law, "The Force" in *Star Wars* terminology. Wisdom entails recognizing this truth and living in accordance with it. Although both asha and rita are sometimes represented as deities and some schools of Hindu thought teach that a supreme God is responsible for order, still there is no concept in Zoroastrian or Hindu thought of divine punishment for transgressions or violations of the cosmic order. Instead, this cosmic order itself automatically punishes the transgressor. In Zoroastrian thought, transgressors will suffer in the afterlife until resurrection. In Hindu thought transgressors will suffer in subsequent lifetimes until they recognize the truth. Rebirth into a lower status as a result of violations of rita, or into a higher status as a result of living in accordance with rita, results automatically, in accordance with laws of cause and effect known as **karma**. Actions in accordance with the cosmic truth bring positive effects; actions that violate the cosmic order bring negative effects. Although some traditions hold that gods can assist people in their efforts, ultimately people are responsible for their own destinies.

In Chinese thought, the concept of the inherently orderly working of the universe is known as **Tao**, "the Way." As we shall see in Chapter 8, Tao is a much broader concept than asha, rita, and karma. It is Ultimate Reality; it is the source of all that is. It is inexpressible in words, but it is knowable in actions. Still, it is the basis of morality. Living in accordance with Tao is right; violations of "the Way" are wrong and, again, ultimately futile.

Authority and Power

Many religious traditions also designate authority figures to assist and, in some cases, lead the community in various ways. Again we find a great variety in the roles and qualifications for authority figures in the world's religions.

Among the most commonly recognized authority figures are people thought to influence the forces that control our lives but over which we have no direct control. Generically called **shamans** or **priests**, these authorities' tasks vary depending upon what forces their communities rely upon for survival. Ancient societies that depended upon successful hunting and protection from wild animals often valorized those who were believed to be capable of influencing the spirits that control animals.

As we shall see in Chapter 5, some of the earliest evidence of human activity appears in caves dating from **Paleolithic** times (the Old Stone Age), before people learned to grow food crops. Like other animals, they were hunters. Their survival depended upon their ability to kill animals to eat, and avoid being eaten by other animals. The evidence that we have of these people consists of pictures of both kinds of animal.

The oldest "cave drawing" is in the Chauvet Cave in southern France. Dating from around 30,000 years ago, the drawings depict a number of species, including both the kind that were hunted for meat (like horses and reindeer) and the kind that hunted the hunters (like lions and bears). Most of the pictures are realistic but some of them show combinations of human and animal characteristics. Some scholars believe that the purpose of the pictures was to represent the spirits of the animals, so that a shaman could influence them to help the community to survive.

As we saw above, Yoruba priests represent a different approach to authority. They are believed to be capable of communicating with the gods who control the various aspects of our lives. They may even embody these gods. Santeria (also known as Lukumi), the Yoruba-based religion that developed in Cuba, recognizes a number of gods, each with important responsibilities. Besides the creator god Obatala and the royal ancestor god of the Yoruba, Shango, chief among the Santeria gods are Eleggua (also known as Eshu and by several other names in diverse Yoruba-based traditions), who protects travelers and escorts the dead to the afterlife; Ogun, who is in charge of hunting and war; Oshun, who presides over love, beauty, and wealth; Oya, who creates storms, earthquakes, and other harbingers of change or chaos; and Yemaya, who is mother ocean and protects children.

In traditions with written texts (scriptures), being able to read, interpret, preserve, and transmit the texts is a prerequisite for elite status. We see this pattern in Judaism's **rabbis** – meaning those who teach (the scriptures). Before the destruction of the Temple in Jerusalem by the Romans, when animal sacrifices were still offered to please God, the

FIGURE 2.4 Hammurabi before a god. © Ivy Close Images/Alamy.

elites in charge of that were kohanim – priests, which is where we get the common Jewish name "Cohen." But sacrifices are no longer a feature of Jewish practice; study of the sacred texts is the most important undertaking and rabbis are the dominant elites. The same is true in Islam, where the "scholars" of the sacred texts – ulama and fuqaha – are the primary religious authorities.

In some traditions, the person who is most closely associated with the gods takes on not just moral authority but also coercive power. He not only interprets and articulates what people should or should not do, but can make sure that people obey. He is the king. An early example of this pattern is Hammurabi (1792–1750 BCE), king of Babylon (in modern-day Iraq). Hammurabi handed down a set of 282 laws known as the Code of Hammurabi, including "an eye for an eye," and "a tooth for a tooth." The basis of his authority? He said that the chief gods of the land called upon him, because he was a righteous prince, "to bring about the rule of righteousness in the land." The pharaohs of ancient Egypt were authorized to rule because they were the sons of important gods. Later on, pharaohs were believed to actually be the all-important god Horus in human form.

Although we have these examples of rulers with combined religious authority and coercive power, it is more common throughout history to find religious authority and coercive power – that is, control of the government – in separate hands. Sometimes the two spheres of life are entirely distinct, as in traditions such as Baha'i that reject political involvement, but often religious authorities cooperate with governmental authorities, and even empower them, giving official religious approval. The crowning of the Holy Roman emperor by the **pope** is a case in point. In the year 800, on Christmas day, Pope Leo III crowned the invading Frankish (proto-French) King Charlemagne as the Imperator Augustus, or Revered Emperor.

Later in Europe, 16th-century French philosopher Jean Bodin articulated the idea of **divine right kingship**, according to which the king has power because God wills it. No earthly authority can challenge the king's power. However, religious authority and political power often come into conflict, as happened after the Christian Reformation and in modern Islamic history. Such conflicts raise more questions for religious communities.

In some cases religious authority is hereditary, as in **Shi'i Islam** (see Chapter 6). It may be relatively informal, as in Judaism and Islam, where individuals may choose to undertake advanced study of the religious texts and then may or may not be recognized by their communities as authorities. In other cases the route to positions of religious authority is highly formalized, as in Roman Catholicism, with its strict hierarchy of clergy ranging from priests through bishops and cardinals to the pope. In the medieval Church, the scholars who interpreted the Bible and formulated Church doctrines and laws called themselves the *magisterium*, the teaching authority, of the Church. In 1870 Pope Pius IX went one step further by declaring himself infallible – unable to make a mistake – when he taught about matters of faith and morals.

The Role of Ritual

A final aspect common to religions that we shall consider is ritual. Rituals are actions, often symbolic, repeated systematically by individuals and groups for specific purposes. The purposes may be very practical, such as to heal someone, to bring success in a new endeavor, or to ward off evil. They may mark time or the passage of seasons; many traditions include rituals to celebrate the beginning of a new year, for example, or the coming of spring. Rituals may symbolize phenomena or events important in the community's traditions, such as when Christians reenact Jesus' last meal of bread and wine. Rituals may be performed to initiate individuals into the community, as in naming ceremonies and baptism. They are often used to mark significant events in individuals' lives, such as becoming an adult, getting married, achieving a high status within the community like priesthood or kingship, and, not surprisingly, death. Rituals may also be performed simply to please a god who is believed

Prayer for the Auto Industry

Many religious traditions have prayers for their everyday needs. In Christianity, the Lord's Prayer asks God for "our daily bread." When people's livelihoods are threatened, as in the economic downturn that began in 2008, many turn to prayer, private and public. In this service at the Greater Grace Temple in Detroit, Michigan, the "Motor City," Christians surround three S.U.V.s in the sanctuary to pray that God will save the auto industry.

FIGURE 2.5 Prayer for the auto industry. © Carlos Barria/Reuters/Corbis.

to appreciate the actions or because the god commanded his community to perform them. Such rituals often include the offering of gifts or sacrifices.

Most generally, rituals are performed for a combination of reasons, including an individual's desire to feel closer to her or his god. Rituals are the occasion for profound spiritual and emotional experiences each time they are performed.

Ritual actions may be described in foundational myths or developed by authorities within the community. They may entail travel or **pilgrimage** to a particular place with special significance to the community, such as where they originated. Rituals may include dance or other formalized actions, such as bowing or moving from one position to another in systematic ways. Ritual actions may also be more unique and specific to a single tradition, such as throwing stones at a pillar representing the devil, as Muslims do during the annual pilgrimage to Mecca.

As well, rituals often include formal prayer, which is another feature common to many religions (although not all prayer is ritualized). Prayer – calling upon a god or other cosmic force to express concern, ask for assistance for oneself or someone else, express gratitude or sorrow for offenses, acknowledge submission and dependence or awe – may be performed privately and informally. But when it is performed in ways specified by the tradition, it is considered ritual.

The repetitive and systematic nature of rituals also serves to reinforce the group's beliefs about their identity and the nature of the world in which they live. At the same time, rituals reinforce solidarity within the group. Rituals therefore bring together our discussions of religion as reflecting humans' social nature and as responding to the human need for order, the need for life to make sense and be at least somewhat predictable. Scholars have noted that very little about human life remains static; change is inevitable and everywhere evident not just in individuals but in communities. Our ways of making a living, our customs, even our languages change. But rituals are peculiarly resistant to change. We like our rituals to be carried out the same way each time. This sameness, this predictability and regularity creates, in effect, little universes of order and gives a comforting rhythm to our lives.

Conclusion

Religions help us deal with life. As Albert Einstein said, "Our situation on this earth seems strange. Every one of us appears here involuntarily and uninvited for a short stay, without knowing the whys and the wherefore." Religions make life less puzzling by giving people a big picture of who they are, what the world around them is, and how they fit into it. They give people a *worldview*. (Scholars often use the German term for this word, *Weltanschauung*.) They allow us to see meaning in life. As well, they help us order our communities, providing ethics and laws and institutions.

We could have organized our description of the various aspects of religion in any number of ways. Many people would begin an explanation of religion with something about belief in the supernatural. Others might focus on questions of ultimate truth and the symbolic nature of religious language and practice. Still others would emphasize individual experience, particularly perceptions of contact with the supernatural, commonly known as "religious experience."

Fortunately, there is no "orthodoxy" in Religious Studies. As we noted in Chapter 1, the field is multi-disciplinary; its scholars come from many areas of expertise including history, philosophy, sociology, anthropology, and psychology. The views about what constitutes religion are many and varied. German-American theologian Paul Tillich (d. 1965) famously described faith as "the state of being ultimately concerned." (Tillich 1957, 1) However, "faith" is not the same thing as "religion." Faith – believing in something that one is unable to demonstrate logically or rationally – is among the phenomena studied by Religious Studies scholars. But there are many others. Philosopher Ninian Smart (d. 2001), a major figure in Religious Studies, identified seven elements typical of religions: doctrine, myth, ethics, ritual, experiences, institutions, and material culture.

As we shall see in the chapters that follow, Smart's taxonomy is a late development in over two centuries of scholarly efforts to characterize religion.

In Chapters 3 and 4, we shall trace the development of Religious Studies, highlighting major contributors and their theories. In the remaining chapters, we shall then demonstrate the application of many of their theories in a survey of the world's religious traditions. We shall conclude with a chapter highlighting recent developments in the ongoing effort to understand religion.

DISCUSSION QUESTIONS

1. Do you know what religion is?

2. Do you think that everyone has a religion?

3. Do you think that everyone should have a religion? If so, why?

4. Can there be a religion of one? Could an individual have her or his own religion, or is religion by nature a group phenomenon?

5. Think about the terms ethics, morals, and rituals or rites. "Ethics" is related to "ethos," a term without normative judgments but just meaning the basic character or spirit of a group. "Morals" is related to "mores," another term without implied value judgments but just describing the way a group does things. "Ritual" and "rite" come from Latin terms that originally meant simply the way a particular group does something. Only gradually did the terms take on the connotation of things that have to be done in a particular way or else they are not "right" and will not be effective in achieving their purpose. What might these verbal relationships tell us about the importance of the group in religion?

6. Do you believe in ghosts? If you belong to a religious group, does that group's teaching include anything about ghosts?

7. Have you ever checked your horoscope or done anything else with astrology? If you belong to a religious group, what is that group's attitude toward astrology?

8. If you belong to a religious group, check into its teachings about life after death, and compare those teachings with the different accounts of life after death in this chapter.

REFERENCE

Paul Tillich, *The Dynamics of Faith*. San Francisco: HarperCollins, 1957.

FURTHER READING

Stephen Mitchell, translator, *The Book of Job*. New York: HarperPerennial, 1992.
Hiroshi Obayashi, editor, *Death and Afterlife: Perspectives of World Religions*. Westport, CT: Praeger, 1992.
Ninian Smart, *Worldviews: Crosscultural Explorations of Human Beliefs*. Englewood Cliffs, NJ: Prentice Hall, 2nd ed., 1995.
Rodney Stark, *Discovering God: A New Look at the Origins of the Great Religions*. New York: HarperOne, 2007.

THE EARLY DEVELOPMENT OF RELIGIOUS STUDIES

"*Theologian? You guys are always fun.*"

FIGURE 3.1 © Charles Barsotti 2004/The New Yorker Collection/www.cartoonbank.com.

The Religion Toolkit: A Complete Guide to Religious Studies, First Edition. John Morreall and Tamara Sonn.
© 2012 John Morreall and Tamara Sonn. Published 2012 by Blackwell Publishing Ltd.

Religion is regarded by the common people as true, by the wise as false, and by the rulers as useful.

SENECA, ANCIENT ROMAN PHILOSOPHER

3

Overview

Religious Studies is a modern academic field. It grew in part out of the ancient disciplines of philosophy and theology.

- Greek philosophers such as Xenophanes noted the anthropomorphism in religion – the tendency to think of the gods as like human beings.

- Aristotle talked of doing "theology," study of the gods. For him, this was a branch of philosophy.

- Aristotle's kind of theology, practiced later by thinkers such as Thomas Aquinas, rationally examined reasons for and against various religious beliefs. Today it is often called Philosophy of Religion.

- Another kind of "theology" is not part of Religious Studies. It is learning the teachings of one's own religious tradition in a non-critical way, as a kind of training.

The invention of the printing press in the mid-1400s raised many questions for those who wanted to translate and print Bibles, and therefore had an impact on the study of scriptures.

- Baruch Spinoza's objective study of scripture led him to question some major beliefs in Judaism and Christianity, such as that Moses wrote the first five books of the Bible. The study of the sources of scripture is now called Source Criticism.

Philosophy, Theology, and Religious Studies
  The Relationship between Philosophy and Theology
  Two Kinds of Christian Theology

Scriptural (Biblical) Studies and the Impact of the Printing Press
  Baruch Spinoza: The Beginnings of Source Criticism
  William Robertson Smith: Historical Criticism

The Rise of Modernity and New Academic Disciplines: Oriental Studies, Anthropology, Sociology, and Psychology
  Max Müller: Oriental Studies and Religion
  Edward Burnett Tylor: Anthropology and Religion
  James Frazer: Evolution and Religion

Negative Views of Religion
  Karl Marx: Religion as the Opiate of the Masses
  Sigmund Freud: Religion as Neurosis

Sociology of Religion
  Emile Durkheim: Modernization Theory
  Max Weber: The Protestant Ethic and the Secularization Thesis

Conclusion

- William Robertson Smith was a pioneer of "historical criticism" of the Bible. He showed that the ancient Israelites had many similarities with their neighbors, including the worship of many gods.

The Protestant Reformation and the subsequent emergence of modern European states was accompanied by competing interpretations of scripture. Scholars began to study the process of interpretation, how reason works, and how to determine when it can be trusted. As well, modern states' global explorations led scholars to look for counterparts to Christianity in other cultures.

- These developments, collectively known as the rise of modernity, gave rise to new academic disciplines, including Oriental Studies, anthropology, sociology, and psychology.
- Orientalist Max Müller, scholar of Sanskrit, identified the new field of Religious Studies in the 1870s as the Science of Religion. Just as scholars examine the world's languages objectively, he said, they should also examine the world's religions.
- Edward Burnett Tylor, the first major anthropologist of religion, defined religion as belief in spiritual beings and theorized that the essence and origin of all religions was animism – the tendency to perceive everything that moves as alive and having a soul.
- James Frazer explored the myths and rituals in many cultures and concluded that early cultures evolved from magic to religion, and that "acuter minds" would eventually move on from religion to science.

Some early scholars of religion believed that religion is actually harmful.

- Philosopher Karl Marx, focusing on Christianity at the time of the Industrial Revolution, called religion "the opiate of the masses." Like a drug that numbs pain, he said, Christian belief and ritual allow factory workers to cope with the suffering in their lives.
- Sigmund Freud, the inventor of psychoanalysis, believed that religion is based on illusion – belief grounded in wishful thinking. Religion allows people to feel secure in a dangerous world.

Sociology

- Emile Durkheim was an early sociologist who traced all religions back to totemism, a tribe's veneration of the image of an animal that represents that tribe.
- Durkheim believed a highly influential theory that religion distinguishes between the sacred and the profane. In Durkheim's analysis, the sacred represents the social group, and the profane represents individual concerns.
- The function of religion, according to Durkheim, is to bring people together and motivate them to contribute to the group. Durkheim's theory is a functional theory: it explains religion by describing its function.
- Durkheim's theory is also reductionist: it reduces religion to its function.

- Max Weber described three ideal types of religious leader: the magician, the priest, and the prophet.
- Weber theorized that early Protestantism made capitalism possible.
- Weber was also an early proponent of the "secularization theory," which predicted that in industrialized countries religion would steadily decline.

Philosophy, Theology, and Religious Studies

Religious Studies as an academic field is recent – there have been departments of Religious Studies in universities only since the 1960s. Long before then, however, people were studying the beliefs, rituals, and history of their own traditions, as part of their religious training. Some spent years in training in order to qualify as religious authorities within their traditions. While such study involves a great deal of time and effort, being trained in one's own religious tradition is not what we mean by Religious Studies. As we saw in Chapter 1, Religious Studies is not study aimed at improving the spiritual or moral status of the student – although this may indeed happen. Instead, it is an intellectual activity, like other sciences, aimed at increasing the person's understanding of the world.

To examine a religion in this scientific way, a certain attitude of objectivity is required. This involves openness to new discoveries, including discoveries that may run counter to our current beliefs. Like physics, biology, and psychology, Religious Studies does not claim to have a set of truths that will never be refuted. The best we can have, as in the natural sciences, are solid claims that are backed by data. If new discoveries call these claims into question, then we should be willing to consider them and to update our ideas. As we have said, the claims in question are not about the truth of specific beliefs or the correctness of particular practices, but rather about whether people actually hold such beliefs and follow such practices, and whether our descriptions and explanations of them are accurate. As well, Religious Studies examines the reasons people believe and practice as they do, and the nature of religion itself.

Here is an example of objectivity in the natural sciences. At the beginning of the 20th century, most geologists believed that the continents have always been about where they are now. But then some researchers pointed out how the eastern coastline of South America and the western coastline of Africa could almost fit together. They suggested that those two continents had once been joined. By the 1960s, more observations like this had led to the theory of Pangaea. According to this theory, 225 million years ago there was just one big continent, which then broke up and moved around the globe to form the separate continents. This theory has since been confirmed by thousands of observations, and so it is now standard theory in geology.

To study religion in a similarly objective way, we have to base our ideas on solid evidence. We must observe our subject matter closely, think carefully about it, try to define important terms, and develop explanations for what we observe. We have to demand of our explanations the same clarity, coherence, and credibility demanded of other scholarly claims. First, is the idea clear? Second, is it coherent? (Do the parts of the idea fit together and do they fit with closely related ideas?) And third, is it credible? Do we have good reasons to believe the claim? We call these questions about clarity, coherence, and credibility the three "C" questions.

This approach to the study of religion is actually older than the modern discipline of Religious Studies. It can be traced all the way back to classical Greek philosophy. The word "philosophy" comes from the Greek *phila*, love, and *sophia*, wisdom. Philosophy is the love of wisdom, or the pursuit of wisdom. Notice that the field is not called Wisdom. That is because philosophers do not take an idea, even a great idea, lock it in their minds, and throw away the key. They are always willing to revise what they think.

The very earliest philosophers asked questions about what we now call physics, but a new approach was taken in the 5th and 4th centuries BCE by Socrates (d. 399 BCE), his student Plato (d. 347 BCE), and Plato's student Aristotle (d. 322 BCE). They concentrated on human life, and many of their questions come under our categories of religion, psychology, and ethics. Are emotions beneficial or harmful? How can people be genuinely happy? What is the best way to live? What happens at death? Socrates and Plato spent most of their time discussing such questions, because they thought that answering them was essential to personal fulfillment. Socrates' motto was "The unexamined life is not worth living." The most important thing in life, he taught, is "care of the soul."

The Relationship between Philosophy and Theology

For the Greeks, philosophy covered the pursuit of all organized knowledge. This included all the sciences, logic, ethics, and political theory, as well as theology. (It is because philosophy originally included all branches of academic knowledge that the highest degree in any of them is a "Ph.D.," a Doctor of Philosophy degree.) *Theos* in Greek means "god," and *logos* in this context means "study of." So theology was the study of the gods.

As the Greek philosophers thought about the gods, they called into question many popular beliefs and stories about them, such as those found in the great epics (hero stories) of Homer, the *Iliad* and the *Odyssey*. For example, almost all philosophers rejected the anthropomorphism (assigning human characteristics to the gods) of their culture's religions. An early critic of anthropomorphism was the poet Xenophanes (d. 480 BCE), who disapproved of the way "[m]ortals suppose that gods are born, wear clothes, and have a voice and body." In one poem, he sounds as if he is mocking anthropomorphism.

> The Ethiopians say that their gods are flat-nosed and black,
> But the Thracians say that theirs have blue eyes and red hair.
> Yet if cattle or horses or lions had hands and could draw…
> then the horses would draw their gods
> Like horses, and cattle like cattle.
> http://www.thehumanist.org/humanist/
> 09_jan_feb/March.html

FIGURE 3.2 Aristotle. The Art Archive/Alamy.

Worse than just describing the gods as if they were humans, Xenophanes said, people tell stories about the gods in which they have human vices. The great Homer was especially objectionable when he "attributed to the gods all sorts of things that are matters of reproach and censure among men: theft, adultery, and mutual deception." Homer tells stories, for example, in which Aphrodite, the goddess of beauty and love, deceives her husband and has affairs with other gods.

Xenophanes does not offer positive details about what the gods might be like, but he is positive that they would not have the vices and shortcomings humans have. In one tantalizing line, he refers to

> One god greatest among gods and men,
> not at all like mortals in body or in thought.
> http://plato.stanford.edu/entries/
> xenophanes/

Xenophanes appears to think of this supreme deity as aware of everything, able to influence everything through his thought, and able to change things without himself changing, a view close to later monotheistic ideas about God as Perfect Being.

Two centuries after Xenophanes, Aristotle worked out a more detailed theology. He agreed with Xenophanes that anthropomorphism is a mistake, because the divine would not have the imperfections of material things. He also presented one of the first philosophical arguments for the existence of God. The changes happening in the natural world, he says, point to a First Cause of change, and this First Cause could not itself change – otherwise it would need yet another cause. Anything material changes, furthermore, so the First Cause must be non-material. Unlike material things, too, this First Cause has no "potentiality" (meaning that it will not change or develop from a lesser to a greater form), but is pure "act." This means that, like energy, this First Cause is entirely active. Also like energy, it is neither created nor destroyed; it is timeless, eternal. The essential activity of the First Cause, Aristotle says, is thinking. And since the highest thing to think about is itself, the First Cause contemplates itself.

We can use the word *God* for this unchanging, eternal, non-material First Cause. Simply put, God is Perfect Being.

This understanding of God as Perfect Being carried over to early Christian thinking and helped shape Christian theology.

Two Kinds of Christian Theology

While the word *theology* started out with the meaning "philosophy about the gods," it came to have another meaning when it was adopted by early Christians. So we need to explain the different ways in which Christians came to use the term "theology."

Christianity started in the Roman Empire, where the international language was Greek and where Greek philosophy was admired. In the early centuries of Christianity, when its members were spreading their message around the Roman Empire, leaders often used Greek philosophical terms and ways of arguing. This was useful because they lived in a culturally diverse world where a number of religions and philosophies competed for people's attention. There were Greek and Roman religions, with their dozens of gods to worship. "Mystery religions" promised practical benefits to people upon being initiated into their secrets. According to the philosophy of Stoicism, the best way to be happy was to reduce emotional attachment to things, while the philosophy of Epicureanism held that the goal of life is pleasure. In this competitive marketplace of ideas, Christians used Greek concepts and arguments to show that their new beliefs could answer the three C questions – about clarity, coherence, and credibility. They tried to make clear what they believed, especially about Jesus. To explain what they meant in calling Jesus "the Son of God," for example, they said that, unlike ordinary sons, Jesus is *agenetos*, uncreated. Christians also wanted to show that their beliefs fit together into a coherent whole, so that, for example, Jesus' divinity is compatible with his humanity. Thirdly, they tried to show that their beliefs were credible, so that it was reasonable to accept them.

In the 4th century, Christians' ability to articulate and defend their beliefs became even more important. Until then Christianity was seen as an upstart religion, a deviation from mainstream Judaism at best. Many Christians suffered persecution. Then, as we shall see in Chapter 6, the emperor Constantine (r. 306–337) made it legal to practice Christianity. However, in the light of day, it turned out that various Christian groups around the

Mediterranean held divergent views. This is when Christians began trying to work out their differences and agree on a single set of beliefs. In 325, Constantine called together various Christian leaders (bishops) at Nicea to develop this creed (list of beliefs). This list of beliefs, known as the Nicene Creed, then became the criterion for belonging to the religion. Those who accepted it were Christians; those who did not were heretics (people holding beliefs that are considered incorrect).

In their deliberations at Nicea and at councils after that, the leaders of the Church used Greek philosophical language and arguments. They talked theology. Once the bishops had agreed on the dogmas (official teachings) of Christianity, however, the word "theology" came to be applied to these dogmas themselves, understood as a fixed set of truths. This is sometimes called dogmatic theology. Roman Catholic seminarians, for example, spend four years studying this kind of theology. They do not analyze and critique the doctrines they are taught, the way Aristotle would have. They learn the official teachings and rational defenses of these teachings as part of their training.

Dogmatic theology is not considered a part of Religious Studies. But theology in the original sense – philosophizing about God – remains part of Religious Studies. An activity in which people consider various alternatives and look for reasons to adopt or reject them, it is sometimes called natural theology, since it starts from observations about the natural world rather than from religious beliefs derived from the Bible. Another heading to put it under is philosophy of religion.

The work of medieval philosopher Thomas Aquinas (d. 1274) is a good example of natural theology. In his *Summa Theologiae* (*Compendium of Theology*) Aquinas starts each section not with a doctrine to be accepted but with a question to be discussed. The most obvious question to him: "Does God exist?"

Aquinas begins the discussion by saying, "It seems that God does not exist," and giving the strongest arguments he knows for atheism. One of them is a version of the Problem of Evil. If there were an infinite, all-good being, Aquinas says, that being would not allow evil to exist. Infinite good would crowd out evil. But obviously, there is evil in the world. Another argument he gives for atheism (rejection of belief in gods) is that, if something can be explained in a simple way or in a complex way, we should prefer the simple way. And, Aquinas says, we can explain everything in the world either through natural causes, as in the sciences, or through human causes. So there is no need to appeal to a God.

After presenting these arguments for atheism, Aquinas presents five arguments for theism (belief in the existence of a god or gods). The first one he got from Aristotle, and we saw it above. It is that the changes in the world must be traceable to a First Cause of change. Aquinas' "second way" is similar. The things we see around us have causes for their existence, he says, and these causes themselves have causes. But the chain of caused causes cannot go on forever. There must be a First Cause, itself uncaused, for the existence of everything in the world. Aquinas begins his fifth argument for the existence of God with the observation that animals and plants act in ways that show intelligence, even though they are not intelligent themselves. Birds fly south for the winter, and this helps them survive, even though they do not understand that cold weather is coming and would probably kill them. So, Aquinas says, there must be an intelligent agent who is directing all the unintelligent animals and plants – and this is God. (For full discussion of the Five Ways, see Copleston,

1956, 114–130.) Having presented his five arguments for the existence of God, Aquinas goes back to the two arguments for atheism with which he started, and he responds to them.

This philosophical method of rational discussion of the reasons for and against various beliefs, as we said, remains a component of Religious Studies. In fact, many schools house their Religious Studies programs in departments of philosophy or theology. But the philosophical method is only one approach to the study of religion in the modern discipline known as Religious Studies.

Scriptural (Biblical) Studies and the Impact of the Printing Press

The multi-disciplinary field of Religious Studies as we know it today developed under the impetus of a number of innovations in early modern Europe. The first of these was the printing press. The printing press, developed in Europe in the mid-1400s, had a profound influence on Christianity. In this deeply religious world, people considered the Christian Bible to be the most important book, and wanted to put it in print form. Before that, each Bible had to be copied by hand. This task kept the scribes (people who write) employed, but there was little in the way of systematic quality control. Copying from their own master copies, different monasteries used diverse writing styles and ways of abbreviating terms. And given human fallibility, slight differences inevitably developed among the many hand-copied versions available at the time.

But human error was not the only source of variations among the manuscripts. The Bible had been translated into Latin from its original Hebrew and Greek as early as the 2nd century BCE. An official translation had been produced in the 4th century CE. But even then scholars had worked with diverse sources. So scholars began the process of comparing manuscripts, determining the sources of variations among them, and producing a text they believed was accurate according to the earliest available version. During this process, they discovered another complication. They recognized that it was hard to recapture the meanings of terms as they were used at the time the Bible was first written down; meanings and usage of terms can change over time. Asking questions about the accuracy of transmission and translations of biblical texts in order to produce an accurate copy for the newly invented printing press, then, was a first step in the development of Religious Studies.

Eventually, scholars began to identify variations in both the substance and style of even the earliest versions of scripture they could find. These observations led to the development of new fields in scripture study. Scholars involved in "source criticism," for example, figured out that books previously assumed to be the work of a single author may well have been the work of several authors, or that work attributed to diverse authors may well have been based on a single source. As well, through advanced methods of study, scholars were able to determine that some books of Judaic and Christian scripture were written long after the events they reported, raising questions about their historical accuracy and purpose. These developments represented another step away from the insistence on the timeless truth of scripture – and our ability to access it – that is characteristic of traditional theological studies.

Baruch Spinoza (d. 1677): The Beginnings of Source Criticism

Baruch Spinoza of Amsterdam is a good example of this approach to scriptural studies. Among both Jews and Christians, it was standard belief that Moses wrote the Pentateuch, the first five books of the Hebrew Bible – Genesis, Exodus, Leviticus, Numbers, and Deuteronomy. But Spinoza read the Bible carefully, along with several commentaries, especially that of Abraham ibn Ezra (d. 1164). Spinoza then put together several arguments that Moses did not write the first five books of the Bible. The simplest argument is about the book of Deuteronomy, which ends this way:

> There in the land of Moab Moses the servant of the Lord died, as the Lord had said. He was buried in a valley in Moab opposite Beth-peor, but to this day no one knows his burial-place. Moses was a hundred and twenty years old when he died; his sight was not dimmed nor had his vigor failed. The Israelites wept for Moses in the lowlands of Moab for thirty days; then the time of mourning for Moses was ended…. There has never yet risen in Israel a prophet like Moses.

It seemed obvious to Spinoza that Moses could not have written about his own death and funeral.

FIGURE 3.3 Baruch Spinoza. Imagno/Getty Images.

Another argument Spinoza presented was that Deuteronomy 27 says that the whole book of Moses was written on the circumference of one altar. But the Pentateuch is well over 200 pages long. To fit on the surface of an altar, Spinoza said, what Moses wrote must have been much shorter. Many passages in the first five books of the Bible, too, are written about Moses in the third person, such as "Moses talked with God" and "Moses was the meekest of men." Why would Moses write about himself in the third person rather than saying, "I talked with God"?

Spinoza also looks at place names in the Pentateuch. Some names for places, such as "Dan" for a certain city, did not exist until long after Moses was dead. Spinoza concludes, "From what has been said, it is thus clearer than the sun at noonday that the Pentateuch was not written by Moses, but by someone who lived long after Moses." (Spinoza 1951, 124)

For his critical thinking about the Bible, and for his unorthodox philosophical ideas, Spinoza was expelled from the Jewish community in Amsterdam in 1656. But "source criticism" – the scientific study of the sources of scripture – remains a significant area of specialization within Religious Studies. Indeed, over the next two centuries, scholars continued to work on the sources of the Pentateuch. Today, biblical scholars generally accept what is known as the "documentary hypothesis," developed by German theologian Julius Wellhausen (d. 1844), according to which the "Books of Moses" are an amalgam of four independently authored sources. As well, scholars have developed sub-specializations in examining the literary forms of scripture ("form criticism") and on the impact of scripture's editors ("redaction criticism").

William Robertson Smith (d. 1894): Historical Criticism

As more scholars pursued source criticism, the field broadened and came to be known as "higher criticism" (by contrast to "lower criticism" or "textual criticism," which focuses on removing any human errors in transcription or transmission of texts). Some scholars focused on the historical contexts in which scriptural reports developed, relying on sources outside scripture in order to better understand the meaning of the texts. This area of specialization in Biblical Studies is therefore often called "historical criticism." William Robertson Smith is a major figure in the development of this field.

Robertson Smith offered descriptions of ancient Near Eastern life and religion in order to contextualize scripture. The people of Israel, he said, were far from unique in their religious ideas and practices. They were Semites, speakers of a Semitic language, a group which includes Hebrew, Aramaic, and Arabic. So to understand the Bible, the Prophets, and Jesus, we must understand the Semitic culture they lived in.

One tradition that was already solidly in place when the Israelites appeared on the historical scene was the sacrificing of animals by priests. The writers of the Old Testament do not explain these rituals, as if they were a new idea, Robertson Smith writes, because everyone in the ancient Near East had long assumed "that sacrifice is an essential part of religion."

When we look at other details of the religion of ancient Israel, we find other similarities with neighboring Semitic cultures. In fact, when we study Israel before the sixth century

BCE, "nothing comes out more clearly than that the mass of the people found the greatest difficulty in keeping their national religion distinct from that of the surrounding nations." (Smith 1923, 5) As we shall see in Chapter 6, Solomon was famous for building the Temple to Yahweh in Jerusalem, but he also built shrines to the goddess Asherah (2 Kings 18:22). And over the next four centuries, the Temple itself came to have altars and shrines to Asherah, Baal, and other deities (2 Kings 23:4–13). Thus, he concludes, the early people of Israel were not monotheists, believers in only one god. Elijah's contest with the 450 prophets of Baal and 400 prophets of Asherah in the First Book of Kings (18:19–40) demonstrates this. There could not be 950 prophets of other gods if Yahweh were the only god worshipped in Israel.

The Rise of Modernity and New Academic Disciplines: Oriental Studies, Anthropology, Sociology, and Psychology

Related to the development of the printing press was the Protestant Reformation, which led to another step in the development of Religious Studies. As we shall see in Chapter 6, the Protestant Reformation began when various reformers disputed some of the teachings of the Roman authorities. Since the Roman authorities based their teachings on their interpretations of the Bible, it was up to the Protestants to justify their views with different interpretations of the same scriptures. Although theologians in each camp were convinced of the accuracy of their own interpretations, some scholars got the idea that there was more than one plausible interpretation of scripture. It became another step in the development of Religious Studies.

Another less obvious but related phenomenon contributing to the development of Religious Studies was the breakdown of central authority and rise of independent countries in Europe. In Europe's pre-modern era, political power was legitimated through religious authority. As we noted in Chapter 2, from the time Pope Leo III crowned Charlemagne (800 CE), the Church had theoretically been the source of political legitimacy. That is, people had to obey the emperor and his representatives because the Church said so. If a group became disloyal, the emperor could send his armies to enforce allegiance. However, the economy was changing and the emperor did not have infinite resources to support either his loyal vassals or his troops. As various regions of Europe developed economic independence, they began to demand political autonomy as well. Since the emperor's power was legitimated based on the Roman Church's authority, it was up to those who wanted independence to either reject religion or defend their positions with new religious justifications.

Europe's various regional leaders chose the latter option, starting with Henry VIII in England. Instead of separating government from religion, he created the Church of England, independent of the Church of Rome. He had no disagreements with the pope concerning doctrine. And it is true that Henry wanted a divorce because his wife had produced no male heirs. But more importantly, Henry did not want the income from local churches going to Rome, while he had to pay the salaries of local clergy. So he made himself the head of the Church of England – a position still held by the British monarchs.

Other regions began to declare independence and express loyalty to new interpretations of Christianity – those of Luther or Calvin, or example. This process began the development of Europe's modern countries. But the birth of these states was not easy. ("States" are geopolitical entities with fixed borders, in contrast with "nations" or "empires" that do not necessarily have fixed boundaries.) There was a great deal of conflict over who got to lead them and how to establish the borders between them. For over a century, Europe's "Wars of Religion" raged. Various Protestant and Catholic factions battled for control across Europe, culminating in the horrendously bloody Thirty Years War. Finally, in 1648, the combatants agreed to stop fighting and recognize a formula that had been developed nearly a century before in a failed effort to bring peace. According to this "Westphalia formula" (named after the city where it was articulated in 1555), each ruler had the right to determine the religion of his own territory. So parts of what would become Germany (established in 1871) became officially Lutheran, Switzerland was Calvinist, and so on.

Political implications aside, what this period again highlighted to scholars was the human element in scriptural interpretation. The existence of multiple and conflicting interpretations of a single scripture prompted scholars to examine the very process of interpretation and, more specifically, how people reason. The need to demonstrate rules of careful reasoning became a serious responsibility. This examination of how people reason, in fact, became a preeminent concern of modern philosophers. They wanted to identify how reason worked and under what conditions it could be trusted.

Another major concern of modern philosophy was political theory. Under the pre-modern system, people's responsibility was to obey the clerks of the realm, who were often the clergy (the two terms are related). As we saw in Chapter 2, obedience was owed because the leader was under divine sanction. In the modern age, by contrast, sovereignty ultimately resides in the people (the meaning of "democracy"). Everyone is endowed with dignity, freedom, and the wits to order their own lives under normal circumstances. Since their efforts are most effective when used cooperatively, modern philosophers developed the idea of a "social contract" whereby people agreed to give up some of their personal autonomy to a government that rules in accordance with the collective will of the people. Even so, it is considered "self-evident" – as the United States Declaration of Independence put it – that people have the right to "life, liberty, and the pursuit of happiness." However, religious authorities had denied some of these rights and had legitimated governments that denied them. (In fact, the Roman Catholic Church was opposed to democracy until the 1920s.) So Europe's modern political thinkers based their revolutionary thoughts on what they believed was valid human reason – rather than on religious authority. This is the source of the separation of religious authority from political authority.

This heightened confidence in reason, in turn, contributed to the development of Religious Studies, particularly when combined with data flowing in from Europe's global explorations in the 15th and 16th centuries. Until then, the only attention paid by European Christian scholars to religions other than their own had been efforts to demonstrate the superiority of their own religions. The paradigm of this genre was Thomas Aquinas' *Summa Contra Gentiles*, written in the mid-13th century allegedly to refute Muslim teachings.

The explorers' mandate was not always explicitly religious, although spreading Christianity was a common motivation for their efforts. Their major task was to find sources of wealth (and potential conquests) accessible to their European sponsors. In the process, however, they discovered cultures entirely new to them, and their reports spurred some scholars to examine them.

The academic fields of Classics, Oriental Studies, and anthropology developed in this context. Classics, the study of ancient Rome and Greece, had been a feature of Europe's young universities since the 16th century, as had Oriental Studies, with experts in such "oriental languages" as Hebrew, Arabic, and Aramaic. But the fields expanded to include other languages and cultures, including religions, during the 17th and 18th centuries. During the 19th century, the field of anthropology developed, with the goal of understanding human beings, their cultures, languages, and religions. As we shall see, early representatives of these disciplines struggled with ethnocentrism – a preference for their own group's ways, including its religion. Moreover, their research methods were primitive compared with those of later scholars. However, the goal of identifying and describing others' religious traditions as objectively as possible, in order to contribute to the understanding of the phenomenon of religion as such, became central to Religious Studies.

Max Müller (d. 1900): Oriental Studies and Religion

Among the most significant of the early Orientalists was Max Müller. He is best known for identifying Religious Studies as a field of specialization on its own. He named it *Religionswissenschaft* – the Science of Religion.

A specialist in Sanskrit, the language of ancient India, Müller left his native Germany to work in England. Britain controlled India at the time, and its agents had collected hundreds of Sanskrit texts. Müller translated and published many of them as a 50-volume set he called *Sacred Books of the East*. At the University of Oxford, he became Professor of Comparative Philology (the study of languages and literature), and then Oxford's first Professor of Comparative Theology.

Müller wanted his observations of Indian traditions to be well informed and rational, as objective as any other scientific study. He wanted scholars to put aside whatever religious commitments they might have had, and study other people's traditions simply as well informed, rational observers. This kind of objectivity is what Müller hoped to achieve in the "Science of Religion."

In pursuing this ideal of a Science of Religion, Müller was inspired by the new science of language, Linguistics. Linguists study many languages, comparing and contrasting them, and looking for general patterns. This is how scholars should approach the world's religions, according to Müller. Another promising similarity is that linguists treat all languages as valid and interesting.

FIGURE 3.4 Max Müller. Hulton Archive/Getty Images.

Müller thought scholars should take this same attitude toward the world's religions. Just as any language gives a group of people a set of concepts with which they make sense of their lives, so too does any religion. "The Science of Language has taught us that there is order and wisdom in all languages," Müller said, and he hoped that the Science of Religion would search for the order and wisdom in all religions. (Müller 1869, Vol. 1, 21)

The comparative method, which is essential to Linguistics, became essential to Müller's study of religion, too. As we saw in Chapter 1, he insisted that with both languages and religions, "He who knows one know none." The person who simply speaks a language or practices a religion does not have what is necessary to understand the general phenomenon of language or the general phenomenon of religion.

Müller's own study of Sanskrit and Indian traditions was a model for the scientific approach he preached. Similarities between Sanskrit words and words in Latin, ancient Greek, and modern languages led him to conclude that there are similarities between various religions. The Sanskrit word for god, *deva*, is related to the English word *divine*. In the Rig Veda (one of the four "Vedas," the oldest of India's sacred texts), there is the father god Dyaus Pitar. His name is related to Zeus Pater, the father god in ancient Greece, and to Jupiter, the father god in ancient Rome. (If you say these three names fast, you can hear the similarity.) Müller spent decades studying the Vedas, in part to find the origin of the gods of Greece, Rome, and Europe, and the roots of religion in general.

While Müller's attempts at objectivity were noble first tries, it is not surprising that, as a pioneer of this approach, he did not have a perfect score. In several of his writings, the influence of his Christian upbringing is obvious. For instance, Müller defined religion as "a mental faculty… which… enables man to apprehend the Infinite." This works well for Müller's own Christianity, but not for Buddhism or for many other traditions. Müller's grounding in Christianity is also evident in his comment that

> The Science of Religion will for the first time assign to Christianity its right place among the religions of the world; … it will restore to the whole history of the world, in its unconscious progress towards Christianity, its true nature and sacred character.

A few pages later, Müller says, "Every religion, even the most imperfect and degraded, has something that ought to be sacred to us, for there is in all religions a secret yearning after the true, though unknown, God." (1869, Vol. 1, 30)

Whatever shortcomings Max Müller may have had, though, his contribution to Religious Studies was enormous. He set the bar high for everyone who followed, by saying that the academic study of religion should be a science.

Edward Burnett Tylor (d. 1917): Anthropology and Religion

Some of the same dynamics that gave rise to *Religionswissenschaft* also influenced the development of other new academic disciplines, among them anthropology – "the study of human beings." Among the common phenomena Europeans observed as they explored the "new worlds" (which, of course, were not new to the peoples who lived there) was what appeared to be religious activity. Many early contributions to Religious Studies came from this new field of study.

One of the first people to study religions scientifically was also one of the first anthropologists, Edward Tylor. Tylor held the first chair in anthropology at the University of Oxford. His best known book is *Primitive Culture*. Today we do not call oral cultures "primitive," because it has a negative connotation. But in Tylor's perspective, "primitive" simply meant "early" or "uncomplicated."

When Tylor's book came out in 1871, most European scholars saw Europeans as advanced far beyond the other cultures. This is how they justified their colonizing of Africa, Australia, Asia, and the Americas. Darwin's *On the Origin of Species* had only recently been published and was becoming popular among intellectuals. Tylor applied its theory of evolution – the idea that more complex forms of life develop from simpler ones – to cultures. Tylor thought that cultures could be ranked, based on how far they had "evolved": Australian, Tahitian, Aztec, Chinese, Italian, and upwards toward his own culture.

Another evolutionary idea of Tylor was that, as cultures developed into more advanced forms, they sometimes preserved older tools, language, customs, and beliefs. He called these old things that had been preserved in modern culture "survivals." Archery is now a sport, for example, but it began as a technology for hunting and war. It is therefore a "survival" of earlier methods of hunting. When someone sneezes today, we say, "God bless you." This is a "survival" from centuries ago, when people believed that the soul escapes the body when one sneezes. "God bless you" is a kind of prayer that God will put your soul back into your body quickly.

Today this belief is outdated and considered quaint, but some beliefs that have survived from early human cultures are still taken seriously, particularly in what Tylor called *animism*. For Tylor, animism was the first "general philosophy of man and nature," and religions all over the world were based on it.

Animism is seeing everything that moves as having an *anima*, a soul or spirit that animates it. Indeed, the words *animate* and *animal* are built on *anima*. Animals have *animae* (plural of *anima*), and so do trees, rivers, volcanoes, and anything else that moves. Some cultures even attribute *animae* to things such as tools.

Tylor had an evolutionary explanation for animism. He said that it developed in stages. Early humans observed that the difference between a living person and a dead person is that a living person breathes. So our distant ancestors thought that it was breath that made people be alive, Tylor said. This is why in many languages the word for "soul" is the word for "air" or "breath." The English word "spirit" is from the Greek *spiré*, which means "breath." The biblical words for "soul" are the Hebrew *nefesh* and *ruah*, and the Greek *spiré* and

FIGURE 3.5 Edward Burnett Tylor. Granger Collection/ Topfoto.

pneuma; and the Qur'anic terms are the Arabic *nafs* and *ruh* – which are all words for "breath" or "air." So for Tylor, the first stage of animism was to think of the anima, the soul or spirit, as something that makes a person be alive.

Early people who thought this way, Tylor said, naturally thought of death as the departure of the anima, the soul or spirit, from the body. But that was not the end of it. Once free of the body, our ancestors thought, the soul or spirit continued on its own. This is the second stage of animistic thinking: the soul is what leaves the body at death and goes on by itself.

The third stage of animism, according to Tylor, was to think of the anima, the soul or spirit, as what appears to us when we dream about a dead person, or have a vision of a dead person. After a loved one dies, we do not erase them from our memories, of course. It is common to dream about someone who has died, or even see an apparition of that person while we are awake. An important public person such as a religious leader might even appear to many people at the same time in different places. If a person's dying is their soul leaving their body, then it is natural to think that what appears to us in our dreams of dead people, and in their apparitions to us, is their soul, which has left their body. This soul, their anima, now free of the body, has become a phantom or a ghost – a person without its old physical body.

A dream or apparition is obviously not as solid or stable as the living person was, so the phantom is thought of as made of a very lightweight, translucent kind of matter, like a mist that can hold a shape. Tylor described it as "a thin, unsubstantial human image… a sort of vapour, film, or shadow." Like a living person, it takes up space, has a shape, and moves, but it weighs almost nothing and it can pass through walls and doors, and travel across great distances in an instant.

To summarize, then, the anima, soul, or spirit is

- what makes a person be alive
- what leaves the body at death
- what appears to us in dreams and apparitions of dead people.

Once early humans had this idea of the anima, Tylor says, they extended it beyond people. If human beings have souls that make them be alive, they thought, then animals have souls that make them be alive, too. Similarly, if having a soul means being alive, and being alive is characterized by the ability to move, then the movement of trees blowing in the wind, rivers, volcanoes, and anything else that moves may be attributed to their having souls. Indeed, Aristotle thought that even the stars were moved by souls.

The next stage was to think of souls that had never been in bodies. These "pure" souls are gods, angels, and demons (disembodied souls that have evil tendencies). Having the "spirit of God" move you is having an outside anima take control of your body. The same is true of being possessed by a demon, an idea found in a number of the world's religious traditions.

Tylor said that the development of religious thought was largely the development of animism. In the beginning, each god, each disembodied anima, was local. It was associated with a particular thing or place – this river, or that village. But then people developed the idea of gods with wider domains. Ceres became the goddess of cereal grain – not just the grains in Rome, but all grains everywhere. Poseidon became the god of all the seas, not just the ones around Greece.

The anima, soul, or spirit is essential to ideas about life after death. In the monotheistic traditions, there are two main ways of looking at death. The older one is that death destroys people for a while, but at the end of the world people will be brought to life again; God will give them life (or breath) again. They will be "resurrected." After the notion that human beings are a material component animated by a spirit or soul (dualism) began to influence Christianity, Christians tended to identify themselves with their souls. Then they thought of death in a different way – that their souls survive death and wait somewhere until the Last Day. Some monotheists believe that their souls will be with God right after death and later will be rejoined with their bodies; for others, souls remain in the grave until the Last Day. Then they will be rejoined with their bodies, their lives will be judged, and they will be consigned either to happiness in heaven or punishment in hell.

In Hinduism and Buddhism, and in many traditions of Asia and Africa, a common belief about death is that the anima leaves the body and then animates a different body on earth. As we saw in Chapter 2, this is called reincarnation. Some believe that the souls of male relatives must be revered lest they become troublesome ghosts.

According to Tylor, all these ideas of life after death are based on thinking of the soul as what makes a person be alive and as what survives death. And all ideas of gods, angels, and demons are also based on that way of thinking. So believing in animae is the basis of all religions. This allows Tylor to present a simple theory of religion. Religion, he says, is "the belief in spiritual beings."

Tylor maintains that the most advanced religions are monotheistic, because they have just one God as the creator and controller of everything. Apparently uninfluenced by theories of evolution in this regard, he figured that the simplest religious structure, rather than the most complex, is the most advanced. On the other hand, he did think that religion was evolving. And since animism was "primitive" – an idea that began in the "childhood of the human race" – it should now be discarded. As science has developed, he thought, explanations involving souls, spirits, phantoms, and ghosts have all but disappeared in educated people's discussions.

It should be noted here that Tylor is assuming that religion is a universal phenomenon. He was brought up in a culture that distinguished between religion and other aspects of life, and he assumed that all cultures make the same distinction. Further, since religion in his culture was associated with belief in God and the soul, he looks in other cultures for belief in "spiritual beings" in order to understand what he assumes is their religion. We shall see other scholars who make the same kinds of assumptions, and in later chapters we shall see that these assumptions are questioned by contemporary scholars of religion.

James Frazer (d. 1941): Evolution and Religion

The most famous student of Edward Tylor was James Frazer. In 1890 Frazer published what would become one of the first classics of Religious Studies, *The Golden Bough: A Study in Magic and Religion*. Over the next 25 years, he expanded *The Golden Bough* to twelve volumes, in an exploration of the myths, cults, and rituals of many cultures.

Like Tylor and others, Frazer saw human cultures as evolving through stages. As we noted, in their view their own cultures were the most advanced and, by comparison, others were at earlier stages of development. For many such thinkers, it was Christianity that marked European culture as the most advanced. They saw monotheism – or at least Christianity – as the most highly developed stage of religious thinking. Communities with multiple gods were primitive, and their beliefs and rituals were based not on reason but only on superstitions. They represented an early stage of human development. They were examples of **magic**.

At the heart of magical thinking, Frazer says, is the belief that certain actions guarantee certain results. Expressed as a formula,

Do A, and B will happen.

This idea is found not just in magic, of course, but in science and human thinking generally. What distinguishes magic is that its formulae for what action will cause what result do not reflect empirically verifiable and readily duplicated patterns of cause and effect. Instead, they are based only on associations between ideas of A and B.

In magical thinking, if the idea of A is associated with the idea of B, then A and B are related in the real world. And so one can manipulate A to have an effect on B. One way that A and B might be associated is that A is a part of B. If I want to hurt you, and I have some of your hair, I might do something to that hair as a way of doing something to you. Another kind of association is similarity. If I draw a picture of you and then burn the picture, this may hurt you. Some scholars believe that prehistoric cave drawings served in this way. Perhaps people tried to influence the animals by appealing to the pictures of the animals. This kind of magic is often called "sympathetic magic."

However, magic is not entirely predictable. It does not always work, and this became problematic for ancient peoples, says Frazer. In his view, it was the realization of the fallibility of magic that led to the development of a more advanced kind of thinking – religion.

For Frazer, religion involved appealing to supernatural powers to influence those things over which we have no direct control. As Daniel Pals explains,

> Instead of magical laws of contact and imitation, religious people claim that the real powers behind the natural world are not principles at all; they are personalities – the supernatural beings we call the gods. Accordingly, when truly religious people want to control or change the course of nature, they do not normally use magical spells but rather prayers and pleadings addressed to their favorite god or goddess. Just as if they were dealing with another human person, they ask favors, plead for help, call down revenge, and make vows of love, loyalty, or obedience. (Pals 2006, 38)

Frazer's analysis of Christianity provides a good example of the evolution from magic to religion. One of the many similarities he found between ancient magical rites and Christian practices concerned what he called the Corn King. He believed that some early agrarian cultures developed elaborate rituals to ensure that their grain crops would come back each spring. He describes their choosing a man to personify the crop for one year. He calls this

Cargo Cults and Magic

Cargo cults are the classic example used by scholars of the associative kind of reasoning in magic. "Cargo cults" is the generic name for a phenomenon that developed in the South Pacific following the arrival of Japanese and then Allied forces in World War II. Both groups had introduced kinds of equipment and quantities of supplies previously unimaginable to the islanders. The local people witnessed the periodic arrival of food, medicines, weapons and other supplies via ships and airplanes. It appeared that these shipments occurred following certain actions by the soldiers: speaking into an electronic device, writing numbers on sheets of paper, and marching in formation on an airstrip, for example. After the war and the evacuation of the soldiers, the supplies no longer arrived. Some of the islanders reasoned that the deliveries had stopped because no one was doing the things the soldiers used to do. Some islanders attempted to restart the deliveries by imitating the actions of the soldiers. Researchers observed them fashioning models of radio communication devices and airplanes, shuffling papers on models of desks, and marching up and down runways just as the soldiers had done before supplies were delivered. It appeared to them that these actions had pleased the gods, who in response delivered the supplies from the sky or the sea. Surely, they would respond again provided the actions were performed properly.

FIGURE 3.6 Cargo cults. Paul Raffaele/Rex Features.

person the "Corn King" ("corn" here meaning any grain). The Corn King was identified with the crop, and so he was treated very well through the growing season. But in the fall, when it came time to break up the dried stalks and scatter the seeds, the Corn King was killed and his body was chopped up and scattered across the fields. This ritual was believed to insure that the seeds would sprout and come up in the spring.

Frazer found "survivals" (to use Tylor's term) of the ancient beliefs in Christian teachings. In the Gospels Jesus uses the image of the grain dying and then bringing forth new life: "Unless a grain of wheat falls into the earth and dies, it remains alone. But if it dies, it bears much fruit" (John 12:24). And New Testament writer Paul uses the image of grain dying and coming back to life to explain how humans would be resurrected (I Corinthians 15). Frazer also suggests that the idea of Jesus being crucified for the good of the human race evolved from the ancient Corn King ritual.

Frazer's general conclusion is that Christianity superseded ancient magical practices, replacing unpredictable magical thinking with religious belief in a God who controlled

Frazer and the Evolution of Christian Beliefs

Frazer believed there were many similarities between ancient myths and Christianity. The ancient Greeks and Romans, for example, worshipped a vegetation god, Attis, and his mother, Cybelé, who, some accounts say, was a virgin. In Greece and Rome, Cybelé was called "Mother of the Gods." Christianity taught that, since Mary was the mother of Jesus, and Jesus was God, Mary was the Mother of God. So it made sense that when Christians built a church on the site of the old temple of Cybelé, "Mother of the Gods," they dedicated it to Mary, the "Mother of God."

The death and resurrection of Attis were celebrated in early spring. Frazer describes a ritual in which worshippers of Attis mourn his death, but then

> the sorrow of the worshippers was turned to joy. For suddenly a light shone in the darkness: the tomb was opened: the god had risen from the dead.… The resurrection of the god was hailed by his disciples as a promise that they too would issue triumphant from the corruption of the grave.

To Frazer, this sounds like Easter. Frazer also sees similarities between Christmas and ancient rituals celebrating the Birth of the Sun around December 21, when after six months of the days getting shorter, they finally start to get longer.

> Thus it appears that the Christian Church chose to celebrate the birthday of its Founder on the twenty-fifth of December in order to transfer the devotion of the heathen from the Sun to him who was called the Sun of Righteousness. (Frazer 2009, 370)

human destiny. However, rather than jettisoning all previous practices, Christians "compromised," and transformed the earlier practices to fit the new thinking.

While Christianity and other religions were an improvement on magic, Frazer thought, the outcome of religious rituals is not always predictable either. When they pray to gods, religious people realize that their requests are not always met. However, religious people have a number of explanations for these instances. Maybe they have not made the proper offering required by the god. Perhaps they displeased the god earlier and have not yet made amends. The list of possible reasons for not having your prayers answered is a long one, and so, Frazer says, the religious person does not expect automatic results.

Frazer said that religion was therefore an improvement over magic. When they do not get the results they seek, religious people can explain why, as believers in magic cannot. However, Frazer thought, religion has problems of its own because it presumes that God or the gods interfere in nature. That means that there are not any rigid patterns in nature such as the laws of physics and laws of chemistry. Suppose that during an earthquake a rock is falling through the air. A physicist would say that it will continue to fall until it hits something. But if the rock is heading toward a baby carriage and the mother has just asked God to protect her baby, then, according to religious believers, the rock might change direction. Therefore, if prayer works, then the laws of physics are not as fixed as we might think.

According to Frazer, recognizing this problematic aspect of religion prompted some "acuter minds" to move on from religion to a still more advanced way of thinking – science. Like magic, science posits correlations between events, but through observation and experimentation science arrives at correlations that are consistent and readily duplicated, while magic does not. Both magic and science are attempts to control the world, then, but science is more reliable.

It is not terribly surprising that Frazer expressed so much confidence in science and the power of reason. He was living in an age of stunning scientific and technological progress. His confidence was shared by many in his generation and beyond. As well, the evolutionary model introduced by Darwin was extremely influential. The combination of modernity's confidence in reason and Darwin's theory of evolution resulted in the belief that religion is but a stage in human evolution, destined to be outgrown. This view of religion was expressed most provocatively by two major thinkers: Karl Marx and Sigmund Freud.

Negative Views of Religion

Karl Marx (d. 1883): Religion as the Opiate of the Masses

Instead of trying to understand a variety of religions, Karl Marx concentrated on European Christianity in his own time. As a philosopher contending with the negative effects of the Industrial Revolution on working people, his main concern with religion was its impact on society. And he believed it was very negative. Religion was not his only target. His condemnation of capitalism made him extremely unpopular with those who benefited most from it: the wealthy industrialists. And in his fierce criticism of religion – especially

FIGURE 3.7 Karl Marx. © Bettmann/Corbis.

the Christianity dominant in industrial Europe – he was not alone. His slightly younger contemporary Friedrich Nietzsche (d. 1900) gained notoriety for postulating that "God is dead." However, Nietzsche's work was so idiosyncratic and unsystematic that it had little lasting impact on Religious Studies. The influence of Marx, on the other hand, is still palpable in the field.

To understand why Marx had such a negative view of the Christianity of his own time, we need to understand what life was like in 19th-century Europe and North America. The Industrial Revolution was changing society in unprecedented ways. People were moving from rural areas, where they had done farming and craft work, into big cities, where they worked in factories and lived in cramped apartments or row houses. In 1800, 20% of Europe's population lived in cities, but by 1851, that figure had nearly doubled.

The workweek was six days, and the workday ten to twelve hours. There were no minimum wage laws and no government rules about safety. Accidents were common, and hundreds of workers died each year. Factory owners could run their factories as they pleased, to make maximum profits. Children as young as five worked in the textile mills: mines could legally employ ten-year-olds. Factory smokestacks belched tons of filthy smoke, without restrictions. For workers who were injured or laid off, there were no benefits to help them get by. And when a worker became too old to work, there were no pensions or social safety nets. In some industries such as mining, the factory owner maximized his profits by building a "company town," so that he owned all the houses and the stores, where workers were forced to buy their food and clothing at high prices. Many workers were in constant debt, so that no matter how miserable the job, a worker could not afford to quit, because, as an old song says, "I owe my soul to the company store." The lives of factory workers, in short, were little, if any, better than the lives of slaves. They had next to nothing – except their labor, which they sold each day to the factory owner.

Marx knew firsthand what this system was like, because his friend Frederick Engels was the son of a factory owner and together they visited many factories. In his book *Das Kapital* (*Capital*), Marx analyzed the society produced by the new industrial capitalism and compared it with earlier societies.

Capital is something a person owns to make a profit. In ancient and medieval times, before manufacturing, farming was the basic form of production. Food crops and livestock were the basic commodities, and so land was the basic form of capital. Those who owned the land had the peasants working on it to produce a profit in the form of crops and livestock. Landowners could also rent out some of their land to make a profit. Most people who did not own land did not have any capital. Peasants had to make do with whatever food and shelter the landowners allowed them.

With this division between rich and poor, life in ancient and medieval societies was hard for the lower classes, Marx says. But medieval life looked almost pleasant compared with the lives of 19th-century factory workers. For one thing, most medieval workers lived in rural areas, where they were surrounded by fresh air and the natural world. In crowded 19th-century cities such as London and New York, people lived in filthy tenements, breathed polluted air, and drank polluted water.

Another difference was that in ancient and medieval times at least the landless poor had craft skills from which they derived satisfaction. Craftspeople such as seamstresses and blacksmiths worked hard, but they could take pride in what they produced. Indeed, they took enough pride in it to make the name of their craft their last name. Dozens of last names even today are the names of crafts: Weaver, Potter, Cook, Taylor, Carpenter, Shepherd, Farmer, etc. *Smith* is an extremely common name just because in the Middle Ages "smith" was the general term for a craftsperson.

In contrast with the pride people took in craftwork, Marx says, people who work in industrial economies, trading their labor for wages, are "alienated" from their labor. Rather than the satisfaction they might have derived from the process of making a unique product from beginning to end, workers in the capitalist system receive only wages. One worker's wages are distinguishable from others' wages only in amount. So laborers cease to derive a sense of identity from their work, and begin to identify with their wages and what they can acquire with them. They relinquish a sense of being someone who does something in particular, and make do with an identity based on what they own. In Marx's view, this "identity of having" is inherently unsatisfying, since the only way to distinguish oneself is by "having" more than someone else. This sets up a dynamic in which people are in constant competition to own more than their neighbors. Thus, the capitalist system has negative effects on social relations, as well as personal identity. People become, in effect, slaves of the economic system.

Marx believes that religion is an integral part of industrial capitalism's ability to control societies. He says that religion keeps the oppressed workers cooperative and submissive, willing to spend six days a week at mind-numbing, physically exhausting toil. Religion – and he meant specifically Christianity – does this by convincing people that we serve God by doing our daily work and obeying those in authority – the mayor, the bishop, and the foreman at the factory. Our work is hard, but our earthly lives will be over soon. If we have been submissive and obedient, we shall go to heaven, where we shall be rewarded with comfort and all our needs will be fulfilled. "Eye has not seen, nor ear heard, neither has it entered into the heart of man, the things which God has prepared for them that love him." (I Corinthians 2:9)

Without religion, Marx thinks, factory workers would confront the misery of their lives and do something to change it. They might well revolt against the oppressive factory owners. However, Marx says, religion dulls their sense of suffering as they focus on the life to come. In short, religion works like a strong painkilling drug. It is the "opiate of the masses."

If we look back through history, Marx observes, religion has always taken the side of the rich owners of capital against the poor workers. Marx calls the owners of capital the *bourgeoisie* and the workers the *proletariat*. The Hebrew Bible not only permitted slavery but regulated it, as did Judaism, Christianity, and Islam. But again, Christianity was his primary target. Christianity that taught, "Slaves, obey your earthly masters with fear and trembling, in singleness of heart, as you obey Christ" (Ephesians 6:5–9) and "Let every soul be subject to the governing authorities. For there is no authority except from God, and the authorities that exist are appointed by God. Therefore whoever resists the authority resists the ordinance of God, and those who resist will bring judgment on themselves." (Romans 13:1–2) Marx concludes:

> The social principles of Christianity justified the slavery of Antiquity, glorified the serfdom of the Middle Ages, and are capable… of defending the oppression of the proletariat… The social principles of Christianity preach the necessity of a ruling and oppressed class… preach cowardice, self-contempt, abasement, submission, and humility….

> The social principles of Christianity declare all the vile acts of the oppressors against the oppressed to be either a just punishment for original sin and other sins, or trials which the Lord, in his infinite wisdom, ordains for the redeemed.

Marx's critique of religion was harsh indeed, but it certainly was taken seriously by the Russian revolutionaries who overthrew the Czar in 1917, and by the revolutionaries who took control of China in 1949. Both tried to eliminate religion from their new Communist states.

Sigmund Freud (d. 1939): Religion as Neurosis

FIGURE 3.8 Sigmund Freud. © Bettmann/Corbis.

Sigmund Freud, who developed psychoanalysis, the basis for psychiatry, had an equally negative assessment of religion, but for very different reasons. Freud revolutionized our understanding of the human mind, and when he applied his new ideas about the mind to religion, it came out looking far from noble or virtuous.

Before Freud, most people thought of the mind as something that gives us the truth about the world and about ourselves. It was generally assumed that people could reliably report on their own beliefs, emotions, and motivations. However, from his studies of people with psychological problems, Freud concluded that the mind is not a truth device but a coping device. Its function is to help us cope with our problems and get through each day.

Some things that are in our minds do not cause anxiety and so we may be fully aware of them. If asked about the weather, for example, most people could give an honest answer. Things like this are in the conscious part of the mind. However, many things in the mind are saturated with emotions, and so they are not known objectively in the way we know whether or not it is raining. Imagine a child who has been abused by her father. If she is asked, "Do you love your father?" her feelings about her father may not be readily available in her conscious mind. Rather, Freud says, her negative feelings about her father have probably been repressed – pushed out of her conscious mind into her unconscious mind – so that she may well not express her hatred for her father. Admitting such a thing would be very uncomfortable and could have extremely negative repercussions. So she is likely to say "Yes, I love my father," and may even believe it in her conscious mind. This helps her cope with her problems for the moment. Her hatred for her father, which is locked away in her unconscious mind, however, will cause her psychological problems later on, such as difficult in forming healthy relationships with other men or trusting people in positions of authority. Indeed, Freud says, virtually all our psychological problems stem from our early relationships with our parents.

The new techniques of psychotherapy that Freud developed were designed to bring thoughts and feelings out of the unconscious into the conscious mind, where they could be faced and dealt with. One of them was the analysis of patients' dreams. In our dreams, Freud says, thoughts and feelings that are repressed in waking life are expressed.

This new understanding of psychological problems and of the mind as a coping device influenced Freud's understanding of religion. He sees religion as arising not from the rational conscious mind, but from the unconscious mind. Religious beliefs, he says, are not based on what we have found to be true. They are based on what we would like to be true. Religion is a way for us to cope with problems and get through life. As a coping device, religion works to a certain extent, but it causes major problems of its own, just as the child's repression of her negative feelings for her father does. Freud's overall assessment of religion is that it is a kind of neurosis, that is, a mild form of mental illness.

Freud wrote three books on various aspects of religions. In *Totem and Taboo* (1950) he presents a theory of how religion originated, and in *Moses and Monotheism* (1939) Freud presents a new interpretation of the story of Moses in the Bible. It is his *The Future of an Illusion* (2010) that presents a general assessment of religion in culture.

The basic motive for religious belief and ritual, Freud says, is fear of the dangers in life, and a desire to be reassured that everything will be all right. Early humans faced a dangerous and often confusing world every day. The two main sources of their anxiety were other human beings, on the one hand, and nature, with its many surprises and threats, on the other. Early on, they learned to handle social problems by making agreements, setting up rules, and showing consideration for other people. When they wanted something from other people, for example, they would be polite and offer them something in return.

As early humans faced the natural world, Freud said, they carried over their ways of dealing with other human beings. They treated volcanoes, thunder, and rain, for instance, as if they were the actions of gods with whom they could make polite requests, negotiate, and do the other things that worked with people. If they needed rain for their crops, they could sacrifice something to make the rain god happy. If the volcano was rumbling, they could beg the volcano god to calm down. By believing in gods and praying to them, they made the natural world an extension of their social world, and this gave them a feeling of control over natural events.

According to Freud, the gods had three functions: to exorcise the terrors of nature, to reconcile people to the cruelty of fate, and to compensate them for what they endured and what they gave up by living in society. Originally, humans believed in many gods, but eventually monotheism evolved to streamline polytheism. Instead of having dozens of gods, each controlling a different area of life – the crops, sailing, childbirth, etc., now there was a single God, who was not just all-knowing and all-powerful, but a Father who cares about his children. They showed him respect, prayed to him, offered him sacrifices, and followed his commands. All of this belief and practice made life feel more secure and, at the same time, laid down the moral rules that made civilization possible.

Whatever benefits religion brought long ago, however, Freud says that we now have better ways than praying and sacrificing to deal with illness, crop failures, and other natural forces. These better ways come under the heading of science. In science we try to figure out patterns in nature and we check them with experiments. When we come up with a hypothesis, we test it against the data, and we accept the hypothesis only if it fits the data. In religion, on the other hand, we accept beliefs because they make us feel secure. We believe that a Heavenly Father is watching over us, for example, not because we have discovered this to be true, but because we want it to be true.

Freud has a name for a belief based on such wishful thinking. He calls it an "illusion." Normally, that word implies that a belief is false, but Freud uses the term in a different way. His term for a simple false belief is "delusion." In ancient times, for example, people believed that the earth is flat. When this was shown to be false, most people switched to the belief that the earth is round. This kind of correctable false belief is a delusion. However, religious beliefs are not correctable, Freud says, because people do not check them against their experience. Rather, they accept those beliefs for the way they make them feel. This makes religious beliefs illusions rather than delusions.

This analysis of religion in *The Future of an Illusion* has drawn many more responses than Freud's ideas about Moses or his theory of how religion began. This is because the ideas presented in the other two books were based mostly on speculation about what may have happened in the past. They were therefore "unscientific." However, his claim that religion is based on a reassuring belief in a father figure is testable, and it is criticized because – for one thing – it does not work for all religions. Buddhism and Taoism, for example, do not have a divine father figure. Even in the Western monotheistic religions, God is not always portrayed as a loving Father. In some interpretations of Christianity, as we shall see (Chapter 6), God is strict and authoritarian, and he punishes the whole human race for the sin of the first human beings. Indeed, because of Original Sin, everyone deserves eternal torment in hell. This is hardly the kind of belief people accept because they want it to be true.

So Freud's theory of religion does not seem to cover all religious traditions, nor even all forms of Christianity. But it does reflect the kind of evolutionary thinking combined with utmost confidence in reason that characterizes modernity. And in their very boldness, such negative theories of religion helped separate the scholarly study of religion from the normative or devotional approaches that characterize dogmatic theology. In particular, they reflect the 19th-century hypothesis that religion represents an intermediate stage of human development that is bound to be replaced with more advanced, non-religious – scientific – approaches to life's challenges. Less pessimistic but likewise evolutionary theories of religion are evident in the work of the founding fathers of yet another modern field of study: Sociology.

Sociology of Religion

Emile Durkheim (d. 1917): Modernization Theory

Psychology – the study of people's mental states and behavior – did not originate in Europe. It had precursors in classical Greek and medieval Islamic thought. Similarly, sociology – the scientific investigation and critical analysis of how society operates – has representatives among classical Greek and medieval Islamic thinkers. However, as an independent field, based on supreme confidence in human reason, sociology is quintessentially modern European, and Emile Durkheim is generally regarded as its founder. He established the first department of sociology, at the University of Bordeaux in 1895.

Durkheim studied all aspects of human social organization, including religion. In fact, he believed that religion is essentially social. In *The Elementary Forms of Religious Life*, he describes what he considers the earliest and simplest religion as totemism, the veneration of totems by tribes. A totem is an animal with which a tribe identifies. The Native Americans of the Pacific Northwest, for example, carve totem poles featuring bears, crows, and whales. Sometimes they name themselves after the totem animal. Modern sports teams do something similar when they name themselves the Lions or the Dolphins, but totems have a deeper meaning to the group than the simple symbolism of a mascot. As we saw in Chapter 1, the totem often figures in the foundational stories held sacred by the group and is believed to have a metaphysical or spiritual relationship with the group.

The function of totemism, Durkheim says, is to meld people into a cooperative group. By focusing on the group identity through rituals about the totem, their religion encourages them to override their selfish concerns, for the good of the group. The function of these rituals is "to bring individuals together, to increase contacts between them, and to make those contacts more intimate." (Durkheim 1915, 348)

Durkheim thus defines religion as "a unified system of beliefs and practices relative to sacred things, that is to say, things set apart and forbidden." (Durkheim 1915, 47). This distinction between "sacred" and "profane" things was readily accepted within the field of Religious Studies. "Sacred" meant "holy" or "special" and therefore to be treated with reverence; it is to be treated differently from everyday "profane" things. Whether it is a totem or other object, or a place, a person, or even a name or word, its specialness must be marked. In this sense it is "forbidden" to the uninitiated. In Durkheim's terminology, the sacred totems are *taboo* – something that should not be touched except under special conditions.

We shall see in Part II that diverse traditions identify a wide variety of sacred things, and often the thing or person or word is considered sacred because of its connection with the supernatural. But for Durkheim the sacred is not something supernatural. The sacred is the realm of the social, where people are concerned with the common good.

Because the totem represents the group, what people are actually venerating in their religious rituals is their own social group. In Durkheim's words, "The sacred principle is nothing more nor less than the society transfigured and personified." (Durkheim 1915, 347). The term "profane," by contrast, covers people's everyday activities such as work, in which they are concerned only with themselves and their families. So Durkheim concludes his definition of religion: It is "a unified system of beliefs and practices relative to sacred things, that is to say, things set apart and forbidden – beliefs and practices which unite in one single moral community called a Church all those who adhere to them." (Durkheim 1915, 47)

This theory of Durkheim is called "functionalist" for the obvious reason that it defines religion in terms of its function. But whereas some functionalist analysts believe that the function could be fulfilled by things other than religion, Durkheim sees the role of religion in promoting group solidarity as irreplaceable. Without the solidarity engendered by religion, he fears that we would find ourselves back in social chaos. In fact, in his studies of suicide, Durkheim suggests that one of its causes is the loss of social orientation provided by religion.

Durkheim was one of the key figures in the development of what is called "modernization theory," which forecasts that all societies would inevitably develop industrialized economies just as Europe had. With industrialization, societies reorganize. They build cities (urbanize), and develop new institutions (bureaucracies) to organize their lives. Durkheim also observes that, as societies modernize, individuals develop increased autonomy and a correspondingly decreased sense of group identity. He worries that, without the strong sense of belonging to a group, individuals may lose the sense of wellbeing provided by group solidarity. The other great figure in the development of sociology, Max Weber, likewise theorized about the role of religion in social evolution, but attributed a different role to religion.

Max Weber (d. 1920): The Protestant Ethic and the Secularization Thesis

One of Max Weber's contributions to Religious Studies is his naming of "ideal types" of leadership. In *The Sociology of Religion* (1922) he discussed three ideal types of religious leader. First is the "magician," which Weber describes as the shaman or healer, who has a charismatic style of leadership. The magician gets to be a leader by convincing people through sheer force of personality that he can offer practical benefits such as healing for their illnesses and rain for their crops. The second ideal type of leader is the "priest." While magicians gain authority based on personal charisma, priests' authority is a function of the official positions they hold. And while the magician is a one-person operation who does whatever seems appropriate to him, the priest is part of a bureaucracy that has extensive training, many rules, and a system of pay and promotion. Weber's third ideal type of religious leader is the "prophet," from the Greek terms meaning to "speak" (*phao*) "for" (*pro*). The prophet speaks for a god. Even more than magicians, prophets' authority comes from their personal charisma. They are respected because they convince people that they are speaking for a god. If the audience does not hear the god's voice in the message of someone who claims to be a prophet, she will not be recognized as a prophet.

However, Weber's best known contribution to Religious Studies is his theory that early Protestantism made modern capitalism possible. As he studied various European cultures of his own time, he noticed that the leaders of business and banking were overwhelmingly Protestants. Catholics tended to be workers and tradespeople or, if they were in the middle class, doctors, lawyers, or teachers. So Weber asked, "What is the connection between modern business and Protestantism?" "And why did capitalism start in Europe rather in India or China, and in the 1600s rather than earlier or later?" His reflections on these questions became his most famous book, *The Protestant Ethic and the Spirit of Capitalism*.

Weber's explanation is that the new beliefs and practices taught by Luther and Calvin (see Chapter 6) fostered in people attitudes and habits that made them want to be successful in business. The "spirit of capitalism," Weber says, was for "the earning of more and more money, combined with the strict avoidance of all spontaneous enjoyment of life." (Weber 1958, 53)

The Christian tradition of medieval Roman Catholicism that came before Luther and the Protestant Reformation did not valorize worldly success. Indeed, it warned of the dangers of being concerned with money. Jesus, after all, said that it is "easier for a camel to pass through the eye of a needle than for a rich man to enter heaven." In Catholicism, Weber observes, a religious life is oriented to the world to come, heaven, not to this world. And so the fully religious person is a priest, a monk, or a nun, not a banker or a factory-owner. Because worldly success was suspect, Catholic laypeople tended to be farmers, lower-level workers, doctors, lawyers, and teachers.

In Weber's analysis, the Protestant leader whose ideas did the most to foster capitalism was John Calvin (see Chapter 6). In his *Institutes of the Christian Religion* he wrote that, because of the "original sin" of Adam, all human beings are born in a morally corrupt state. We inherit an "innate depravity from our very birth." We are born so depraved, in fact, that we are incapable of doing anything good on our own. We have no free will. All we can do by ourselves is sin. In this dreadful condition, the whole human race deserves eternal damnation, Calvin said. Every baby is naturally headed for hell, and without God's intervention, all would end up there. However, fortunately for some, God has absolute freedom to do whatever he wants, and he chooses to save some people. They are called "the elect." They are no better than anyone else, but God predestines them for eternal happiness in heaven.

Understandably, those who accepted Calvin's teachings, such as the Puritans, were anxious about their eternal fate. Since everyone deserved damnation, death was scary. Unlike Catholics, who believed in free will and in the value of "good works," Calvinists thought they were incapable of doing anything to help themselves reach heaven. Catholics had the Mass and other sacraments, they prayed to the saints to intervene with God for them, and they said special prayers to address special needs. But Calvinists had none of these techniques for calming their anxieties about damnation. There was one thing they did have, however, that could allay their worries about whether they were saved or damned. This was success in their work.

Here is how Weber explains the connection between work and salvation. The world exists for only one reason, Calvin taught, and that is to glorify God, its creator. The main way we do this is through our daily work. Our religious calling is not, as in Catholicism, to withdraw from worldly activities and pray. It is to be successful at our jobs. We are on earth to work. The harder we work and the more successful we are, the more we glorify God, and the more likely it is that God has predestined us for heaven rather than hell. Success in business does not *earn* people salvation; success simply *indicates* that they are already favored by God and predestined for salvation.

This new worldview produced what Weber calls the **Protestant Ethic**. It valorized hard work and career success, and cast a doubtful eye on play and leisure. The virtues it praised were self-control, self-denial, the ability to delay gratification, thrift, and simple living. Weber calls this "inner-world asceticism." It made Protestants well suited to starting businesses, opening banks, engaging in trade, building factories – all the things that helped promote modern capitalism in Europe and North America.

Weber's articulation of forms of religious leadership and his thesis that Protestantism made capitalism possible were two of his major contributions to the analysis of religion. A third was his introduction of what is called the **secularization thesis**. Again, reflecting modernity's overarching confidence in reason, as well as the influence of Darwin's theory of evolution, Weber characterizes the modern world (and the "spirit of capitalism") as "calculating" or rational. Modernization is a process of "intellectualization" of life, and a reciprocal decline in reliance on "mystery" or the unpredictable promises of religion. He calls this process "disenchantment" (*Entzauberund*) and "secularization." Secularization is thus characterized by diminishing appeals to the divine in daily life, especially in practical and economic matters, and the declining influence of institutionalized religion. We shall return to this topic in Chapter 10.

Conclusion

Weber's secularization thesis is treated by many scholars as more than a description; it is treated as a prediction. As Rodney Stark, a leading critic of the theory, pointed out in 1999, Weber was not alone in his prediction. Stark traces this line of thinking as far back as the 18th-century theologian Thomas Woolston, who predicted the end of Christianity by 1900, and Frederick the Great, who wrote in the 18th century that religion "is crumbling of itself." In the same century Voltaire gave religion fifty more years of life; and Thomas Jefferson wrote in 1822 that every "young man now living in the United States" will abandon Christianity for Unitarianism. Stark summarizes: "For nearly three centuries, social scientists and assorted western intellectuals have been promising the end of religion. Each generation has been confident that within another few decades, or possibly a bit longer, humans will 'outgrow' belief in the supernatural." (Stark 1999)

However, the dire predictions for religion contained in the secularization thesis turned out to be false. As we shall see in Part II, religion continued to thrive, and new religions continued to be born. As a result, Religious Studies continued to develop as an autonomous field, although it remains multi-disciplinary. In the next chapter we shall survey approaches to the study of religion that became fundamental to Religious Studies.

DISCUSSION QUESTIONS

1. What are some reasons that it took so long for educated Europeans to begin to study religion scientifically?

2. Discuss William Robertson Smith's response to opponents of source criticism: "A book that is really old and really valuable has nothing to fear from the critic, whose labours can only put its worth in a clearer light, and establish its authority on a surer basis." (Smith 1892, 17)

3. In 1900 the Catholic Church was opposed to source criticism and other modern methods of studying the Bible. The pope insisted, for example, that Moses had written the first five books of the Bible. However, by 1950 Pope Pius XII approved of modern methods of biblical criticism. What might this change of position say about how religious teachings develop?

4. Can the idea of anima or soul that Tylor described still be found in religions today?

5. Can ideas that Frazer called magical thinking still be found in religions today?

6. Can you think of examples of religious teaching today that justify Marx's critique of Christian churches during the Industrial Revolution?

7. Can you think of examples of religious behavior today that justify Freud's view of religion?

8. Does Durkheim's claim that the essential function of religion is to promote social solidarity match any contemporary religions?

9. What are some contemporary examples of religious leaders who fit into Weber's three ideal types?

REFERENCES

Emile Durkheim, *The Elementary Forms of the Religious Life*. New York: Macmillan, 1915.

Emile Durkheim, Mark S. Cladis, editor, Carol Cosman, translator, *The Elementary Forms of Religious Life*. Oxford: Oxford University Press, 2008.

James George Frazer, *The Golden Bough: A Study in Magic and Religion*. Oxford: Oxford University Press, 2009.

Sigmund Freud, *Totem and Taboo*, standard ed. New York: Norton, 1950.

Sigmund Freud, *The Future of an Illusion*. Eastford, CT: Martino, 2010.

Sigmund Freud, *Moses and Monotheism*. London: Hogarth, 1939.

Max Müller, "Preface," in *Chips from a German Workshop*. New York: Scribner's, 1869. Vol. 1.

Daniel Pals, *Eight Theories of Religion*. Oxford: Oxford University Press, 2006.

William Robertson Smith, *The Old Testament in the Jewish Church*. London: Black, 1892.

William Robertson Smith, *Lectures on the Religion of the Semites*, 2nd ed. London: Black, 1923.

Baruch de Spinoza, R.H.M. Elwes, translator, *A Theological–Political Treatise*. New York: Dover, 1951.

Rodney Stark, "Secularization, R.I.P. – Rest in Peace," *Sociology of Religion*, 60, No. 3 (Fall 1999), 249–273.

Edward Burnett Tylor, *Primitive Culture*. Ithaca, NY: Cornell University Press, 2009.

Max Weber, *The Sociology of Religion*. Tübingen: Mohr (Siebeck), 1922.

Max Weber, Talcott Parsons, translator, *The Protestant Ethic and the Spirit of Capitalism*. New York: Scribner, 1958.

FURTHER READING

F. C. Copleston, *Aquinas: An Introduction to the Life and Work of the Great Medieval Thinker (Penguin Philosophy)*. New York: Penguin (Non-Classics), 1956.

Richard Elliot Friedman, *Who Wrote the Bible?* San Francisco: HarperOne, 1997.

Karl Marx, Eugene Kamenka, translator, *The Portable Karl Marx*. Harmondsworth: Penguin, 1983.

Jon R. Stone, *The Essential Max Müller: On Language, Mythology, and Religion*. New York: Palgrave Macmillan, 2002.

RELIGIOUS STUDIES IN THE 20TH CENTURY

"I had a nice chat with my trainer today about Allah."

FIGURE 4.1 © Donald Reilly 1997/The New Yorker Collection/www.cartoonbank.com.

The Religion Toolkit: A Complete Guide to Religious Studies, First Edition. John Morreall and Tamara Sonn.
© 2012 John Morreall and Tamara Sonn. Published 2012 by Blackwell Publishing Ltd.

Every religion is true one way or another. It is true when understood metaphorically. But when it gets stuck in its own metaphors, interpreting them as facts, then you are in trouble.

JOSEPH CAMPBELL

4

Overview

The field of Religious Studies matured in the 20th century, losing some of its bias in favor of European culture. However, it retained diverse views about the nature and purpose of religion. Some theories of religion say that it fulfills functions that can be fulfilled by other things. These theories are called reductionist. Durkheim's theory, for example, reduces religion to its function of promoting social cohesion. In his view, something else, such as belonging to a sports team, could do what religion does. Other theories say that religion has its own distinct essence that cannot be replaced by anything else. These theories are called essentialist. Essentialist views of religion have their roots in modern philosophy.

- In the 20th century, some philosophers practiced "analytic" philosophy. Emphasizing the analysis of language, they looked at religious statements and asked the three C questions: Is it clear? Is it coherent? Is it credible?

- Antony Flew was in a school of analytic philosophy called logical positivism. For him a statement is a meaningful assertion only if some experience could count as evidence for or against the statement. If nothing could verify or falsify a statement, then it is not a meaningful assertion.

Back to Philosophy
Analytic Philosophy: Antony Flew (d. 2010)
Phenomenology and Religious Studies

Philosophy of Religion
John Hick (b. 1922)
William Lane Craig (b. 1949)

Anthropology of Religion
Clifford Geertz (d. 2006)
Mary Douglas (d. 2007)

Sociology of Religion
Peter L. Berger (b. 1929)
Robert N. Bellah (b. 1927)

Psychology of Religion
William James (d. 1910)
Carl Jung (d. 1961)

Conclusion: Theories and Methods
Philosophical Theories
Genetic/Historical Theories
Functionalist Theories

- Some religious statements, such as those about history, are verifiable and falsifiable, and so they are meaningful assertions. "Jesus rose from the dead" is an example.
- However, other statements, such as "God is a loving father," seem unverifiable and unfalsifiable and are not, therefore, meaningful assertions.
- Another kind of philosophy in the 20th century was phenomenology. It was based on carefully describing the way things appear to us, while "bracketing" (putting aside) questions about what is real or true.
  - Rudolf Otto had a phenomenological theory of religion in which the source of all religion is an encounter with the Holy. Otto analyzes the experience of the Holy as a feeling of utter creature-dependence. The object of this feeling is *mysterium tremendum et fascinans* – a scary and fascinating mystery.
  - Mircea Eliade also studied religion phenomenologically. As an essentialist, he thought that religion was *sui generis* – its own kind of thing – and not reducible to anything else.
    - Eliade was most interested in old nature-based religions. He said that they reveal the essence of the Sacred better than later "historical religions," which locate the Sacred in time and space.
    - Manifestations of the Sacred are called hierophanies.
    - For Eliade, the Sacred lies outside time and space, and is more real than the things described by science and history.
    - People think about the Sacred mostly in their myths, stories about things that may not have ever happened but that are true nonetheless.
    - Religious myths around the world show many similarities and reveal the deepest concerns that human beings have.
    - Human beings are by nature religious; *homo sapiens* is *homo religiosus*.

Still other philosophers in the 20th century practiced what is called philosophy of religion. They examined the credibility of religious claims such as that God exists.

- John Hick presented a number of arguments that the Christian doctrine of the Atonement is not credible today because it is based on outmoded ideas about God as a king.
- William Lane Craig presented a new version of the Argument from Design for the existence of God. It is based on the way the universe seems to have been "fine-tuned" to prepare it for producing living beings like ourselves.

Anthropologists also studied religion in depth in the 20th century.

- Anthropologist Clifford Geertz said that religion is at the heart of culture. It offers people a system of symbols that creates a worldview for them. This worldview in turn produces moods and motivations in them so that they know how to react to situations in life, especially problems and suffering.
- Mary Douglas studied religious ideas about purity and impurity. The basic idea of the impure or "dirty," she said, is that something is out of place. Religions such as Judaism

classify certain animals as unclean because these animals do not fit certain concepts of what animals should be like.

Sociologists, like anthropologists, study religion as the experience of social groups.

- Sociologist Peter Berger talks about "the social construction of reality." Our ideas about the world, he says, are partly determined by our social group. Religions are especially influential in shaping our ideas about what is real and what is important.

- In his early work, Berger embraced secularization theory and predicted that religion would decline in importance over time. However, later he admitted that he had been wrong: he said that the 21st century will be just as religious as previous centuries.

- Robert Bellah expanded the idea of religion to include "civil religion" – the way of life of people such as Americans whose worldviews provide a sense of history, a set of values, and rituals, without necessarily involving belief in supernatural forces such as God.

The psychology of religion began in the late 1800s.

- William James, an early practitioner, was especially interested in mystical experiences – those moments in which all reality seems to be one, and even the distinction between subject and object breaks down.

- Carl Jung believed that, besides the individual's unconscious mind, there is a single "collective unconscious" for the whole human race. In it are "archetypes" – universal ideas found around the world, especially in myths.

A theory is a way of looking at something that makes it more understandable. There are three main kinds of theory in Religious Studies.

- The first are philosophical theories, which try to give definitions of terms such as "religion," offering necessary and sufficient conditions for applying these terms.

- Second are genetic/historical theories, which make religions more understandable by explaining where they came from and how they developed.

- Third are functional theories such as those of Durkheim and Freud, which explain what functions religions have for people.

By the dawn of the 20th century, the scholarly study of religion was evolving into the multi-disciplinary field it is today. The bias in favor of European culture and Christianity found early in Religious Studies was declining, and soon no reputable scholar would write about "primitives" or "savages." Scholars from diverse fields of expertise continued to be divided about the nature and purpose of religion. Some continued to argue that religion is gradually becoming obsolete as human beings discover more efficient ways to fulfill their needs and find meaning in life, but many scholars became convinced that religion fulfills a unique function in life and is here to stay.

This second idea is called the "essentialist" approach to religion. It says that religion is *sui generis* (its own kind of thing). That is often contrasted with "reductionist" approaches. Durkheim's idea that religion's job is to promote social cohesion is an example of a reductionist approach. It "reduces" religion to its social function, a function that could be fulfilled by something else, such as nationalism. The essentialist approach – the idea that religions do something for people that nothing else can do – has its roots in a branch of modern philosophy called phenomenology.

Back to Philosophy

We mentioned in Chapter 3 that modern philosophy reflected an abiding confidence in humans' ability to reason, provided the reasoning in question is carried out properly. Therefore, modern philosophers tried to identify just what constituted reliable reasoning. One of the key figures in this project was Immanuel Kant (d. 1804). Kant struggled with the conclusions drawn by another famous modern philosopher, David Hume (d. 1776), who stressed the importance of sense perceptions as the basis of knowledge. Hume was so committed to grounding knowledge in sense perception that he denied the objective reality of things such as cause and effect. He said we cannot observe cause and effect; we can observe only that something routinely happens after something else – such as a billiard ball moving after we hit it. We say that the movement is "caused" by hitting the ball, but we cannot see the transfer of anything. Kant rejected this radical skepticism. He argued instead that there are things that we know without having to observe them. For instance, we know that a square has four sides and that material things have dimensions. We know such things *a priori*, meaning that we know them without having to observe them. He included causality – the idea that all effects have causes – among our *a priori* concepts.

However, Kant continued, we must recognize that this kind of *a priori* reasoning resides in the reasoner, not in the thing being observed. The "thing being observed" is usually called the "thing in itself" (*Ding an sich*, in Kant's German). In philosophical language, it is called the noumenon (pl. noumena). And Kant said we cannot expect to know it. All we can know, according to Kant, is the thing as it appears to us. He called this – the thing as it appears to us – the phenomenon (pl. phenomena). Our impressions consist of the things we observe as they are interpreted through our *a priori* categories of understanding – such as causality. We can then manipulate these impressions. We can analyze them – reduce them to their constituent components. And we can synthesize them – put them together with other impressions. Either way, we must be very careful to follow rules of logic if we want our efforts to result in valid claims.

Some philosophers continued in this line of reasoning, with stress on the importance of validating claims (or "propositions," as philosophers like to call them). Some thinkers concluded, in fact, that the entire goal of philosophy was to validate claims through careful reasoning. These thinkers developed what is known as analytic philosophy.

According to the basic standards of analytic philosophy, all claims should be subject to three questions, which may be called the "three Cs." These questions, as we saw in Chapter 3, are: "Is the claim clear?" (Are the terms used to make the claim explained carefully, so that anyone who hears the claim can understand just what is being asserted?) "Is it coherent?" (Do the parts of the claim fit together in reasonable ways?) And "Is it credible?" (Does the claim follow accepted rules of reasoning so that we have good reasons to believe it?)

The three Cs seem very reasonable, of course, but when religious claims are subjected to them the results can be problematic, as we shall see in the work of analytic philosopher Antony Flew.

Analytic Philosophy: Antony Flew (d. 2010)

Antony Flew represents a movement within analytic philosophy known as logical positivism. Logical positivists try to clarify statements, identifying those that are meaningful and those that are not. Among the criteria they use are "verifiability" and "falsifiability." In order for a statement to be considered meaningful, logical positivists hold that there must be a way to demonstrate its truth or falsehood. In the natural sciences, if someone claimed to have a hypothesis but nothing would count as evidence for or against it, then it would not really be a hypothesis. It would be meaningless as a claim. The logical positivists extended this criterion beyond science to claims in philosophy and religion.

Applying it to philosophy, they concluded that a number of traditional philosophical claims are meaningless. The position called Materialism – that everything is material – is one of these statements. And so is Idealism – that everything is made up of minds or ideas. No possible test could show that either of these positions was true or false, and so they are not really claiming anything.

Flew applied the falsifiability test to religious claims. In books such as *God and Philosophy* (1966/2005), *The Presumption of Atheism* (1976), and *Atheistic Humanism* (1993), he concludes that many religious statements that seem to say something about God are not meaningful claims at all, because no event could prove them to be either true or false.

Some religious statements are testable and so meaningful as assertions. "Jesus rose from the dead" is one of them. We can imagine verifying this statement, as by discovering historical documents proving that Jesus was resurrected. We can also imagine falsifying this statement, as by discovering historical documents proving that Jesus' followers made up the story of the resurrection. However, other religious statements cannot be verified or falsified, and these are meaningless as assertions, according to Flew. Jews, Christians, and Muslims, for example, often say that God loves the human race. Indeed, Christians call God our loving Father. This sounds like a claim, much as you might say of your neighbor, "Clive is a loving father." But suppose that when you said that Clive is a loving father, someone pointed out that when Clive's children all came down with life-threatening swine flu he did nothing about it, even though he had the money and time to get them to a doctor. If you continue to insist that Clive is a loving father but you cannot explain his obvious dereliction of paternal duty, then your claim is not a meaningful assertion.

Flew applied the same argument to claims about God's goodness. Throughout history millions of people have lived miserable lives plagued by disease and poverty that could have been prevented by an all-powerful being. According to UNESCO, 35,000 children starve to death each day. The person who continues to insist that "God is a loving father," despite the clear evidence to the contrary, is describing a fiction she has chosen to believe, rather than making a meaningful assertion, Flew says. Meaningful assertions are revisable in light of evidence, so that if certain things happened, we would deny what we now assert. Flew's question to religious believers is, "What would have to occur or to have occurred to constitute for you a disproof of the love of, or even the existence of, God?" (Flew 1955, 99) If the answer is, "Nothing," Flew says, then their statements about God are meaningless as assertions. At best, these statements simply express comforting ideas that religious believers choose to maintain for reasons unacceptable to analytic philosophers.

It should be noted that Flew's rejection of claims about the existence of a loving father God did not preclude his belief in God. Following the dictates of reason, he came in his later years to believe that there is sufficient scientific evidence to support claims for the existence of God as the purposeful creator of our magnificently complex cosmos.

Phenomenology and Religious Studies

Not all philosophers limited valid claims to those that can be verified and falsified. Some looked at the distinction between noumena (things as they are in themselves) and phenomena (things as they appear to us) and proposed a new kind of study that focuses on phenomena. They called this study **phenomenology**.

Edmund Husserl (d. 1938) is usually regarded as the father of phenomenology. Rather than limit philosophy to things that are objectively verifiable, as the logical positivists did, Husserl believed that philosophy should concern itself with subjective things – those things that are functions of human consciousness. Emotions and memory and intention are all considered subjective phenomena and worthy of study.

But how can subjective phenomena be studied systematically? Husserl proposed a new method: **bracketing**. When we study phenomena, he said, we pay careful attention to what appears to us or is described to us, but we should not ask whether it is real or true beyond our experience of it. We put such questions "in brackets," ignoring them for the purposes of our study.

This method of carefully describing how things appear and not asking what is objectively true has become a dominant method in Religious Studies – so much so that phenomenology of religion has become a special kind of phenomenology.

Rudolf Otto (d. 1937)

Early representatives of phenomenology of religion focused on identifying phenomena associated with religious experience. Rudolf Otto went beyond describing to asserting that religious experience has a unique essence.

Otto was deeply influenced by the German theologian Friedrich Schleiermacher (d. 1834). Schleiermacher described the source of religion as a powerful feeling of dependence people have on something infinitely greater than themselves. Worship is their response to this feeling. It is the acknowledgment that everything they are comes from the divine. In his groundbreaking 1917 work, *The Holy: On the Irrational in the Idea of the Divine and Its Relation to the Rational*, Otto describes the source of religion as encounter with "the Holy."

The Holy is something we feel rather than something we understand. Our experience of the Holy, he says, is a "non-rational, non-sensory experience or feeling whose primary and immediate object is outside the self." To analyze the experience of the Holy, he describes what it feels like. He invents a new term for the object of this experience. He calls it the

numinous, and analyzes the numinous as something that, when experienced, evokes feelings of frightening and fascinating mystery. His Latin phrase is *mysterium tremendum et fascinans*.

Religious experience, Otto says, is negative and positive at the same time. There is awe and fear in it, but also attraction and fascination. It is beyond the experience called sublime, the sense of awe and wonder that one might feel when viewing a huge waterfall or a stunning work of architecture. Experiencing the Holy makes one feel utterly insignificant in the face of the Infinite, as when Abraham addresses God with the words, "Let me take it upon myself to speak to the Lord, I who am but dust and ashes." (Genesis 18:27)

Otto calls this sense of utter dependence "creature consciousness." "It is the emotion of a creature, submerged and overwhelmed by its own nothingness in contrast to that which is supreme above all creatures." (Otto 1958, 8–11) There are phenomenologists who do not concern themselves with whether or not the "religious experience" is caused by some transcendent reality, but Otto was convinced that religion is the human response to encounters with the ultimate reality, the Divine.

It is interesting to note here the drift away from using terms specific to one religious tradition in identifying the source of religious experience. Phenomenologists tend to use terms such as the Holy, the Sacred, Ultimate Reality, and the Divine rather than God. Otto says the Holy is not "the 'philosophic' God of mere rational speculation, who can be put into a definition." Rather the source of *mysterium tremendum* is a force "which is urgent, active, compelling, and alive." (Otto 1958, 24). It is common to all religious experience, around the world, and only to religious experience. This is why Otto is called an essentialist.

Mircea Eliade (d. 1986)

The universality of religious experience developed as a central feature of Religious Studies through the work of Mircea Eliade. Many people count him as the most influential scholar of religion in the 20th century. Eliade was editor of the *Encyclopedia of Religion*, and as a professor at the University of Chicago he mentored dozens of young scholars who went on to become professors.

He was also an essentialist. Criticizing prevailing views in Religious Studies, he was especially hostile to *reductionism*, explanations of religious phenomena that present them as nothing more than social, psychological, or economic phenomena. Against such thinkers as Durkheim, Freud, and Marx, Eliade insisted that religion is a distinct and unique phenomenon (*sui generis*). It reflects not merely the psychological and social dimensions of life, but another dimension – the Sacred. So religion should be explained "on its own terms," and

FIGURE 4.2 Mircea Eliade. Michael Mauney/Time & Life Pictures/Getty Images.

not be "explained away" as some other kind of phenomenon. Any reductionist explanation of religion, Eliade said, "is false; it misses the one unique and irreducible element in it – the element of the sacred." (Eliade 1963, xiii)

In applying a phenomenological approach, Eliade proceeded historically. Rather than simply describing the current phenomena, he traced various manifestations of the Sacred throughout history. For this reason, his methodology is known as History of Religions (or HR).

His primary interest was in older, nature-based religions, the kind that are often called "archaic." He thought that these ancient traditions show the essence of religion that lies deep within all traditions. Unlike the historically based traditions of Western monotheism, which identify manifestations of the Sacred in specific times and places, archaic religions treat the Sacred as in a special realm outside of history.

In *The Sacred and the Profane* (1957), Eliade says that the Sacred and the profane are different planes of existence. The profane is our ordinary world of physical objects in space and time. The Sacred lies outside of ordinary time and space; it is eternal and transcends the ordinary world described by history and science.

People think about the Sacred mostly in their myths – which Eliade describes as stories of events occurring in a special time not recorded by clocks and calendars. The aboriginal peoples of Australia call it "Dream Time." Renowned astrophysicist Carl Sagan (d. 1996), quoting 4th-century philosopher Sallustius, calls myths "things which never happened but always are." (Sagan 1977, 8)

Religious myths help people make sense of their lives and deal with life's problems. People connect themselves with myths by attending to hierophanies – manifestations of the Sacred in our world – and they perform rituals to reenact sacred events. However, for Eliade, rituals do not just imitate sacred events; they are not merely symbolic of events that were important in the past. Rituals allow people to transcend the ordinary world to actually participate in these sacred events themselves over and over, according to Eliade.

As Eliade studied hundreds of myths in the world's religions, he identified a number of patterns. Fertility and growth are important to people around the world, for example, and many cultures tell of a great cosmic tree from which things grew. Some archaic religions venerate an actual tree as the great cosmic tree, and say that it is the center of the universe.

Another myth found in many cultures is the story of how the human race started out in a paradise but then "fell" from that ideal state into the world we see today. A major motivation in religion, Eliade said, is to return to that original golden age, and so many religions have savior figures who rescue human beings from their fallen state and bring them to paradise. Again, from Eliade's viewpoint, these stories reflect awareness of the dual planes of existence, and the human urge to transcend the profane and live in the presence of the Sacred. Even in the "historical" traditions, Eliade says, there is a sense of sacred time in rituals such as the Passover Seder, which reenacts the Hebrew people's escape from enslavement in Egypt; the Sacrifice of the Mass, which reenacts Jesus' death on the cross in payment for human sinfulness; and Eid al-Adha, the Islamic festival commemorating Abraham's willingness to sacrifice his son when God told him to.

According to Eliade, religious myths and symbols reflect the deepest concerns of human beings, and so the Sacred is the most important dimension of human life. If we adopt the ordinary attitudes of Western culture since the Enlightenment, we may think of science and history as telling us the way things "really are." But actually, Eliade says, the Sacred is more real than everyday things and events. In order to appreciate the Sacred, we have to go beyond our ordinary thinking, especially its linear sense of time and its commitment to logic. Religious thought works with symbols, metaphors, and imagination, not with rational assertions. It is more like aesthetic experience, the thinking in poetry, music, and painting, than the thinking in science or engineering.

People living with modern technology in big cities have largely lost a sense of the Sacred, Eliade thinks, even if they say they are religious. They are hungry for the deep meaningfulness that the Sacred confers on life, especially the shared emotions with their fellows that religious rituals evoke. And almost as if he were prescribing a cure for the modern sense of alienation, he insists that people will never find satisfaction without it. This is because he believes that all people, by nature, seek the Sacred. As he put it, humans are naturally "religious" – *homo religiosus*. Eliade's views remain highly influential but, as we shall see in Chapter 10, his claims about *homo religiosus* have come under serious criticism.

Philosophy of Religion

Not all modern philosophers who are concerned with religion practice analytic philosophy or phenomenology. Some examine the credibility of religious claims. They practice the kind of philosophical theology traditionally known as philosophy of religion. Reflecting its Christian origins, philosophy of religion is practiced almost exclusively by Christian thinkers. John Hick and William Lane Craig are examples.

John Hick (b. 1922)

John Hick, an ordained Presbyterian minister with a Ph.D. in philosophy from Oxford, has spent decades analyzing Christian ideas philosophically. An example is his critique of the standard Christian teaching that Jesus died for our sins, in a book chapter titled "Atonement by the Blood of Jesus?" (Hick 1993) Like Thomas Aquinas, Hick starts with a question. He asks whether the traditional Christian doctrine of the Atonement makes sense today. According to this doctrine, Jesus' death on the cross paid the penalty owed by the human race to God for Original Sin. In Hick's words,

> The basic notion is … that salvation requires God's forgiveness and that this in turn requires an adequate atonement to satisfy the divine righteousness and/or justice. This atoning act is a transaction analogous to making a payment to wipe out a debt or cancel an impending punishment.

Hick points out that the doctrine of the atonement originated around 1100 when Anselm of Canterbury wrote his book *Why Did God Become Man*? Before Anselm, Christians had other ways of explaining what the death of Jesus had accomplished. As we shall see in Chapter 6, according to a popular view, the human race became the property of Satan after the sin of the first man and woman, just as slaves are the property of their masters. To redeem human beings, God offered Satan a bargain: he would trade his son's life for the human race. Satan eagerly accepted the bargain and released the human race. However, three days after Jesus died on the cross, God tricked Satan by bringing Jesus back to life.

This explanation of Christian redemption was popular for 700 years, but it "is only embarrassing today," Hick comments. As Anselm said, it was silly to think that the Devil could own the human race without God's permission. Anselm suggested instead that God, as a king, deserves obedience from his subjects, the human race. When Adam and Eve disobeyed God, they dishonored the King, and were required to "pay back the honor" of which they had deprived God. However, God is no ordinary king. He is infinite, and therefore the dishonor he suffered from the sin of Adam and Eve was infinite. This called for an infinite payment, which, of course, finite human beings could not make. The only infinite thing is God himself, and so only God could pay the infinite debt owed by the human race for the sin of Adam and Eve. He did this by becoming human (the "incarnation" of God into Jesus) so that he could represent the human race, and pay their debt. His dying on the cross constituted a blood sacrifice in payment of humanity's debt to God. The ritual that reenacts this payment is thus called "The Sacrifice of the Mass" by Catholic Christians.

Over the centuries, Hick points out, Christian theologians have modified Anselm's atonement theory in minor ways. The Protestant reformers Luther and Calvin said that sinners are like people convicted of crimes who have to "pay their debt" by serving time in prison or by being executed. After the sin of Adam and Eve, all humans were born guilty of their offense, and so all had to "pay their debt" to God. They could not do this themselves, Luther and Calvin said, so Jesus paid their debt for them by dying on the cross, following the pre-modern system that allows one person to be punished or executed in place of another.

Although many Christians have accepted various versions of the atonement theory for 900 years, Hick says, the theory makes four assumptions that no reasonable Christian today should accept:

> *Assumption 1* Sinning creates a debt owed by a person to God that can be paid by another person.

In non-moral matters, such as financial debt, it makes sense that someone could pay a debt for someone else. But in moral matters, we cannot pay another person's debt. We cannot serve another person's prison sentence, or go to the electric chair in their place. Hick says, "The idea that guilt can be removed from a wrongdoer by someone else being punished instead is morally grotesque." (Hick 2009, 104) Similarly, purposely punishing one person for what another person did is problematic, as when Christians say that God (the Father) punishes God (the Son) for the wrongdoing of Adam and Eve.

> *Assumption 2* God cannot forgive a sin unless the debt it created is paid.

Anselm based his atonement theory on medieval rules about people insulting the honor of a king, but Hick says that we cannot impose rules of 12th-century European society on the all-powerful Creator of the universe. If a sinner repents to God and humbly begs for forgiveness, who is Anselm to say that God cannot forgive this person fully? Similarly, Luther and Calvin based their versions of the atonement theory on 16th-century criminal law, but who are they to tell God under what conditions he can and cannot forgive a repentant sinner?

What Anselm, Luther, and Calvin are talking about, Hick says, is not really God's forgiving sin. Instead they are talking about God's demanding full payment for sin. Forgiving something means agreeing to overlook it and not demand a penalty for it. What is wrong with all versions of the atonement theory, Hick says, "is that they have no room for divine forgiveness. For a forgiveness that has to be bought by the bearing of a just punishment, or the giving or an adequate satisfaction, or the offering of a sufficient sacrifice, is not forgiveness, but merely the acknowledgement that the debt has been paid in full." (Hick 2009, 110)

Hick contrasts all such ideas of atonement as payment with the forgiveness that Jesus talked about and practiced. To the penitent thief crucified next to him, Jesus said simply, "You will be with me in paradise" – not "You will be with me in Paradise right after you pay off all the debt owed for your sins." Similarly, Hick says,

> In the Lord's Prayer we are taught to address God directly as our heavenly Father and to ask for forgiveness of our sins, expecting to receive this, the only condition being that we in turn forgive one another. There is no suggestion of the need for a mediator between ourselves and God or for an atoning death to enable God to forgive. (Hick 1993, 113)

Assumption 3 After Adam and Eve committed the first sin, the debt for this sin was inherited by all their descendants.

According to Hick, "The idea of an inherited guilt for being born as the kind of being that we are is a moral absurdity." (Hick 2009, 101)

Assumption 4 God paid the debt that was owed to him, to himself, by becoming a human being and having himself crucified.

The idea of paying a debt to oneself also seems absurd to Hick. Because of these and other unsolvable conceptual problems, Hick concludes that "the idea of the atonement is a mistake." (Hick 1993, 113)

William Lane Craig (b. 1949)

One of the popular traditional "proofs" for the existence of an all-powerful and intelligent Creator-God is called the *argument from design*, or the **Teleological Argument**, from the Greek *telos*, which means "purpose." The argument dates to medieval Christian thought (as we shall see in Chapter 6), and it was revived in the 18th century by William Paley. Paley's argument compared the world to a watch. If we found a watch on the ground, Paley said, we would naturally assume that it had been designed by an intelligent person, since all of its parts fit together to tick off the hours and minutes. And when we look at the natural world, Paley continued, we find vastly more design and organization. So it is reasonable to conclude that, just as the watch had a watchmaker, the world had a world-maker.

The most famous critic of the argument from design in modern philosophy was David Hume (d. 1776). He said that there is little similarity between the world and the things humans make, such as a watch, a house, or a ship, and so making conclusions about how the world started from what we know about how these things are made, is not sound reasoning. Even if there were a strong similarity between the world and things we make, this would not prove the existence of a single, omnipotent, omniscient, all-good God. Watches, houses, and ships are made by many craftspeople rather than just one. So if there were a strong similarity between a watch and the world, we would be as justified in concluding that several gods made the world as in concluding that a single God made it.

In the mid-19th century, Darwin's theory of evolution cast further doubt on the argument from design. It sketched an explanation for how simple forms of life could evolve into complex forms, by a process called "natural selection." According to this theory, all living things produce random genetic variations. Those variations that aid the survival of a species and are heritable (able to be passed from one generation to the next) will naturally be replicated, without external guidance.

The argument from design got a boost in the late 20th century when physicists and biochemists were able to discover some amazing facts about the universe. They suggested that the universe as we know it began to emerge – actually, explode – from some enormously dense state about 14 billion years ago. This is known as the "Big Bang" theory. Scientists then speculated that if things had been only slightly different, the universe would not have been able to produce living things. So either life is a totally random development, or the universe was "fine-tuned" to develop organic materials and then intelligent life.

William Lane Craig – philosopher, theologian, and biblical scholar – rejects the possibility that life is a random development and argues that the universe must have been designed by an intelligent God. In physics, for example, much has been discovered about the "strong force" that binds together protons and neutrons in the nucleus of an atom. If that force had been just 1% stronger than it is, almost all the carbon in the universe would have turned into oxygen. An increase of 2% would have made it impossible for protons to form, so that there wouldn't even be any atoms. If, on the other hand, the strong force had been 5% weaker than it is, the universe would have consisted only of hydrogen.

Or consider another force in atoms, the "weak force." Craig says that if it had been slightly weaker then the universe would have consisted entirely of helium. If gravitation had been slightly greater, then all stars would have been red dwarves, which are too cold to support planets where life could evolve.

What happened in the first moments of the Big Bang had to happen exactly as it did, Craig argues, or the universe as we know it would have never come about. The astrophysicist Stephen Hawking estimated that even a decrease of one part in a million million in the rate of expansion would have led to the universe's collapsing in on itself long ago. A similar increase in the rate of expansion would have prevented the galaxies from condensing out of the expanding matter. In either case, there never would have been stars and planets, and so life.

A more familiar set of features of matter are found in water, which is essential to all living things. Water expands as it changes from a liquid into a solid. This is why ice floats on the top of ponds and lakes. This feature of water is essential to life, for if ice were heavier than water, it would sink to the bottom of ponds and lakes, where it would remain until those bodies of water froze solid. In the actual universe, the heaviest water remains liquid at 4 degrees Celsius at the bottoms of ponds and lakes, where animals such as fish and frogs can live through the winter. Craig argues that the best explanation for such fine-tuning of the universe is that the universe was designed by an intelligent being – God.

Anthropology of Religion

As we saw in the previous chapter, among the earliest scholars of religion were the first anthropologists. Anthropologists continue to be highly significant in Religious Studies, contributing both methods of studying and theories of how religions work. In the work of two of the most influential anthropologists of religion in the 20th century, we shall see that anthropology tends to treat religion as a universal phenomenon, and it looks for diverse examples of religion.

Clifford Geertz (d. 2006)

First published in 1973, Clifford Geertz's *The Interpretation of Cultures* is a classic of Religious Studies. Geertz compares a culture to a work of art. It means something to people, and our task is to interpret this meaning. We need to go beyond simply describing what people do in religious rituals to what he calls "thick description." Geertz did not invent "thick description" (he borrowed the phrase from philosopher Gilbert Ryle), but his application of it to anthropology and Religious Studies has established it as a dominant method in these disciplines. A thick description involves being as thorough and specific as possible in one's descriptions, including not just what one observes but explanations from those being observed regarding their actions and motivations.

Geertz is also known for his insistence that religions are at the heart of culture. He defines a culture as "a system of inherited conceptions expressed in symbolic forms by means of which people communicate, perpetuate, and develop their knowledge about and attitudes toward life." (Geertz 1973, 89) Cultures are systems of symbols by which people make sense of their lives. Other animals are born with instincts to do most of the things they will need to do in life, but humans are born utterly helpless, have only a few instincts, and must learn all the skills they will need to survive. This is what culture provides for people, and religion is central to it.

Geertz describes religion as a system of symbols that provides a worldview, a picture about "a general order of existence." Symbols are anything that stands for something else; they can be words, pictures, rituals, statues, songs, etc. The worldview created by religious symbols is both descriptive, and prescriptive or normative. It describes both the way the world is, and the way the world should be.

Through their worldviews, religions produce "moods and motivations" in people, prompting them to think, feel, and act in certain ways. Many of these motivations are moral

FIGURE 4.3 Rangda the Witch, mask, Bali. J. Marshall – Tribaleye Images/Alamy.

virtues, such as courage, compassion, and generosity. Geertz gives the example of the puberty rites of the Native Americans known as the Plains Indians. To become a man, a boy must go on a "vision quest" that requires "endurance, courage, independence, perseverance, and passionate willfulness" – exactly the traits that he will need as a man to get through life. The vision quest is a mini-rehearsal for his life as a man.

Geertz presents detailed discussions of how religious rituals create worldviews that produce "moods and motivations." One involves a ritual on the island of Bali, in Indonesia. This ritual is a wild struggle between two mythical figures. The first is Rangda the witch, a vicious hag who snatches babies from their mothers and causes strife wherever she goes. Rangda represents all the evil that happens to the people of Bali. Geertz describes the person playing Rangda in the ritual:

> Her eyes bulge from her forehead like swollen boils. Her teeth become tusks curving up over her cheeks and fangs protruding down over her chin. Her yellowed hair falls down around her in a matted tangle…. Her long red tongue is a stream of fire. And as

she dances she splays her dead-white hands, from which protrude ten-inch claw-like fingernails, out in front of her and utters unnerving shrieks of metallic laughter. (Geertz 1973, 114)

Rangda's opponent is the Barong. He is a monster, too, but a friendly, comical one who helps the human race. The Barong is a four-legged figure who is played by two men in a horse-like costume and a wooden mask with chattering teeth. Geertz describes him as a "cross between a clumsy bear, a silly puppy, and a strutting Chinese dragon."

The ritual begins with Rangda threatening the village. Men with short swords come together to attack her, but she casts a spell over them. Then the Barong comes to the rescue, engaging Rangda in fierce combat. Sometimes he subdues her, sometimes she gets the better of him, but neither wins for very long.

The lesson in this ritual is that life is full of danger and struggle, and we have to cooperate if we are going to survive. However, life is not an epic struggle calling just for seriousness. As the ritual shows, there is considerable room for playfulness as well. Geertz says that the Barong embodies "the Balinese version of the comic spirit – a distinctive combination of playfulness, exhibitionism, and extravagant love of elegance, which, along with fear, is perhaps the dominant motive in their life."

As we have seen, religions handle evil in diverse ways. Many have a less comic approach and a more heroic approach, as in epics or tragedy. However, whatever stories and symbols religions use, they provide an overall picture of the world that makes sense of the suffering and struggle, and they provide coping mechanisms. They are therefore central to every culture.

Mary Douglas (d. 2007)

Mary Douglas produced another classic of Religious Studies, *Purity and Danger* (1970). In it she observes that most religions' worldviews contain ideas about what is pure and what is impure, and she proposes an explanation that has been highly influential.

In *Purity and Danger*, Douglas relates notions of purity and impurity to ideas of "clean" and "dirty." The basic idea of "dirty," she says, is that something is out of place.

Shoes are not dirty in themselves, but it is dirty to place them on the dining-table; food is not dirty in itself, but it is dirty to leave cooking utensils in the bedroom, or... clothing lying on chairs; out-door things in-doors; upstairs things downstairs.... In short our pollution behavior is the reaction which condemns any object or idea likely to confuse or contradict cherished classifications. (Douglas 1970, 48)

The opposite of "dirty" is "clean." Cleaning is putting things in order. This means putting things where they "belong." Where things belong can be rather arbitrary, but within any given system (or worldview) things belong in designated places determined by categories. In systems that consider rats to be dangerous vermin, one would not expect to find them in a religious building. However, there are worldviews in which rats are seen as receptacles of the souls of deceased nobles, or indeed as the nobles themselves, waiting to

FIGURE 4.4 Rats at Karni Mata, "Rat Temple," in Rajasthan, India. Rafal Cichawa/Shutterstock Images.

be reborn as humans. People who organize their lives according to such worldviews worship in temples that are sanctuaries for rats.

Everyone needs to classify things into categories, Douglas points out, in order to know how to act toward them. If we cannot label something as belonging to a class we recognize, then we do not know what to do with it, if anything. "It is part of our human condition to long for hard lines and clear concepts," she says. When we experience things that do not fit into our categories, we are puzzled and uncomfortable. We tend to avoid them or even condemn them.

Religions play key roles in establishing people's categories, says Douglas, to help us organize our world. The Hebrew Bible's Book of Leviticus, Chapter 11, and Deuteronomy, Chapter 14, for example, list creatures and tell us which ones we can eat, and which ones we cannot eat because they are "unclean." Here are a few:

> These are the living things which you may eat among all the beasts that are on the earth. Whatever parts the hoof and is cloven-footed and chews the cud, among the animals you may eat. Nevertheless among those that chew the cud or part the hoof, you shall not eat these: The camel, because it chews the cud but does not part the hoof, is unclean to you. And the rock badger, because it chews the cud but does not part the hoof, is unclean to you.... And the swine, because it parts the hoof and is cloven-footed but does not chew the cud, is unclean to you....

These you may eat of all that are in the waters. Everything in the waters that has fins and scales, whether in the seas or in the rivers, you may eat. But anything in the seas or the rivers that has not fins and scales… is an abomination to you….

Every swarming thing that swarms upon the earth is an abomination: it shall not be eaten. Whatever goes on all fours, or whatever has many feet, all the swarming things that swarm upon the earth, you shall not eat; for they are an abomination.

We can make sense of this classification into clean and unclean animals, Douglas says, if we consider the categories of animals that the ancient Israelites had. The animals with which they were most familiar were the ones they raised – sheep, goats, and cattle. These shared two features: they had split hooves and they chewed the cud. The first passage from Leviticus above makes those two features requirements for mammals that are to be eaten. If an animal is close enough to sheep, goats, and cattle, in having split hooves and chewing the cud, then we may eat it. But if it lacks either of these essential features, then we should avoid it. The pig, for example, has split hooves, but does not chew the cud. It does not fit into our accepted classification system. It is therefore potentially dangerous; it is impure or "unclean."

Many people today say that monotheistic scriptures forbid the eating of pigs because they can carry diseases such as trichinosis, but there is no hint of this explanation in the Hebrew Bible or the Qur'an (which also forbids the consumption of pork). The real reason, Douglas says, is that the pig is not similar enough to sheep, goats, and cattle, the animals that the nomadic peoples of scripture had always eaten. It was strange, out of place, and so unclean.

The second passage above is about things that live in the sea and in rivers. The paradigm of a water animal presented is a fish. The essential features of a fish are its fins and scales. So the passage above makes fins and scales requirements for water creatures that are to be eaten. A clam, for example, does not have fins or scales, it does not swim, and it does not even have eyes. Lobsters have eyes, but they are like land animals in having legs and walking. They cross categories, combining land animal features with water animal features. They do not fit neatly into either category, and so they are rejected as "an abomination." If the ancient Israelites had ever seen penguins, Douglas suggests, they would have called them unclean, too, because they are birds but do not fly like standard birds. Instead, they walk like land animals and swim like water animals.

The third passage above condemns animals that creep, crawl, or swarm. What is wrong with them, Douglas explains, is that they move in an indeterminate way that does not fit the Bible's description of land animals. A land animal is supposed to have four legs and move by hopping, jumping, or walking. But a snake or a worm has no legs at all and slithers. A centipede has way too many legs that move much too fast to see clearly. A reptile has the right number of legs but it does not walk on them. Instead, like a snake, it slides its body across the land. Not just the writers of the Bible, but most people even today find something disturbing about all these forms of locomotion. Douglas's explanation helps explain why the verb "to creep" is at the root of the adjective "creepy," and why Radiohead named its classic 1992 song "Creep."

Douglas' most influential theory, then, is that the basis of religions' purity rules is systems of categories. These are fundamental concepts, generally presented in religions' worldviews, with which people sort the things they experience, and so make sense of the world.

Sociology of Religion

Like anthropologists, sociologists look at religion as a collective experience. Indeed, their fields overlap significantly.

Peter L. Berger (b. 1929)

Peter Berger is best known for his work on the **social construction of reality**, which is the title of one of his most famous books (co-authored with Thomas Luckmann in 1966). The idea is that our concepts are influenced by our social contexts. Berger does not say that our thinking is completely determined by social context, but he does reject the idea that our thinking can be utterly independent of that context. We learn through language, and the use of language involves countless connotations and associations. (Think, for example, of terms such as "liberal," "conservative," "Muslim," and "Jew," and how each of them would be described by people from different groups.) We learn attitudes and value judgments as we learn our languages within our communities, Berger observes. We learn about our environments through these inherited meanings, and we learn about ourselves the same way. So even our self-perceptions are products of our social contexts.

However, meanings and the concepts based on them are not static. They develop over time. Human beings create societies, which then become their own realities complete with meaning-laden language to describe themselves and to ensure their survival. Berger calls this the "objectification" of society. These objectified societies then impact individuals within them. Societies transmit to their members the meanings and values of things, understandings of who they are as members of the group and what is expected of them, as well as what they can expect. (Compare, for example, the self-perceptions of someone who grows up being called "Your Highness" with someone who grows up being called a "foreigner.") The individuals then can reflect upon these experiences, and either repeat the meanings in future interactions or attempt to reinterpret the received meanings. Thus, the individual, although a product of society, can also impact society.

The vehicle through which meanings are conveyed, again, is language. Through language people share communities of meaning. Berger uses the term "knowledge" for these collective meanings and therefore describes his work as sociology of knowledge. Knowledge in this sense is also involved in an interactive process: it is a product of society but can also be used to change society.

Thus, according to Berger, people create their societies and are created by their societies through a process that plays out over generations. This is how we order our lives. Religion plays a significant role in this process, particularly at the stage of "objectification" of society. Religions are the means by which societies "reify" society, or "make it into something" of which individuals can feel a part and to which they can give their loyalty. Using terms such as "the Community of Saints" and "the People of God," they "sacralize" or sanctify the social order.

In another of his famous works, *The Sacred Canopy: Elements of a Sociological Theory of Religion* (1967), Berger explains that religions are social constructs serving specific functions. They establish contexts in which individuals can find meaning in their lives, and thus engender commitment to the "sacred community." They are, in other words, not "real" in the sense that that a tree or a cat is real; instead, like the societies they serve, they are constructs shared by groups in their "communities of meaning."

The consciousness of being members of a sacred community shared by individuals is thus based on fiction – something that human beings have made. It is a useful fiction, however. It gives us a sense that the world is indeed in order. Life is not chaotic and our lives are not just random accidents. Again, we see the connection between what is good and what is orderly in religion. In Berger's early career, he believed that sufficient reflection on this reality would allow societies to transcend the need for religion. He publicly embraced secularization theory, and predicted the demise of religion in accordance with the spread of modernity and its all-powerful rationality. However, in his later career he admitted that history had proven him wrong. In *The **Desecularization** of the World: Resurgent Religion and World Politics* (1999) he stated that "the whole body of literature by historians and social scientists loosely labeled 'secularization theory' is essentially mistaken." Berger predicted that the 21st and subsequent centuries would be just as religious as any other, perhaps more so, but not necessarily in the same ways. Indeed, he concludes, "Those who neglect religion in their analyses of contemporary affairs do so at great peril." (Berger 1999, 18)

Berger's admission of error about secularization does not detract from the significance of his contributions to sociology of religion. His theories regarding the relationship between individual and society and especially his focus on the role religions play in creating universes of meaning remain highly influential. As well, Berger's method of studying religions remains useful. Part of this method is "methodological atheism," which he proposed in *The Sacred Canopy*. Similar to our "willing suspension of belief," methodological atheism in the study of religion does not entail rejection of one's own religious positions and identity but, as Husserl would say, "bracketing" them in a conscious effort to view religious claims without preconceptions or prejudgment (prejudice).

Robert N. Bellah (b. 1927)

Robert Bellah's treatment of secularization is quite distinct from that of Berger. Rather than make predictions about the decline of religion, he expands the definition of religion to include contemporary developments.

Bellah is best known for his description of "American civil religion," the title he gave in a 1967 article to what many citizens of the United States see as simply their way of life. For Bellah, this way of life involves holidays and rituals such as the Thanksgiving meal and the Fourth of July fireworks. These rituals reinforce a worldview complete with group loyalties, and motivations to behave in accordance with specific values. These values, such as courage in the face of tyranny, individualism, and selflessness, are supported by founding myths and heroes (think of George Washington and the cherry tree). For Bellah, the lack of a supernatural element in American civil religion is irrelevant.

Civil religion does not replace traditional religions necessarily; it exists parallel to them. As Bellah put it, "While some have argued that Christianity is the national faith … few have realized that there actually exists alongside… the churches an elaborate and well-institutionalized civil religion in America." (Bellah 1967, 1)

In describing civil religion, Bellah effectively turned the study of religion on its head. Traditionally, scholars looked at examples of phenomena that people identified as religious, and then tried to construct definitions broad enough to encompass all the phenomena involved. Bellah took a broad description of religion and then found examples of human activity that fit the description, even if they were not identified by the people involved as religious. This opened the way for analysis of numerous "varieties of civil religion," as he elaborated in a 1982 book by that title.

Bellah believes that the development of civil religion is one aspect of secularization in the United States. Individualism is another. He views individualism as a corollary of secularization, which he described as "the emptying out of any religious content of culture." America has always been individualistic, Bellah observes, but, without a public presence of religion in culture, individualism may become excessive.

Participating in a religious community can moderate excessive individualism, Bellah believes, but he also worries that identification with a religious community can itself become excessive. As he wrote in *Uncivil Religion: Interreligious Hostility in America* (1987), despite secularization, religions in America remain focal points of communal and individual identity. He focuses in particular on antagonism between Christians and Jews, between Protestant and Catholic Christians, and between liberals and conservatives of all traditions. As with his treatment of individualism, Bellah here is concerned with both the positive and negative effects of religion.

Psychology of Religion

As we saw in the previous chapter, one of the founders of the field of psychology, Sigmund Freud, dealt in passing with religion, but focused almost exclusively on what he considered its negative impacts. Another father of the field of psychology focused more extensively on religion and, by contrast to Freud, saw in religion both positive and negative aspects.

William James (d. 1910)

Unlike Bellah, William James was not worried about religion becoming private or personal; personal religious experience was his primary interest. Indeed, he defined religion as "the feelings, acts, and experiences of individual men in their solitude; so far as they apprehend themselves to stand in relation to whatever they may consider divine." (James 2008, 31)

James believed that psychologists should study these intense kinds of religious experience, because they show us extreme forms of normal mental patterns. He even speculated about

PART I THE TOOLS

the experiences of ancient religious figures, those who influenced the development of the religion with which he was most familiar, Christianity. What did the experience of religious revelation feel like to them? When Abraham first heard the call from Yahweh to leave his home and move to a new land, what form might that experience have taken? When Moses experienced God in the Burning Bush, or Job heard the voice of God in the whirlwind, what was that like? By thinking about "the inner experiences of great-souled persons wrestling with the crises of their fate," James said, we can discover something about religion in general.

William James (the brother of novelist Henry James) was not concerned with whether or not the divinities people described were real. However, he said, "If there be higher spiritual agencies that can directly touch us, the psychological condition of their doing so might be our possession of a subconscious region which alone should yield access to them." In other words, if there really are higher powers such as God, then communicating with them – or "experiencing" them – might require special mental abilities or attitudes. Perhaps it is possible for people to cultivate those abilities or attitudes.

James was especially interested in mystical experiences – the kinds of intense mental or emotional experiences some people report and interpret as having resulted from experience of the divine. To induce such

FIGURE 4.5 William James. Paul Thompson/FPG/Getty Images.

experiences himself, he took drugs such as chloral hydrate, nitrous oxide, and peyote. He then developed a scientific description of mystical experiences. Mystical experiences, James said, have four features. First, they are "ineffable," meaning they cannot be described to someone who has not experienced them. Second, they have a "noetic quality"; they are so intense that they make us feel that we are understanding a truth or learning something, perhaps for the first time. Third, mystical states are transient: they come and go rather quickly. Fourth, during a mystical experience, people feel passive: they feel that some external agent is acting upon them. They do not feel that they themselves are creating the experience.

As James explored many kinds of religious experience, he thought that some fostered mental health while others did not. His terms were "the religion of healthy-mindedness" and "the sick soul." The healthy-minded religious person appreciates "the goodness of life" and is optimistic, while the sick soul is pessimistic. Even when the sick soul seems happy, "something bitter rises up: a touch of nausea, a falling dread of the delight, a whiff of melancholy." (James 2008, 106) (Scholars have observed that this description seems to reflect James' personal experiences with depression and thoughts of suicide.)

Some sick souls, he said, are converted to healthy-mindedness – he calls such people the "twice-born." Citing as examples Augustine of Hippo and Leo Tolstoy, James said that the twice-born person reaches a "state of assurance" with "the loss of all the worry, the sense that all is ultimately well, …the peace, the harmony, the *willingness to be*, even though the outer conditions should remain the same." (James 2008, 185)

As a philosopher and psychologist, James eventually came up with a general assessment of mystical and other religious experiences. He said that on the whole they are beneficial. Indeed, they are "amongst the most important biological functions of mankind." In religious experiences, "the further limits of our being plunge, it seems to me, into an altogether other dimension of existence from the sensible and merely 'understandable' world." (James 2008, 373–374)

Carl Jung (d. 1961)

Carl Jung is another towering figure in psychology who took religion very seriously. Early in his career, Jung collaborated with Sigmund Freud, accepting Freud's basic ideas about the importance of experiences and perceptions of which we are not conscious (because they are stored in the "unconscious"), the role of dreams in revealing what is happening in the unconscious, and the origin of psychological problems in early childhood experiences. However, after five years, Jung and Freud parted ways. While Freud is considered the founder of psychoanalysis, Jung is the founder of a school of psychotherapy called "analytic psychology." Freud gave us terms such as the "ego" and the "unconscious." Jung gave us the term "complex" to name mental problems, as in "inferiority complex," and the concept of introverted and extroverted personalities.

After his split with Freud, Jung resigned his teaching job and deliberately withdrew into his own private mental world. As a child, he had often had vivid dreams and fantasies, and now he gave free rein to the irrational, unconscious part of his mind. He took careful notes about his dreams and fantasies, and developed theories about what they meant. All this became important in Jung's method of psychotherapy, a method he called "individuation." Its goal was to have patients strip away social conventions to discover their unique true selves.

In our dreams and fantasies, Jung said, there are personal elements that arise from our individual experiences, but there are also universal elements found in the "collective unconscious," a part of the mind that is shared by everyone, in all cultures and all historical periods. Jung called the ideas in the collective unconscious **archetypes**. They include "the father," "the mother," "the child," and a patriarchal figure Jung called the "god-archetype."

According to Jung, these archetypes in the unconscious mind are the source of the thinking that is at the root of all religion. Religious myths are expressions of these ideas found in everyone's mind. To understand the world's religions, Jung thought, we need to analyze their symbols and myths, and trace them to the archetypes.

Jung studied many religious traditions, but was especially interested in Christianity and its role in shaping European culture. This culture had developed in three stages, he said – the religious, the scientific, and the psychological. In each stage people handled the archetypes in the collective unconscious differently. In the Middle Ages, about 500 to 1500, the archetypes were expressed in religious images such as God, Jesus, and the Virgin Mary. This is obvious in medieval art, architecture, and literature. In the Renaissance and the

Enlightenment, roughly 1500–1900, the emphasis was on the conscious rational mind. So the unconscious with its archetypes was neglected and even repressed. Science was valorized as the highest form of thought, and religious thinking and anything else based on the unconscious were considered obsolete. The last stage of European culture, according to Jung, is the psychological era, starting around 1900, when scientists such as Freud and he discovered the unconscious mind. Now, at last, Jung said, we can acknowledge the importance of the unconscious mind and study it scientifically. Since religion is based on archetypes in the unconscious mind, we shall finally be able to understand religion across all cultures in an objective way, by studying the various expressions of the archetypes.

Jung influenced a number of important scholars of religion who focus on the meanings of myths. Joseph Campbell (d. 1987) is chief among them. Campbell, who was also influenced by James Frazer (see Chapter 3) and Rudolf Otto, developed an immensely popular documentary, televised in six parts, called "The Power of Myth." In it he discussed "hero types" – his version of a Jungian archetype, using Jesus, the Buddha, and movie heroes as examples, and a massive array of other aspects of traditional and popular culture.

Conclusion: Theories and Methods

In the final chapter, we shall see that the scholarly study of religion continues to develop. Before this, however, we shall survey the major religious traditions, giving examples of the use of the theories and methods – the "tools" – of Religious Studies. These tools are what we have been discussing in this and the previous chapter.

Many of the tools of scholarship are named for the people who developed them. For example, scholars speak of Freudian or Marxist or Weberian interpretations. However, theories and methods can also be classified more generically.

A theory – from the Greek *theorein*, which means "to look at" – is a way of looking at something that makes it more understandable. We can make something more understandable in several ways, so scholars identify several kinds of theory.

Philosophical Theories

A philosophical theory of X attempts to say exactly what X is; it attempts to "define" X. A definition states the essential features of X. It is important to remember that "essential" is a technical term in philosophy. It is an adjectival form of the word "essence," and refers to those features of X without which X would cease to be X. For example, a square is essentially a rectangle with equal sides. Its size and color are not essential to the description of a square, but in order for something to be a square, it has to be a rectangle with equal sides. And anything that is a rectangle with equal sides has to be a square. Those are what philosophers call "necessary and sufficient conditions" for being a square.

Unfortunately, it is not easy to give a philosophical theory of religion. In the previous chapter we saw one philosophical theory of religion, that of Edward Burnett Tylor. He defined religion as "the belief in spiritual beings." This fits many religious traditions, but not all of them. As we shall see in Chapter 7, early Buddhism, for example, did not require belief in souls, gods, or other spiritual beings. So either we have to disqualify Buddhism as a religion or we have to disqualify Tylor's definition for not giving us necessary features of religion. Nor does his definition give us the sufficient conditions of religion. There are many people who believe in spirits but this does not make their belief a religion. It is perfectly possible to believe in ghosts, for example, but belong to no religion at all.

If "belief in spiritual beings" is neither necessary to religion nor sufficient for religion, then it is not a workable theory of religion. Many people after Tylor have offered other philosophical theories of religion, but none has been accepted by all scholars. In fact, as we said in Chapter 1, there is no universally accepted philosophical theory of religion. Some thinkers even say that there are no essential features shared by all religions.

Genetic/Historical Theories

Another way to make something more understandable is to explain where it came from. This kind of explanation can be called a genetic theory, from the Greek word *genesis*, meaning "origin." We can also call it a historical theory. Such theories make their subject more understandable by describing its origins and development through history.

Genetic or historical theories of religion that trace current religions back through time to early forms of religion work in this way. To refer to Tylor again, his genetic or historical explanation for all of today's religions was that they began with belief in *animae*, souls, and developed from there.

A corollary of genetic or historical theories of religion is that religious traditions are related to one another. We saw this expressed directly in the work of Mircea Eliade, who developed one of the most prominent 20th-century approaches to Religious Studies, known as History of Religions (or HR, for short).

Functionalist Theories

A third way to make something more understandable is to explain what its function is. Functional theories are very common in our everyday life. We may not know how to define light or explain how it originated, but we can describe what it does. Knowing that light bounces off things and hits our eyes, allowing us to see them, helps us understand light, even if only minimally.

In the 20th century, there were several theories that tried to make religion more understandable by explaining what its functions are. The two main kinds of function that scholars focused on were psychological functions and social functions. As we saw, Freud said that the basic function of religion is to make people feel more secure, while Marx said the basic function of religion is to make people submissive to economic oppression.

As we have seen, theories can also be contrasted as either reductionist or essentialist. According to reductionist theories, religion can be "reduced" to something else, as Freud did when he claimed that religion makes people feel secure. Such theories are called "reductionist" because they claim that the functions performed by religions could just as well be performed by something else, such as a loving family or a therapist (in Freud's case). Essentialist theories, on the other hand, claim that religion is *sui generis* – it is its own kind

PART I THE TOOLS

of thing. In essentialist theories, religion does something that nothing else can do. As we saw, Otto and Eliade provide good examples of essentialist theories of religion.

In Part II, we shall apply some of these theories and methods to various religious traditions of the world, as we try to understand what religions are, how they arose and developed, and what they do for people.

DISCUSSION QUESTIONS

1. Antony Flew said that some statements in religion are unfalsifiable – that religious people do not allow anything to count against them. Can you think of any other kinds of statement or belief that people stick to, no matter what? Would you count them as meaningful?

2. Rudolf Otto's description of religious experience seems accurate for some religious experiences. Can you think of any religious experiences for which it is not accurate?

3. Mircea Eliade said that religious myths reveal the deepest concerns that human beings have. Can you think of an example from a religion you know?

4. John Hick argued that the Christian doctrine of the Atonement no longer makes sense. Can you think of ways to respond to Hick's criticism?

5. William Lane Craig argued that the universe had to be "fine-tuned" by an intelligent Creator, or human beings would not have appeared on Earth. Do you see any weaknesses in this argument?

6. Clifford Geertz said that religions evoke moods and motivations in people. Can you think of examples in your own experience?

7. Mary Douglas said that something is impure/unclean if it violates our ideas about what things are supposed to be. Can you think of examples in your own experience?

8. Would Durkheim agree with Berger's theory about the objectification of society?

9. Robert Bellah analyzed American patriotic holidays such as the Fourth of July as rituals. In what ways does this seem reasonable, and in what way does it seem inaccurate?

10. Together with at least five people, try to reach agreement on a definition of religion.

REFERENCES

Robert Bellah, "Civil Religion in America," *Journal of the American Academy of Arts and Sciences*, 96 (1967), 1–21.

Robert N. Bellah, *Uncivil Religion: Interreligious Hostility in America*. New York: Crossroad, 1987.

Robert N. Bellah and Phillip E. Hammond, *Varieties of Civil Religion*. San Francisco: Harper, 1982.

Peter L. Berger, *The Sacred Canopy: Elements of a Sociological Theory of Religion*. Garden City, NY: Doubleday, 1967.

Peter L. Berger, editor, *The Desecularization of the World: Resurgent Religion and World Politics*. Grand Rapids, MI: Ethics and Public Policy Center and Eerdmans, 1999.

Peter L. Berger and Thomas Luckmann, *The Social Construction of Reality: A Treatise on the Sociology of Knowledge*. Garden City, NY: Doubleday, 1966.

Mary Douglas, *Purity and Danger: An Analysis of the Concepts of Pollution and Taboo*. Harmondsworth: Penguin, 1970.

Mircea Eliade, *The Sacred and the Profane*. New York: Harcourt Brace Jovanovich, 1957.

Mircea Eliade, *Patterns in Comparative Religion*. Lincoln, NE: University of Nebraska Press, 1963.

Antony Flew, "Theology and Falsification," in *New Essays in Philosophical Theology*, Antony Flew and Alasdair MacIntyre, editors. London: SCM Press, 1955.

Antony Flew, *God and Philosophy*. Amherst, NY: Prometheus, 1966/2005.

Antony Flew, *The Presumption of Atheism*. New York: Barnes and Noble, 1976.

Antony Flew, *Atheistic Humanism*. Amherst, NY: Prometheus, 1993.

Clifford Geertz, *The Interpretation of Cultures*. New York: Basic, 1973.

John Hick, *The Metaphor of God Incarnate*. Louisville, KY: Westminster John Knox, 1993.

John Hick, *Who Or What Is God? And Other Investigations*. New York: Seabury Books, 2009.

William James, *The Varieties of Religious Experience*. Rockville, MD: Arc Manor, 2008.

Rudolf Otto, *The Idea of the Holy*. New York: Oxford University Press, 2nd ed., 1958.

Carl Sagan, *Dragons of Eden*. New York: Random House, 1977.

FURTHER READING

Robert N. Bellah, *Beyond Belief: Essays on Religion in a Post-Traditionalist World*. Berkeley: University of California Press, 1991.

William Lane Craig, *Reasonable Faith: Christian Truth and Apologetics*. Front Royal, VA: Crossway, 3rd ed., 2008.

Mircea Eliade, Rosemary Sheed, translator, *Patterns in Comparative Religion*. New York: Meridan, 1958.

Mircea Eliade, Willard R. Trask, translator, *History of Religious Ideas, Vol. 1: From the Stone Age to the Eleusinian Mysteries*. Chicago: University of Chicago Press, 1981.

Mircea Eliade, *Myth and Reality (Religious Traditions of the World)*. Long Grove, IL: Waveland, 1998.

Antony Flew and Alasdair MacIntyre, editors, *New Essays in Philosophical Theology*. London: SCM Press, 1955.

John Hick, *Philosophy of Religion*. Upper Saddle River, NJ: Prentice Hall, 4th ed., 1989.

William James, *William James: Writings 1902–1920 – The Varieties of Religious Experience, Pragmatism, A Pluralistic Universe, The Meaning of Truth, Some Problems of Philosophy, Essays*. New York: Library of America, 1988.

Carl G. Jung, Joseph Campbell, editor, R. F. C. Hull, translator, *The Portable Jung*. Harmondsworth: Penguin, 1976.

PART II
USING THE TOOLS

Surveying World Religions

EARLY TRADITIONS

"Couldn't be a man. Must be a god!"

FIGURE 5.1 © Al Ross 1989/The New Yorker Collection/www.cartoonbank.com.

The Religion Toolkit: A Complete Guide to Religious Studies, First Edition. John Morreall and Tamara Sonn.
© 2012 John Morreall and Tamara Sonn. Published 2012 by Blackwell Publishing Ltd.

A belief in all-pervading spiritual agencies seems to be universal.

CHARLES DARWIN

5

Overview

Our species, *Homo sapiens*, has existed for about 150,000 years. For most of that time, they lived as hunters and gatherers.

- Archaeological evidence suggests that early hunters had an intimate knowledge of the animals they ate and the animals that might eat them.

- Some scholars say that this sensitivity to animals led early humans to *animism* – the tendency to think of everything that moves as alive.

- In addition to their sensitivity to animals, early humans were sensitive to other human agents, who also might benefit them or harm them.

- According to some scholars, that sensitivity to human agents naturally led to anthropomorphism – the tendency of humans to think of other things as like humans.

- Animism and anthropomorphism help explain the development of religion, because beings like us tend to perceive events in nature, such as thunderstorms, as the actions of agents. And so early humans might have believed in agents other than living human beings, such as spirits, ghosts, and gods.

- Thinking of natural events as coming from agents allowed early humans to feel that they could influence

Prehistoric Religions?
  Animism and Anthropomorphism
  Death Rituals
  Fertility Goddesses
  Hunting Rituals
  Shamans
  Ancient Traditions, Oral Traditions, and Religion

The Neolithic Revolution and the Rise of Historic Religions

Conclusion

such natural forces as the rain and the sun, sickness and health. They could do this by persuading these agents to help them, as by sacrificing something of value.

- In the Upper Paleolithic period (10,000–35,000 years ago), we find considerable archaeological evidence of activities that can be called religious. Most of them involved death, hunting, or fertility, all major concerns of early human beings.

- Early death rituals indicate a belief that humans survive death and need food and tools in the next life.

- There is evidence of the concern of early humans with fertility in about 200 figurines made between 20,000 and 27,000 years ago. They have large breasts, wide hips and prominent vulvas. Some scholars say that they served as "fertility goddesses."

- The concern of early humans with prey animals and with predators shows up in several European caves where between 11,000 and 30,000 years ago early artists drew detailed images of bison, bulls, and other animals.

- A few images from caves seem to represent figures that are part animal and part human, something like the shamans in various religions later on.

- The animism and anthropomorphism of oral tribal cultures today may be similar to the thinking of early humans.

About 12,000 BCE, some human groups made the transition from hunting and gathering to agriculture and herding. This is called the **Neolithic Revolution**.

- In the new agricultural way of life, the control of land became important, and so men's ability to fight did too. From land ownership and war, some scholars say, came empires, slavery, and men's domination of women.

- From the time of the earliest empires and states, government and religion have been linked.

While several features of early human cultures, like features of oral tribal cultures today, seem similar to what we now call "religion," those cultures seem to lack some basic distinctions that are made by religions. Those include the distinctions between natural and supernatural, sacred and profane/secular, and religious/non-religious.

There is a traditional Gospel song called "Old-Time Religion." The first verse is "Give me that old-time religion. Give me that old-time religion. Give me that old-time religion. It's good enough for me." The kind of religion referred to is Evangelical Protestantism, which goes back almost three centuries. But what if we wanted to find really old-time religion?

Our species, *Homo sapiens*, has been around for 150,000 years. But the oldest institutionalized religions we have today, Hinduism and Judaism, were created only three to six thousand years ago. According to the Jewish calendar, 2011 CE is year 5771, and the Hindu calendar puts it at 5112, but that leaves about 97% of human history unaccounted for. However, many scholars of religion – especially essentialists such as Otto and Eliade (see Chapter 4) – believe that religion is an "essential" aspect of human life. If this is the case, then it should be evident even in the earliest societies. So they look at evidence of earlier human activity that might be called religious. They look at objects and images that early humans made, and figure out if they might have had religious significance.

Calendars

Many ethnic groups have traditions that explain the origins of their world and their group. Many also date their history from this beginning point. Many peoples' calendars have fallen into disuse and been lost to history. But there are still more than 40 calendars in use worldwide. The Christian calendar begins with the birth of Jesus, and is known as *anno domini* (AD), "year of the Lord." It uses "BC" to refer to the time before Jesus was born. ("BC" refers to "before Christ.") Since the Christian calendar is the most widely used calendar today, its dates are often referred to by scholars as "common era" dates (CE).

Prehistoric Religions?

As we mentioned in Chapter 1, some of our earliest evidence of human beings seems to depict what modern Western observers identify as religious ritual. About 17,000 years ago, for example, our distant ancestors created images such as those in Figure 5.2 in caves in Lascaux, France. There are over 2,000 images on the walls in these caves: 600 are drawn or painted, and 1,500 are engraved into walls. To make some of the images on the ceilings, archaeologists say, the painters must have climbed up on scaffolding. Of the figures represented, the most common are horses – 364 of them, and stags – 90 of them. There is only one representation of a human. The most famous figures are four huge bulls, one 17 feet long.

What can we say about images like these? One thing they show is that early humans knew well the shape of some animals. They were familiar with their muscles, horns, and other body features. This suggests that they often looked at animals up close, studied their features, and watched them move. This makes sense since at this time our ancestors lived not by farming, but by hunting and gathering food. To be successful at killing prey, they had to know what different species looked like and how they moved, where their most vulnerable points were, and how they defended themselves. Hunters would track animals, sometimes for days, figuring out their movements from clues such as footprints and odors. And when they closed in for the kill, they had to attune their movements to the animal's, to prevent it from escaping. With large prey, such as bull and bison, they had to respond quickly to the animal's aggressive movements or they would be gored or trampled. To do all this, they had to be sensitive to the animal's every move.

Another reason that early humans had to be sensitive to animals is that the animals also hunted them. Imagine what it was like for early humans living on the East African grasslands to sleep on the ground at night, surrounded by lions, leopards, and hyenas. They had to be alert to every rustle in the grass and every sound that might be coming from a predator's throat. Quieter, smaller threats from poisonous snakes and spiders were common, too. Our first ancestors, in short, had to pay close attention to what they might kill, and to what might kill them.

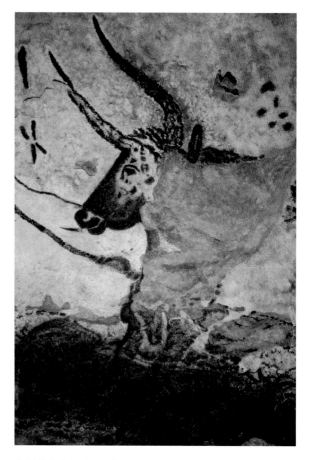

FIGURE 5.2 Caves in Lascaux, France. © Photononstop/ SuperStock.

Animism and Anthropomorphism

This sensitivity to animals, some scholars say, led early humans to *animism*, which, as we saw in Chapter 3 in our discussion of E.B. Tylor, is the tendency to see everything that moves as somehow alive. *Animé* is Greek for "soul"; it is the term that gives us our words "animate" and "animal." Animism was a survival strategy for the first humans. Understandably, under the circumstances it was safest to assume that, if something moves, it is either a predator or prey, unless you know otherwise. Treat all movements as coming from "agents" – living things that see you and can hurt you or benefit you. People who thought this way were perhaps a little paranoid, but, with dangerous animals all around, paranoia could be a good survival strategy.

Adding to early humans' sensitivity to animals was their sensitivity to other people – who also could hurt them or help them. Until a few thousand years ago, everybody lived in tribes, as many people still do. Human babies then, as now, were utterly helpless and completely dependent on other people to survive – first their mother, then their family, then the wider social group. So they quickly learned to distinguish their mother's face, and voice, from everyone else's. As they grew, they learned which faces were in their tribe and which were not, and which were friendly and which dangerous.

A large part of the right brain of humans – the part of the brain that deals primarily with visual, audio, and spatial recognition and manipulation – is devoted to identifying faces. In fact, because we are so attuned to faces, we tend to see them everywhere – not just on people. In Figure 5.3 is a rock formation on Mars in which people have "seen" a human face.

This hypersensitivity to other humans led to another *ism*, anthropomorphism – the tendency to see things as human. The word is from the Greek *anthropos*, human being, and *morphé*, shape. The roots of anthropomorphism probably go back long before our ancestors were *Homo sapiens*. Three million years ago in southern Africa, pre-human members of the group *Australopithecus* weighed only about fifty pounds as adults, and had brains about one-quarter the size of ours. Archaeologists discovered in one of their camps a small reddish-brown jasper stone (Figure 5.5) that was from an area several miles away. Apparently, an Australopithecus had picked up this stone and carried it to a camp miles away. We cannot say for sure what they were thinking, but it seems plausible that they brought it home because it looked as if it had a face.

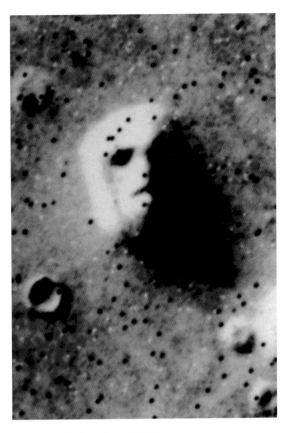

FIGURE 5.3 Face in rock – Mars. © 1989 Roger Ressmeyer/NASA/Corbis.

What, if anything, do animism and anthropomorphism have to do with religion? Contemporary psychologist Pascal Boyer, confirming some of the theories of early anthropologists such as Tylor and Frazer, claims that early humans had a highly sensitive *agency-detection system* in their brains. They naturally tended to perceive any movement as the action of a living thing – this is the animism. And they tended to think of anything alive as like themselves – this is the anthropomorphism. If tree branches moved suddenly, or something rustled the grass, or the ground rumbled, they became alert and observed carefully. Their muscles might have tensed as they went into a fight-or-flight mode. They got ready to confront whatever it was, or to run away from it. Anyone who has slept alone in a creaky old house during a storm, with the wind making weird noises and lightning casting strange shadows on the walls and ceiling, may well have experienced their own agency-detection system at work. They probably tended to interpret all these movements and sounds as the actions of an animal or person. If that interpretation was right and a rat or a burglar was coming toward them, then their animism and anthropomorphism paid off, since they were better prepared to deal with the threat. If, on the other hand, the disturbance was only a branch brushing against the window, then all they wasted was a little adrenaline and anxiety.

The Nun Bun

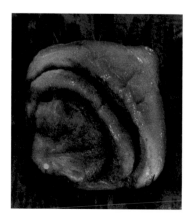

FIGURE 5.4 Nun Bun, Tennessee 1996.
AP Photo/Nashville Tennessean/Bill Steber.

In 1996 in Nashville, Tennessee, a customer in the Bongo Java Coffee Shop noticed that the bun pictured above looked like Mother Teresa. Within a week, photos of the "Nun Bun" were appearing in news media around the world. Bob Bernstein, owner of the shop, had the bun coated with shellac and put in a glass case. In 2005, someone broke into the shop and stole the bun.

FIGURE 5.5 The Makapansgat cobble/pebble.
© The Natural History Museum, London.

Employing aspects of Darwin's theory of natural selection (see Chapter 3), thinkers such as Boyer believe that those early humans who were ultra-sensitive to possible agents around them survived longer and produced more offspring than those who were less sensitive. So over tens of thousands of years of evolution, our species ended up with a hypersensitive agency-detection system. This is why we might easily mistake a rock for a bear, but we are much less likely to mistake a bear for a rock.

This hypersensitive agency-detection system in early humans naturally led them to look for an agent whenever anything happened, especially something important. If someone died suddenly, and no animal or person had attacked them, early humans might think that some special kind of agent was at work. That agent might be a jealous mate who used some special power to kill them. It might be the ghost (see Chapter 2) of an angry relative. It might be some cosmic or supernatural payback for some offense.

The First Work of Art?

FIGURE 5.6 Rock person, Morocco. Robert G. Bednarik.

In 1999 the rock pictured above was found in Morocco. Its original shape was somewhat human, and 400,000 years ago, before *Homo sapiens* evolved, someone carved grooves into it to better define this shape. They also added ochre, a dark red coloring, to it. Anthropologists speculate that whoever reshaped and colored this rock did so because they saw it as like themselves.

This tendency to attribute bad events to an agent – natural or supernatural, mundane or cosmic – is still found today in traditional religions. "Traditional religions" is what scholars call religious traditions that are indigenous to particular areas, continue to be transmitted orally from one generation to the next, and have not spread beyond their native areas. (There are many traditional religions in Africa and Australia, for example. We shall look at one example of Native American traditional religions in Chapter 9.) It is common in traditional religions to treat death as a result of agency. When someone dies, people say that some agent must have killed them. If no one stabbed or poisoned them, then it may have been someone with extraordinary power – a **witch** casting an evil spell, or a spirit getting revenge, or a god or cosmic force administering justice. Even if their community knows that the person died from pneumonia or cancer, they still ask who killed them – killed them by giving them pneumonia or cancer.

Sacrifice

The first book of the Hebrew Bible tells the story of the first two children: Cain and Abel, sons of Adam and Eve. The Qur'an, Islamic sacred scripture, tells the story as well. The two decide to offer sacrifices to God. Cain gathers some of his best grain and burns it on an altar. Abel slaughters a perfect lamb and burns it for God. The smoke from his offering goes straight up, while the smoke from Cain's offering drifts sideways. Taking it as a sign that God has rejected his offering, Cain becomes jealous of Abel and kills him. Whether or not offering sacrifices to please a god is a universal phenomenon, it certainly is a part of Jewish, Christian, and Islamic tradition. Scholars have generalized from this example that offering sacrifices to gods is a major feature of religions.

Traditional religions in today's world are not identical to the first religions of the human race, of course, but some anthropologists believe they show a basic way of thinking that may have contributed to the development of religion. If this approach is correct, then perhaps religions grew out of the natural human tendency to interpret events as actions, and to understand actions as motivated by something, just as human actions are motivated by something. When a volcano rumbled, when lightning struck, when the rain came, our distant ancestors saw this as someone doing something. And when the volcano went quiet, the storm stopped, or the rain failed to come as expected, they interpreted this as someone's refraining from acting.

This way of thinking not only allowed early humans to explain the world around them, but also made them feel they had a way to influence it, maybe even control it. As Freud speculated in his book *The Future of an Illusion* (see Chapter 3), human beings early on became skilled in dealing with other people. As they faced problems with the natural world, they tried to use the same techniques. If the volcano or the rain was someone's action, then they could ask that someone to stop the volcano or start the rain. They could do something to please the one who was performing the actions so that this agent would do what was asked. And if the request was granted, they could thank the agent. If the agent did not grant the wishes or answer the prayers, it might have been because they had failed to please the agent or had offended the agent somehow. The next step might be to offer other gifts or **sacrifices**, or to apologize and ask for forgiveness. By seeing events around them as the actions of persons, they could deal with the natural world in all the social ways they dealt with other people.

Death Rituals

Those who offer these suggestions about the origins of what we understand as religion would be much happier if they could find archaeological evidence for their claims, but, unfortunately, there is almost no archaeological record of what religions may have been like between 2.5 million years ago, when the earliest members of our genus, *Homo*, evolved, and 35,000 years ago, the Upper Paleolithic period. All we have from this long period are some animal bones arranged in special patterns in human encampments, and some remnants of ochres (common colors found in the earth) that early humans may have used to decorate their skin.

When we get to the Upper Paleolithic period of 35,000 to 10,000 years ago, however, we find more archaeological evidence of activities that can be interpreted as religious. Most of these concerned death, hunting, and human fertility – all major concerns of human beings trying to survive in a scary and unpredictable world. As we saw in Chapter 2, dealing with basic concerns is an important part of what religions do for people.

The oldest evidence of actions performed systematically for no obvious practical reason but with some kind of symbolic significance – what we call rituals – comes not from *Homo sapiens*, our species, but from *Homo neanderthalensis*, or Neandertals, cousins of ours who lived from about 200,000 years ago to about 30,000 years ago. Evidence from caves suggests that Neandertals had rituals for disposing of dead bodies, some of which were curled up in a fetal position. One commonly cited Neandertal burial is Shanidar 4, known as "Old Man," in a cave in Iraq. Soil samples show significant amounts of pollen from a wide range of wildflowers, some having medicinal value. Before he died, he was blind and partially crippled, and so he would have needed to be cared for. The suggestion is that his group took care of him in life, and then covered his body with flowers when he died. Just what did these people believe about death and what did they think their rituals would accomplish? We do not know for sure, but it is possible that they thought of the dead person as still existing in some way.

The evidence for funeral rituals gets stronger with our species, *Homo sapiens*, about 20,000 years ago. There are almost 100 examples from Europe and Asia of people being buried in caves and open-air sites, often with "grave goods" – things for them to use after death – such as stone or bone tools, shells, beads, animal bones, and red ochre. One male buried in Arena Candide, Italy, was nicknamed the "Young Prince." His body was dusted with red ochre and decorated with pendants carved from mammoth ivory, shells, and a 9-inch flint blade placed in his left hand. Some burial sites had several bodies, perhaps families buried together.

Fertility Goddesses

Another intriguing set of artifacts made between 20,000 and 27,000 years ago consists of hundreds of nude female figurines found across the ancient world. Ranging from 1.57 inches to 10 inches in height, they typically have large breasts, wide hips, and prominent vulvas. The most famous, in Figure 5.7, is called "Venus of Willendorf" – after Venus, the Roman goddess of love, and the town in Austria near where the figure was found in 1908.

When these figurines were made, food was not abundant. A long winter or a few disappointing hunting expeditions could

FIGURE 5.7 Venus of Willendorf.
Caro/Alamy.

mean starvation for some or all of the group. So a woman who was as plump as this Venus would have been rare indeed. Rather than representing an actual woman, these statues seem to represent an ideal type – the fertile, probably pregnant, female with a wide pelvis, large breasts, and plenty of stored body fat. This is the perfect body for bearing and nursing children. The fact that there are so many of these figures spread over a wide area suggests that they were made not occasionally and randomly, but often and for a definite purpose. The most likely purpose would have been in rituals to ensure fertility for women in the group.

Hunting Rituals

In the Magdalenian period, 11,000 to 17,000 years ago, we find evidence of rituals associated with hunting. This is the period when the paintings of bulls and bison were done on cave walls. Some of the animals in the paintings appear to have arrows stuck in them. In several caves in Europe, too, bear skulls have been placed in special locations, often along with bones. Some scholars say that these hunting peoples had bear cults that today might be called religious. Considering the size of the bears of that time, it is easy to see how early humans, armed only with primitive spears and arrows, would find them awesome and perhaps even worship them. Archaeologists tell us these animals were twice as tall as today's bears, and weighed more than half a ton.

Shamans

Not only are there indications that early hunters had rituals associated with animals, but there are intriguing images on cave walls of characters who are part animal and part human. In Figure 5.8 is a touched-up image from a cave in Ariège, France, of a man/stag, painted and engraved about 13,000 BCE.

This figure has antlers like a stag, eyes like an owl, ears like a wolf, paws like a bear, a tail like a horse, and human feet and penis. There is no evidence that people lived in this cave, or that it was used on a daily basis, so this image does not appear to have been just a part of some cave dweller's decor. The cave seems to have been a special place used only on special occasions, like a synagogue, mosque, church, or temple today. Many scholars call this image "The Sorcerer," interpreting it as a shaman. As we saw in Chapter 2, shamans (or priests) – those recognized for their skill in influencing agents who have power over people but over whom we have no direct control – appear to be the first authority figures recognized in human society. Shamans performed rituals to insure success in hunting and to initiate young men into the fellowship of adult hunters.

There are still shamans today. They typically wear special dress and go into altered mental states. In these special states, they are believed to be able to learn things – such as where the good hunting is – and to get power from spirits to help members of their group. In Figure 5.9 is a shaman from a Native American tribe in Alaska in the early 20th century performing a ritual to cure a sick boy.

The roles and duties of shamans – if not their supernatural powers – are similar to those of religious authorities who conduct systematic, symbolic activities in modern religions, even today.

FIGURE 5.8 Image from a cave in Ariège, France, of a man/ stag, painted and engraved about 13,000 BCE. World History Archive/Alamy.

Ancient Traditions, Oral Traditions, and Religion

Do the similarities between some of the elements of prehistoric societies just discussed and what we call religion today justify the claim that they are early forms of religion? As we have seen, scholars who hold an evolutionary view of religion believe so. They think that what we recognize as religious activities arose in bands or tribes of hunter-gatherers long before the development of writing. These ancient ancestors of ours were concerned with the animals they hunted for food, and with the predators that hunted them. They were concerned with death and sometimes marked it with rituals. They were also concerned with birth because it replenished their numbers, so the fertility of their women was important. They tended to think animistically and anthropomorphically: that is, they thought of moving things as alive and like themselves.

If we look at the people today who are the most similar to humans in the Upper Paleolithic age, we can see all these features in their cultures. There are still hunter-gatherer

FIGURE 5.9 Photo of shaman. Library of Congress.

tribes living in South America, Australia, and Africa. Like humans before agriculture, their lives depend on killing prey, and on not being killed by predators. So rituals connected with hunting and avoiding predators are prominent. Human death is a major concern, so they mark it with rituals. Like early human groups, too, these tribes are small, and so the fertility of their women is essential. They think animistically and anthropomorphically, too, describing rivers and volcanoes, for example, as living things, and attributing human thoughts and motives to animals. While today's oral hunter-gatherer cultures cannot be assumed to have all the same features as the first tribal cultures had, they may help us understand some of the ways that early humans thought and acted.

PART II USING THE TOOLS: SURVEYING WORLD RELIGIONS

Common Features of Oral Cultures

- The survival of the tribe is the main value.
- Human fertility is important.
- Animals and plants are central.
- Rites of passage mark life-transitions – birth, puberty, marriage, death.
- Thinking tends toward animism and anthropomorphism.
- They have no word or concept "religion."
- There is no distinction between religion and politics.
- The leader may be religious, political, and medical.
- Each tradition is local; there is no expectation that other groups will share their beliefs and rituals.
- There is no distinction between literal uses of language, on the one hand, and metaphors and other non-literal uses of language.
- There is no doctrine.
- There is no distinction between natural and supernatural.
- Knowledge is stored in proverbs – easy to remember sayings.
- Dreams and visions are considered sources of knowledge.

For example, the absence of writing in non-literate societies today means that there are no birth certificates, marriage licenses, or other records of life-events. So in order to have people remember important events, those events are marked by public rituals. Memorable ceremonies announce to the tribe that a baby has joined the group, that a child has become an adult, that two people have married, and that someone has died. Scholars call these transitions from one life-stage to another **rites of passage**. It is reasonable to assume that early humans would also have developed rites of passage as a way of acknowledging and remembering important events in people's lives.

Another feature of oral tribal traditions today is that they are local. There are no traditions for the whole world. No one expects the tribe on the other side of the river to tell the same stories and perform the same rituals as they do. Conversely, everyone who is in the tribe is "in the tradition." There are no "non-believers;" to not participate in the rituals would be to leave the community. Without writing, there are also no official teachings and so no orthodox beliefs, or heretical beliefs; there is simply belonging to the community or not belonging to it. (As we saw in Chapter 3, pioneer sociologist Emile Durkheim focused on community as the most important factor in religions, both ancient and modern.) All these features of oral tribal traditions today may well have characterized our early ancestors. But does either set of traditions represent religion?

Why not just describe both sets of traditions simply as typical of oral cultures? Literature scholar Walter Ong's groundbreaking book *Orality and Literacy: The Technologizing of the Word* (2002) outlines the characteristics of oral societies. They include a number of characteristics we have seen in these ancient traditions, such as the tendency to think practically rather than abstractly – to view things in terms of their use rather than some intellectual category; to view life as a seamless whole rather than in distinct segments such as "political," "economic," or religious; and to store and transmit knowledge in proverbs.

Whether "religious" or simply "oral," the relative simplicity of early hunter-gatherer cultures would change drastically when humans settled down to an agricultural way of life. And many of those changes are reflected in the traditions we identify as religious.

The Neolithic Revolution and the Rise of Historic Religions

Around 12,000 BCE, some humans figured out how to produce crops year after year in the same place, rather than having to wander around looking for food. This first happened in Mesopotamia, the land between the Tigris River and the Euphrates River in what is now Iraq. The first plants grown as crops were grains: barley, then wheat, rye, and rice. From being nomadic hunter-gatherers, people settled in places suitable for farming and herding animals. This change is called the Neolithic ("New Stone") Revolution.

With crops planted in the same fields each year, people had to control access to this land and protect it from invaders. They claimed ownership rights to specific plots of land and, because there were frequent disputes about who had the rights to which property, men's fighting skills became more important than they had been in the hunter-gatherer economy of Paleolithic ("Old Stone") times. While hunter-gatherers had lived in tribes of twenty to thirty, agriculture made possible villages of hundreds and then cities of thousands. The chief of a hunter-gatherer tribe was not elevated far above his relatives, but a king ruling over cities was. And the king was usually the man who had led warriors successfully in maintaining control of their group's territories. His leadership was linked not just to his military skills but to his ownership of land and stores of food, since these were what induced people to be loyal to him.

Those who lost battles often became slaves of the winners. These slaves included not just the losing warriors, but their women and children, too. So now aggressive men owned not only land, but people. And they often took female captives as their concubines (slaves with whom they had sex and whose offspring they could claim as their rightful heirs) or wives. From there it was an easy step to thinking that a man owns not only his land but his wife and children, along with his slaves. Thus, according to many scholars, **patriarchy** – rule by strong father-figures – became a common pattern.

As patriarchy became part of societies after the Neolithic Revolution, it also characterized what would come to be called religions. Instead of venerating fertility goddesses and wild animals, as Paleolithic peoples had done, Neolithic peoples came to picture their supernatural guardians as being like their leaders – strong male warriors and kings. And just as the strongest fortresses were located on high ground where it is possible to see what your enemies are doing, so the gods were thought to live at the highest level of all – in the sky, "the heavens." The goddesses associated with fertility receded in importance. A new kind of fertility became important – fertility of the land – and new gods emerged representing that fertility. And both kinds of fertility deity were perceived as subservient to the dominant warrior gods.

The transitions in the stature of gods and goddesses sometimes were described in dramatic terms. For example, in Greek mythology, Zeus was the king of the gods, the ruler of Mount Olympus, and the god of the sky whose weapon was lightning. But he was not always so powerful. Zeus was the youngest child of the Titans, Cronus and Rhea, both children of the earth, Gaea. But Cronus, the king of the Titans, had been told that he would be overthrown by his son, just as he had overthrown his own father. In order to prevent this, he swallowed each of his children as they were born. Rhea became tired of losing her children this way, so before the last one was born she wrapped up a rock and handed this to Cronus, pretending it was the baby. Cronus swallowed it and Zeus was saved. When he grew up, Zeus forced his father to vomit up his siblings. His brothers were so grateful that they let him have control of the sky and the thunderbolt. The siblings then did battle with the Titans, banishing them to the underworld – except for Atlas, who was punished for fighting Zeus by having to hold up the sky. Then Zeus and

Social Revolutions Reflected in Myth: Cain and Hephaestus as Villains

Above we saw the story of Cain and Abel as an example of sacrifices being accepted or rejected by gods. Scholars also see in the story of Cain and Abel a reflection of the conflict between herders and farmers. When people claim plots of land so that they can raise crops, shepherds find their grazing lands reduced and their livelihood threatened. In the biblical/Qur'anic story, Cain's offering was grain; he was a farmer. Abel's offering was an animal; he was a shepherd. Cain is depicted as the evil one. He became so angry that he killed his brother – showing that the story is told from the viewpoint of the nomadic shepherds, which, of course, the ancient Hebrews were. This was an ancient range war – like those between the farmers and cattlemen in the Old West of the United States. Negative depictions of blacksmith gods – such as Hephaestus, who fashioned Zeus's punishments – may also reflect the viewpoint of a nomadic culture in conflict with farmers, since it was settled societies that developed smithing and metalwork.

his brothers Poseidon and Hades drew lots for the rest of the world – Poseidon got the waters and Hades got control of the underworld. Zeus then set about marrying his sisters, putting them under his control. But one of them refused him. There are many versions of Greek mythology, but according to one popular version, Hera conceived a son all by herself, just to spite Zeus. Zeus was so angry that when the child was born, he threw him into the sea from the top of Mount Olympus, crippling him. There (or on an island, according to some versions) the son, Hephaestus, became a master blacksmith and submissive servant of Zeus. Later, when Zeus was outraged by men (this was before there were women) because they had collaborated with the Titan Prometheus, he commissioned Hephaestus to fashion the worst possible punishment: a box that when opened, released Pandora, described as "woman, that curse from which men would never escape."

The characterization of women as treacherous, devious, and conniving is common in traditions after the Neolithic revolution. Often, in fact, we find the character of goddesses transformed, from benignly powerful to jealous and spiteful – and powerful. That is what happened to Hera, the sister and wife of Zeus who defied him. The Indian goddess Kali (as we shall see in Chapter 7) is another example – often depicted with blood and corpses or body parts around her, she is associated with death and destruction, unpredictable and to be feared. The unreliability of females, then, leaves the field clear for males to dominate. Indeed, the idea of dominating became central in many ancient traditions. In the Hebrew Bible, for instance, Yahweh is described as "Lord of Hosts (Armies)," and as a super-king ruling over the whole world.

In ancient Mesopotamia, the most powerful warriors and the priests were at the top of society. The farmers, craftspeople, and slaves were at the bottom. The king's authority was legitimated by the priests, who confirmed that he spoke with the authority of the gods. To allow the leaders to rise even closer to the gods, step-pyramids called *ziggurats* were built. Scholars believe rituals were performed at shrines at the top of these monuments.

Not far west and south of Mesopotamia was Egypt, and it also developed a patriarchal culture after the Neolithic Revolution, along the Nile River. Ancient Egypt had about 700 gods and goddesses, but – as is typical for Neolithic societies – the gods dominated. The Egyptian leaders went further than Mesopotamian rulers, declaring that the Pharaoh – the king – *was* a god. He was associated with Horus, the son of the sun god Ra.

As a god himself, of course, the pharaoh wielded great power. A later Egyptian tradition even said that at death the Pharaoh became Osiris, a god who was in charge of life after death. Obviously, this would be someone to stay on good terms with. Egyptian ideas about the afterlife changed over time, but constant was the belief that the body had to be preserved for the person to live after death. This is why the Egyptians developed the art of turning corpses into mummies. The pharaoh's mummy was shown further respect by being entombed in a pyramid.

Mesopotamia and Egypt were not the only places where civilizations developed after the Neolithic Revolution. The Indus River Valley in southwest Asia and the Yellow River Valley in China were two more. In the next three chapters we shall see how seven religious traditions developed in these places – the seven commonly called "world religions" by scholars. From the ancient Middle East came Judaism, Christianity, and

The Divine Right of Kings – an Early Version

FIGURE 5.10 Wall carving from the Temple of Horus at Edfu in Egypt. © Luke Daniek/iStockphoto.

The idea that rulers get their power from gods is an ancient one. In this wall carving from the Temple of Horus at Edfu in Egypt, two goddesses crown the pharaoh with a new crown made by combining their individual crowns. The temple was built between 237 and 57 BCE during the Ptolemaic period.

Islam. From the Indus River area came Hinduism, out of which evolved Buddhism. And from China came Confucianism and Taoism.

Conclusion

We have seen that some Religious Studies scholars try to find examples of religion in prehistoric cultures. Like non-literate tribes today, prehistoric peoples seem to have been concerned with animals and human fertility, no doubt in order to assure the group's survival. They may well have anthropomorphized animals and other natural forces, seeing them as what would later be called supernatural powers or gods. They may also have believed it possible to communicate with and encourage such powers to help their group, by offering gifts (sacrifices) and compliments (worship) and then making requests (praying). They may have recognized certain individuals as more adept at this kind of thing than others. They may even have believed that some individuals can channel the supernatural power and so perform extraordinary feats such as healing. In other words, they may have had priests or shamans. As well, they seem to have marked life-transitions, especially the death of members of the group.

However, we have no evidence that our prehistoric ancestors recognized a fundamental distinction between what we call the supernatural and the natural. Nor do we find evidence that they distinguished sharply between various spheres of daily tribal life such as political, economic, public, and private – much less religious and non-religious.

What we call "religion" today seems to be more specific and more complex than either what the first humans did or what oral tribes today do. Religion seems – at the very least – to distinguish between parts of life that are within its realm and parts of life that are outside its realm. To use the language of many of the thinkers in Part I, religion seems to distinguish between the sacred and the profane, or the sacred and the secular parts of life. ("Secular" refers to the things of everyday life, the things that exist "in time," as distinguished from the timeless or "eternal" realm of divinity.) In the next chapter we shall survey the traditions in which that distinction emerged: the Western monotheistic traditions of Judaism, Christianity, and Islam.

DISCUSSION QUESTIONS

1. Do you see evidence of animism and anthropomorphism in modern life? Think about how we name ships and hurricanes, for example.

2. Do you believe in ghosts? If you do, and you also belong to a religion, is your belief in ghosts compatible with this religion?

3. Among early human beings, death rituals seem to have involved the belief that dying is going to another world that is much like this one. What would the religions that you know say about that idea?

4. After the Neolithic Revolution, many scholars think, the control of land became important, and so there was an emphasis on war and conquest. Do you see any evidence of this in the religions that you know?

5. After war and conquest became important for group survival, warriors – typically male – became dominant in many societies. Do you see a correlation between the importance of war and the secondary status of women?

6. Do you think that the dominant status of males is inevitable in society?

7. Unlike early humans, few of us are hunters. But animals still seem important in our lives and in our thought. Can you think of examples? Are there any examples of things that are part animal/part human in modern thought?

REFERENCES

Sigmund Freud, *The Future of an Illusion*. Eastford, CT: Martino Fine Books, 2010.
Walter Ong, *Orality and Literacy: The Technologizing of the Word*. London: Routledge, 2nd ed., 2002.

FURTHER READING

Pascal Boyer, *Religion Explained*. New York: Basic, 2002.

H. and H.A. Frankfurt and John A. Wilson, *Before Philosophy: The Intellectual Adventure of Ancient Man*. Harmondsworth: Penguin, 1967.

Jack Goody, *The Logic of Writing and the Organization of Society*. Cambridge: Cambridge University Press, 1967.

Edith Hamilton, *Mythology*. New York: Back Bay, 1998.

Gerda Lerner, *The Creation of Patriarchy*. Oxford: Oxford University Press, 1997.

THE FAMILY OF WESTERN MONOTHEISMS

Jewish, Christian, and Islamic Traditions

"I'm calling it 'Genesis.' It's part of a five-book contract."

FIGURE 6.1   Mort Gerberg 1998/The New Yorker Collection/www.cartoonbank.com.

In the name of God The Compassionate, The Merciful. Praise be to God, Lord of the Universe, The Compassionate, the Merciful, Sovereign of the Day of Judgment. You alone we worship, and to You alone we turn for help.

OPENING OF THE QUR'AN

6

Overview

This chapter surveys the family of traditions that trace their origins to revelation received by Abraham. Followers of the "Abrahamic traditions" believe that the source of this revelation is the only God; they believe in no other. (They are therefore called monotheists. *Monos* is Greek for "one," and *theos* means "god." This God is not gendered but is generally referred to in masculine terms.) The Abrahamic traditions share a good deal of history, many values, and a number of other beliefs as well:

- God created the universe, loves his creatures, and periodically sends messages to them through "prophets," revealing what he would like his creatures to do.

- These revelations, which include instructions for how God would like to be worshiped and how God wants people to treat each other, comprise at once the will of God and law for human beings.

- At some point God will bring life as human beings know it to an end, and will judge people's success or failure at fulfilling the divine will. Those who implemented God's will (followed God's law) will be rewarded eternally; those who failed to do so will be punished.

Jews, Christians, and Muslims have diverse opinions about just what the revealed will of God is, so the various groups have differing laws. Although some believe that each

Unit I Judaism

The Torah, the Hebrew Bible, the Old Testament
The History and Teachings of Judaism
The Rituals of Judaism
Judaism Today

Unit II Christianity

The History and Teachings of Christianity
Christian Rituals
Christianity Today

Unit III Islam

The History and Teachings of Islam
Islamic Rituals
Major Divisions Today

Unit IV The Impact of Religious Studies on the Western Monotheisms

Biblical Studies
Theology
Conclusion

community is entitled to follow its own interpretations of the law, leaving judgment to God, many believe that their own community's interpretations are superior to the others, leading to a number of conflicts among these "siblings" throughout history.

Employing a "history of religions" ("HR") methodology, our survey of the three major monotheistic traditions includes the following.

- **The history of the tradition.** How did it begin? How did it change over time? What major groups evolved within each tradition, and how do they stand today? We base this history on both religious (or "sacred") sources and scholarly sources from outside the traditions (secular sources), and will note when there are significant discrepancies between the two kinds of source.

- **The teachings of the tradition.** We shall include both metaphysical teachings (teachings about gods, souls, survival of death, etc.) and moral teachings (teachings about what is right and wrong).

- **The rituals of the tradition.** As we saw in Chapter 2, rituals are systematically repeated actions that are believed to please a deity (god) or accomplish a goal such as healing. This is their religious purpose. Scholarly secular analysis demonstrates that rituals also promote group solidarity and reinforce the beliefs and the values of the group. We shall highlight both aspects of ritual.

We shall conclude the chapter with comments about how Religious Studies has impacted the monotheistic traditions.

Unit I Judaism

We call Judaism, Christianity, and Islam a family because they all trace their origins to the experiences of a man named Abraham, believed to have lived almost four thousand years ago, and they share many stories, beliefs, and moral rules. (We shall look at the youngest member of this family, Baha'i, in Chapter 9.)

Over the centuries, some members of each of these traditions have been hostile to members of the other two. In a series of invasions of the Middle East beginning in the late 11th century known as the Crusades, European Christians killed thousands of Muslims and Jews. In 1492, the king and queen of Spain declared that all non-Christians living in Spain had to convert or leave the country. There have also been similar conflicts within each of the monotheistic traditions. In 1208, for example, Pope Innocent III launched a crusade against the Cathars, a group of Christians in Southern France, whom he declared heretical. Many people today are aware of the current conflicts between Sunni and Shi'i Muslims in Iraq. Fewer are aware that in Israel today there are often legal battles between Orthodox Jews and Jews who are not Orthodox.

Despite all the conflicts within and between various Christian, Jewish, and Muslim groups, however, they have a great deal in common. All of them started in the Middle East and are based on what are believed to be God's words (revelation) as recorded in scripture (sacred or holy writings). The Christian New Testament accepts the Hebrew Bible and builds on it, and Islamic scripture – the Qur'an (archaic: Koran) – accepts and builds on both the Hebrew Bible and the New Testament. The Qur'an refers to Jews and Christians as "People of Scripture" or "People of the Book."

For all three traditions, there is only one God, who created the world, loves his creatures, and has given people certain orders or "commandments" (things they must do) as well as prohibitions (things they must not do). All consider God to be far above and beyond human characteristics, but each of the traditions generally uses the masculine singular pronoun "he" when referring to God. He is omnipotent (all-powerful), omniscient (all-knowing), just, and merciful. And God will judge people at the end of time based on their obedience to his commandments and prohibitions.

These three traditions also share a linear view of time and history. Time begins with the creation of the world and goes in just one direction, like an arrow in flight, so that each moment in history happens just once. (This contrasts with the cyclic view of time in South Asia, as we shall see in Chapter 7.)

For the People of the Book, God revealed himself at specific times in history, and he has spoken through many prophets. The messages of the prophets in all three traditions are the major sources for people's understanding of who they are, why they were created, what they are supposed to do and what they must not do, and what will happen to them when they die.

The Torah, the Hebrew Bible, the Old Testament

The foundation for the worldview in Judaism, Christianity, and Islam is in the **Torah**, the first five books of the Hebrew Bible. "Bible" comes from the Greek word for "book," *biblos*, but the Bible is not one book. It is a collection of books written at different times and places for different reasons. It is more like a small library than a single book. As we saw in Chapter 3, biblical scholars have researched the language, style, and sources for the text in excruciating detail. They have determined that most of it was circulated in oral form for centuries before being written down. The story of Saul, the first king of the Israelites, for example, happens in the 11th century BCE, but it was probably first written down in the 6th century BCE. Other parts of the Hebrew Bible were written down much later.

There were no printing presses at that time, of course, so even when the stories were written down, they were copied by hand any number of times and circulated among communities. Scholars believe that both the oral transmission of stories, and the hand copying of manuscripts, once the stories were recorded, could well have led over time to some variations in the accounts. Some scholars suggest that this is why scriptures as we now know them sometimes contain more than one version of the same event. They believe that when the people who recorded the scriptures (scribes) encountered variations in the story of an event in oral or hand-written versions, they simply included all the variations, rather than trying to determine which were the "true" versions. That is, many scholars believe that scribes considered the overall themes of the stories more important than the details. For example, there are two creation stories in the book of Genesis, the first book of the Hebrew

Bible. In Chapter 1 of this book, God makes things by speaking. He creates light, for instance, by saying, "Let there be light." He makes Adam and Eve by saying, "Let us make humankind in our image." In Chapter 2, God creates things in a different order and he makes people by shaping them out of dirt, rather than by speaking. Nevertheless, the story of creation is considered to be a single story of the divine origin of all that exists.

Scholars have also determined that the various books of the Bible served different purposes. While Genesis contains mostly stories that explain the origin of the world, the human race, and the people of Israel, the Psalms are not stories but religious songs addressed to God. The book of Joshua is mostly history. Leviticus presents rules for the people of Israel to live by, such as the prohibition on eating pork and shellfish. Ecclesiastes is a philosophical essay on how hard it is to make sense of life. The book called Song of Songs is about romantic love, and does not even mention God.

Over time, different religious groups collected and copied different scrolls (hand-written copies of the texts). In the early centuries of the common era, some writings were put onto codexes, flat sheets bound together like books. The religious authorities – the rabbis – also looked through the many scrolls and codexes and decided which ones would be included in the **canon**, the group of writings considered authentic, what we now call the Hebrew Bible.

The Hebrew Bible presents a history of the human race from creation to classical times. It starts with God creating everything in six days and resting on the seventh. He creates the first humans, Adam and his mate Eve, puts them in a beautiful garden, and gives them dominion over all other creatures. However, he tells them not to eat from the tree at the center of the garden, the Tree of the Knowledge of Good and Evil. They disobey him and so are expelled from the garden. From then on, their lives, and human life generally, will be a struggle: childbirth will be painful, they will have to work hard, and they will die.

This story of Adam and Eve is taken literally by some, while others read it as an explanation of how it is that human beings – alone among all creatures – have the ability to make terrible mistakes as they attempt to progress through their lives. Another way to put that is to say that the story describes the fact that human beings – again, unlike other creatures – have the right and responsibility to make choices; they have free will. The first human beings chose to violate their creator's command and were therefore punished. Scholars see in the story a perfect example of one of the major goals of religious stories: providing an explanation for suffering and death (see Chapter 2).

Later generations of human beings continue to violate God's commands and make bad choices. God becomes so disgusted that he decides to wipe out the human race with a flood. However, then he has mercy on the family of Noah, and saves them, along with animals to repopulate the earth after the flood.

The next major event, and the one central to Judaism, Christianity, and Islam, is that God chooses one man, Abram, to be the father of a new nation that will have a special relationship with him. He tells Abram to leave his home in Ur in today's Iraq and "go to a country that I will show you. I will make you a great nation, I will bless you." (Genesis 12:1–2) Though this one group are God's "Chosen People," they will also serve as role models for the rest of the human race. "By you all the families of the earth will bless themselves." (Genesis 12:3) Abram moves to Canaan, where at first he is an outsider. However, then God makes a covenant (agreement) with him. If he and his descendants will worship God and follow his laws, he says, "I will give you and your descendants after you the land in which you now are aliens, all the land of Canaan." (Genesis 17:8) God changes Abram's name to Abraham and, as a sign of the covenant, commands that all the males in his household be circumcised. And though Abraham and his wife Sara are very old, God promises them a son.

Abraham and Sara are at first skeptical about the possibility of having a child. Sara suggests that Abraham and their maid Hagar might be able to reproduce, and this they do. Hagar's son is named Ishmael. However, then Sara also gives birth to a son. She banishes Hagar and Ishmael, and Sara and Abraham then concentrate their attention on their son Isaac.

God then tests Abraham by telling him to sacrifice his son. Abraham agrees, but at the last minute an angel appears and substitutes a ram as the sacrificial animal. As we shall see, there is disagreement between Jews and Muslims about which son was involved in the near-sacrifice. In the Jewish telling, it is Isaac, with whom God later renews the covenant, promising that "I will make your descendants as many as the stars in the sky; I will give them all these lands." (Genesis 26:4) Isaac's son Jacob is given the name "Israel," which means "the one who wrestled with God," and this becomes the name of the people he leads. Jacob has twelve sons, and they become the heads of the twelve tribes of the people of Israel.

Famines cause the descendants of Jacob to leave Canaan for Egypt, where they are slaves for four centuries. As their oppression worsens, a great leader arises, Moses. God tells him to lead his people out of Egypt and back to Canaan. To force Pharaoh (the Egyptian ruler) to release them, God inflicts terrible plagues on the Egyptians, the last of which is the slaughter of their firstborn children. The Hebrews mark their doorposts with lamb's blood, so that this plague skips their houses or "passes over" them. It is this event that the feast of Passover commemorates. The escape of the Hebrews from Egypt is called the Exodus (meaning "emigration"), and this is also the name of the biblical book describing it.

A note about dates: The Hebrew Bible does not specify dates for most events, although, as we saw in Chapter 5, the Judaic calendar places the events described in the Book of Genesis – in particular, the creation of the world and the first humans – some 5770 years ago. As we have seen, scholars consider the earth and the human species much older than that. The difference between the two is a good example of the contrast between "sacred history" and literal or "secular history," a distinction that scholars of religion are careful to highlight. For example, we have no evidence apart from sacred history of the lives of the specific people mentioned in the Hebrew Bible up to this point in our story: the Exodus. We do know there were countless nomadic tribes in the Middle East, and that periodic wars and droughts caused some tribes to wander far from their traditional pasturelands, so the emigrations from Iraq and Canaan would not have been unusual. Indeed, scholars trace the term "Hebrew" to its root meaning, "immigrant from the other side of the river." Further, comparing historical evidence from Egypt with the accounts given in the Hebrew Bible, scholars place the emigration from Egypt back to Canaan around 1300 BCE.

Back to sacred history: The journey across the Sinai Desert to the Promised Land of Canaan takes forty years, according to scripture. During this time, God appears to Moses at Mount Sinai and gives him a set of laws, including the Ten Commandments. These laws will be supplemented in subsequent books of scripture, particularly Leviticus and Deuteronomy. All the laws together are known as Mosaic Law, and it will become the constitution of the

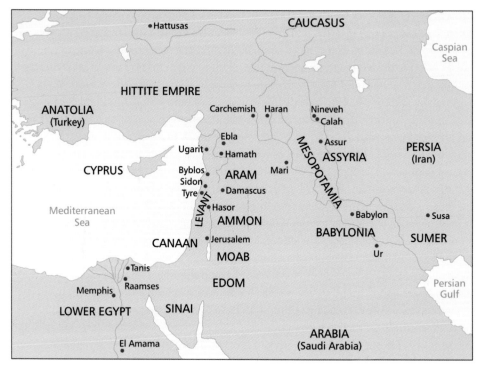

MAP 6.1 Map of the Ancient Near East.

people of Israel. Next to the establishment of the covenant with Abraham, God's communication of the Law to Moses is the central event in the history of Judaism.

The Israelites finally enter Canaan, but not until Moses has died. His protégé Joshua leads them into the land of Canaan. However, there are many groups already living there. God directs his people to undertake a series of battles against the Canaanites. In the first two, the Israelites (the "people of Israel," another name for the Hebrews) are commanded to exterminate the inhabitants of the cities of Jericho and Ai. When they win battles, they say that God is blessing them for obeying him, and when they lose battles, they say that God is punishing them for disobeying him. However, they eventually prevail over the local inhabitants, and cease their nomadic lifestyle.

After Joshua, the people of Israel are no longer led by tribal leaders (people descended from Abraham and Isaac), but instead by people well versed in the law. They are called judges. However, finding themselves content with settled life, the people want to become a kingdom, like other settled groups. God agrees, and Saul becomes the first king. However, when Saul displeases God, David replaces him as king. By this time – which scholars place around 1000 BCE based on archaeological evidence – the twelve tribes have coalesced into two major groupings. The northern ten tribes are identified as the Tribes of Israel, and the southern two tribes are called the Tribes of Judah. David creates a united kingdom of the tribes of Israel and Judah. His son Solomon succeeds him as king and builds a temple in Jerusalem that becomes the center of worship. The united kingdom does not last long,

Is This Religion?

Scholars search early Hebrew scriptures in vain for terms that correspond to the modern term "religion." The term translated as religion is *din*, but this term actually means "judgment" (see Chapter 1). The law delivered by God to the people of Israel through Moses is not limited to any particular part of life. It pertains to all aspects of life – devotion to God, family and social relationships, and practical aspects of life such as nutrition and making a living, as well as governance. As nomadic people living in tribal communities, they had no need to accommodate other people's ways of doing things. Scholars hypothesize that the distinction between religious (or sacred) and non-religious (or secular) aspects of life developed only gradually, as people changed from nomadic to settled life. In settled communities (villages, towns, cities), tribal groups had to interact with others who had their own norms. In some cases the interaction took the form of violent competition for dominance. The most successful settlements were those in which diverse groups developed space for multiple "lifestyles" – to use modern terminology. To do this, they identified certain areas of the law, such as worship and family matters, as pertaining only to them. Over centuries, these areas of life would be reserved for "religious law." Other aspects of life, such as economic and political, became "neutral" – or secular – territory, in which diverse peoples would negotiate and reach compromises acceptable to the majority. We shall see examples of this pattern throughout our survey of religious traditions.

though. When Solomon dies, the northern tribes become the kingdom of Israel, and the southern tribes become the kingdom of Judah.

By this time in the story, the people of Israel have had three kinds of leader: patriarchs such as Abraham, Isaac, and Jacob; judges; and kings. They will still have kings for several centuries, but around 900 BCE a new kind of religious leader emerges, the prophet. A clear example of one of Weber's ideal types (see Chapter 3), the prophet's power and authority are not inherited, but come from the voices he hears and the visions he has, along with his charisma in communicating these experiences to the people. Early prophets included Elijah, Elisha, and Nathan. Later prophets included Amos, Isaiah, and Jeremiah.

A central message of the prophets to the people is that they must be faithful to one god. Since the exodus from Egypt, the Israelites have referred to this god as YHWH or Yahweh, since this is how he identified himself to Moses during one of their conversations (Exodus 3:14). The reason the prophets had to insist on one god is that the people had other gods, as well. The Hebrew Bible tells us that two fertility gods, Baal and Asherah, also had altars within the temple in Jerusalem. (2 Kings 23:4–13) Baal, also called Tammuz, is an agricultural god of death and rebirth. Asherah is a fertility goddess who, like Baal, is mentioned in numerous ancient sources in addition to the Hebrew Bible. Although we have

FIGURE 6.2 Clay figure of Asherah.

Z. Radovan/BibleLandPictures.

no archaeological evidence of the temple itself, numerous figurines of Asherah have been found, so we know that she was represented as a tree on the bottom and a woman on the top. King Solomon is famous for building the first Temple in Jerusalem, but the Bible indicates that he built shrines for Asherah, as well. (2 Kings 18:22)

As the northern kingdom of Israel and the southern kingdom of Judah are threatened by powerful empires around them, they become more loyal to Yahweh. The constant message of the prophets is that the Israelites are not following Yahweh's laws, and will suffer great punishment if they do not return to his ways. The First Book of Kings (18:19–40) tells how the prophet Elijah challenges 450 prophets of Baal and 400 prophets of Asherah to a contest. Each side prepares the wood for a sacrificial fire, kills a bull and cuts it up, and places the pieces on top of the wood. However, instead of lighting the fire, they will pray to their gods to light it for them. The prophets of Baal pray to him for hours, but no fire appears. Elijah mocks them, suggesting that "he has wandered away, or he is on a journey, or perhaps he is asleep and must be awakened." Then Elijah prays to the God of Abraham and

the fire of the Lord fell and consumed the burnt offering, the wood, the stones, and the dust, and even licked up the water that was in the trench. When all the people saw it, they fell on their faces and said, "The Lord indeed is God; the Lord indeed is God." Elijah said to them, "Seize the prophets of Baal; do not let one of them escape." Then they seized them; and Elijah brought them down to the Wadi Kishon [a river valley], and killed them there.

Despite such dramatic displays by the prophets, the people of Israel do not turn completely to Yahweh, and catastrophe does come. In 722 BCE the Assyrians – a Semitic people from Mesopotamia – conquer the northern kingdom of Israel, killing thousands and driving many refugees into the southern kingdom of Judah. (These tribes are known as the Lost Tribes of Israel; subsequent history focuses on the Tribes of Judah, from which we get the term "Jew." However, alternate sources indicate that not all members of the northern tribes were killed or dispersed. The Samaritans [see below] claim to be among their descendants.) The prophet Jeremiah presents his theodicy (see Chapter 2): this disaster was God's punishment for disobedience. Afterwards, worship of Yahweh increases in the southern kingdom, and prophets and kings suppress the worship of all gods other than Yahweh. Hezekiah, who was king at the time of the Assyrian invasion, destroys images associated with other gods, and concentrates the worship of Yahweh at the temple in Jerusalem. A few years later, King Josiah bans all worship that is not in the temple. He also goes through the temple and gets rid of all the altars and shrines dedicated to Asherah, Baal, and other gods, along with their priests. From then on, the people of Israel are largely monotheistic and their worship is based strictly in the temple.

Names for God

The Hebrew Bible employs a number of terms commonly translated as "God." In the earliest books, the term "Elohim" is most common. Elohim is a plural form of the term "El." Scholars interpret its plural form as a special usage like the "royal 'We'" – a usage appropriate for royalty, although Elohim is sometimes used in reference to generic spiritual beings (1 Samuel 28:13) or to gods other than the One God. (See, e.g., Genesis 6:2, Exodus 20:3.)

The singular form "El" is the designation for the god of the ancient religion of Canaan. In a temple in Syria dating from 2300 BCE, he is described as the oldest or supreme or father of the gods. He is the husband of the important goddess Asherah, although El is used extensively for the One God in Psalms and the Book of Job. The term sometimes appears as El Shaddai, "God of the mountains" or "God Almighty." Many scholars believe that El is the name given to the god of Abraham.

YHWH or YHVH – the Tetragrammaton ("four letters") commonly written as Yahweh, may have been the name of an ancient Canaanite storm god (referenced in Psalm 29). However, it is also considered God's designation of himself. It is the first person singular of the Hebrew verb "to be." In Exodus 3:14 God answers Moses' question as to his identity, using this term twice: "I am what I am" or "I am that I am," or simply, "I am." In Exodus 6:2–3, God explains, "I revealed myself to Abraham, to Isaac, and to Jacob as El Shaddai but was not known to them by my name YHWH."

Still, YHWH is not like a normal name. Jews believe it conveys a truth about God so profound that it may never be known fully by human beings. Reflecting the infinity (unlimited-ness) and ineffability (unspeakable-ness) of God, the term is considered sacred and not to be pronounced. It is never used in Jewish religious rituals. Instead, the term Adonai, meaning "my Lord," used throughout the Hebrew Bible to express the greatness and power of God, is the most common designation for God in Jewish rituals. Ha Shem or Hashem – "the Name" is the term used most commonly by Jews outside of prayer. Like Adonai, ha Shem allows people to avoid using the Tetragrammaton and thus violating its sanctity.

Christian scriptures, written in Greek, use the term *ho theos* (Deus, in Latin translation) in unambiguous reference to God, the one God. However, God is not considered a name; it is a designation of the supreme being. Human beings can know what God has revealed about himself but, being infinite, "God" cannot be defined (or "delimited") as would be the case if "God" were a normal name. Therefore, as in Judaic practice, descriptive terms such as Lord, King, and Father are commonly used.

Islamic scripture, the Qur'an, is written in Arabic, a Semitic language related to Hebrew. The term for God, *al-ilah*, "the [only] god," is very similar to the

Hebrew *el. Al-ilah* is pronounced "allah" and that is how it is transliterated in the Latin alphabet. However, again, Allah is not considered a personal name. There are countless attributes of God, and these are sometimes called "names." According to one tradition, God has 3000 names. The angels know 1000 of them; the prophets Abraham, Moses, and Jesus know 1000 of them; the Torah, the Psalms, and the Gospels each contain 300; and the Qur'an contains 99. The last name – the greatest – is known only to God.

Nonetheless, things worsen for the kingdom of Judah when in 586 BCE the Babylonians invade Jerusalem, destroy the temple, and take the leaders east to Babylon. Although they are far from home, many of the Israelites prosper there. With no temple, they can no longer base their religion on sacrificing animals and other temple rituals. So they turn to other activities, such as writing down the books that would later be called the Bible. The **Babylonian Captivity**, as this period is called, lasts about fifty years, and then another emperor, Cyrus of Persia, defeats the Babylonians (for which the prophet Isaiah [45:1] dubbed him "messiah"). Cyrus lets the Jews return to Jerusalem and live according to their own law, but they are still under Persian control. Not all the Jews do go back to Jerusalem. Those who stayed in Babylon have descendants there, in Iraq, even today.

Those who go to Jerusalem build a Second Temple. (The remains of the Second Temple are a sacred site in Jerusalem, known as the Western Wall; some Christians call it the Wailing Wall.) Now without a king, they are led by Ezra and Nehemiah, appointed by the Persians to govern the Jews. According to tradition, the books of the Hebrew Bible are organized and edited in this time by a group of scholars called the Great **Synagogue** (assembly), organized by Ezra. In 444 BCE Ezra officially announces the Law of the Torah as governing the people of Israel. From then on, the main religious acts in Judaism are following the Torah and studying it. Rituals of sacrifice are still held in the new temple, but they are not as important as they were in the first temple. And Jews could perform public prayer anyplace there is a **minyan**, a quorum of ten Jewish men, rather than only in the temple.

The people of Israel in Jerusalem live under Persian domination for two centuries, but they yearn for independence. Prophets have apocalyptic visions. As we saw in Chapter 2, "the apocalypse" refers to the events associated with the end of the world as we know it, and scholars often interpret stories associated with this event as reflections of anguish and a sense of helplessness. The fact that the Jewish prophets during this time had visions of God destroying the world and creating a new one in which the Israelites are rewarded and God's enemies are destroyed clearly fits this profile. Before the apocalypse, the prophets predict, God will send a great king, descended from King David, to defeat his enemies and restore peace and justice. A man was made a king by being anointed (dabbed with oil), and so this hoped-for king is called the **Messiah**, which means "the Anointed One."

In 331 BCE, the Persians are defeated, not by a Jewish Messiah but by Alexander "the Great" from Greece. Life under Greek rule turns out to be no better than life under Persian rule. By this time the Greeks control the entire Middle East and Egypt; the Jews are ruled first by a Greek governor from Egypt, then one from Syria. In 168 BCE the Greek Syrian governor changes the temple from one dedicated to the worship of Yahweh into one dedicated to Zeus, the supreme Greek god. In 166 BCE there is a Jewish rebellion against this **sacrilege** (violation of a sacred object), led by the Maccabee brothers. They rededicate the temple to Yahweh, an event commemorated in the feast of Hanukkah. For the next century, Judah is an independent state, but not a strong one, and then in 63 BCE the Romans make it part of their empire, calling it Judea.

The History and Teachings of Judaism

The story just outlined is about the ancestors of those who now call themselves Jews, as well as Christians and Muslims. All three groups trace their roots back to Abraham and accept the Torah as God's revelation. The story of Judaism as a tradition separate from Christianity and Islam begins in the first century of the Common Era.

The First Five Centuries

In the first century, according to first-century historian Josephus, there were a number of schools of thought among Jews. The most popular were the **Pharisees**. They were largely from the middle class, and drew followers from middle and lower classes. Those familiar with the Christian Gospels have heard the Pharisees described as nitpicking hypocrites, but these slurs were written long after the time of Jesus, when his followers were splitting away from Judaism. In Jesus' time, most Pharisees did not interpret scripture or the Mosaic Law narrowly and rigidly. Instead, they wanted to make the law reasonable and something that people could follow. So they said that some rules are more important and some less. In making moral judgments, they considered people's intentions, and not just their outward behavior. They were not just concerned with "the letter of the law." In these ways, they were like Jesus. Like him, too, they believed in a Messiah, a new world that would be governed by God, a resurrection of the dead, and a final judgment.

The Pharisees said that in addition to the written law – the Torah of scripture, God had revealed to Moses an oral law – or Oral Torah – that was then passed down from generation to generation in commentaries about the written law. This oral law would eventually be written down as the **Talmud**, as we shall see.

The **Sadducees** were a second group. In contrast to the Pharisees and the followers of Jesus, they were in the upper class of Judean society and they cooperated with the Romans. They conducted the operations of the temple, and wanted everything done "by the book." Disagreeing with the Pharisees, they denied the resurrection of the dead, because it is not taught in scripture. They also denied that there was an Oral Torah. This group disappeared around 60 CE.

The **Essenes** were Jews who withdrew from society to live in monastic communities (groups living apart from the mainstream population, pursuing spiritual matters) under strict

FIGURE 6.3 Yochanan Ben Zakai Synagogue in Jerusalem's Old City. AKG Images/Israelimages.

rules of priestly purity. What we know about the Essenes comes mostly from their writings in the **Dead Sea Scrolls**, documents found by two Palestinian shepherds in caves near the Dead Sea in the 1940s. (Following the initial discovery, archaeologists began systematic excavation of the area and within ten years had identified some 900 scrolls.) The Essenes considered themselves the true faithful children of Israel, and they hoped to reconquer the promised land from gentiles (non-Jews) and Hellenized Jews (those who had adopted Greek ways).

There were other schools of thought, as well, including those messianic Jews who believed Jesus was the messiah. It may sound odd to count them as Jews, but Jesus was indeed Jewish and thought of himself as Jewish, as did his **disciples**, as his followers (or students) are usually called. Even today, there are messianic Jews who believe that Jesus is the messiah. (There are perhaps 250,000 messianic Jews in the United States, and some in Israel, although, as we shall see, not all Messianic Jews believe Jesus was the messiah.) However, the fourth group mentioned by Josephus was the **Zealots**, revolutionaries who conducted guerilla warfare against the Romans. They launched a revolt in 66 CE, which the Romans crushed, destroying the Second Temple in 70. A second Jewish revolt in 132–135 was also put down, killing perhaps half a million Jews and destroying almost a thousand villages. This time the emperor rebuilt Jerusalem as a Roman colony and banned Jews from entering it.

From then on, the Jews were in **diaspora**, a Greek word that originally meant a scattering of seeds, but now means the dispersing of people from their homeland. Within a century, Jews were settled as far west as Spain and as far east as India. By this time, the followers of Jesus no longer considered themselves Jews, and the Sadducees, Essenes, and Zealots had disappeared. So there was one kind of Judaism left, that of the Pharisees. Theirs was the foundation of the Judaism led by rabbis that we still have today.

After the destruction of the Second Temple, as after the destruction of the First Temple, worship could not be centered in a temple or in Jerusalem. And sacrificing animals was obsolete. Jewish practices had to be portable, so that they could be conducted anywhere that Jews might find themselves. This portable form of Jewish practice had been developing since the Babylonian Captivity. It consisted of following the Mosaic Law, praying, and studying the Torah. Judaism was now carried out mostly in people's homes and in meeting places called synagogues.

"Torah" is perhaps the most important word in Judaism. It has a range of meanings. In the narrowest sense, it is the first five books of the Bible, the Pentateuch. In a wider sense, Torah is the Scriptures, the Hebrew Bible. The Bible is also called Tanakh, which is an acronym in Hebrew formed from the first letters of the three parts of the Hebrew Bible – the Torah (the first five books), the Nevi'im (Prophets), and the Ketuvim (Writings) – hence *TaNaKh*.

In a still wider sense, Torah includes the Written Torah (the Bible) and the Oral Torah (Talmud). According to the Pharisees, the Oral Torah is the part of God's revelation at Sinai that Moses did not write down but passed on to his successors by word of mouth. They in turn passed it on to their successors. When it was eventually written down, the Oral Torah took the form of the **Mishnah** and the **Gemara** (see "Law and Life" in box below). The Gemara consists of commentaries on the Mishnah.

There are two major talmuds. The first is the Talmud of Jerusalem, which was compiled around 400 CE. A second, more sophisticated Talmud was compiled around 600 CE in Babylon (Iraq), where many Jews continued to live after the end of their captivity there. Since 600, rabbis have added more comments to these texts, creating even richer talmuds.

The Talmuds are commentaries on the law, which covers all aspects of life. It contains all Jewish teaching about what is right and wrong, what should and should not be done, including rules about cleanliness, suitable foods, and cooking.

The Talmuds became the heart of Jewish education. Students learned what important rabbis had said about various questions, and learned to debate in favor of and against various positions. Today in **yeshivas**, Jewish schools, students pair up to interpret and debate the traditional questions. On a typical page from a Talmud, there is at the center a passage from the Mishnah outlining the opposing positions of early rabbis Hillel and Shammai on some rule. Above this is a passage from the Gemara offering comments by later rabbis. Then around the edges of the page are still more comments.

With the Bible and the Talmuds, the Jews now had a rich body of texts that guided every aspect of life. Being Jewish meant studying these texts, following the law as presented in them, and thus making their lives holy.

The Middle Ages (500–1500 CE)

In the fourth century the Roman emperors made Christianity legal and then made it the official religion of the Empire. With their new power, Christian leaders often treated Jews harshly. John Chrysostom, one of the most revered of the **Church Fathers** (influential thinkers in the early centuries of Christianity, whose views are considered authoritative; also known as

Law and Life

The Mishnah is a law code written about 200 CE that interprets the **mitzvot** – the plural of **mitzvah**, "commandment." For example, the Mishnah discusses the kinds of work that are prohibited on the Sabbath (the "seventh" day, commemorating the day on which God rested after creating the world). The Bible does not prohibit "work" in general on the Sabbath. It prohibits *melachah*, which is the word used in Genesis for God's creating the world. Since God rested from melachah on the seventh day, the rabbis reasoned, we should rest from similar kinds of work. The rabbis also found the word *melachah* in Exodus 31, where it is applied to the building of the sanctuary. There God emphasized that no one should engage in melachah on the Sabbath – under penalty of death. So the rabbis concluded that what God meant in banning melachah on the Sabbath were the kinds of work involved in building the sanctuary. What kinds of work were these? The rabbis came up with this list of thirty-nine kinds:

1. Sowing
2. Plowing
3. Reaping
4. Binding sheaves
5. Threshing
6. Winnowing
7. Selecting
8. Grinding
9. Sifting
10. Kneading
11. Baking
12. Shearing wool
13. Washing wool
14. Beating wool
15. Dyeing wool

16. Spinning
17. Weaving
18. Making two loops
19. Weaving two threads
20. Separating two threads
21. Tying
22. Untying
23. Sewing two stitches
24. Tearing
25. Trapping
26. Slaughtering
27. Flaying
28. Salting meat
29. Curing hide
30. Scraping hide

31. Cutting hide up
32. Writing two letters
33. Erasing two letters
34. Building
35. Tearing a building down
36. Extinguishing a fire
37. Kindling a fire
38. Hitting with a hammer
39. Taking an object from the private domain to the public, or transporting an object in the public domain.

Ultimately, the rabbis counted 613 mitzvot.

FIGURE 6.4 First page of the Babylonian Talmud. AKG Images/Israelimages.

"Doctors" of the Church), said that because the Jews had killed Jesus and Jesus was God, the Jews had killed God. Because of this offense, Chrysostom said, God rejected the Jews once and for all, so that they were a doomed people who deserved to suffer. This comment ignores the historical fact that Jesus was executed by the Romans and not "the Jews," of course, but such anti-Jewish arguments became common across Christian Europe in the Middle Ages. Many church synods (meetings of bishops) passed laws surprisingly similar to the laws that Hitler created in Nazi Germany. In 306 the Synod of Elvira prohibited Christians from marrying Jews, or even eating with them. The Synod of Clermont in 535 banned Jews from holding public office. A synod in Toledo, Spain in 681 ordered the public burning of the Talmud and other Jewish books. Other synods forbade Christians from visiting Jewish doctors, and said that Jews could not be plaintiffs against Christians in court, or serve as witnesses against Christians. The Fourth Lateran Council of 1215, a meeting in Rome to which all bishops were invited, declared that Jews had to mark their clothing with a special badge. The Synod of Breslau in 1267 set up compulsory ghettoes – areas where Jews were required to live. The Council of Basel in 1434 said that Jews were not permitted to obtain university degrees.

As we shall see, Christianity underwent a revolution in the 16th century called the Protestant Reformation. It was designed to correct what its leaders saw as deviations from Christian principles in the actions of the Roman Christian rulers. However, unfortunately, anti-Judaism remained a feature even of "reformed" Christianity. Here are some of Martin Luther's proposals:

> What then shall we do with this damned, rejected race of Jews? … First, their synagogues or churches should be set on fire, and whatever does not burn up should be covered or spread over with dirt so that no one may ever be able to see a cinder or stone of it…. Secondly, their homes should likewise be broken down and destroyed…. Thirdly, they should be deprived of their prayer-books and Talmuds in which such idolatry, lies, cursing, and blasphemy are taught. Fourthly, their rabbis must be forbidden under threat of death to teach any more…. If however we are afraid that they might harm us personally … let us drive them out of the country for all time. (Luther 1543, Part XI)

While Jews suffered great discrimination in the Middle Ages and later in Christian Europe, they did much better in areas ruled by Muslims. As we shall see, in the 7th century, Islam arose on the Arabian Peninsula and spread west across North Africa to Spain, and east to India and beyond. The Muslims rejected the claim that the Jews had killed Jesus or God. Their theology, like Jewish theology, was a simple monotheism with no division of God into three persons. They accepted the Torah as God's revelation. And many of their laws were similar to Jewish laws, such as their prohibition on eating pork and other dietary rules. Jews did especially well in Spain while it was governed by Muslims from 711 to 1492. There they made up more than 5% of the population (in the United States today Jews are around 2% of the population).

One of the most important Jewish thinkers, Moses Maimonides (d. 1204), lived in Muslim Spain. In this relatively open multicultural environment, there was a great deal of interaction between Jews, Christians, and Muslims – interaction that included discussions of religious matters. In this context, Maimonides felt compelled to extract basic Jewish beliefs from the Mishnah. He identified 13 basic Jewish beliefs:

1. God is the perfect Creator of all things.

2. God is one in a unique way.

3. God is not physical.

4. God existed before everything else, and exists after everything else.

5. God and only God is to be worshipped.

6. Prophets are special creatures who speak for God.

7. Moses is the greatest of the prophets; he spoke to God face to face.

8. God revealed the Torah to Moses.

9. The Torah is complete.

10. God knows all human actions.

11. God rewards and punishes people in this life and in the world to come.

12. The Messiah will come.

13. The dead will be resurrected.

Many rabbis initially rejected Maimonides' novel, philosophical approach, so different from the traditional style of commentary on the law. However, these thirteen basic principles eventually were accepted by the majority and remain central in Judaism to this day.

Another approach to Judaism that arose in the Middle Ages was the mystical tradition known as **Kabbala**. Its most famous document is the Zohar, "The Book of Splendor," written in Spain around 1275 by Moses de Léon, who claimed that it came from a rabbi of the 2nd century. The Zohar is a mystical commentary on the first five books of the Bible, and discusses the nature of God, the universe, human souls, and good and evil. In the Zohar, God is described as complex rather than simple, and dynamic rather than unchanging. God has emotions. What is more, God has male and female aspects, and they must be joined to maintain harmony in the universe.

A later movement spawned by mystical Judaism was **Hasidism**, which arose in Eastern Europe in the 18th century. It emphasized the emotional side of religion, so that music, dancing, and states of ecstasy could be part of worship. This tradition centered around a leader who had a simple, pious love of God. Hasidic Jews believe that this holy man has a special relationship to God, and following his teachings will bring blessings. The most famous contemporary Hasidic group is the Lubavitcher movement of Rebbe Menachem Schneerson (d. 1994) of Brooklyn, New York. Since his death in 1994, many of his followers have thought of him as the Messiah.

The Modern Period (1750 to the present)

The Enlightenment

Until the 18th century, all Jews were what we would today call Orthodox. They believed that the entire Torah was revealed by God in just the words we have now, so that whatever it says is literally true. They followed the rules in the Mosaic law and lived apart from Christians in Europe. However, in the 18th century new developments in European philosophy, science,

FIGURE 6.5 Rebbe Menachem Schneerson. Z. Radovan/ BibleLandPictures.

and culture changed the lives of many Jews, much as they changed the rest of European culture. The general name for these changes is the Enlightenment, and the Enlightenment within Jewish culture is called **Haskelah**.

The Development of Reform Judaism

The intellectual and political changes brought by the Enlightenment influenced Jewish thinkers in the 18th century. With the flowering of democracy, North American and some European governments granted civil and political rights to Jews. This led many Jews to reject their traditional segregation from the rest of society. In the 19th century, more and more Jews stopped thinking of themselves as outsiders; they wanted to live as full citizens of their countries. They stopped dressing in special ways and speaking in Yiddish, a dialect of German traditionally used by European Jews. They pursued careers in law, medicine, and university teaching. They began to integrate into the cultures where they lived and immerse themselves in the intellectual and cultural life of their nations. Many came to prominence, including some of the scholars mentioned in this study – such as Karl Marx, Sigmund Freud, and Emile Durkheim.

As Jews began to integrate into their national cultures, some aspects of the traditional laws receded in importance. Indeed, the changes in European society brought by the Enlightenment led to a rethinking of Judaic practice that resulted in Reform Judaism.

Reform Judaism is a movement that started in Germany and France in the 19th century, but flourished in the United States. Whereas traditional Judaism had emphasized the Talmud, Reform Jews emphasized the study of scripture. And instead of reading the Bible as word-for-word dictation from God, they read it in a new way. (As we shall see,

The Enlightenment

The Enlightenment was a broad set of intellectual developments that accompanied socioeconomic and political changes in Europe, beginning in the 17th century. Four significant areas experiencing change were (1) cosmology, our understanding of the universe, (2) epistemology, our understanding of how we know, (3) ethics (or morality), and (4) political thought. All these developments had important consequences for religion.

First were changes in cosmology. From ancient times through the Middle Ages, people thought of the earth as the center of the universe, with the sun, the moon, and the stars circling around it. This, of course, made humans feel important. A few passages in the Bible seem to back up this geocentrism (earth-centered view), and the 2nd-century thinker Ptolemy made it into a complete system of astronomy. However, starting around 1500, astronomers such as Copernicus and then Galileo proposed that the earth moves around the sun. With the invention of better telescopes, scientists came to see that the universe is immense, and that the Earth is far from the center of everything. This realization challenged the geocentrism of the Bible.

Second were changes in epistemology, the study of knowledge and belief. In the ancient and medieval world, the authority of revelation was taken for granted. People believed something was true based on who said it was true – a characteristic of oral cultures. Revelation, considered to be the word of God, was the ultimate source of truth. Those who were accepted as legitimate interpreters of revelation, such as rabbis and priests, were also respected authorities. On issues on which scripture was silent, the word of non-religious authorities was often taken as definitive. Aristotle, the ancient Greek philosopher, said that heavy objects fall faster than light objects, for example, and people accepted this as the truth. However, when the traditional belief that the sun goes around the earth was questioned, people started asking what other traditional beliefs might be incorrect. Instead of taking Aristotle's word for it that heavy objects fall faster, Galileo dropped balls of different weights from the top of a ship's mast, and found that they hit the deck at the same time. Such experiments were the start of the modern scientific method, in which the basis of certainty is not an individual's or an institution's word. Instead, reason, based on empirical observation and experimentation, became the source of certainty.

If experts such as Aristotle and Ptolemy could be wrong about physics and astronomy, what about experts in matters of religion? Should people accept the interpretations of scripture offered by the religious authorities, or were individuals – using their own reason – able to understand scripture's teachings? For that matter, how do we know that the version of scripture we are reading was copied correctly? Are we sure that we know the exact meanings of the words in scripture, especially if we are reading a translation from an ancient text?

A third major development in the Enlightenment was in people's understanding of right and wrong – ethics or morality. In the Hebrew Bible, doing what is right is doing what God commands, and doing what is wrong is doing what God forbids. Ethics is a matter of obedience and disobedience. (As we saw in Chapter 3, this is known as "Divine Command" Ethics.) This understanding was questioned by Enlightenment thinkers. They reasoned that when God commands something, either he has a reason for giving that command or he has no reason. If God gives commands for no reason, then he is a despot or an autocrat, terms with a rather negative connotation in Enlightenment Europe. Since people think of God as good, it must be that God gives commands for a reason. Furthermore, most divine commands – such as those calling for honesty and concern for the needy, and those forbidding murder and theft – obviously serve to benefit human beings. So, as Enlightenment thinkers examined issues of right and wrong, they looked for the effects of actions on people, for the ways an action would harm or benefit someone. If there were rules that benefited ancient people but would not benefit people today, Enlightenment thinkers tended to consider these rules as no longer applicable. They must have been beneficial at some point in human history, but they were no longer pertinent. They had become obsolete.

There were also changes in political thought. Before the 18th century, the standard understanding of how leaders got their authority was that God gave it to them. This idea came to be called the Divine Right of Kings, but it goes back at least to the Bible, where God chooses Saul, then David, and so on. In the Christian New Testament, Paul says that all authority is from God (Romans 13:1). However, 18th-century thinkers, many of them devout Jews and Christians, developed a new view of political authority – democracy or "rule by the people." Enlightenment thinkers argued that the authority to govern people comes from those people themselves. A government that ruled without this authority would not be legitimate. This idea led to a number of revolutions, including the American Revolution in 1776 and the French Revolution in 1789. It is in this context that we begin to see a clear distinction drawn between religious and political authority – and with it, a distinction between religion and politics.

Christian scholars were doing the same thing.) In this perspective, the Bible was indeed divine revelation, but it was not taken as literal history or science. It was read as a guide for people living in specific cultures and historical eras, as a source of wisdom about purposeful human existence. Reform Jews also changed their synagogue rituals to be more accessible to the congregation. Instead of Hebrew, they used the vernacular, the local language.

In the new Reform movement, as in traditional Judaism, the most important feature of religion was ethics. However, the emphasis was now on the ethical principles of the

Kashrut

Judaic dietary laws are known as *kashrut*. This is the system of rules about what foods are acceptable and unacceptable, and how certain foods must be prepared. Of the animals that live in the water, only those that have both fins and scales are acceptable. So fish are **kosher** (proper), but clams, oysters, and lobsters are *trefa* (or *tref*, literally meaning meat that was killed by wild animals rather than being properly slaughtered, but generally applied to all food that is forbidden). Of the four-legged animals that live on land, only those that have split hooves and chew the cud may be eaten. So sheep and cattle are kosher, but not pigs or foxes.

Acceptable animals must be slaughtered according to a specific ritual called *shehitah*. The slaughterer says a prayer and then draws a razor-sharp knife across the animal's neck to sever the main arteries. Blood may not be eaten, so after most of the blood is drained from the carcass, it is soaked and salted to eliminate any residual blood.

A prohibition in Exodus 23:19, Exodus 34:26, and Deuteronomy 14:21 says, "You shall not boil a kid in its mother's milk." From this passage, the rabbis derived the rule that meat and dairy products may not be eaten at the same time, or even be prepared together. Further, a household should keep separate dishes, cutlery, and table linens for serving meat and dairy products.

Many Jews follow modified kosher laws, such as avoiding pork and shellfish, but not keeping separate dishes and utensils for meat and dairy.

Muslim dietary laws concerning meat are virtually identical to those of Jews. Acceptable meat is called **halal** (as opposed to forbidden or **haram** meat). In areas without halal butcher shops, Muslims often shop for kosher meat.

These rules were derived from the Bible, mostly the books of Genesis, Exodus, Leviticus, and Deuteronomy. As we saw in Chapter 4, anthropologist Mary Douglas thinks that these prohibitions were based on the Bible's categories for things God created. The "unclean" animals are those that do not fit neatly into the Bible's categories.

Enlightenment, which were moral rules that any reasonable person could discover. Many of the 613 mitzvot were seen as obsolete in Reform Judaism. God wants us to tell the truth, be honest in our business dealings, help the poor, and be concerned about social justice. However, whatever purpose had been served by, for example, the rule against *shatnes* – wearing clothing made of two materials – that rule is now obsolete. So the ethics of Reform Judaism looked much like the ethics of other religious groups influenced by the Enlightenment. Central was an emphasis on social justice. Instead of worrying about observing 613 rules, Reform Jews had a simpler ethics captured in the ancient prophet Micah's saying, "What does the Lord require of you but to do justice, love mercy, and walk humbly with your God?" (Micah 6:80)

While Reform Judaism was at first strongest in Germany, various branches of government there would recognize only a single kind of Judaism, and this was usually traditional Orthodoxy. However, in the United States, with its strict separation of religion and politics (or church and state), there were no such restrictions, and Reform Judaism was able to flourish. In 1885, American Reform Jews gathered in Pittsburgh to draft a statement of principles. We can summarize them this way.

1. Every religion attempts "to grasp the Infinite," and in every book of revelation there is "the consciousness of the indwelling of God in man." Judaism has developed "the highest conception of the God-idea."

2. The Bible records the consecration of the Jewish people to its mission as the priests of the one God. This makes the Bible "the most potent instrument of religious and moral instruction." Modern scientific discoveries are not incompatible with the teachings of the Bible, which was written at a time when people did not understand as much as we do now about how nature works.

3. The 613 Laws of Moses were designed for "the Jewish people for its mission during its national life in Palestine." Many of these laws are no longer "adapted to the views and habits of modern civilization," and do not "elevate and sanctify our lives." The only parts of the Mosaic Law that are still binding are the general moral laws.

4. All the Mosaic and rabbinical laws that "regulate diet, priestly purity, and dress originated in ages and under the influence of ideas entirely foreign to our present mental and spiritual state. They fail to impress the modern Jew with a spirit of priestly holiness; their observance in our days is apt rather to obstruct than to further modern spiritual elevation."

5. The time of "Israel's great Messianic hope for the establishment of the kingdom of truth, justice, and peace among all men" is approaching. "We consider ourselves no longer a nation, but a religious community, and therefore expect neither a return to Palestine, nor a sacrificial worship under the sons of Aaron, nor the restoration of any of the laws concerning the Jewish state."

6. Judaism is "a progressive religion," changing over time to spread the message of monotheism and morality. Christianity and Islam grew out of Judaism, and "we appreciate their providential mission, to aid in the spreading of monotheistic and moral truth." "We extend the hand of fellowship to all who cooperate with us in the establishment of the reign of truth and righteousness among men."

7. While Judaism teaches that the soul is immortal, "We reject as ideas not rooted in Judaism, the beliefs both in bodily resurrection and in Gehenna and Eden (Hell and Paradise) as abodes for everlasting punishment and reward."

8. Social justice is the central concern in Judaism. "In full accordance with the spirit of the Mosaic legislation, which strives to regulate the relations between rich and poor, we deem it our duty to participate in the great task of modern times, to solve, on the

basis of justice and righteousness, the problems presented by the contrasts and evils of the present organization of society."

The Central Conference of American Rabbis met in 1937 in Columbus, Ohio. Under the impact of the horrific persecution of Jews in Europe, they revised parts of the Pittsburgh Platform. They re-emphasized the idea that Jews are a people, bound by a common history and religious heritage. They also stressed the importance of the synagogue and encouraged the use of Hebrew in liturgy.

Moses Mendelssohn (1729–1786)
The Father of Haskelah, the Jewish Enlightenment

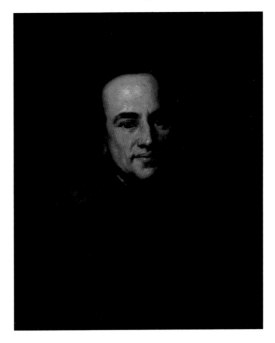

FIGURE 6.6 Moses Mendelssohn. Imagno/Getty Images.

The first Jew to become widely known across Europe was Moses Mendelssohn. He studied not only his own tradition, but also the Enlightenment thinkers of the time. His brilliance was recognized in 1763 when he entered a literary contest and won the Prize of the Prussian Academy of the Arts, defeating the philosopher Immanuel Kant. While traditional Judaism had emphasized the Talmud, Mendelssohn said that the Bible should be the basic text in Jewish education. He helped to write a translation of the Bible into literary German, and within a generation most Jewish households in central Europe had a copy of this Bible. Two of Mendelssohn's grandchildren – Felix and Fanny – had outstanding careers as composers of music.

Conservative Judaism

By 1880 Reform Judaism had become the most popular form in the United States, and if the population had simply grown without immigration, then the number of more traditional Jews would have dwindled even further by the mid-20th century. However, between 1880 and 1920 there was a huge Jewish immigration into the United States from Russia, Poland, and Eastern Europe. These people were mostly traditional Jews whose religious views had not been affected much by the Enlightenment. They did not want to drop traditional customs and laws. As they moved into American cities such as New York, however, many did see the appeal of being a part of the culture around them. And so many, while not becoming Reform Jews, became less traditional than Orthodox Jews, those who stayed committed to the traditional interpretations and practices of Jewish life. By the early 20th century, there was a new kind of Judaism for them. It was called Conservative Judaism in the U.S. and **Masorti** (traditional) Judaism elsewhere. It would keep many of the traditional elements of Judaism – Hebrew as the language of prayer, kosher dietary laws, observance of the Sabbath – but would let people adapt themselves to modern culture and to science. In 1902 in New York, Solomon Schechter founded the Jewish Theological Seminary to train rabbis in the new Conservative movement.

Reconstructionist Judaism

One of the more influential rabbis at the Jewish Theological Seminary was Mordechai Kaplan (d. 1983), who taught there for over fifty years. Born in Lithuania, he started his career as an Orthodox rabbi. Judaism, he said, "is the sum of everything about Jewish people," not just their religious beliefs and rituals. He promoted the idea of Jewish community centers, where the whole culture of Jews would be fostered. He especially wanted to reach the many secularized Jews he saw all around him, people who had stopped observing religious rituals but who still considered themselves Jewish.

In 1922 Kaplan founded the Society for the Advancement of Judaism, and in 1934 he published *Judaism as a Civilization*. Gradually he developed a new form of Judaism that he called Reconstructionism. The major difference between this movement and Orthodox, Reform, and Conservative Judaism is its **religious naturalism**, the tendency to stress ethical values and spirituality as natural parts of human life, rather than stemming from supernatural sources. Kaplan taught that God is not a supernatural person, but a force or energy that improves human life. "God is the power that makes for salvation," the sum of all natural processes that allow humans to live meaningful, fulfilled lives. Kaplan wrote that "to believe in God means to take for granted that it is man's destiny to rise above the brute and to eliminate all forms of violence and exploitation from human society." (Kaplan quoted in "Reconstructionist Judaism," http://en.academic.ru/dic.nsf/enwiki/15963). He also rejected the idea that the Jews are God's Chosen People. This claim, he said, only alienates Jews from the rest of humankind.

For many Jews, Kaplan's naturalism was incompatible with the Torah as revelation from a personal God, and so Reconstructionist Judaism has never attracted many members. Worldwide, there are fewer than 100 Reconstructionist synagogues. In 1945 the Union of Orthodox Rabbis of the United States and Canada accused Kaplan of "atheism [and]

heresy," and of "disbelief in the basic tenets of Judaism." He was excommunicated and his *Sabbath Prayer Book* was burned during a ceremony at a hotel in New York City.

The Rituals of Judaism

Jewish life centers on sanctifying everyday life – that is, making it holy. The center is the family, and so many rituals are observed in the home, such as the weekly Sabbath dinner, the Passover Seder, and Hanukkah celebrations.

The *shabas*, or Sabbath, is observed each week from sunset Friday to sunset Saturday. Members of the family finish their work on Friday afternoon, bathe, and put on fresh clothes. After sundown, the family gathers in the home for a meal prepared earlier. The food is blessed and there are other prayers. On Friday evening or Saturday morning the family goes to the synagogue or temple in the morning, where they worship and hear readings from the Torah. Orthodox Jews follow the traditional laws forbidding work during the Sabbath. Since driving is considered work, Orthodox and Conservative Jews often walk to the synagogue for services. Many consider turning on electrical devices to be work, and so they use pre-set timers.

The most important object in any synagogue or temple is the Torah scroll. It is kept in the **ark**, an ornamented cabinet at the front of the hall where a lamp burns to mark its presence. An important part of the service is opening the curtains in front of the ark and removing the Torah scroll to read it to the congregation.

Like most traditions, Judaism has rituals to mark the major events in life. Eight days after a boy is born, there is the **bris**, circumcision. The transition to adulthood is marked by a **Bar Mitzvah** for boys and a **Bat Mizvah** for girls (in non-Orthodox communities) at age 12–13. *Bar* means son, and *Bat* means daughter; *Mitzvah* means commandment. So Bar Mitzvah or Bat Mitzvah means that the young man or woman is now bound by the law. While no ceremony is required to mark this transition, and none is mentioned in the Talmud, over the last century most Jewish families have chosen to have a ceremony in a synagogue or temple, and then a reception in a party setting. At Sabbath services the young man or woman is called up to recite a blessing over the Torah reading, and perhaps to lead the congregation in prayers. They may also give a short speech that begins, "Today I am a man/woman."

FIGURE 6.7 At his Bar Mitzvah ceremony, a young man holds the Torah Scrolls. © CapturedNuance/ iStockphoto.

There are also rituals for Jewish weddings, such as having the couple stand under a **chuppah** or canopy, and having the groom crush a glass with his foot at the end.

At death there is a simple ceremony and burial in a plain pine coffin. Jewish law forbids embalming and requires that the body be buried within 24 hours. Just before the funeral begins, the immediate relatives of the deceased tear their garments, or the rabbi may hand them torn black ribbons to pin on their clothes, to symbolize their loss. Traditionally, after the burial, there is a seven-day period of mourning called **sitting shivah**.

In the Jewish calendar, there are several feasts associated with the seasons. The New Year is **Rosh Hashanah** in the fall. Then nine days later is **Yom Kippur**, the Day of Atonement. Together, these Days of Awe, also called the High Holy Days in the U.S., mark the season of penitence. Also in the fall is **Sukkot**, the Feast of Tabernacles, a harvest festival for which the family builds a shelter outside, covers it with branches or fronds, and eats their meals inside it. Then in December is **Hanukkah**, which commemorates the victory of the Jews rebelling against their Syrian overlords in the second century BCE. In the spring is Passover, the celebration of the liberation of the people of Israel from bondage in Egypt, as told in Exodus. At a special dinner called the **Seder**, the family eats unleavened bread to commemorate the speedy exit of the Hebrews from Egypt. The wine is blessed and there are special prayers.

Judaism Today

Today there are 13.3 million Jews worldwide. Half live in the Americas, with some 6.5 million in the U.S. About 37% live in the State of Israel and 12% in Europe and Russia. In the U.S., according to the 2000 National Jewish Population Survey, 35% of Jews identify themselves as Reform, 26% as Conservative, 10% as Orthodox, and 2% as Reconstructionist. In the United Kingdom there are about 350,000 Jews. Some 20% are Reform or Liberal, an approach to Reform Judaism that developed in the U.K.

As we have seen, Judaism has changed significantly over the centuries. Indeed, until the late 15th century, there was no such term as "Judaism." There were Jews, of course, and the laws by which they lived. They were a people – spread across the globe and thus diverse in culture, but related nonetheless by being members of "a great nation" who struggled to maintain fidelity to the one God. However, the term "Judaism" refers to an ideology (set of ideas) reinforced by practices and rituals and supported by institutions. It was coined in Europe, as a parallel to the term "Christianity" – a term coined only a few centuries earlier to refer to the *raison d'être* for "Christendom" (Christian religio-political institutions and the vast domains they governed). As we saw in Chapter 4, this kind of terminology signals what Peter Berger would call "objectification" or "reification" of a people's way of life – making the dynamic flow of a people's ways of acting and thinking "into a thing" (from the Latin *res*, "thing"). We shall see in the next section that the reification of Christianity led to a kind of rigidity: significant changes in the structure of Christianity became difficult at best. They often required revolutionary action.

However, this is not the case in Judaism. There have been many interpretations of Judaic teachings, and diverse interpretations coexist among Jews today. While most religious Jews accept the traditional language of God, covenant, Israel, Messiah, and the World to Come, they are flexible in their interpretations of these words. Reconstructionist Jews do not believe in a personal God, for example, and neither do some Reform Jews, including rabbis. Conservative Judaism requires belief in God, but leaves the description of "God" quite open. Similarly, the Messiah is understood by many Jews to be a better time in the future, rather than a liberating king. And many do not believe literally in an apocalyptic World to Come, or even in a personal life after death.

Yet the core teaching of Judaism from ancient times to the present remains that the people of Israel were chosen by God to be "a kingdom of priests and a holy nation." God established a covenant with Abraham and renewed it with Moses at Sinai, and the "people of Israel" – Jews – are bound by it today. As God's People, they have a special responsibility, and by carrying out this responsibility they make their lives holy and set an example for the rest of the world to follow.

Unit II Christianity

The History and Teachings of Christianity

Origins

What we now call Christianity was started by Jesus of Nazareth in the first century. From birth to death, he was a Jew and presented himself as a Jewish reformer. He did not call himself "Christ" – this is a title used later by his followers. "Christ" is the English form of *Christos*, the Greek translation of "messiah," meaning "one who is anointed (as king)." As we saw, the idea that a messiah would come to liberate Jews from foreign oppressors became important in the centuries before Jesus' birth. The Messiah, it was said, would be a Jewish king descended from King David.

What we know about Jesus' life comes mostly from what was written about him, decades after his death, in the **gospels**, from the Old English word for "good news." Biblical scholars (see Chapter 3) disagree about the exact dating of the gospels but generally agree that they were written at least forty years after the events they describe. Biblical scholars also generally agree that none of the Gospels was written by people who knew Jesus personally, even though two of the four gospels are attributed to the friends of Jesus whose names they bear: Matthew and John. Still, working with scripture and other historical documents, scholars believe they can discern some facts about Jesus' life and teachings.

Jesus grew up in the lower class in Nazareth, a town in Galilee in the northern part of Palestine (the name the Romans had given to the parts of the land of Canaan between the Jordan River and the Mediterranean Sea, now known as the state of Israel and the Palestinian territories of the West Bank and Gaza). When he was about thirty, Jesus began preaching about "the kingdom of God," "kingdom" here being a translation of the Greek word for "reign" or "rule." (Although Palestine was ruled by Rome at the time, the language of learning was still Greek. The gospels were therefore written in Greek.) The Kingdom or Reign of God would be a world in which people lived the way God has told them to live.

FIGURE 6.8 Statue of Jesus Christ the Redeemer above Rio de Janiero, Brazil. Mark Schwettmann/Shutterstock Images.

Like many preachers at the time, Jesus spoke of an "apocalypse," a catastrophic ending to the world as we know it. He said that when this happens, God will judge everyone and then reward those who have followed his will, and punish those who have not. Many of Jesus' followers thought that he was the Messiah, but he did not appear to be a kingly figure, much less a political liberator, as most people expected the Messiah to be. Jesus did not tell his followers to overthrow Roman rule, and even told them to pay their taxes to the Romans. His preaching was not about politics, but about morality. Nor did he speak as a theologian discussing doctrine or as a rabbi discussing details of the law. He preached in simple stories – called **parables** – about how people should live. When he said that people should love their neighbors, for example, and someone asked, "Who is my neighbor?" Jesus did not define "neighbor," but showed what he meant by telling the parable of the Good Samaritan (Luke 10:25–37).

Samaritans Today

There are still Samaritans today. Many live near Mount Gerizim – known as Jabal Tur, in Arabic, located in the West Bank city of Nablus – which is biblical Shechem. Samaritans believe Mount Gerizim is where Abraham almost sacrificed his son. They therefore hold it sacred.

In that story a Jewish traveler is beaten by bandits and left for dead at the roadside. Two religious authorities pass by, one after the other, but neither stops to help the victim. Then a Samaritan comes by, nurses the man's wounds, takes him to an inn and instructs the innkeeper to take care of the man until he is well, and pays the man's bill.

The Samaritans – "people of Samaria"– claimed that they were descended from the tribes of Israel (see above). However, this claim was rejected by the Jews who returned to Jerusalem from Babylonian captivity, and the two communities had been bitter enemies ever since. So Jesus' using a Samaritan as an example of highly moral behavior would have seemed strange to his Jewish audiences, who were used to dealing with morality exclusively within their own community. There have been numerous religious interpretations of the parable over the centuries, but scholars see in its emphasis on an inclusive moral community a major step in the development of what would become Christianity as distinct from Judaism.

Another significant distinction between the two traditions can be seen in the Sermon on the Mount in Matthew 5–7. Believed by scholars to be a summary of major themes in Jesus' overall teaching, it begins with eight "Beatitudes," statements about how people are "blessed" when they do God's will even though they suffer for it. He praises those who are gentle, who forgive others, and who are willing to be persecuted for the sake of justice. By following the will of God they embody the Kingdom of God.

While for many people at the time, being a good Jew was carefully following the 613 mitzvot, Jesus emphasizes what is called the "Great Commandment" from Leviticus 19:18: "You shall not take vengeance or bear a grudge against your kinsfolk. Love your neighbor as yourself." He skips hundreds of mitzvot, including those about purity, diet, and observing the Sabbath. Rejecting the biblical law of retaliation ("An eye for an eye and a tooth for a tooth" – Exodus 21:23–25; Leviticus 24:19–21), Jesus says, "Do not resist an evildoer." While the Hebrew Bible sanctioned retaliation (or vengeance), Jesus stresses love. He says, "You have heard it said, 'Love your neighbor and hate your enemy.' But I tell you: Love your enemies and pray for those who persecute you." (Matthew 5:43–44) This emphasis will comprise another distinction between the Judaic and Christian traditions.

As we shall see, some aspects of these teachings will be reinterpreted by later Christians as circumstances change, but certain aspects of Jesus' teaching remain central to the Christian tradition throughout history, including his focus on love, as well as doing the will of God. As he put it when he gave an example of how to pray,

The Beatitudes, from the Sermon on the Mount

Blessed are the poor in spirit, for theirs is the kingdom of heaven.
Blessed are those who mourn, for they will be comforted.
Blessed are the meek, for they will inherit the earth.
Blessed are those who hunger and thirst for righteousness, for they will be filled.
Blessed are the merciful, for they will receive mercy.
Blessed are the pure in heart, for they will see God.
Blessed are the peacemakers, for they will be called children of God.
Blessed are those who are persecuted for righteousness' sake, for theirs is the kingdom of heaven.

Matthew 5:3–10 (NRSV)

Our Father in heaven, hallowed [holy, revered] be your name. Your kingdom come, your will be done, on earth as it is in heaven. Give us this day our daily bread, and forgive us our offenses, as we also have forgiven those who offend us. And do not lead us into temptation, but rescue us from evil. (Matthew 6:9–13; Luke 11:2–4)

The important things in life, Jesus continues, are not material possessions, which can wear out or be lost. What is important is striving to carry out God's will. Like a good father, God knows that you need such things as food and clothing, and he will provide them if you do his will.

The Gospels present more than just what Jesus taught. They also describe what he did, such as miraculously healing blind and paralyzed people, and bringing dead people back to life. The writers of the Gospels said that they were including these miracles to show that Jesus spoke and acted with authority from God, and many people were attracted to his teachings as a result.

As Jesus attracted more and more followers, some of whom called him the Messiah and King of the Jews, the Roman rulers of Palestine became suspicious. They feared that he would lead a revolution. So Pontius Pilate, the Roman governor of Judea (the province where Jesus lived), tried Jesus and sentenced him to death by crucifixion. The Gospels say that three days after Jesus died he came back to life (was "resurrected"), spent 40 days among his followers, and then ascended ("went up") into heaven. His followers expected him to return soon – as Messiah. However, when this did not happen, different understandings of who Jesus was evolved, and an entire movement developed around his teachings.

The Development of Christian Doctrine

The most influential person after Jesus in the new movement was Paul of Tarsus ("last names" or surnames are a modern invention; in the olden days people were often identified by where they lived – such as Tarsus, in what is now Turkey), who lived from about 3 to about 66 CE. He was a Pharisee who had adapted to the Greco-Roman world. Paul was the first to write anything that is now in the New Testament – his Letters or **Epistles**, which he used to spread the new movement beyond Palestine to Greece and Rome. The first Christians thought of themselves as Jews, and so required that non-Jewish men joining their group be circumcised. However, Paul says that this is a new movement and should include not only Jews but anyone else who is willing to follow Jesus' teachings. As more and more non-Jews joined, eventually Christians came to think of themselves as a separate tradition.

Paul never met Jesus and says very little about the details of Jesus' life. His epistles mention some aspects of Jesus' moral teaching. In his first letter to his followers in Corinth, for example, he writes about love so beautifully that it is among his most quoted passages:

> If I speak in tongues of men and angels, but have not love, I am only a resounding gong or a clanging cymbal. If I have the gift of prophecy and can fathom all mysteries and all knowledge, and if I have a faith that can move mountains, but have not love, I am nothing. If I give all I possess to the poor and surrender my body to the flames, but have not love, I gain nothing.
>
> Love is patient, love is kind. It does not envy, it does not boast, it is not proud. It is not rude, it is not self-seeking, it is not easily angered, it keeps no record of wrongs. Love does not delight in evil but rejoices with the truth. It always protects, always trusts, always hopes, always preserves.
>
> Love never fails. But where there are prophecies, they will cease; where there are tongues, they will be stilled; where there is knowledge, it will pass away. For we know in part and we prophesy in part, but when perfection comes, the imperfect disappears. When I was a child, I talked like a child, I thought like a child, I reasoned like a child. When I became a man, I put childish ways behind me. Now we see but a poor reflection as in a mirror; then we shall see face to face. Now I know in part; then I shall know fully, even as I am fully known.
>
> And now these three remain: Faith, hope and love. But the greatest of these is love.
> (I Corinthians 13:1–13)

Even U.S. President Barack Obama quoted from this passage in his inaugural speech. However, Paul's primary emphasis is on the cosmic significance of Jesus' life and death. He describes Jesus as redeeming human beings – that is, saving them – from their natural sinfulness, especially through his death and resurrection.

Over the first three centuries of the common era, as Christianity spread through much of the Middle East, Northeast Africa, and southern Europe, a number of opinions developed about the identity of Jesus and the meaning of his mission. It was common to refer to Jesus as "Son of God." "Son of God" is a standard phrase in the Hebrew Bible, meaning someone who follows God's will, as when Jesus tells his followers to "love your enemies and pray for those who persecute you, so that you may be sons of your father in heaven." (Matthew 5:44–45) Some Christian groups believed that Jesus was literally the "Son of God," and that he had no beginning in time as normal sons have. He was the Eternal Son of God.

Baptism

The Gospels of Matthew and Mark say that, at the beginning of his public life, Jesus was baptized by his cousin John in the River Jordan. As in many traditions, in Judaism the ritual of being immersed in water – **mikvah** – is a symbol of purification. It is required after coming into contact with substances that are considered impure. As we saw in Chapter 4, these typically include blood and other bodily fluids, as well as corpses. When a non-Jew wants to become a Jew, s/he must undergo this symbolic purification after living a life not protected from impurity by the following of Judaic law. It thus symbolizes a monumental change in status – for the better. Jesus' baptism became a symbol of a similar change in status; baptism indicates acceptance of Jesus' teachings. In Matthew 28:19, he commissioned his apostles to "make disciples of all nations, baptizing them in the name of the Father, and of the Son, and of the Holy Spirit."

FIGURE 6.9 Woman baptized in the Jordan River. Eddie Gerald/Alamy.

This teaching was based on the Gospel of John, which starts: "In the beginning was the Word, and the Word was with God, and the Word was God."

There were other ideas about Jesus, as well. Some early Christian groups believed that Jesus was divine, but that he was not eternal because he had been created. Some said that he was the adopted son of God – created as a man but then made divine by God. These and many other ideas about Jesus circulated among early Christians in over fifty documents.

FIGURE 6.10 *In hoc signo vinces.*

They included the four gospels most Christians are familiar with (Matthew, Mark, Luke, and John), as well as the Gospel of Thomas, the Gospel of Peter, the Gospel of the Ebionites, the Gospel of the Nazareans, and the Gospel According to the Hebrews. Early Christians also had the letters of Paul and James (another of Jesus' followers), which are now in the canonical (official) Bible. However, there were letters of other early Christian preachers, as well, such as Clement, Ignatius, Barnabas, and Polycarp. Known as the Apostolic Fathers, they did not know Jesus but they did know the original twelve **apostles** – Jesus' closest students and messengers – and so their 1st- and 2nd-century writings are considered authoritative. As well, besides the now canonical Apocalypse of John, early Christians had the Apocalypse of Jesus' great friend Peter. With input from so many diverse sources, it is not surprising that early Christian thought reflected multiple viewpoints. There was, in these early centuries, no orthodoxy in Christian thought.

The Institutionalization and Politicization of Christianity

This lack of orthodoxy would change with the development of Christianity as a political force. During the first three centuries of Christianity, several Roman rulers had ordered the persecution of Christians. In 64 the emperor Nero blamed the Christians for the fire that burned much of Rome, and he started killing Christians in the Roman Coliseum in horrible ways for public entertainment. He even devised a tunic impregnated with a flammable liquid, so that the Christian **martyr** (literally, a "witness" but more generally, someone who maintains commitment to a cause even in the face of death) would slowly burn to death to the delight of the crowd. The last major persecutions were in the early fourth century, with thousands of Christians killed.

However, in 312, the Emperor Constantine, whose mother was Christian, became interested in the movement. Constantine led a life full of warfare. He fought with other generals for leadership of the Roman Empire, and led battles against European tribes that did not want to be part of that empire. According to one story, before a major battle he had a vision of the Greek letters *chi* and *rho*, the first two letters of the Greek word for "Christ," superimposed on one another. Under this were the words *In hoc signo vinces* – "in this sign you will conquer."

Taking this vision as a divine message, Constantine had his troops paint these symbols on their shields, and they won the battle. After this he signed an edict that allowed Christians to practice their religion openly, instead of in hiding as they had done during the persecutions.

The Christian population of the Roman empire was, of course, extremely grateful to Constantine. And their allegiance to Constantine no doubt strengthened his political

The Expanded Nicene Creed

We believe (I believe) in one God, the Father Almighty, maker of heaven and earth, and of all things visible and invisible. And in one Lord Jesus Christ, the only begotten Son of God, and born of the Father before all ages. (God of God) light of light, true God of true God. Begotten not made, consubstantial to the Father, by whom all things were made. Who for us men and for our salvation came down from heaven. And was incarnate of the Holy Spirit and of the Virgin Mary and was made man; was crucified also for us under Pontius Pilate, suffered and was buried; and the third day rose again according to the Scriptures. And ascended into heaven, sits at the right hand of the Father, and shall come again with glory to judge the living and the dead, of whose Kingdom there shall be no end. And (I believe) in the Holy Spirit, the Lord and Giver of life, who proceeds from the Father (and the Son), who together with the Father and the Son is to be adored and glorified, who spoke by the Prophets. And one holy, catholic, and apostolic Church. We confess (I confess) one baptism for the remission of sins. And we look for (I look for) the resurrection of the dead and the life of the world to come. Amen.

authority *vis à vis* rival claimants to power in Rome. However, Constantine found the disagreements among the various Christians in the empire to be troublesome. In 325, therefore, he organized a conference of bishops in Nicea (in today's Turkey), in order to get agreement among Christian authorities.

At the time, various Christian communities around the Mediterranean were led by **presbyters**, a Greek term that means "elder" and is often translated as "bishop." One of them, Arius of Alexandria (Egypt), said that Jesus had been created by God. However, at the Council of Nicea, that idea was voted down in favor of the view that Jesus, like God the Father, was uncreated. By the end of the conference, a majority of bishops had agreed on an official statement saying that Jesus was uncreated and was the same substance as the Father. The document also referred to the "Holy Spirit" – terminology found in Talmudic literature referring to God or to God's communication to prophets. The official statement became known as the **Nicene Creed**. At a later council in Constantinople in 381, it was expanded into the familiar creed that is now accepted by almost all sects of Christians.

Once this creed was official, Arius and his followers were branded heretics. "Arian" Christianity and other forms of Christianity continued, mainly in the Middle East, as minorities outside the official control of Rome.

At around the same time, Christian leaders rejected more than half of the gospels and epistles used by the various Christian communities. By the mid-300s they had determined an official list, a canon, of the 27 books that are now called the **New Testament**.

Christianity and Faith

Being a Jew means living in accordance with the laws of God. One becomes a *bar* or *bat mitzvah* ("son" or "daughter" of the law or "commandments"). Similarly, being a Muslim means living in accordance with Islamic law. In the case of Christianity, the identifying factor is having correct beliefs. This is, in fact, the core meaning of "orthodoxy," from the Greek words for "straight" and "teaching." The rite of passage into adulthood in Christianity is Confirmation – a ceremony in which one affirms one's "faith" or "belief in" the teachings of the Church. This is why Christianity is often called a "faith." While specific beliefs are central to both Jewish and Muslim identity, it is less common to refer to either Judaism or Islam as faiths.

Christianity, its basic literature and doctrines newly established, became the state religion of the Roman empire in 380. That meant that it was central to the government's legitimacy; its leaders approved of the government and acceptance of its official teachings became the measure of full membership in the Roman state. Those who did not accept official Christian teaching were not only excluded from the rights of citizenship; because they did not accept the state ideology, they were considered politically suspect – possibly traitors. This politicization of Christianity marked the beginning of anti-Jewish sentiment discussed above.

Two more councils of the Christian Church were held, to further define correct understandings of Christian doctrine, in 431, and 451. They declared that Jesus is fully God and fully human, one person with a divine nature and a human nature, and that he always was and always will be God. The Holy Spirit was declared to be equal to the Father and the Son. The Father, the Son, and the Holy Spirit make up the **Trinity**, which comes from the Greek and Latin root *tri-*, meaning three. Yet the Trinity does not compromise the monotheism of Christianity. Christians believe in only one God – which has three "persons."

From these early councils to today, the issue of orthodoxy versus heresy has been important in most Christian groups. When members within a group had major differences in their beliefs, they usually split into different sects or churches. This splitting has led to today's 34,000 Christian sects.

Eastern and Western Christians

Once Christianity was the state religion of the Roman Empire, it had support from the government and its leaders had considerable political influence. In the 3rd century, the bishops of Jerusalem, Antioch in Syria, Alexandria in Egypt, and Rome were called patriarchs. In the 4th century, when Constantine moved the imperial capital to Byzantium, in today's Turkey, its bishop became the fifth patriarch. Starting in the 3rd century, the bishops of Rome argued that they were more than local patriarchs, since they had inherited their authority from Rome's first bishop, Peter, and Jesus had chosen Peter to lead his new church. So, they said, the Bishop of Rome was a super-bishop, the leader of all

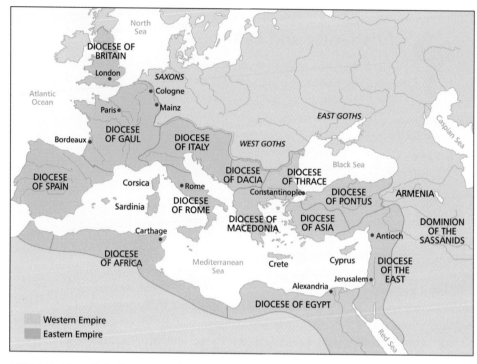

MAP 6.2 Map of the Roman Empire – East and West.

Christians. The other four patriarchs disagreed, especially the patriarch of Byzantium, which Constantine had renamed after himself – Constantinople, "City of Constantine." Eventually, the bishop of Rome would establish himself as the patriarch of the **Roman Catholic Church** and call himself the pope, from *papa* for father. He ruled over the Western or Latin Church with its headquarters in Rome. The bishop of Byzantium (Constantinople) would be the patriarch of the Byzantine Church, now called the Orthodox or Eastern Orthodox Church. The Orthodox Church is a group of self-governing regional churches, including Greek, Romanian, Bulgarian, and Russian. Various smaller churches, such as the Coptic Church in Egypt, have their own patriarchs.

THE WESTERN/ROMAN CHURCH Early on, the Roman Church started calling itself Catholic, that is, universal. Being in the western center of the Roman Empire gave the Bishop of Rome prestige and power. In the 400s the Roman Empire in Europe was disintegrating under the impact of invasions by Germanic tribes. As a result, the bishop of Rome became even more powerful, as he assumed some of the roles that kings and princes had had in the Empire. Through the Middle Ages, the Roman Catholic Church was a central institution in Europe, and church law, developed from Roman Law, provided social stability. The officials of the church served as local clerks of the empire. In fact, the term "clerk" comes from the same root as "clergy," the religious hierarchy.

In matters of doctrine, the western Roman churches and the eastern Byzantine churches agreed on most issues, but they emphasized different things. Starting with Augustine of

Hippo (now in Algeria; d. 430), Western churches emphasized the "fallenness" of the human race after Adam and Eve's disobedience – the idea that human beings are by nature prone to serious error (are "sinful") and cannot overcome this condition on their own. They need to be rescued ("saved"); they have to let God do for them what they cannot do for themselves. This rescue (or "salvation") was accomplished by Jesus' death on the cross. It is sacrificial and salvific (it saves them). As we shall see, this concern with sinfulness and guilt came to dominate medieval European Christianity and then Protestant thinkers such as Martin Luther and John Calvin.

Psychologists of religion often see Augustine's concern with sinfulness as linked to his negative views about sex. As a teenager, he was undisciplined and out of control. The woman he lived with had a baby when he was 14. During his twenties, in an effort to get control of himself, he began to follow the teachings of Mani (d. 276), a religious figure who taught that the human soul is good and made of light, while the body is bad and made of dark earth. Adding to Augustine's negative view of the human body was his reading of philosophers influenced by Plato who saw the soul as striving for good and the body pulling us toward evil. When Augustine became a Christian and then a bishop in his thirties, he felt guilty for his sinful early years and came to view sex itself as evil. It is through sexual intercourse, he said, that the Original Sin of Adam and Eve is passed on to each succeeding generation. According to Augustine, even within marriage, sex engaged in for pleasure is sinful; sex is only acceptable as fulfilling the task of continuing the human race. What is more, since women were the source of all his sexual temptations, Augustine thought of them as morally dangerous. So the morally superior choice for a Christian man would be to avoid sex, even in marriage; even better is to live a celibate life as a priest or monk.

Augustine's thinking influenced Christian theology in other ways, as well. One was his rationalism, his confidence in the ability of the human mind to figure things out. As a Christian, he saw the need for faith, of course, but reason can work with faith, he said. His motto was "Faith seeking understanding." Augustine's books combined references to the Bible with quotations from philosophers and his own philosophical reflections, in a way that showed confidence in the power of reason to clarify matters of faith and to establish truths of its own. In the Middle Ages Christian thinkers inherited this confidence in reason. Christians believe that God exists, for example, but theologians such as Anselm of Canterbury (d. 1109) and Thomas Aquinas (d. 1274) worked out arguments to prove the existence of God. With these arguments, they said, we can go beyond merely believing that God exists to knowing that he does. They also thought carefully about the nature of God, examining questions about God's knowledge, power, and goodness, and his relationship to the human race. Starting in the 11th century, the Catholic Church established universities in Western Europe, and in them Theology (the study of the existence and attributes of God) was called the "Queen of the Sciences."

Another major development in the Christian Middle Ages was devotion to saints – individuals recognized for their extraordinary goodness. In early centuries Christians remembered those who had stood out for their piety, such as martyrs who had died for their faith. Relics of saints, such as their bones, were treasured, and each altar had at least one relic built into it. Eventually, the church worked out an official list of saints and a procedure for adding new ones. One requirement was that miracles be attributed to the person, such

Popular Religion, Folk Religion, Lived Religion

Popular religious practices are sometimes known as **folk religion** – beliefs and practices of people that are not strictly part of their religion but are not in conflict with it either. Often passed down through local communities and so varying from region to region, folk beliefs and practices generally reflect practical concerns such as health and prosperity. For example, people may carry an image of a particular saint believed to be a specialist in safe travels, or recite a prayer to a personal angel to keep them safe during sleep.

Many scholars of religion view such beliefs and practices as part of **lived religion**. The study of lived religion de-emphasizes organized religion in favor of less formal expressions of people's spiritual concerns. One of the major proponents of the study of lived religion was Wilfred Cantwell Smith (d. 2000). He taught that religion should not be thought of as an abstract set of beliefs and practices but as the lived experience of individuals in their relationship to the transcendent.

Some scholars see the category "folk religion" as derogatory, as if such practices are somehow of a lesser order than "official" or orthodox religion. As well, some see it as a reflection of the inadequacy of the term "religion" in the first place. They argue that "religion" is a category based on a Christian paradigm that requires certain components and excludes others – some of which may well be as important to the people who practice them as, for example, sacraments are to Christians. We shall return to this discussion in Chapter 10.

as someone's being cured of a disease or infirmity after praying to the dead person to intercede with God for them. People prayed to specific saints for specific things, and even visited ("made pilgrimages to") places associated with their lives and therefore considered holy (their "shrines") to ask for favors. St. Cecilia, for example, had been a talented musician and so was prayed to by musicians. St. Joseph, the foster father of Jesus, was a carpenter and so became known as the "patron saint" of carpenters. It is in this context that we see aspects of what scholars call **popular religion** – religious practices that are not necessarily grounded in official doctrine but enjoy widespread popularity – develop in Christianity. In many countries today, for example, Joseph is also the patron of house hunting and selling. People who want to sell their home may bury a statue of Joseph in their yard. Similarly, St. Jude is considered the patron saint of "lost causes" and he requests that his favors be acknowledged publicly. So the "Personal" sections of newspapers often have notices that say, "Thanks to St. Jude for favors received." The calendar of the Catholic church still celebrates hundreds of saints' feast days.

The mother of Jesus, Mary, is also highly important in Christianity. The church authorities said that Jesus was God, and Mary was his mother, so the Council of Ephesus in

451 declared her to be the Mother of God. She is a figure of enormous popular devotion, particularly in Roman Catholicism and Orthodox Christianity.

THE EASTERN ORTHODOX CHURCHES   As the Roman Catholic Church was growing in Western Europe through the Middle Ages, the traditions now known as **Orthodox** developed in Greece, the Middle East, Africa, and Russia. In Greece, the Byzantine Church flourished from the 4th century to 1453, when the Ottoman Turks conquered Constantinople, changed its name to Istanbul, and made it the capital of their Islamic empire. Since Islamic law protected religious freedom, Christianity continued to thrive. In 988 the leaders of Russia adopted a Byzantine form of Christianity.

Though there were tensions between these Eastern churches and the pope in Rome over theological and political issues, they were all considered to be in the same tradition until 1054, when disagreements between the Patriarch of Constantinople and an emissary of the pope led them to excommunicate (declare someone to be no longer a member of the community) each other. From this **Great Schism** on, the Orthodox churches have considered themselves separate from the Roman Catholic Church. During the Crusades, Western Catholics captured and looted Constantinople, an outrage that has not been forgotten by Eastern Christians.

Whereas the Western Christians remained unified under the leadership of the pope in Rome until the Protestant Reformation, Eastern Christians did not have a central authority. They organized regionally, resulting in a strong connection between the religious leaders, the national political leader, and the national language. This bond is reflected in the names of the churches, such as the Greek Orthodox Church, the Russian Orthodox Church, the Serbian Orthodox Church, the Bulgarian Orthodox Church, and the Romanian Orthodox Church. There are also Oriental Orthodox Churches based in Egypt, Syria, Ethiopia, Eritrea, and India.

Besides this political difference, Eastern Orthodox Christians differ in other ways from Roman Catholics – and from Protestants. One is that their religious rituals are longer and more ornate. The priests wear richly ornamented vestments (garments), icons (painted pictures of Jesus, Mary, and the saints) are important, and incense is burned as an offering to God. Most of the rituals are sung rather than recited, and musical instruments are not used. On about half the days of the year, too, Orthodox Christians are required to fast (abstain from food and drink) to some degree.

In their theology, Eastern Orthodox Christians rely heavily on the writings of early Greek Fathers such as Gregory of Nyssa, St. Basil the Great, and St. John Chrysostom. These men lived long before Anselm of Canterbury (d. 1109) created the Atonement Theory of Jesus' crucifixion. That theory said that Jesus's death paid the debt owed by the human race for the Original Sin of Adam. By the time Anselm, and later Martin Luther and John Calvin, were teaching the Atonement Theory, Greek Orthodox Christians had split away from Western Christianity. So they never adopted the Atonement Theory. This makes their explanation of what Jesus did, and what Christian life is, different from what Catholics and Protestants believe.

In Orthodox theology, God created human beings in his image and wanted them to grow in likeness to him. The central goal of life is **theosis**, becoming like God and unified with

FIGURE 6.11 Greek Orthodox priests, Palm Sunday procession. © Hanan Isachar/SuperStock.

God. Jesus became the God–man in order to bring humanity and divinity together. As St. Athanasius of Alexandria said, Jesus "was made man that we might be made God." Therefore, in the Orthodox perspective, Jesus saved the human race not by paying a debt for sin, but by allowing people to join more fully with the life of God.

The Protestant Reformation

At the end of the Middle Ages there was another major split among Christians, the **Protestant Reformation**, when the German monk Martin Luther (d. 1546) challenged Roman Catholic authorities over what he considered corrupt practices and false doctrines. In 1517 he wrote a list of **Ninety-Five Theses** and circulated them among friends and bishops he thought would be sympathetic to reforming the church. According to legend, he also nailed his document to the door of the church in Wittenberg.

A major complaint of Luther's was about the church's selling **indulgences**, which are reductions in the time a dead person would have to suffer in **Purgatory** before entering heaven. According to a Christian teaching articulated at the First Council of Lyon in the 13th century, Purgatory is a state of suffering endured by the dead whose sins keep them from being fully reconciled with God. The effects of their sins are "purged" by a fire like that of hell. When people received an indulgence from the church, this would shorten their time in Purgatory after they died; a plenary (full) indulgence would eliminate their time in Purgatory altogether. The church taught that indulgences could be earned by saying certain prayers, by doing good works, and by contributing money to the support of good works. By Luther's day, abuses of the sale of indulgences had become widespread. Indulgence salesmen traveled the countryside, with little accountability for the funds they collected.

Luther also objected to several of the church's teachings. One was that both faith and good works are necessary for salvation. Luther taught that faith in Jesus' redemptive death alone (*sola fides*) is necessary for salvation. Following Augustine, he said that because people inherit the effects of Original Sin from Adam and Eve, they are unable to choose good actions without God's favor or "grace." And there is nothing we can do to earn God's grace. According to Luther, people do not even have free will. So when someone does something good, this is a result of God's grace, not of the person's choice. There is nothing people can do to earn salvation; it is totally a gift of God. All that is necessary for salvation is to have faith in Jesus.

Another church teaching that Luther rejected is that both the Bible and church traditions are authoritative. Here he had in mind the documents issued by popes and church councils. Luther said that the Bible alone (*sola scriptura*) is the foundation of Christian belief.

A few decades after Luther launched his reform movement in Germany, John Calvin (d. 1564), a French lawyer, started another movement in France and Switzerland. Even more than Luther, Calvin emphasized the devastating effects of Original Sin.

> Good men, and beyond all others Augustine, have labored to demonstrate that we derive an innate depravity from our very birth…. Even before we behold the light of life, we are in the sight of God defiled and polluted. (Calvin, 1964, book II, i, 6–7)

For Calvin, every newborn baby deserves unending punishment in hell for its depravity. Not only is there no free will and therefore nothing people can do to help themselves, but from all eternity God knew whom he would choose to save and who would be damned. This teaching is called **predestination**. Different groups influenced by Calvin came to be known as Calvinists, Reformed Christians, Presbyterians, and Puritans.

In England, too, there were major disagreements with the Roman Catholic Church, but they centered around church authority rather than doctrine. So through the Reformation period, the Church of England remained "catholic," and is still known as the Anglican Catholic Church (or A.C., for short).

In the 17th through 19th centuries, hundreds more Protestant groups arose – Baptists, Methodists, Quakers, Mennonites, Seventh-Day Adventists, etc. Each had its own pattern of beliefs and practices, but all had some disagreements with the Catholic Church. The major things challenged by the reformers were teachings about Purgatory, the authority of the pope, devotion to the saints, mandatory celibacy for priests, **monasticism** (the renunciation of worldly life and withdrawal to a "monastery" to live a life devoted to spiritual development), most of the sacraments (see below), and infant baptism.

Christian Rituals

Among the 34,000 sects of Christians, there is a wide variety of rituals. Quakers assemble in a simple room and sit quietly waiting for divine inspiration before they speak. Russian Orthodox liturgies involve elaborate vestments, icons, and incense, and they can last hours.

The Roman Catholic Church has seven special rituals called **sacraments**. The Catholic understanding of sacraments is that they are rituals established by Jesus that have spiritual effects on participants. The seven are Baptism (which is believed to neutralize some of the negative effects of Original Sin), Holy Communion (or Eucharist – re-enacting Jesus' last meal and his sacrificial and salvific death), Penance (or Confession or Reconciliation – telling a priest one's misdeeds and receiving forgiveness), Confirmation (marking the passage to adult moral responsibility), Matrimony, Holy Orders (ordination into the priesthood), and Anointing of the Sick (or Extreme Unction, which includes forgiveness of sins). Most Protestant denominations have only two sacraments: Baptism and Holy Communion, also called the Lord's Supper or the Eucharist.

Christianity Today

As we saw in Chapter 1, there are now 9,000 denominations that call themselves Christian, and they are subdivided into 34,000 sects. Some of these groups trace their lineage to Jesus and the Apostles, but thousands more, such as the Church of Jesus Christ of Latter-day Saints (Mormons), were started in the 19th and 20th centuries. The process of churches splitting that launched the Protestant Reformation is still common today. As we write this, some members of the Episcopal Church are planning to split off from that church because of the consecration of V. Gene Robinson, the first openly gay Episcopal bishop.

In the 20th century, many Christian churches went in the opposite direction from splitting, in what is known as the "ecumenical movement." They emphasized what Christian groups had in common rather than their differences. They held conferences and conducted services together. Some groups even fused. The best known ecumenical group is the World Council of Churches, which has members from 349 Christian groups in 120 countries. In 1999, the Lutheran World Federation Council and the Roman Catholic Church put to rest one of the biggest disagreements between Protestants and Catholics over the last five centuries – the nature of justification (the process of God's making people righteous before him). Wrapping up discussions between Lutherans and Roman Catholics that started in the early 1970s, the two groups signed a joint declaration on the nature of justification. The Methodist Church added its signature to this declaration in 2006.

The number of Christians worldwide is about 2.1 billion, making Christianity the largest religion. In different parts of the world, the power and influence of Christian churches varies considerably. In Britain and Western Europe, people's identification with churches and attendance at rituals have dropped considerably in the last century. In the U.S., evangelical Protestant churches have grown in numbers and strength each year, as traditional Protestant churches such as the Lutherans and Methodists have lost members. The largest increase in church membership is taking place in the developing world – especially in Africa – where 23,000 people a day join a Christian church.

The largest Christian denomination is Catholicism, with 1.1 billion members – half of all Christians and one-sixth of the world's population. Although usually identified with the "Latin Rite" – the rituals familiar to European and American Catholics – the Catholic Church includes 22 Eastern rites too, such as the Coptic Catholic rite that originated in Egypt.

Unit III Islam

The History and Teachings of Islam

Core Teachings

The history of Islam is, in the Islamic perspective, the history of monotheism. This is a core assumption in Islamic scripture, the Qur'an ("Koran" in archaic spelling). The Qur'an refers to the stories of Adam and Eve, Noah and the flood, Abraham and the covenant, Moses and the Torah, Jesus and the Gospels, and many other prophets and figures from the Hebrew Bible and the Christian New Testament, but it does not tell the stories in detail or even in chronological order. Instead, the Qur'an says that it is reminding people of these stories. These stories comprise the background to the messages conveyed in the Qur'an. They are part of the history of the community of those who believe in the one and only God. The term for "god" in Arabic, which is the language of the Qur'an, is *ilah*. The Qur'an refers to God as "*the* god," *al-ilah* or **Allah**, saying repeatedly that "there is no god but God." God created human beings and immediately began communicating with them about how to live successfully and fulfill the purpose for which they were created. All human beings are called upon to submit to the will of God by establishing justice. In doing so, they will be following the **din**, the term used by the Qur'an to summarize the core of the monotheistic tradition.

We have seen that the Hebrew Bible uses the same term. This is not surprising, since Hebrew and Arabic are closely related Semitic languages. What is perhaps surprising, though, is that neither the Hebrew Bible nor the Qur'an uses a term that translates easily into the English term "religion." As we saw in Chapter 1, *din* in both Hebrew and Arabic means "judgment" – in particular, divine judgment.

Human beings will all be judged on the Last Day, the *yom al-din*, "the day of judgment." And all people are called upon to make their own decisions in light of that reality. So *din* is

FIGURE 6.12 Indian Muslims praying. Fredrik Renander/Alamy.

like justice; it is both the goal or purpose of human existence, and the means of achieving it. People are called upon to live in accordance with the "true *din*," the *din* of Abraham and of all prophets. They all lived their lives and made their decisions based upon – in Islamic terminology, "in submission to" – the will of God. The term for "submission [to the will of God]" in Arabic is *islam*. Therefore, the Qur'an says that *islam* is the true *din*. When translated into English, this becomes "Islam is the true religion." (Qur'an 3:19) However, it is important to understand that, from the perspective of the Qur'an, this does not mean that other religions are false. Rather, it conveys the idea that Islam is the culmination of the monotheistic (or Abrahamic) tradition. The message brought in the 7th century CE by Muhammad, the prophet of Islam, confirmed the messages of earlier messengers, corrected some misinterpretations of those earlier messages, and completed or finalized the transmission of messages from God to humanity.

Muslims refer to their prophet as Prophet Muhammad and, in order to show respect, add the blessing "Peace be upon him" (PBUH or, more correctly, "The peace and blessings of God be upon him," in Arabic abbreviated as SAW). However, Muhammad is actually considered the last of the prophets of Islam, not the first. Muslims consider Adam to be the first prophet of true Din. The Qur'an mentions Adam 25 times, referring to human beings as the "children of Adam." Adam is considered a prophet because through him God delivered a message to humanity. Human beings are the creatures of God, created to be stewards, his delegates on the earth. The term used for steward is khalifah. (In English this becomes "caliph." This term is later politicized, as imperial rulers take upon themselves the

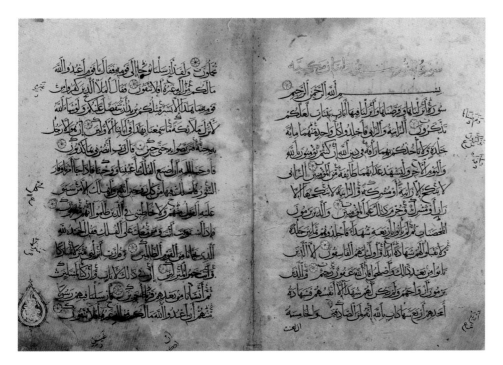

FIGURE 6.13 A page from a 14th-century Qur'an. Christie's Images Ltd./SuperStock.

responsibility to be divine stewards or viceroys, to be obeyed by everyone else. As a result, the term *khalifah* often is translated as "successor" to Prophet Muhammad, since the caliphs took over leadership of the community after Muhammad died, but this translation is misleading when applied to the Qur'anic use of the term *khalifah*.) Thus, Creation is the beginning point of the history traced in the Qur'an.

The Qur'an, the ultimate authority on all issues in Islam, is believed to be the accurate record of the precise words revealed by God to humanity through Prophet Muhammad. It was memorized and parts of it were written down during the lifetime of Prophet Muhammad (570–632 CE), and it was recorded and canonized (put into official form) within twenty years of Muhammad's death. Muslims are therefore fully confident that it is free of error (inerrant) in its Arabic form – and it is considered to be truly the Qur'an only in Arabic. Prophet Muhammad said and did many things that were not considered to be revelation and are therefore not recorded in the Qur'an. However, they are nonetheless considered important, often complementary to the Qur'an. Reports of these words and deeds are called **hadiths**. The hadith reports circulated among the Muslim community in oral form for two to three centuries but were then recorded, scrutinized for authenticity, and codified. There are several official collections of hadiths, three of which are considered to be quite reliable (two for **Sunni** Muslims and one for **Shi'i** Muslims [see below]). Taken together, the hadith reports comprise the example set by Muhammad to guide Muslims in their efforts to implement the message of the Qur'an. This example is called the **Sunna**. The Qur'an and the Sunna are the foundational sources for Islam.

Muslims believe that the Qur'an's message is meant for all humankind, but it was addressed specifically to the community in the environs of Mecca and Medina in Arabia (now Saudi Arabia) in which it was delivered. That community was organized into tribes – some of which were settled in oasis towns, and some of which were nomadic – and included Jewish tribes, Christian tribes, and tribes devoted to specific lesser gods (gods that were recognized as patrons to their tribes but who were not universal; they were one among many). The people of Mecca and Medina were also familiar with other traditions, such as that of the Sabeans of southern Arabia (now Yemen), known also as Sheba, whose queen is associated with the story of Solomon in both the Hebrew Bible and the Qur'an. The Qur'an addresses itself to people who represent all these traditions, acknowledging they have received true revelation, but challenging some of their interpretations as well as their failure to live in accordance with the guidance they have been given.

This multi-religious region provides the context for the Qur'an's unique orientation toward other religious communities. Instead of condemning them, it addresses what it considers their misinterpretations of the revelation they have received from earlier prophets, and offers correctives. The Jews, it says, mistakenly assumed that the Torah was meant for them alone. The Qur'an rejects the notion of a "chosen people" and affirms that the messages received through Abraham, Moses, and the other prophets are meant for all humanity (5:18–19). Muslims also believe that the son involved in the story of Abraham's sacrifice was Ismail (Ishmael), rather than Isaac, but this is not considered a major issue. Both Jews and Christians are criticized for rejecting each other as true believers, even though they both claim to believe in the same God (2:113). The Qur'an also rejects the Christian belief that God procreated and that Jesus was the result. Instead, the Qur'an teaches that Jesus was a great prophet and the Messiah (although it does not specify what that term means), and his mother Mary was miraculously a virgin even in childbirth, but Jesus was human, like all other prophets (5:17). Nor did the Jews crucify Jesus, the Qur'an says, even though it appeared as if he had been crucified (4:157). Likewise, the Qur'an rejects the idea of the Trinity, stressing the importance of recognizing that there is only one god (4:171; 5:73).

The purpose of all these correctives is to guide people in true belief on the assumption that believing the truth and living virtuously are integrally related. In the Qur'anic perspective, the virtuous actions required for reward in the afterlife result from true belief. The Qur'an characteristically mentions good deeds and true belief in tandem. However, at the same time, the Qur'an does not call for a single religious community. The Qur'an says that all people have been given specific laws and rituals (5:48); this is considered part of the divine plan. God created people in different communities so that they could learn from one another. The Qur'an says there can be no compulsion in matters of the Din (2:256). Rather, peoples of various communities should come together in agreement (3:64), and compete with one another in good works (5:48).

Good works are, therefore, the focus of the Qur'an's teachings. The clearest indicator that communities have failed to implement the teachings of the earlier prophets is the social dysfunction that Muhammad sees all around him: rampant poverty, wealth controlled by a privileged and greedy few, widows and orphans exploited, women treated as property and disrespected to the extent that girls were often killed at birth because they were considered an economic burden. So the Qur'an continually reminds people of the teachings of the Torah and the Gospels, and places the measure of piety in the treatment of others:

> Goodness does not consist in turning your faces towards the East or West [in prayer]. The truly good are those who believe in God and the Last Day, in the angels, Scripture, and the prophets; who give away some of their wealth, however much they cherish it, to their relatives, to orphans, the needy, travelers and beggars, and to liberate those in bondage; those who keep up the prayer and give charity; who keep promises when they make them; who are steadfast in misfortune, adversity, and times of danger. These are the ones who are true, and it is they who are aware of God. (2:177)

However, the core of Islamic teaching is monotheism. The Arabic term **tawhid** means that there is only one God, and that God is unitary, rather than a Trinity. This emphasis on monotheism is found in what is called the first "pillar" of Islam, the **Shahada**. The Shahada is literally a "bearing witness." It is conveyed in the vow, "I bear witness that there is no god but God and Muhammad is the Messenger of God."

The significance of the Shahada goes beyond mere belief or creed. It entails committing oneself to demonstrating one's belief in actions, actions that are intended to carry out (or "submit to") the will of God. The importance of the second half of the Shahada, "...Muhammad is the Messenger of God," is that Muhammad brought the Qur'an, which guides believers in their efforts to carry out the divine will. So the Shahada commits a person to working to establish the kind of community envisioned by the Qur'an.

As we saw, the Qur'an focuses on belief that is demonstrated in actions. In the Qur'an's worldview, the divine origin of all creatures is to be reflected in the way people treat one another. There is only one God, and that God created all human beings. All people are equal in the sight of God, and the human challenge is to create a society that reflects the equality all people share in the eyes of their Creator. This is the reason human beings were created – as we saw, to be "stewards" of God's creation. And this is the basis upon which human beings will be judged.

Two terms are important here: intention and effort. The Qur'an promises reward for those who submit to the divine will, and punishment for those who reject it. However, the Qur'an also stresses that this challenge is not meant to be a burden for human beings. The Qur'an presents God as ultimately compassionate and merciful, always providing guidance and assistance for those who seek it. No individual is expected to single-handedly end poverty and oppression. However, every person must make the intention (*niyyah*) and the effort (*jihad*).

Muslims believe there are two levels of divine judgment, one in history and one at the end of time. Divine judgment in history is reflected in the belief that a just society will be strong and healthy, while an unjust or oppressive society will eventually be destroyed. The Qur'an provides numerous familiar examples, such as Sodom and Gomorrah, the communities warned by Lot to end their evil ways. When they did not, they were destroyed. Individuals will also be judged on the Last Day. At that time, each will stand alone, with conscience laid bare and no one to intercede. Punishment or reward will be earned on the basis of one's intention and effort to contribute to a society that reflects the will of the one God.

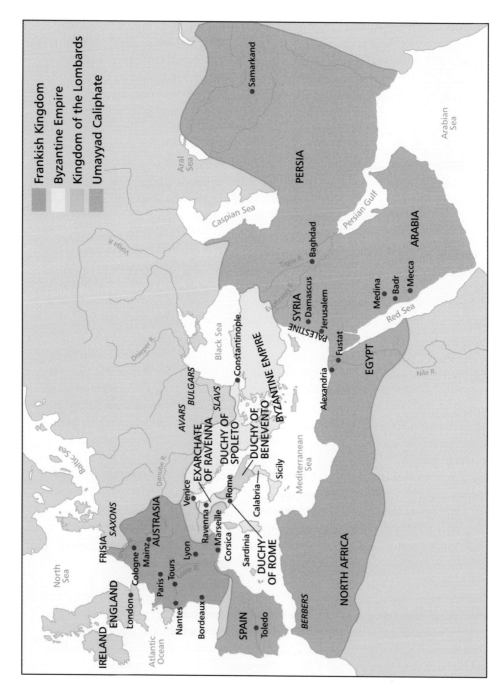

MAP 6.3 Spread of Islam in the 1st century.

Jihad
The Most Misunderstood Term

The term **jihad** comes from a verb that means "to exert strenuous effort." The Qur'an repeatedly tells people to "struggle in the way of God," and the way of God is described as "doing good and preventing evil." The Qur'an gives countless examples of how to struggle to do good and prevent evil. These include being truthful and sincere, generous, responsible, and hard-working. In certain circumstances, the struggle may be military. If a community is under attack, military jihad may be called for. The community in question need not be one's own; most Muslim authorities believe that military jihad is not exclusively for self-defense. Defense of another community may require it. However, Islamic law strictly controls military jihad. It may only be called by a duly constituted government, it may only be waged with due warning and after efforts to settle the conflict peacefully, non-combatants must be protected, buildings and natural resources must not be attacked, and if the enemy requests peace it must be declared.

For these reasons, terrorists attacks such as 9/11 have been condemned by virtually every Muslim religious authority, publicly and repeatedly. These condemnations of terror are readily available on the internet, and have been compiled by scholar Charles Kurzman at http://www.unc.edu/~kurzman/terror.htm.

Many Muslims believe there is an interim period, between death and the Last Day, when people undergo a kind of torture or "punishment of the grave" if they have committed grievous offenses. This is based not on the Qur'an, however, but on traditional literature (hadith). There is also widespread speculation about the nature of rewards and punishments. The Qur'an describes the afterlife in graphic detail – hideous torments in hell and luxurious physical comforts in heaven. This includes "pure companions," houris. The topic of wild speculation in traditional literature, the houris have entered the folk imagination as 72 voluptuous virgins for deceased martyrs. Scholars stress the metaphorical nature of language about the "pure companions." Some trace it to the ancient Zoroastrian notion of a pure conscience appearing in angelic form. (See Chapter 9.)

Islam's moral teachings revolve around the Qur'an's commitment to justice. This commitment is comprehensive, beginning within the family and extending to society at large. The family is the core social unit, so the Qur'an teaches that families must be based on loving concern between spouses. Sex is restricted to married couples, in order to protect the family unit. Modesty is required of females and males, and extra-marital sex is severely punished. (False allegations of extra-marital sex are also severely punished; according to Islamic law, four adult male Muslim witnesses must be produced in order to prove an allegation of adultery. Otherwise, the person who makes the allegation is punished.)

Marriage is a solemn commitment in Islam. Among the many reforms instituted by the Qur'an was a prohibition of buying and selling wives; the "bride price" or dowry is required to be given to the bride herself, rather than to her family. The unlimited polygyny (multiple wives) of pre-Islamic times is limited. The Qur'an advises that marrying one woman is best, but allows men to marry up to four, if that is necessary in order to protect orphans and provided the wives are treated equitably. Divorce is discouraged, and the Qur'an recommends reconciliation efforts in troubled marriages. However, if reconciliation efforts fail, then divorce is permitted and men are advised to provide what support they can for the divorced wife. Men are responsible for the support of their offspring. Women are required to wait to make sure they are not pregnant before remarrying, again, for the sake of protecting offspring. Children and spouses – including females – are guaranteed inheritance shares.

As noted above, Islamic values are worked out in greatest detail in Islamic law, **Sharia**. Sharia is like Judaic law, in that it attempts to guide every aspect of life through the ages. As such, it includes the requirements and prohibitions found in the Qur'an, but it also includes human efforts to interpret Qur'anic values for circumstances not specifically covered in the Qur'an. While Shariah in general is considered sacred, divinely inspired law and therefore perfect and unchanging, the human interpretations of Sharia are subject to ongoing discussion and revision. This discussion is carried on by highly trained scholars, who are guided by the **maqasid** or goals of Sharia. There is a great deal of disagreement among scholars about many of the details of human interpretations of Sharia. However, all agree that the goals of Sharia are the preservation and protection of life, religion, family, property, and reason (or human dignity). These *maqasid* guide interpretations of specific manifestations of Islamic moral teaching in diverse contexts.

Early History: The Life of Muhammad and the Rashidun Caliphs

Prophet Muhammad was an orphan by age six. He was taken in by relatives and became a skilled and successful trader. At around age 40 he felt the religious call and began to preach to the people of Mecca. His message immediately resonated with the impoverished masses and even with a few of the wealthy people. However, most of the wealthy people felt threatened by his call for social justice. They therefore boycotted and persecuted the Prophet and his followers. However, the popularity of the message continued to spread.

In 622 CE Muhammad was inspired to accept an invitation to move to Medina, a city some 200 miles north of Mecca. This emigration (**hijra**) became the turning point in the young community's life, so much so that it marks the beginning of the Islamic calendar. It marks the transition from preaching the importance of submitting to the will of God (*islam*) to actually establishing institutions designed to promote and protect social justice. The Prophet immediately established a constitution whereby all the clans and tribes of Medina and the newcomers would form a single community. Each would retain authority to deal with internal matters, but all would join in mutual defense if the town were attacked. Significantly, the constitution identified Muslim, Jewish, and polytheistic clans as signatories to the agreement, and guaranteed religious freedom for all. Any disputes between groups would be referred to Muhammad who, with divine guidance, would settle them.

Muslims and Jews

Some of the people who collaborated with the Meccans against Muhammad's community in Medina were members of Jewish tribes. As a result of the collaboration, these tribes were evicted from Medina. In one case, the men of the tribe were executed and the women and children were made slaves. Despite the fact that other Jewish tribes continued to live in peace among Muslims, some people have interpreted these early battles as evidence of anti-Semitism in Islam.

Muslims reject this claim, demonstrating that throughout history Islamic law has guaranteed religious freedom and Jews have lived in Muslim lands in peace and security. Yet current political conflicts in the Middle East have indeed led some Muslims to express anti-Jewish views. The best known is Iranian President Mahmoud Ahmadinejad, who has publicly denied the Holocaust. Many Muslim leaders therefore struggle to reaffirm Islam's commitment to religious pluralism. Eboo Patel, Muslim community leader and founder of the Interfaith Youth Core in Chicago, says that anti-Jewish statements "blacken the heart of anyone who says or thinks or feels them, and I want my religious community to have nothing to do with those sick attitudes." Shaykh Hamza Yusuf, one of the most prominent young American Muslim leaders, believes that Holocaust denial undermines Islam. Patel reports that the voices of people such as Shaykh Hamza "are having an increasing influence within the American Muslim community for a very simple reason – they reflect the attitude of the majority of American Muslims, who have felt both sickened and silenced by the minority of Muslims who speak of anti-Semitism as if it were a core tenet of Islam." (http://newsweek.washingtonpost.com/onfaith/eboo_patel/2007/09/on_muslim_antisemitism.html)

The **Constitution of Medina** proved to be effective in resolving the disputes that had plagued the city for some time. It also became an attractive model to other communities in the region, and a number of local tribes established agreements with the Prophet. The Medinan community prospered, but the Meccans continued their hostilities. There were instances of collaboration between the Meccans and members of three Medinan tribes, and a number of battles. However, by 628 the two cities established a truce, and in 630, the ruling tribe of Mecca relinquished its claim and accepted the leadership of Muhammad. Muhammad entered the city, rededicated the ancient sanctuary at its center, the **Kaaba**, to Allah, and from then on Mecca was the religious center of the Muslim world.

Medina continued to be the political capital briefly, but disputes over leadership after Prophet Muhammad died in 632 led to political changes. Muslims consider Muhammad the final prophet, but some members of the community believed leadership of the community should remain in the Prophet's family. Muhammad died leaving no sons; the closest male relative was his cousin and son-in-law, Ali. The majority of Muslims favored

Muhammad's elder companions Abu Bakr, Umar, and then Uthman. Each of them governed the community in turn, but not without conflict. Abu Bakr had to contend with tribes that refused to pay their taxes once Muhammad died. Umar was highly respected and effective, and led the expansion of Islamic sovereignty into areas previously controlled by the Roman and Persian empires. However, he was attacked and killed by a slave. Uthman continued the expansion of Islamic sovereignty, but he was criticized for excessive control over the provinces, and assassinated by disgruntled Egyptians in 656. The community then chose Ali to be their leader, as his supporters (*shi'ah*) believed he should rightfully have been all along. However, Ali, too, was killed in a battle with the governor of Syria, in 661, who declared himself successor to the Prophet.

The Dynastic Caliphates

The death of Ali marks the end of period when the Muslim community was led by "rightly guided" successors to Prophet Muhammad (**Rashidun**). The Syrian governor's family, the **Umayyads**, then established Damascus as the political capital of the Muslim world and maintained leadership of the Muslim community, dynastic-style, for nearly 90 years. The Umayyads were highly successful in expanding their sovereignty, all the way to Spain in the West and Central Asia, and northwest India in the East. However, by this time, the rulers were no longer considered or even expected to be pious. In fact, they alienated enough of their subjects that they were overthrown in a revolution in 750, which brought in another dynastic caliphate, the **Abbasids**.

The Abbasids built Baghdad as their capital and maintained at least nominal sovereignty until 1258. However, Spain remained autonomous, and many other provinces were virtually independent of the capital. Nevertheless, the dynastic caliphates amassed enormous wealth and maintained relative stability over vast expanses of territory. This wealth and stability allowed the flowering of a magnificent culture that brought together the greatest scholars and artists from across the globe. Building upon the heritage of classical Greek, Roman, African, Persian, Indian, and Chinese cultures, they developed the highest levels of mathematical and scientific knowledge the world had known, and a material culture that was the envy of their contemporaries. Even Charlemagne, crowned Holy Roman Emperor by Pope Leo III in 800, corresponded with the Abbasid caliph Harun al-Rashid (d. 809) in Baghdad, requesting an alliance. Harun rejected the idea but did maintain friendly relations with the European ruler. He sent him magnificent gifts – including carved ivory, a pitcher and tray made of gold, perfumes, beautiful fabric, a robe embroidered with "There is no god but God" in Arabic, and an ornate water clock with twelve carved figures that came out of little windows and brass balls that fell on cymbals to mark the hours. Some of these gifts are on display in European museums. Perhaps the most stunning gift – the elephant that Charlemagne requested – is not; it died after several cold winters in Charlemagne's Germanic capital.

However, Harun's and Charlemagne's successors would eventually become mortal enemies. By the end of the 11th century, Europe was feeling threatened by the expansive Muslim regime. Pope Urban II called for a volunteer army to take the "Holy Land" of Jerusalem back from the Muslims, who were declared infidels. This was the beginning of the

Culture in Islamic Spain

"Commanded by the [Qur'an] to seek knowledge and read nature for signs of the Creator, and inspired by a treasure trove of ancient Greek learning, Muslims created a society that in the Middle Ages was the scientific center of the world. The Arabic language was synonymous with learning and science for 500 years, a golden age that can count among its credits the precursors to modern universities, algebra, the names of the stars and even the notion of science as an empirical inquiry." This is how *New York Times* Science Editor Dennis Overbye characterized the culture of Islam in the Middle Ages. Among its hallmarks were the introduction of Plato and Aristotle to Europe, along with the newly developed algebra (from the Arabic *al-jabr*) and trigonometric algorithms (from the Arabic al-Khwaridhmi, the man who developed it), technical development such as telescopes and microscopes, and new agricultural products such as oranges (from the Arabic *naranj*), lemons (from the Arabic *laimon*), artichokes (from the Arabic *ardi shoki*), cotton (from the Arabic, *qutun*), and sugar cane (from the Arabic *sukkar*). Muslim scientists were cited by Copernicus, and the great historian Ibn Khaldun (d. 1406) continues to be quoted on such issues as tribal solidarity and the relationship between tax cuts and inflation. Historian Arnold Toynbee called Ibn Khaldun's *Muqaddimah* ("Introduction") "the greatest work of its kind that has ever yet been created by any mind."

Crusades, a series of battles over the next two centuries that would pit Christian Europe against the Muslim Middle East. Ultimately unsuccessful in their original goal, the Crusades did have serious impact in the region. They exacerbated tensions among regional rulers, some of whom allied with the Europeans, and weakened the already over-extended Abbasid regime. The Crusades overlapped with the onslaught from the East of the Mongols, headed by the successors of the fearsome Genghis Khan. The Mongols captured and destroyed Baghdad in 1258, effectively ending the Abbasid caliphate.

The destruction of Baghdad marked the end of any semblance of political unity in the Muslim world. However, the momentum of the culture that had developed under the Umayyads and Abbasids was sufficient to survive a massive reordering of the Islamic world. Within a few centuries, the Ottoman Empire was established and ruled North Africa and the Arab Middle East from its base in Turkey. The Saffavid dynasty ruled over Persian lands with their capital in modern Iran. And the Mughal Empire ruled the Indian subcontinent. All three regimes were highly effective during Europe's Middle Ages and the "Age of Religious Wars" that accompanied the Protestant Reformation. However, by the time European Christians settled their religious differences (if not their differences with Jews), the Muslim empires were seriously weakened. The newly organized European states capitalized on their earlier explorations into Africa, the Middle East, and South Asia, and effectively took control of most of the Muslim world by the end of the 19th century.

Taqwa, Spirituality, and Sufism

Muslims believe that sincere belief will be manifested outwardly in righteous actions. However, the core of those actions is still internal. Pious actions result from giving oneself to the divine will, and in so doing committing oneself to do what one can to achieve the divine will. This combination of acceptance and commitment is expressed in the Qur'an as the virtue *taqwa*. The Qur'an never defines the term, in the sense of limiting it to some specific action or actions. Instead, it gives examples of the kind of behavior that stems from a well formed conscience. For example, the Qur'an tells people not to allow other people's unjust actions to lead them to unfair behavior. "So long as [the polytheists] stay true to you, stay true to them. Indeed, God loves those with taqwa." (9:7) *Taqwa* may be described as the willing choice to allow one's conscience to be guided by God, expressed externally through goodness and charity.

Scholars and lawyers can help guide understanding and actions. However, making God's will your own requires spiritual practice. This inward, spiritual aspect of Islamic practice, Sufism, is often called "interior Islam." It can also be described as mature Islam. Whereas a child is motivated to do good and avoid evil based on the promise of reward and the threat of punishment, a mature believer takes personal gratification in virtuous deeds and finds evil deeds personally repugnant. Sufi teachings and practice grew in Islam as a way to help people develop this ability to take joy in virtue.

FIGURE 6.14 Mevlevis, known as Whirling Dervishes for their spinning spiritual dance, are followers of Rumi. © Atlantide Phototravel/Corbis.

Over the centuries Muslims have developed many ways to cultivate spirituality. Religious poetry remains among the most popular, and the 13th century Afghan Sufi Jalal al-Din Rumi is perhaps the most popular poet of all time. Translations of his works by Coleman Barks are best sellers in America today. His poetry expresses the yearning for spiritual freedom that characterizes much of Sufism. It is a desire to be released from the bonds of selfishness, desire, and greed, to be completely absorbed in divine goodness and beauty. The key to spiritual awareness, he says, will not be found in books:

Let the beauty we love be what we do.
There are hundreds of ways to kneel and kiss the ground.

Barks and Barks 1984

The Modern Period: Reform and Recovery

By the time European powers had established control over most Muslim lands, Muslim intellectuals were well aware that the time was ripe for reform. This became clear to some thinkers as early as the Crusades. Legal authority Ibn Taymiyya of Damascus (d. 1328) warned of the need for vigilance and intellectual rigor. The great historian Ibn Khaldun of Islamic Spain (d. 1406) cautioned of the dangers of governments overly concerned with their own power and called for recommitment to justice as the basis of social solidarity and political strength. In the 16th and 17th centuries, reformers such as Ahmad Sirhindi (d. 1624) struggled to refocus the energies of the Indian Muslim community, and in Arabia Muhammad ibn Abd al-Wahhab called for renewed commitment to Islam's core values. However, the warnings of these reformers had been insufficient to motivate the broad reforms that would have been necessary to stop the onslaught of the modernized Europeans.

The 19th century therefore saw both the consolidation of European colonial power and the exponential growth of reform efforts in the Muslim world. Only now the reformers had to struggle on multiple fronts. Added to the issues the medieval reformers had to contend with were the colonial regimes: Britain (Egypt, India), France (Algeria, Tunisia, Syria), later Holland (Southeast Asia), and in the case of Libya, even Italy. What issues to tackle first? Should they try to reform society and then get rid of foreign control, or vice versa? And when they struggle against the foreigners, should they take them all on at once, or work with France against Britain, or Britain against France?

As it happened, the Muslim countries gained independence only in the past half century, and then only one country at a time. France was defeated in a brutal war of independence in Algeria, for example, in 1962. Libya's Italian overlords were defeated in World War II but the country was then placed under international control until 1951. Egypt evicted the British in a military coup in 1952. Syria – which traditionally included the current countries of Syria, Lebanon, Israel, Jordan, and the Palestinian Territories – gained independence piecemeal, as European powers competed over it; this is how it was divided up into several countries, in fact. And that situation was made more complex by the influx of European Jews attempting to escape European persecution. The eventual declaration of the state of Israel in 1948 then displaced hundreds of thousands of non-Jewish (both Muslim and Christian) Palestinians; their numbers have increased so that today the number of stateless Palestinians is estimated at over 6 million. India gained independence from Britain in 1947 but Britain partitioned the country into Hindu-majority and Muslim-majority countries, leaving the status of Kashmir (which was Hindu ruled but with a Muslim majority) unresolved, as it remains today. Indonesia – the most populous Muslim country in the world today – gained independence from the Dutch in 1949, and the state of Malaysia came into being in 1963, after more than a century as a set of disparate British colonies.

In most Muslim countries, independence was achieved through armed struggle, leaving the military dominant, as in many other parts of the formerly colonized world. The rise of military and other forms of non-popular governments in the context of anti-colonial struggles adds yet another layer of complexity to the challenges of modern Islam.

The combination of economic and political challenges facing Muslim societies has given rise to a variety of specifically modern movements. Early 20th-century reformers tended to be secularist, seeking independence and development based on models adopted from Western Europe. The ostensible failure of these models to produce results led to the brief popularity of socialist models in the mid-20th century. At the grassroots level, the most popular approach to reform has been through politicized Islam, known as Islamism, and rejection of secularist models. Continued frustration of people's hopes for economic and political development led, in the late 20th century, to militant radicalization in some sectors. The groups that engaged in terrorist activities in the name of Islam have added yet another set of challenges to those already facing the formerly colonized Muslim world: the need to overcome terrorism as well as the widespread misperception of Islam as a violent religion.

Islamic Rituals

Islamic rituals are relatively simple, compared with those in the other monotheistic traditions. They are usually summarized as the five Pillars of Islam. The first pillar, as mentioned above, is the Shahada. While it is far more than a ritual, requiring commitment to sustained effort to live in accordance with Islamic values in daily life, it does have certain ritual expressions. It is part of the call to prayer (*adhan*; see below), which is whispered into the right ear of a newborn baby, and, ideally, it is the last thing said by a dying person. It is formally declared before witnesses by those converting to Islam.

The second pillar is prayer, Salat. Muslims pray five times daily, at times marked by the position of the sun: just before dawn, noon, late afternoon, just after sunset, and then before retiring. Prayers can be performed anywhere, but many people prefer to pray in a mosque when that is possible. There is no Sabbath in Islam, but Muslims are supposed to gather for the noon prayer on Friday in a mosque. Prayers are preceded by expressing the intention to pray mindfully – by reciting the Bismallah: "In the name of God the most merciful and compassionate." Then Muslims perform a ritual purification by washing (*wudu*) the hands; rinsing the mouth, nose, and head, feet, teeth, and limbs with water. If no water is available, the wudu can be performed symbolically. In cases of "greater impurity" (if the person has had sex, sexual discharge, menstrual period, or has given birth), full ablution (*ghusl*) is required – a complete cleansing including the hair. Prayers are performed in the direction of the Kaaba in Mecca. Because Muslims are supposed to pray in a clean environment, it is common for them to pray on a small "prayer rug" (*sajada*). If none is available, any other material, even cardboard, is acceptable. Prayers consist of recitation of specific passages from the Qur'an, repeated in a specified order, and accompanied by specified postures, including bowing, kneeling, and prostrating (touching the forehead to the floor from a kneeling position). The term "mosque" comes from the Arabic *masjid*, meaning "place of prostration."

The third pillar of Islam is charity, Zakat. Although not technically a ritual, the giving of charity has been regularized to an annual donation of 2.5% of the wealth people have held for a year, not counting the person's house. Many Muslims commonly give more charity than Zakat requires, endowing institutions that serve the community, such as schools and hospitals.

The fourth pillar is fasting (Sawm) from food, drink, smoking, and sexual activity sunrise to sunset during the ninth month of Islam's lunar calendar, Ramadan. Families commonly break the fast together after sunset during Ramadan. Breaking the fast on the last day of Ramadan is the beginning of a happy three-day communal celebration (*Eid al-Fitr*), when families exchange visits and gifts.

The fifth pillar of Islam is the pilgrimage to the Kaaba in Mecca, the Hajj. The Hajj is performed every year during the first half of the Month of Hajj (the last month of Islam's lunar calendar), but Muslims are only required to make the Hajj pilgrimage once in their lifetimes, and then only if they are physically and financially able. However, many Muslims try to make the Hajj as often as possible, finding it an enormously fulfilling spiritual exercise. Muslims may make the pilgrimage to Mecca at any other time of the year, as well, but it does not fulfill the Hajj obligation. On the tenth day of the Month of Hajj, Muslims celebrate the most solemn holiday in their calendar, the Eid al-Adha, commemorating Abraham's willingness to sacrifice his son to fulfill the will of God.

Like Jews, Muslims practice certain dietary restrictions. They are prohibited from eating pork, and may eat only meat that has been properly slaughtered and dedicated to God. (This is called halal – "permitted" – meat; kosher meat is also halal.) As we saw in Chapter 4, Mary Douglas interprets the negative attitude toward pork among Jews and Muslims, as well as shellfish among some Jews and Muslims, as a result of their "crossed categories." Neither pigs nor shellfish are accounted for in the monotheistic creation story so there must be something really wrong with them; they are "impure." Unlike Jews and Christians, Muslims are also supposed to refrain from consuming alcoholic beverages. This prohibition is not a function of purity regulations, however. Its purpose is to preserve people's clear reasoning and prevent the bad behavior that can accompany drunkenness. And like Judaism, Islam calls for circumcision of males, although this is not in the Qur'an. While for Jews circumcision is considered a symbol of belonging to the community, for Muslims it is considered a function of purity. (Some communities, particularly in sub-Saharan Africa,

FIGURE 6.15 Pilgrims walking around the Kaaba in Mecca during the Hajj.
ayazad/Shutterstock Images.

practice female circumcision as well – "female genital mutilation" or FGM – but this is not required by Islam, nor is it practiced only by Muslims.)

The tenth day (**Ashura**) of Muharram, the first month of the Islamic calendar, is traditionally a day of fasting – similar to the Jewish Yom Kippur (observed on the tenth day of the new year). For Shi'i Muslims, Ashura is a day of mourning, commemorating the martyrdom of Imam Hussein, the son of Imam Ali. It is marked by processions of mourners and plays reenacting the suffering of Imam Hussein.

Major Divisions Today

Muslims comprise over one-fifth of the world's population, over 1.5 billion people. Fewer than one-quarter of them are Arabs; the largest Muslim populations are in Indonesia, Pakistan, Bangladesh, and India. Muslims are the second largest religious minority in Europe, and the third largest in the United States.

The vast majority of Muslims – nearly 85% – are Sunni. The second largest branch of Islam are the Shi'a (or Shi'ite) Muslims. Shi'a Muslims trace their roots to the early community who supported Prophet Muhammad's cousin and son-in-law, Ali, as the leader of the community when the Prophet died. They believe he was the first legitimate successor to the Prophet. Sunni and Shi'a Muslims differ little on matters of belief, except that Shi'a believe that members of the Prophet's family were endowed with special spiritual authority, particularly when it comes to understanding how to live in accordance with the Qur'an's teachings. They therefore believe that leadership of the community should have stayed within the Prophet's family, and reject the authority of the first three caliphs chosen by the Sunnis. They refer to legitimate successors to the Prophet as Imams, and Ali was the first one.

Shi'a Muslims traced the descendants of the Prophet through a number of generations, but there were occasional differences of opinion as to who was the rightful Imam. This led to the three main divisions among Shi'a Muslims. The majority of Shi'a Muslims recognize the legitimacy of twelve generations of Imams, ending in the 9th century, and are therefore called **Twelvers** (Ithna Ashari). Twelver Shi'a Muslims comprise the majority of the Iranian population as well as that of Azerbaijan, and smaller majorities in Iraq and Bahrain. **Isma'ili Shi'a** traced the Prophet's lineage through six Imams, but then differed with the majority over the seventh. The Zaidis recognize the first four Imams, but differed from both Twelvers and Isma'ilis over the fifth. Both Isma'ilis and Zaidis are further divided into smaller groups, including the Nizari Isma'ilis, who are led by the Aga Khan. The majority of Shi'a Muslims believe the last Imam, though invisible to human beings, exists in an "occult" form and will return at the end of time as the **Mahdi** or messiah. Many Shi'as believe in the efficacy of prayer to God through the intercession of an Imam, a belief rejected by most Sunni Muslims in favor of prayer directly to God.

All Muslims, whether Sunni or Shi'i, can be **Sufis**. Sufi Islam is often called Islamic mysticism. Not all Sufis are mystics, but they do generally stress the inner, personal dimension of Islamic practice. Sufis try to cultivate deep and abiding awareness of the divine, often through meditation and other spiritual practices. There are many varieties of Sufi practice, often distinguished by the methods they use to develop spirituality. Some are characterized as more austere, calling for fasting, simplicity, and solitude, for example, while others are more "ecstatic" and find music and poetry to be effective routes to heightened spirituality. The "Whirling Dervishes" (technically known as Mevlevis) are famous for their twirling dance to the rhythmic beat of drums as a means to develop spiritual awareness. They trace their origin to the mystic poet and philosopher Rumi.

Unit IV The Impact of Religious Studies on the Western Monotheisms

We have stressed that learning a religion is quite different from studying religions. The scholarly study of religion – Religious Studies – has as its goal understanding what religion is, and how various religious traditions developed, rather than training people in a particular religion. Nevertheless, some of the methods and findings of Religious Studies have had an impact on specific religious traditions, notably Christianity, the religion of so many pioneers of Religious Studies.

Biblical Studies

We saw in Chapter 3 that the academic study of the Bible started in early modern times with scholars such as Spinoza. Then in the 19th century, Biblical Studies became more sophisticated with the method known as Higher Criticism, practiced by people such as William Robertson Smith. Julius Wellhausen formulated the Documentary Hypothesis, arguing that the first five books of the Hebrew Bible – the "Books of Moses" – were actually compiled from four independent sources probably well after the time of Moses. This hypothesis was dismissed by some as an attack on Judaism, but ultimately was accepted – with refinements – by the majority of scholars.

In the 20th century, archaeological discoveries added new materials for scholars to analyze, including documents with particular relevance for Christians. Among the things found were the Dead Sea Scrolls and the Nag Hammadi Scrolls. From these documents scholars learned that in the first three centuries of the common era there were many different Christian and Jewish groups with different scriptures and beliefs. It was only in the 4th century that Christian leaders and Jewish leaders chose certain documents to become their official Bibles, their canons. Before that, Christians had several other gospels besides the now familiar Matthew, Mark, Luke, and John, including the gospels of Thomas, Mary, Peter, Philip, Judas, and one called the Gospel of Truth.

Analyzing and comparing all these gospels, scholars saw that they were a special kind of writing. They were not written as history books but rather as messages of "Good News" – persuasive writings meant to spread various ideas about Jesus, and thereby gain converts. For the first quarter-century, messages about Jesus were passed on by word of mouth. Different communities of Christians had different beliefs and different agendas. Some groups consisted only of Jews; others were mostly non-Jews.

As we saw, the first writings that were eventually included in the New Testament were letters written by Paul in the 50s to communities around the Mediterranean Sea. Then around 70 CE the first gospel was written, the Gospel of Mark. Its author had not known Jesus personally, scholars concluded, but composed the Gospel from material that had been transmitted orally for those 40 years. Mark's is the shortest and simplest of the four Gospels.

The Gospels of Matthew and Luke were written next, in the 80s, and they present a lot of the same material that is in Mark's gospel. Because of their similarities, the gospels of Mark, Matthew, and Luke are called the **synoptic Gospels**. Scholars also noticed that the material reported by Matthew and Luke that is not covered by Mark is similar. That is, Matthew and Luke report similar "non-Markan" material. That led to the hypothesis that there was once a document that the authors of Matthew and Luke both worked from, that no longer exists. Scholars call it *Quelle*, the German word for *source*, or Q for short.

We saw that Judaism is a tradition that integrates religious scholars' commentaries on scripture, generation after generation. And as a practice-based tradition, Judaism does not place a great deal of emphasis on theological analysis. However, it is different in Christianity. The realization that the four canonical gospels were neither the only reports on the life of Jesus, nor complete ones, prompted theologians such as Rudolf Bultmann to return to the Gospels and rethink what can be learned from them.

Rudolf Bultmann (d. 1976): "Demythologizing" Scripture

Rudolf Bultmann, a professor of New Testament studies at the University of Marburg, by the 1940s was considered one of the great scholars of the New Testament. His most famous book, *The New Testament and Mythology*, was published in 1941. Bultmann's scholarly studies convinced him that the basic message of Christian scriptures had been expressed in a way that we can no longer accept.

Bultmann pointed out that the Bible was written at a time when people's understanding of the physical world and of themselves was primitive. It contains many descriptions of nature that science has since overturned. Those outmoded explanations of natural phenomena were not essential to the Bible's message, however, according to Bultmann. The core teachings of scripture are about morality, not about physics or biology or psychology. Today, he says, we need to reinterpret the Bible so that it does not clash with what we know from the study of natural science. Bultmann calls this process "demythologizing" the Bible, that is, taking the myths out of it.

Bultmann notes, for example, that in the Bible the world is imagined as a three-tiered structure, "with the earth in the center, the heaven above, and the underworld beneath."

FIGURE 6.16 Rudolf Bultmann. Ullstein Bild/Topfoto.

Heaven is where God and the angels live, and the underworld is hell, where Satan and his demons live. This **cosmology** (understanding of the universe) can be seen in many medieval paintings and in sculptures above the doorways of medieval cathedrals. In the art of the Middle Ages, Jesus is often represented as seated on a throne in the sky next to God the Father, and people who have been damned are under the earth in a fiery cave being tormented by demons. As well, he notes that in the Bible demons, angels, and God cause many everyday events such as storms, sickness, and recovery from sickness. They even take control of people's minds, forcing them to do what they would not have done otherwise. Often in the New Testament people are said to be possessed by demons. The Book of Exodus, too, explains that when Moses asked Pharaoh to let the Israelites leave Egypt, "the Lord hardened Pharaoh's heart, and he did not let the people of Israel go out of his land." (Exodus 11:10) The clear implication here is that Pharoah was about to let the Israelites go, but God changed his mind for him.

Today, Bultmann says, we know that the earth is not a disk but a sphere, and that if we dig into it, we shall not come to a flaming torture chamber run by horned demons, nor can we take a rocket into the sky and find a golden city with a kingly figure seated on a throne. And our modern understanding of the human mind rules out such myths about human beings as the puppets of good and bad spirits. We now think of people as in control of their own actions, and responsible for these actions. Though these descriptions were helpful for the early audiences of scripture, they should be taken as metaphors for deeper truths.

The New Testament also described the end of the world as just around the corner. Jesus predicts that some people standing in front of him will live to see it. Although this belief that the world would end in a few years was universal among early Christians, it obviously was not literally true. If scripture's teaching about the imminent end was meant literally, then it was wrong, and Bultmann does not want to sacrifice the truth of scripture. It is our understanding of scripture that needs correcting. At the same time, however, Bultmann says we cannot sacrifice our intellect by "accepting a view of the world in our faith and religion which we should deny in our everyday life."

Bultmann has similar objections to the resurrection of Jesus and to the idea that Jesus existed before being born on earth. All of these ideas, he says, were myths created to allow ancient peoples to make sense of their world as they struggled to live morally responsible lives. However, they are not the message of the texts. In his view, their core message is about personal moral responsibility. Bultmann concludes, "If the truth of the New Testament proclamation is to be preserved, the only way is to demythologize it." (Bultmann 1984, 9)

John Dominic Crossan (b. 1934): The Historicity of Scripture

By the later part of the 20th century, many scholars studying the Bible were sympathetic to Bultmann's idea that we need to separate the myths in the New Testament from its moral message. One who furthered the effort to understand these moral teachings was John Dominic Crossen. A former Roman Catholic priest and professor at DePaul University, a Catholic school in Chicago, Crossan wanted to determine what we can reasonably believe about Jesus' actions and words. In 1985, Crossan and Robert Funk started a research team called the Jesus Seminar. Eventually the group came to include over 200 scholars. From 1985 to 1991 they reviewed 1,500 items found in the canonical gospels and other early Christian sources such as the Gospel of Thomas. At their meetings, they gave presentations and debated reasons for accepting and rejecting the quotations attributed to Jesus in the Gospels.

Through a complex process participants in the seminar then calculated the likelihood of authenticity for each quote. The results were published in the 1993 book *The Five Gospels: the Search for the Authentic Words of Jesus*. Of the hundreds of sayings attributed to Jesus, 18% were judged to be likely to be close to something that Jesus actually said. Among them were Jesus' saying not to fret over daily needs such as food and clothing, and his saying that no one can serve two masters. The sayings that were highly questionable included references to Gehenna or hell.

The Jesus Seminar went through the same process regarding the actions attributed to Jesus, as well. The results were published in the 1998 book *The Acts of Jesus*. Of the actions attributed to Jesus in the Gospels, 16% were judged reliable. Those included reports that Jesus was born during the reign of Herod the Great, that his mother's name was Mary, that he was baptized by John, and that he was arrested in Jerusalem and crucified by the Romans. None of the items judged authentic was miraculous. The members of the Seminar did not think it believable that Jesus actually changed water into wine, multiplied the loaves and fishes, walked on water, or raised Lazarus from the dead. The stories of Jesus' own resurrection, the Seminar concluded, were based on visions of Jesus that Peter, Paul, and Mary had.

Beyond leading the Jesus Seminar, John Dominic Crossan has published extensively on his own. His books include *The Historical Jesus: The Life of a Mediterranean Jewish Peasant*, and *Jesus: A Revolutionary Biography*. Crossan applies what we know from history and anthropology to the stories in the Gospels, and, like the Jesus Seminar, Crossan concludes that in the early centuries of Christianity Jesus was commonly understood as a wandering wise man. Crossan also gives more evidence for Bultmann's claim that the Gospels contain many myths. As we have seen, scholars do not consider myths to be fantastic false reports. In Religious Studies, myths are stories that present important teachings, but are not meant to be taken as literal history or science.

Just as the gospel writers made Jesus' birth marvelous in order to support the claim of his greatness, they made his departure from this world marvelous too. They wrote that he rose from his tomb three days after he was buried. According to the Gospels, when his friends went to the tomb, the stone had been rolled back and his body was gone. This story is impressive, Crossan says, but it does not fit with what we know about how the Romans crucified criminals and political troublemakers. This horrible form of torture and execution was designed not just to humiliate the person but to cause maximum anguish and humiliation to their family as well. And so the Romans left the corpse up on the cross for crows, vultures, and dogs to tear to pieces and eat. They did not release the body to the person's family for burial because that would bestow dignity on the corpse and give the family some solace. Therefore, Crossan argues, it is very unlikely that Jesus' family and friends ever got to retrieve his corpse, wash it and place it in a tomb.

Infants and Heroes

A number of scholars have pointed out the apparent coincidence that great leaders throughout history have had extraordinarily perilous adventures as infants and yet somehow managed to survive.

The founders of Rome – Romulus and Remus – were twins whose father was a god and mother was a virgin. Their wicked uncle put them out in the wilderness to die. But they survived – thanks to a wolf who took care of them and nursed them through childhood. Zeus survived the ravenous appetite of his carnivorous father Kronos by being hidden in a cave where he was brought up by a goat or a nymph or a shepherd's family, depending upon which version of the story you read, until he grew old enough to rescue his siblings (from his father's stomach) and take control of Mount Olympus. Moses escaped the Egyptian pharaoh's command that newborns be killed, by being sailed down the Nile in a basket. A princess found him and brought him up in a palace until he was old enough to defy the pharaoh and lead the Israelites out of Egypt. The story of Jesus' birth in an animal's feeding trough (manger) far from home, and rearing by his virgin mother and her elderly caretaker until he went public with his mission to save the world can be seen as another example of a heroic infant myth.

In *Patterns of Comparative Religion*, Eliade (see Chapter 4) points out that stories about specific children's miraculous survival of abandonment is a common mythical pattern, identifying the children in question as heroes from the start.

FIGURE 6.17 Sculpture of Romulus and Remus suckling under a wolf.
javarman/Shutterstock Images.

Fundamentalism

Given the popularity of Ehrman's books and others like it (for example, the 2010 *Jesus Wars: How Four Patriarchs, Three Queens, and Two Emperors Decided What Christians Would Believe for the Next 1,500 Years*, by Philip Jenkins), it seems that critical analysis of biblical sources has entered the mainstream, at least in Western Christianity. However, it is not without opposition. Fundamentalism is a term coined for the modern movement that insists that scripture conveys absolute truth, even in terms of science and history.

Before the rise of modern science in the 17th century, the common European understanding of the universe was based on the Bible, especially the book of Genesis, and ancient Greek science. In this worldview, the Earth was the unmoving center of the universe, with the sun, moon, and everything else revolving around the Earth. However, around 1500 astronomers began challenging this Earth-centered cosmology. Nicolaus Copernicus hypothesized that the Sun was at the center and the Earth revolved around it. In 1632 Galileo published *Dialogue Concerning the Two Chief World Systems*, presenting a cosmology in which the Earth and other planets revolve around the Sun. That book so bothered authorities in the Roman Catholic Church that they put Galileo on trial. He was found guilty of heresy – namely of holding the opinion that the Earth does not lie motionless at the center of the universe. He was imprisoned and his book was banned. In an action not announced at the trial, publication of any other books by Galileo was also forbidden.

Today, Christian churches do not condemn the idea that the Sun is the center of the universe. Many churches, however, reject later scientific ideas about the Earth and the origins of living things. Modern science says that the universe is 14 billion years old and the first forms of life were primitive bacteria in the oceans 3.8 billion years ago; from them all the plants and animals on Earth evolved. Christians who challenge these ideas say that it contradicts the Bible. The Book of Genesis, they insist, is the true description of how living things were created. And Genesis and the rest of the Bible explain that God directly made all living things at about the same time, and did this just a few thousand years ago.

When Charles Darwin published *On the Origin of Species* (1859) and *The Descent of Man* (1871), many Christian churches were initially troubled by the theory that living things had evolved. However, the theory did explain a lot of things, such as the thousands of fossils of prehistoric animals that had been found around the world, and many churches came to see the theory of evolution as complementary to the claim that God created the world. It could explain how God accomplished that creation. God does not do everything directly, they said; sometimes God operates through intermediate causes – in this case, a process

▶

that spanned millions of years. The churches that eventually accepted the theory of evolution – most mainstream Protestant churches and the Roman Catholic Church – explain that the central message of the Book of Genesis is that God made everything and cares about everything, especially human beings, whom he put in charge of the Earth.

However, in the 20th century, some Christian churches rejected the new non-literal approach to the Bible and rallied for laws banning the teaching of evolution. In 1919, the World's Christian Fundamentals Association was founded, largely to oppose modern ideas such as evolution, which it called a "foreign doctrine" undermining Christianity. The term **fundamentalist** was coined in 1920 to refer to those "doing battle royal for the Fundamentals."

Between 1910 and 1915, a 12-volume collection of essays by 64 British and American scholars and preachers was published that was called *The Fundamentals*. Included among the fundamentals is that the Bible is totally accurate, Jesus is divine, his mother was a virgin, his death paid the debt for human sin, he physically rose from the dead, very soon he will return to begin a 1,000-year reign, and then the world will end.

In 1925 the State of Tennessee, which had banned teaching about the theory of evolution in its schools, tried and convicted a high-school teacher named John Thomas Scopes for teaching it. This was the famous Scopes "Monkey Trial."

While fundamentalist churches are in the minority in the United States, the effect of fundamentalist thought has been growing. In a 2005 CBS News poll, 44% of American adults said that "God created the world in six days and rested on the seventh." In six Gallup opinion polls taken in the U.S. between 1982 and 2004, randomly selected adults were asked about creation and evolution. One statement they could agree with was, "God created man pretty much in his present form at one time within the last 10,000 years." Another was that "[m]an has developed over millions of years from less advanced forms of life, but God guided this process, including man's creation." The first position is a rejection of evolution. It was chosen by 44–47% of American adults in the six Gallup polls. (Among scientists, it was chosen by 5%.) The second statement, saying that God's creation is compatible with evolution, was chosen by only 35–40% of Americans.

A striking display of the fundamentalist opposition to modern science is the Museum of Creation, built in Petersburg, Kentucky, in 2007 at a cost of over $25 million. It presents an account of the origins of the Earth and the human race based on a literal reading of Genesis. Displays in the 70,000 square-foot building show the Earth and all living things as being directly created by God over a six-day period, just 6,000 years ago. There are over 80 animatronic dinosaurs, many living side-by-side with humans. One exhibit features a triceratops and a stegosaurus aboard Noah's Ark. Against biologists who say that dinosaurs had been extinct for 60 million years when the first human appeared, Mark Looy, chief spokesperson for the museum, says, "There may not be any fossil evidence showing dinosaurs and people in the same place at the same time. However, it is clearly written [in the Bible] that they were alive at the same time."

Until the late 1970s, *fundamentalism* was applied only to Protestant Christians, and it was often associated with reaction against social and political liberalism. However, in the late 20th century, journalists began using the term for political Islam (see above). Later, *fundamentalism* was applied even more broadly to mean a strict adherence to the conservative or traditionalist forms of any religion or ideology.

FIGURE 6.18 The Creation Museum in Petersburg, Kentucky. Mark Lyons/ Getty Images.

Such miracle stories are of doubtful historicity (historical accuracy), Crossan says, but that does not mean they carry no truth. Instead of being literal reports, they convey meanings that are central to the tradition: that Jesus brought teachings of monumental importance, truths that were recognized as such by his followers but rejected by those with a stake in the status quo. The rulers felt threatened by his revolutionary teachings and therefore executed him. However, the power of his teachings survived his death.

Since the pioneering work of scholars such as Bultmann and Crossan, critical historical analysis of Christian scripture and teachings has become commonplace. Bart Ehrman, a distinguished scholar of religion at the University of North Carolina in Chapel Hill, has produced a number of works challenging traditional Christian teaching – and three have become best-sellers. His *Misquoting Jesus: The Story Behind Who Changed the Bible and*

Why (2005) summarizes the conclusion of textual critics, such as those discussed above and in Chapter 3. *God's Problem: How the Bible Fails to Answer Our Most Important Question – Why We Suffer* (2008) points out inconsistencies in the Bible and argues that it gives several conflicting answers to the question in the title, including that suffering is a punishment, suffering is a test, and suffering is just a part of life. His most recent, *Jesus, Interrupted: Revealing the Hidden Contradictions in the Bible (and Why We Don't Know about Them)* (2010), continues in the same vein as *Misquoting Jesus*.

Theology

Demythologizing scripture and questioning its historicity call into question the purpose of scripture. Scholars such as Bultmann and Crossan claim that the Bible should not be considered literal science or history. Then what is its message? What have we been missing all these years? We shall survey two major approaches to these questions: Liberation Theology and Feminist Theology. According to Liberation Theology, scripture calls for an end to oppression, particularly of the poor. Feminist Theology focuses on ending the marginalization of women as the key to unlocking the message of scripture.

Liberation Theology

In 1965 the Roman Catholic Church concluded its last **ecumenical council** (meeting of all church authorities), the Second Vatican Council ("Vatican II"). The meeting had been called to achieve an "updating" (*aggiornamento*) of the church and to address its relationship to other religious communities. One of the themes stressed by the council was that scripture presented a "preferential option for the poor." By this it meant that the example Jesus set was, above all, helping those in need. Christians should therefore try to follow his example.

In 1968 Catholic bishops in Latin America met at Medellin, Colombia, to discuss implementation of Vatican II's message. The result was a movement that reassessed interpretations of scripture with a focus on intervening in the suffering of the poor. This movement came to be known as Liberation Theology.

Gustavo Gutierrez (b. 1928)

Gustavo Gutierrez, a Catholic priest from Lima, Peru, who is now a professor of Theology at the University of Notre Dame, is a major voice in Liberation Theology. Gutierrez insists that scripture presents Jesus as a reformer. He challenges the interpretations of scripture that allow poverty and oppression to continue. In stories about feeding the hungry and curing the sick, scripture calls upon Christians to actively participate in ending the suffering of others. And this requires intervention in the political and economic structures responsible for oppression.

To those Christians who contend that religion and politics should be kept separate, Gutierrez points out that throughout history Christian churches have supported governments. The dominant theory of government in the Hebrew Bible, the New Testament, and through the Middle Ages is that political leaders get their power and authority from

Traditional Christian Theology Versus Liberation Theology

Leading thinkers in Liberation Theology often contrast it with the traditional theology of Catholic and Protestant churches. Five contrasts are the following.

1. Traditional theology is largely *descriptive*: it describes God and spiritual realities. Liberation Theology is largely *prescriptive*: it prescribes what people should do, especially about poverty and injustice.

2. Traditional theology emphasizes the world to come – heaven and hell. Liberation Theology emphasizes this world.

3. Traditional Theology emphasizes prayer, worship, and other forms of piety. Liberation Theology emphasizes social action.

4. Traditional theology emphasizes the individual's salvation. It answers the question "What do I need to do to get to heaven?" Liberation Theology emphasizes a social vision in which people are concerned with the welfare of others, not just themselves.

5. Traditional theology is often triumphalist. That is, it presents Christianity as having already achieved its central goals of spreading the Gospel and perpetuating itself. Liberation Theology instead sees Christianity as a work in progress which still has much work to do.

God. This came to be called the Divine Right of Kings. Many churches, too, are identified with a government. The Church of England is nominally headed by the King or Queen, who bears the title "Defender of the Faith." The Greek Orthodox and Russian Orthodox churches obviously identify themselves in terms of geopolitical entities. In some countries the clergy are even paid by the government.

In Latin America, the Catholic Church traditionally supported political leaders. Many of the Spanish and Portuguese explorers who came to the Americas in the 1500s had been sanctioned by church authorities who sent missionaries to convert the native peoples. From the beginning, Argentina, Brazil, Peru, and the other colonies were Catholic colonies. The bishops supported the colonial governors and the governors supported them.

The economic and political system imposed on the native peoples in the 1500s, Gutierrez says, was medieval Christian feudalism. The Europeans claimed vast tracts of land, over which they were lords, and the native people were forced to work for them as serfs. They were baptized as Christians and forced into serfdom at the same time. Their new religion taught them to be humble, which made them obedient workers on the plantations, living in poverty while increasing the wealth of the landowners.

In the 1800s, the colonies of Latin America declared their independence from Spain and Portugal, but the feudal system of wealthy lords exploiting poor peasants continued in the new countries. In the 20th century, when peasants tried to organize labor unions and vote for political change, the ruling class used military forces to intimidate and punish them. Thus the wealthy landowners kept their hold on the land, wealth, and political power. In Nicaragua before the 1979 revolution, for example, the ruling Somoza family owned over half the country.

For all of the 19th century and most of the 20th century, the Catholic Church supported these oppressive political systems. However, the 1968 Medellin conference changed things. Looking to scripture, they found a new message. They focused on the concern of God and his prophets for poor and oppressed people. God commands, "You shall not abuse any widow or orphan. If you do abuse them, when they cry out to me, I will surely heed their cry; my wrath will burn, and I will kill you with the sword." (Exodus 22:22–24)

A major example of God's taking the side of oppressed people is in the Book of Exodus, where God liberates the Israelites from slavery in Egypt. He empowers Moses to be their leader and works miracles such as the parting of the Red Sea to get them out of Egypt. After wandering in the desert, they are led to a land where they can live in dignity as free people. This is a message meant for all people, Gutierrez believes. "The liberation of Israel is a political action," he writes in *A Theology of Liberation*. "It is the breaking away from a situation of despoliation and misery and the beginning of the construction of a just and comradely society." (Gutierrez 1977, 17) The message of the prophets – Isaiah, Jeremiah, and Ezekiel, for example – is to take the side of oppressed people, especially the poor, laborers, widows, and orphans.

In the New Testament, Jesus comes as the Messiah – not a monarch but a liberator. Jesus did not overthrow Roman rule and place himself on a throne. He worked for social justice and liberation from misery. Almost every miracle in the Gospels is to provide someone with a basic need such as food (including wine) or health. When Jesus describes how people will be judged at the end of the world, he says that the criterion will be whether they fed the hungry, clothed the naked, and cared for the sick (Matthew 25).

Farid Esack (b. 1959)

Scriptural criticism, though widely accepted by scholars in both Judaism and Christianity, has not received a warm welcome in Islam. Critical studies of the Qur'an have been interpreted as racist slurs and politically motivated attacks on the religion itself, and therefore met with resentment. However, reassessments and liberation-focused interpretations of scripture have very strong representation in Islam. One of its main proponents is Farid Esack, South African scholar and activist. Esack was a leader among Muslims struggling against Apartheid. In 1961 a general "Call of Islam" movement was launched in Cape Town, which set the tone for Islamic activism against injustice with the publication of its principles:

> For too long a time now have we been, together with our fellow-sufferers, subjugated; [we have] suffered humiliation of being regarded as inferior beings, [and] deprived of our basic rights to Earn, to Learn and to Worship. We therefore call upon our

FIGURE 6.19 Farid Esack. Kopano Tlape, University of Johannesburg.

Muslim Brethren and all brothers in our sufferings to unite under the banner of Truth, Justice and Equality to rid our beloved land of the forces of evil and tyranny. (*Muslim News*, 31 March 1961, 4)

There had been many protests against Apartheid policies before this. However, this call for Islamic resistance was unique in a number of ways. First, unlike earlier protests, the new resistance was not against specific rules, such as segregation; it was aimed against an entire system deemed essentially unjust. Second, the injustices being protested were those suffered not by Muslims alone, but by all victims of oppression. The premise was that Islam is above all a struggle against injustice. The purpose of human life as revealed in the Islamic sources is to create a just society.

Just as in other parts of the world, the imposition of colonial rule had shaken South African Muslim activists, and reminded them of the challenge posed by God in the Qur'an: to be stewards, to create and maintain a society reflecting human dignity and equality. Islamic resistance organizations in South Africa from that time on focused on the following issues:

1. explicating the centrality of justice to Islamic values;

2. articulating the implications of this centrality for their daily lives; and

3. defining the entire process as essentially religious activity.

Esack argues against those who feel content that they are good Muslims simply because they fulfill ritual obligations and observe moral prohibitions. He explains that the Qur'an … presents Allah as a being that is concerned with something that people do and with the people who do it, rather than with an abstract entity called faith…. Thus, *muslim* and all its positive connotations (including eschatological) cannot refer to the biological accident of being born in a Muslim family. Similarly, *kafir* cannot refer to the accident of being born outside of such a family. (Esack quoted by Sonn 2004, 112–113)

For Esack, not only is social justice central to Islamic values, but activism in pursuit of social justice is essential. The overall spirit of Qur'anic teaching is personal accountability, Esack argues, not group identity – personal accountability for both the motivations and consequences of one's actions. As Esack puts it: "[E]very deed that we do or refuse to do is a step in our personal transformation." There is no single action or set of actions that encompasses an entire life; moral behavior is an ongoing enterprise, evident in every interaction and choice. It requires ongoing effort. It is continuous responsiveness to injustice in all its forms. For Esack, as for many liberation theologians, this includes gender justice, as well.

Feminist Theology

Feminist theology can actually be considered a form of Liberation Theology and it, too, has strong representation across religious traditions. It grew out of concern for the marginalization of women. Until the late 20th century, major religions around the world were controlled almost exclusively by men. It was only in 1935 that the first woman was ordained a rabbi, and in the 1950s that major Christian denominations began ordaining women. Traditions such as Roman Catholicism still insist that only men may be ordained, and Orthodox Jews as well as traditional Muslims believe that only males are qualified to train as interpreters of the law. Women have been not only blocked from positions of religious authority but also discouraged from studying religion, either their own tradition or anyone else's. This discrimination is a byproduct of the general pattern of patriarchy (see Chapters 5 and 9), rule by father-figures, found around the world.

In the 19th century, some women and men began to question discrimination against women in life generally, and in religion in particular. At a convention in 1848 in Seneca Falls, New York, dozens of women and men came together to discuss the idea that women should be treated as equals. Speakers included Elizabeth Cady Stanton, Lucretia Mott, a Quaker minister, Susan B. Anthony, and Frederick Douglass, the great African-American abolitionist. They produced a Declaration of the Rights of Women that was modeled on the American Declaration of Independence and the Bill of Rights. Here is how that document ends:

Resolved: that the speedy success of our cause depends upon the zealous and untiring efforts of both men and women for the overthrow of the monopoly of the pulpit, and for the securing to women of equal participation with men in various trades, professions and commerce. (http://ecssba.rutgers.edu/docs/seneca.html)

For decades after the convention, the women and men who had attended the conference devoted themselves to gender equality in Christianity, to women's rights, to the

The Woman's Bible

Half a century after the pioneering Women's Rights Convention of 1848, which she helped lead, Elizabeth Cady Stanton and several colleagues wrote *The Woman's Bible*, a set of commentaries on the Bible that prefigure many ideas of contemporary feminists. The introduction stated that:

From the inauguration of the movement for woman's emancipation the Bible has been used to hold her in the "divinely ordained sphere," prescribed in the Old and New Testaments. The canon and civil law; church and state; priests and legislators; all political parties and religious denominations have alike taught that woman was made after man, of man, and for man, an inferior being, subject to man. Creeds, codes, Scriptures and statutes, are all based on this idea.

However, if we read the Bible without sexist assumptions, Stanton wrote, we can interpret it as saying that the feminine is as important as the masculine, and that God includes both. The following section of *The Woman's Bible* presents the story of the creation of man and woman in Genesis 1:26–28, and uses it to argue that God is female as well as male:

And God said, Let us make man in our image, after our likeness: and let them have dominion over the fish of the sea, and over the fowl of the air, and over the cattle, and over all the earth, and over every creeping thing that creepeth upon the earth. And God created man in his own image, in the image of God created he him; male and female created he them. And God blessed them: and God said unto them, Be fruitful, and multiply, and replenish the earth, and subdue it; and have dominion over the fish of the sea, and over the fowl of the air, and over every living thing that moveth upon the earth.

Here is the sacred historian's first account of the advent of woman; a simultaneous creation of both sexes, in the image of God. It is evident from the language that there was consultation in the Godhead, and that the masculine and feminine elements were equally represented. Scott in his commentaries says, "this consultation of the Gods is the origin of the doctrine of the trinity." But instead of three male personages, as generally represented, a Heavenly Father, Mother, and Son would seem more rational.

The first step in the elevation of woman to her true position, as an equal factor in human progress, is the cultivation of the religious sentiment in regard to her dignity and equality, the recognition by the rising generation of an ideal Heavenly Mother, to whom their prayers should be addressed, as well as to a Father. If language has any meaning, we have in these texts a plain declaration of the existence of the feminine element in the godhead, equal in power and glory with the masculine. The Heavenly Mother and Father! "God created man in his own image, male and female." Thus Scripture, as well as science and philosophy, declares the eternity and equality of sex. (http://www.sacred-texts.com/wmn/wb/)

abolition of slavery, and to other issues of social justice. Elizabeth Cady Stanton led a group that published *The Woman's Bible* in 1895. Susan B. Anthony and others worked tirelessly to get women the right to vote. It took seventy years and an amendment to the Constitution before American women were allowed to vote, but the modern feminist movement had begun.

Today there are many approaches to feminism, making the term difficult to define. We shall use the broadest possible description, provided by essayist and broadcaster David Bouchier: "Any form of opposition to any form of social, personal, or economic discrimination which women suffer because of their sex." (Bouchier 1983, 2) The movement is complex, however. Like Liberation Theology, it has a descriptive side and a prescriptive side: it describes how things are, and it prescribes how things should be. While some contend that the academic study of anything should be limited to describing it, when something involves issues of social justice, it is hard to just describe what has happened without commenting on how things should change. That is obvious in studies of slavery, racism, and anti-Semitism, for example, and it is true of feminist studies as well.

In the 1970s a new wave of feminism gained widespread support from women and men, and led to the creation of Women's Studies programs in colleges and universities. Today there are feminist perspectives within most academic disciplines, including literature, fine art, history, philosophy, and Religious Studies.

Of all the institutions that sustain **sexism** (discrimination in favor of one gender over others, characteristic of patriarchy), religions are among the most prominent. Even today, some Orthodox Jewish men say a traditional prayer thanking God that they were "not born a woman." Jews, Christians, and Muslims all think of God as the King of the Universe and the Creator of "man." In Christianity, God and Jesus are Father and Son. The early leaders of the Church are still called the Fathers. Priests are called "Father," too, and "Pope" is English for "Papa." Discrimination against women in Muslim societies is widely publicized in the West.

While some feminists say that sexism runs too deep to be expunged and therefore abandon their religion, others say that sexism is not part of the core message of their religions and so they try to reform them. Liberation Theology as such is not widely represented in Judaism, mainly because Judaic teaching is worked out in legal commentary rather than in theological discussion. However, in the case of feminist issues, scholars from across the the traditions find it necessary to go back to core theological formulations derived from scripture. We shall look at examples from all three of the Western monotheisms.

Judith Plaskow (b. 1947)

Judith Plaskow received her Ph.D. from Yale Divinity School, writing a dissertation that was later published as *Sex, Sin, and Grace: Women's Experience and the Theologies of Reinhold Niebuhr and Paul Tillich*. She has taught at Manhattan College since 1979. In 1972 she became co-chair of the fledgling Women and Religion Group of the American Academy of Religion. In 1981 she helped start the pioneering Jewish feminist group B'not Esh. She was co-founder of the *Journal of Feminist Studies in Religion* and served as co-editor from 1983–1994. In 1997–1998 she was President of the American Academy of Religion. With Carol Christ, Plaskow edited the groundbreaking anthology *Womanspirit Rising* (1979).

With Elisabeth Schussler-Fiorenza, she edited *The Journal of Feminist Studies in Religion*. Over a long and distinguished career, she has offered a feminist perspective on her own Jewish tradition, the wider monotheistic tradition, and religions in general.

Plaskow's earliest work, *The Coming of Lilith* (1972), rewrites an ancient *midrash* (imaginative story based on the Bible) about Eve and Adam's other wife, Lilith. In the story, Lilith is a rebellious outcast. However, when she meets Eve, they become friends, explore the sexism in the world as God has set it up, and think of ways to transform that world. Plaskow's 1982 article "The Right Question Is Theological" argues that *halakhah*, the laws of Judaism, are part of a patriarchal system, a system ruled by men. Those who want to eliminate sexism from Judaism, she says, should reform Jewish theology rather than waste time trying to reform *halakhah*.

In her masterwork, *Standing Again at Sinai* (1990), Plaskow points out that the story of Moses receiving the law from God – the central event in Judaism – does not involve any women. Indeed, in the preparation for receiving the law, Moses warns the men, "Be ready for the third day; do not go near a woman." (Exodus 19:15) More generally, the Torah and Jewish interpretations of history have been written by men in a way that largely ignores the experiences and needs of women. What is needed is a reinterpretation of Jewish history that takes women seriously and treats them as equal to men. Scholars must reread the traditional sources to reveal the experience and actions of women, and they must rewrite Jewish history to include the history of women.

Standing Again at Sinai offers a feminist perspective on the three traditional topics of God, Torah, and Israel. The chapter on God examines the language and images used to represent God. Agreeing with Clifford Geertz that religious language and symbols justify social systems, Plaskow argues that, if God is described as a father, then human fathers thereby become God-like. If God is portrayed as Lord, a dominating male, then male domination becomes acceptable. In her chapter on Torah, she argues that Jewish scripture and history have overlooked much of women's experiences. She is less negative than before about halakhah, seeing law as a necessary part of all human cultures. However, she argues that Jews need to re-think the way that laws are made and interpreted. "Perhaps what distinguishes feminist Judaism from traditional rabbinic Judaism," she says, "is not so much the absence of rules from the former as a conception of rule-making as a shared communal process." (Plaskow 1991, 71) The chapter on Israel sketches the creation of a society in which Jewish women are equal.

Standing Again at Sinai also has a chapter on the theology of sexuality. For Plaskow, sexuality is not a minor detail about a person but part of his or her identity. The world that each of us experiences is body mediated, so that our being human is being sexual as well as being rational. Becoming aware of how experience is mediated through a body, she says, will help us to create a holy attitude towards sexuality, to replace traditional male domination. A new sexual ethics will emerge in which sexual relationships are based not on ownership or hierarchy but on empowerment of each other.

Rosemary Radford Ruether (b. 1936)

Rosemary Radford was educated in philosophy, history, and classics, and she has taught in the theology programs of several seminaries and universities. In her landmark book *Sexism and God-Talk*, she explores how traditional language about God has kept men in control of

FIGURE 6.20 Rosemary Radford Ruether. Used with permission of Pacific School of Religion.

the Western religious traditions. For thousands of years people have talked about God as "Father," "King," and "Lord of Hosts" (Commander of Armies). These words, Ruether says, create an image of God that valorizes fathers over mothers, kings over ordinary people, and warriors over peaceful people. "The God-image serves as the central reinforcement of patriarchal rule." Just as God rules the universe, men rule the earth. They give the orders; women and children obey. In the home, the father is the ultimate authority. In the church, synagogue, mosque, and temple, men interpret the scriptures, conduct the rituals, and manage the finances.

Complementing God as a militarist king and "men" as made in his image are scripture's passive female role models. Ruether notes that women in the Bible are important only because of their relationship to some man, not for what they are in themselves. She points out that in the Bible God speaks directly only to men. Women's access to God is through their husbands or fathers. In Christian scripture the ultimate female is Mary, the mother of Jesus. She is praised not for what she does or thinks, but for what she lets happen to her – becoming pregnant with Jesus – and for what she does not do – have sex. Her greatness is that she does what God and Jesus tell her to do. Church leaders for centuries have held Mary up as the role model for women, an incentive for women to go along with what men want them to think and do.

However, again, this does not make the Bible wrong or misguided. If we probe beneath the sexist language and ideas in the Bible, Ruether says, we can see that the core message is not at all sexist. Sexist language is geared to the social realities at the time of revelation, but it is not prescriptive. It does not mean that society should always be patriarchal. A basic biblical theme is social justice for everyone, and the liberation of oppressed people. This is the point of God's freeing the Israelites from slavery in Egypt. This is what prophets such as Amos are talking about when they protest the mistreatment of widows and orphans. And liberation was the essential feature of the idea of the Messiah.

Not only is sexism extraneous to the original message of the Bible, Ruether says, but it conflicts with what the New Testament says about Jesus. The Gospels portray a man remarkably free of sexism, who speaks to women as equals, has women as friends, and rejects the militarism and hierarchy in his culture.

In order to return to the original message that was meant to liberate both women and men from oppression, Ruether says, we must understand how religious traditions develop. They start, she says, when a group of people have a revelatory experience – when they see a new dimension of reality, a new meaning in life, or a new way of living. Next they describe their experience, using the words and concepts available in their culture. Within the group, leaders emerge who claim authority in expressing and interpreting the revelatory experience, and their interpretations become the central message of the group. For example, the leaders of the ancient Israelites captured their revelatory experience in the writings now known as the Bible.

As the religion grows, each generation applies the central message to its lives, and passes it on to the next generation. Sometimes, however, one generation determines that its leaders are corrupt and no longer acting for the best interest of the group. This happened, for example, when Martin Luther accused the leaders of the Roman Catholic Church of being concerned more with their own power and wealth than with the people they were leading. If the challengers make their case well, they can bring about a paradigm shift, a new way of thinking about the group and its message. This is what happened in the Protestant Reformation, Ruether says, and has recently happened in Christianity and other religions as feminists, both women and men, have challenged patriarchy.

The original revelatory experience of the Bible was interpreted and recorded by men. They experienced transcendent reality, or divinity, and described it as the greatest thing they could think of. In their patriarchal culture, the greatest possible being had to be male. Also, landowners and rulers were a higher kind of being than landless peasants. Lords and kings, who gave orders, were obviously superior to the people who followed those orders. So God had to be not just male but Lord and King. Thinking this way, the writers of the Bible described the divine as a male who, as the King of the Universe, controls everything and everybody. He rules by proclaiming laws, rewarding those who obey, and punishing those who disobey.

Today this understanding of divinity seems obsolete to feminists and other reformers. Many people now reject the idea that monarchy is the natural form of government, that males are naturally superior to females and destined to rule over them, and that morality is following orders, rather than, say, acting out of concern for other people.

We must reinterpret the Bible, Ruether says, to create "an image of God beyond patriarchy." If we want to use a parent image to talk about God, certainly "Mother" is as appropriate as "Father." However, we may want to get rid of all parent metaphors because they promote "spiritual infantilism." That is, they make adults treat themselves and other adults as children. And whether we keep the parent metaphors or not, "God(ess) must be seen as beyond maleness and femaleness."

In building a new feminist theology, Ruether says that we should open our minds and consider all kinds of ideas – not just traditional Christian doctrines, but marginalized and heretical theologies, as well as humanistic philosophies. She also wants to avoid "humanocentric" thinking, and consider the values of the animals and plants on this planet. After all, humans are latecomers on Earth, and our galaxy has 1,000,000,000 stars, so it is highly unlikely that everything exists for us. And even if it does, we should probably take care of it, rather than destroy it through wanton consumerism and warfare.

Amina Wadud (b. 1952)

As in Judaism, theology is not the focus of teachings in Islam. Like Judaism, Islam is a practice-based tradition, so discussion of teachings is generally carried out in the context of legal studies. In the case of teachings about women, this is very appropriate, since the status

FIGURE 6.21 Amina Wadud. © Albert Gea/Reuters/Corbis.

of women is actually controlled by Islamic law. Traditional Islamic law indeed privileges males over females. However, challenges to that privileged status have been part of the many calls for reform in modern Islam over the past century and a half, as we saw above.

As early as the 1870s, reformers were calling for improvement in the status of women in Muslim societies. By the turn of the 20th century, legal scholars were publishing books critical of the secondary status of women in some Muslim societies and describing it as a deviation from the teachings of the Qur'an. However, like most social movements, it took some time for such critiques to reach the mainstream of society.

By the late 20th century, numerous Muslim reformers included the call for improvement of the status of women in their agendas for social reform, basing their arguments on Islamic principles. Amina Wadud, African-American scholar of Islam, is among the best known and most outspoken among them. She acknowledges that women's status in Muslim societies is distinctly beneath that of men, but she refuses to accept that this situation is a reflection of Islamic values. She argues, like most Muslim scholars, that the fundamental Qur'anic teaching is justice and human dignity, and insists that this teaching extends to women as well as men. She believes that Islamic scripture teaches not only that women and men bear equal moral responsibility – a position shared by virtually all Muslims – but that they are intellectually and socially equal as well.

Based on this understanding, Wadud undertakes what she calls a "gender jihad" to bring practice into accord with Qur'anic ideals. Traditionally, Muslim scholars have interpreted the Qur'an as teaching that men have ultimate authority over women. They interpret the Qur'an's description of men as being responsible for their wives and daughters as an overall claim that men are in charge of women. They then explain that this is because women are weaker than men – both physically and intellectually. Besides this, women left to their own devices can tempt men into doing things they otherwise would not do, so it is best for women to be kept in the private environs of home and family. There, their unique talents – such as emotional sensitivity – can be used to greatest effect.

Wadud counters that these conclusions are based on archaic interpretations that must be corrected. She claims that correct understanding of Qur'anic teaching would yield full equality and social empowerment for women. Like others who take a historicist approach to scripture, Wadud says that it is essential to understand the context in which the Qur'an was revealed in order to avoid confusing descriptions of what was going on with prescriptions for the way things should be.

Among numerous examples, Wadud cites one concerning the weight of women's testimony in court. In verses dealing with borrowing and lending, the Qur'an says these transactions are permissible provided they do not involve usury (exploitive interest rates) and that they must be recorded and witnessed so that there will be no misunderstanding about who owes whom what. Specifically, it says that two men should witness the deal, but if two men are not available then one man and two women may do so. That way, if one of the women forgets, the other can remind her. (Qur'an 2:282) From this, the classical scholars inferred that the verse taught that women are only half as reliable as men in general. Wadud argues that this interpretation is based on a lack of understanding. For one thing, it conflicts with countless other verses of the Qur'an that treat women and men as equally responsible. However, beyond this, it confuses description of the context of revelation – when most women were inexperienced in business – with prescription for the way things should always be.

Wadud goes on to apply the same method of interpretation (**hermeneutic**) to other issues, including the right to equal inheritance and the right to a single spouse (**monogamy**), so that the Qur'an's teaching is explained as a fully liberating text.

Conclusion

People who grow up within Judaism, Christianity or Islam often feel that their own tradition is quite distinct from the others. After all, the first two millennia of the Common Era have been marked by violent conflict among the groups. Viewing this history, it is a wonder any of them have survived. However, Religious Studies scholars see things differently. The Abrahamic traditions are a single family. In core beliefs and basic structure, Judaism and Islam are actually closer than either one is to Christianity, but overall, the differences among them are minor, compared with the differences between the Western monotheisms and the traditions of India, China, and Japan – as we shall see in succeeding chapters.

DISCUSSION QUESTIONS

1. Do Jews, Christians, and Muslims pray to the same God?

2. Is it possible to believe one religion is the true religion and continue to respect other religions?

3. Discuss Judaic and Islamic dietary rules from the perspective of Douglas.

4. Discuss bar and bat mitzvah rituals from the perspective of Durkheim.

5. Circumcision is a practice that was so widespread in the ancient Mediterranean world that scholars cannot identify a place or date of its origin. Circumcision is required by Judaic law. It is not mentioned in the Qur'an but it is considered obligatory by most Muslims based on hadith. Circumcision is not a part of Christian law but routine male circumcision is widely practiced in North American societies, despite the fact that the American Medical Association does not recommend it. Discuss the prevalence of circumcision from the perspective of Douglas.

6. Discuss the prevalence of circumcision from the perspective of Tylor.

7. Discuss the origins of Christianity from the perspective of Marx and Weber.

8. Discuss baptism from the perspective of Durkheim and Douglas.

9. Discuss the origins of Islam from the perspective of Marx and Weber.

10. Do you agree with the claim of some feminists that religions have been traditionally used to "keep women in their place"?

REFERENCES

Moyne and Coleman Barks, *Open Secret: Versions of Rumi*. Putney, VT: Threshold, 1984.

David Bouchier, *The Feminist Challenge: The Movement for Women's Liberation in Britain and the United States*. London: Macmillan, 1983.

Rudolf Bultmann, *The New Testament and Mythology and Other Basic Writings*. Philadelphia: Augsburg Fortress Publishers, 1984.

John Calvin, Hugh Kerr, editor, Compendium of the Institutes of the Christian *Religion*. Philadelphia: Westminster, 1964. Book II, i.

Declaration of Sentiments and Resolutions, Women's Rights Convention. http://ecssba.rutgers.edu/docs/seneca.html.

Bart D. Ehrman, *Misquoting Jesus: The Story Behind Who Changed the Bible and Why*. San Francisco: HarperOne, 2005.

Bart D. Ehrman, *God's Problem: How the Bible Fails to Answer Our Most Important Question – Why We Suffer*. San Francisco: HarperOne, 2008.

Bart D. Ehrman, *Jesus, Interrupted: Revealing the Hidden Contradictions in the Bible (and Why We Didn't Know About Them)*. San Francisco: HarperOne, 2010.

Mircea Eliade, Rosemary Sheed, translator, *Patterns of Comparative Religion*. Lincoln, NE: University of Nebraska Press, 1996.

Gustavo Gutierrez, *A Theology of Liberation*. Maryknoll, NY: Orbis, 1977.

Philip Jenkins, *Jesus Wars: How Four Patriarchs, Three Queens, and Two Emperors Decided What Christians Would Believe for the Next 1,500 Years*. San Francisco: HarperOne, 2010.

Martin Luther, *On the Jews and Their Lies, 1543*. http://www.humanitas-international.org/showcase/chronography/documents/luther-jews.htm.

Judith Plaskow, *Standing Again at Sinai: Judaism from a Feminist Perspective*. New York: HarperOne, 1991.

Wilfred Cantwell Smith, *The Meaning and End of Religion*. Philadelphia: Fortress Press, 1991.

Tamara Sonn, "Phases of Political Islam," in *Religious Fundamentalism in the Contemporary World: Critical Social and Political Issues*, Santosh C. Saha, editor. New York: Lexington, 2004, 112–113.

Elizabeth Cady Stanton and the Revising Committee, *Women's Bible, The*. http://www.sacred-texts.com/wmn/wb/.

FURTHER READING

Karen Armstrong, *A History of God: The 4,000-Year Quest of Judaism, Christian and Islam*. New York: Ballantine, 1994.

Patricia Crone and Michael Cook. *Hagarism: The Making of the Islamic World*. Cambridge: Cambridge University Press, 1977.

Hamid Dabash, *Islamic Liberation Theology: Resisting the Empire*. London: Routledge, 2008.

Marc H. Ellis, *Toward a Jewish Theology of Liberation: The Challenge of the 21st Century*. Waco, TX: Baylor University Press, 3rd ed., 2004.

Farid Esack, *On Being a Muslim: Finding a Religious Path in the World Today*. Oxford: Oneworld, 2009.

Farid Esack, *Qur'an, Liberation and Pluralism*. Oxford: Oneworld, 1997.

John L. Esposito, *Islam: The Straight Path*. New York: Oxford University Press, 3rd ed., 2004.

Diarmaid MacCulloch, *Christianity: The First Three Thousand Years*. New York: Viking, 2010.

Jack Miles, *God: A Biography*. New York: Vintage, 1996.

Lisa Miller, *Heaven: Our Enduring Fascination with the Afterlife*. New York: Harper/HarperCollins, 2010.

Jacob Neusner, *Judaism: The Basics*. London: Routledge, 2006.

Jacob Neusner and Tamara Sonn, *Comparing Religions through Law: Judaism and Islam*. London: Routledge, 1999.

Elaine Pagels, *The Gnostic Gospels*. New York: Random House, 2004.

Judith Plaskow, Donna Berman, editor, *The Coming of Lilith: Essays on Feminism, Judaism, and Sexual Ethics, 1972–2003*. Boston: Beacon, 2005.

Judith Plaskow, *Sex, Sin, and Grace: Women's Experience and the Theologies of Reinhold Niebuhr and Paul Tillich*. Lanham, MD: University Press of America, 1979.

Judith Plaskow, *Standing Again at Sinai: Judaism from a Feminist Perspective*. San Francisco: HarperOne, 1991.

Judith Plaskow and Carol Christ, editors, *Womanspirit Rising: A Feminist Reader in Religion*. San Francisco: HarperOne, 1992.

Rosemary Radford Ruether, *Sexism and God-Talk*. Boston: Beacon, 1993.

Amina Wadud, *Qur'an and Woman: Rereading the Sacred Text from a Woman's Perspective*. Oxford: Oxford University Press, 1999.

330 MILLION GODS – OR NONE

Two Traditions from India

"*I imagine serenity's pretty much the same, one season to the next?*"

FIGURE 7.1 © Donald Reilly 1997/The New Yorker Collection/www.cartoonbank.com.

Lead me from the unreal to the Real.
Lead me from darkness unto Light.
BRIHADARANYAKA UPANISHAD

7

Overview

As we turn from Judaism, Christianity, and Islam to the Indian traditions of Hinduism and Buddhism, we find some major differences.

- Indian traditions were started and developed by human beings, without divine intervention.
  - ○ Their scriptures record the wisdom of brilliant human beings who were able to perceive the nature of reality, rather than the word of a god transmitted through messengers.
  - ○ As a result, there are more and less traditional approaches to Hinduism and Buddhism, but there is no orthodoxy.
- Indian traditions are primarily concerned with understanding and living in accordance with the laws of the universe, rather than obeying the laws of a god and achieving salvation.
  - ○ Evil results from incorrect understanding of the nature of reality, rather than displeasing God.
  - ○ Justice is built into the universe itself, rather than imposed by God.
    - Good actions naturally lead to benefits and bad actions lead to harm.
    - The principle of natural justice of the universe is called karma.

Hinduism and Buddhism

Hinduism
   History and Teachings of Hinduism
   Hinduism Today
   Rituals

Buddhism
   History and Teachings of Buddhism
   Buddhism Today
   Rituals

**Conclusion: Religious Studies
   and Indian Traditions**

- Indian traditions do not take ordinary experience at face value, but see it as **maya**, illusory.
  - Ordinary experience is often compared to dreaming, and a major goal in Hinduism and Buddhism is enlightenment, waking up to the true nature of reality.
  - This correct understanding, or "waking up," is true happiness.
- The ways to achieve correct understanding are many.
  - One's spiritual path may involve devotion to a god, but it need not.
  - There are many gods in Eastern traditions. Some people believe in one ultimate God; some believe in many gods; some believe in no gods.
  - Indian traditions generally do not think of the gods and goddesses as ruling the universe by giving people commands.
  - Supernatural beings are more like patron saints in Christianity, sources of aid and comfort.
- Hindus and Buddhists both believe in reincarnation, and believe that karma works itself out through many lifetimes rather than just one.
  - Individuals are born over and over again, into lifetime after lifetime, until they escape the cycle of rebirth by "waking up."
  - Gods and teachers may guide people in their efforts, but they do not "redeem" or "save" them. Ultimately, people's karma is their own.

Despite these differences, scholars see some similarities between Indian traditions and Western monotheisms. However, the application of some Religious Studies categories and methods have been rejected by some members of Indian traditions.

Hinduism and Buddhism

As we said in Chapter 1, "Hinduism" is not the name of one tradition, but a term used to lump together hundreds of traditions that originated in India. Buddhism is somewhat more unified, but from an early stage it had diverse traditions too. There is a huge range of acceptable beliefs in both Hinduism and Buddhism – including idealism (minds and ideas are the only reality), materialism (only material things are real), monotheism, polytheism, pantheism (all things are divine), and atheism. While there have been sectarian clashes over power, caused by specific historic developments, India has generally been known for its religious pluralism.

Indian traditions share a number of commonalities – among them, their ideas about time. In the West, time is thought of as linear, like the flight of an arrow. It has a beginning, a middle, and an end, and goes in one direction only. Time began when God created the world. Time "moves" from past to future, with each event occurring just once. And at some determinate moment in the future, God will bring time and the world to an end. Each person is born physically into earthly life just once, lives for a period of time ranging from minutes to decades, and dies just once, to then be judged.

In the Indian worldview, by contrast, time is cyclic, like the seasons of the year, only with much larger cycles. Western scientists estimate that the universe is 14.5 billion years old. But in Indian thought, the universe has been created and destroyed countless times, with each cycle of creation and destruction lasting much longer than 14.5 billion years. The cycles of creation and destruction are counted as the days and nights of a creator god, **Brahma**. He is a minor god, not to be confused with **Brahman**, Ultimate Reality. A Brahma day is 4,320 million earthly years; a year of Brahma's time equals 3,110,400 million years. And Brahma lives for 100 years. So the whole cycle of Brahma's lifetime is 311,040,000 million years – 311 trillion years. At the end of the cycle, the universe is inhaled into the body of the gods **Vishnu** or **Shiva**, and it stays there until another Brahma develops to start the whole process over again. In Indian thought, in other words, the universe and time had no determinate beginning and have no foreseeable end.

Each of us, too, had no beginning. We have been reborn – "reincarnated" – countless times, not just as human beings, but perhaps also as animals. And we shall probably be reborn countless times in the future, until we develop sufficient awareness to escape the cycle of rebirth. This notion of reincarnation is another major difference between Western traditions and those that came out of India. In Judaism, Christianity, and Islam, life after death happens just once and is something to look forward to (assuming one has lived according to the divine commands). Many Christians and Muslims see living in heaven as the ultimate goal of human life. However, in Hinduism and Buddhism being reincarnated is thought of negatively because it means that you have not reached the goal of human life. Your next life might be as a lowly peasant, for example, or even as an animal, because you acted badly in this life. For Hindus and Buddhists, the goal of life is to *not* be reborn, but rather to escape reincarnation.

Hinduism

The word "Hinduism" is fairly new, and rather imprecise. It covers hundreds of millions of people with amazingly diverse beliefs, moral systems, and rituals. Some "Hindus" are monotheists, some are polytheists, and some are atheists. Some are vegetarian pacifists who refuse to harm any living thing; others fight wars and practice animal sacrifice. It is better to think of Hinduism as a family of traditions rather than as a single religion.

Before the British took over India in the 1700s, few people in India identified themselves as "Hindus." Today, there are large sections of the population who do identify themselves as Hindus, but some Indians resent the term. The word is derived from "Sindhu," an ancient Sanskrit word for the Indus River. When Muslims entered India, they called the people living east of the Indus River "Hindu." Then when the British made India into a colony, they used the word as a convenient label for all the Indians who were not Muslims (or members of the few minority religions in India, such as Jews and Christians).

India today has over a thousand languages written in twenty-four different scripts. Its rituals show a similar diversity. Even when people celebrate a festival under one name at one time, they may have different practices and reasons for performing them. **Navaratri**, for example, is the festival of Nine Nights. In southeastern India, it is mostly

FIGURE 7.2 Men conduct ritual for Durga, who is worshipped during Navaratri. Louise Batalla Duran/Alamy.

a festival for women, who create colorful scenes with dolls representing deities such as Lakshmi and **Sarasvati**. In northwestern India during Navaratri, people light a sacred lamp and do a dance with sticks, like the dance the god **Krishna** did with cowherd girls. For Navaratri in the north Indian town of Ramnagar, young boys reenact events from the **Ramayana**, the epic story about Rama, an avatar ("manifestation") of the god Vishnu. For some Indians, the last two days of Navaratri are for honoring machines: they put garlands of flowers on cars and buses, and bless their computers with special powders.

Amid all this diversity, as we said, Indians have a long tradition of tolerance. There are many paths, they say. What determines whether a particular path is acceptable is not that it conforms with a set of beliefs or doctrines, but that it is effective in helping people live in accordance with the laws of the universe. If your path works for you and mine works for me, then everything is as it should be.

History and Teachings of Hinduism

Unlike Western religions, the family of traditions called Hinduism has no single founder or datable beginning. It developed amid a wave of migrations from Central Asia into India, which brought new influences to one of the oldest civilizations in the world.

Indus Valley Civilization (3000–1500 BCE)

In Pakistan and northwest India, archaeologists have found remnants of a culture that started about five thousand years ago. It stretched across much of Northwestern India (now Pakistan) and had several cities. Some were highly developed and carefully planned, such as Mohenjo-daro and Harappa. Each of these cities was laid out on a grid and had an artificial hill with large buildings on top, which may have been religious or political centers. Mohenjo-daro had a pool on the hill, 17 meters by 7 meters by 3 meters deep, that may have been for ritual bathing. The larger houses in these cities had sewers, plumbing, and even bathrooms on the second floor. Scholars have not yet deciphered their language and do not know for sure what their culture may have been like, but archaeologists have found female figurines and carved stone phalluses (representations of penises) that may have been connected with fertility rituals.

The Aryans and the Vedas (1500–600 BCE)

Between 2000 and 1500 BCE, warrior tribes in central Asia began migrating, some into Europe, and some south and east to settle near Iran. Of the second group, some then moved southeast into what is now Pakistan, and northwest India. They conquered the local peoples, intermarried with them, and ruled over them. They called themselves **Aryans** – "Noble Ones" – and their language was ancient Sanskrit. That language is still used in India today, but for formal purposes only – in rituals, debate, and writing.

The Aryans appear to have had the three social classes common to ancient civilizations (see Chapter 5) – priests, warriors, and peasants. Predictably as well, their rituals included sacrifice to gods. The sacrifices "fed" the gods, so that the gods would make people healthy and prosperous. They offered their gods animals, milk, **ghee** (clarified butter), and honey. Many rituals also involved the making, offering, and drinking of **soma**, a beverage brewed from herbs with stimulant (or perhaps hallucinogenic) effects and considered sacred. The use of stimulants and hallucinogens is another feature common to a number of ancient traditions, although their precise nature and the purpose of their use are difficult to determine from the little evidence found to date.

Over time, the rituals became more complex and the priests, called **brahmins**, insisted that they had to be performed exactly correctly. Some rituals lasted several days and required over a dozen priests. So the brahmins became technical specialists in the proper performance of ritual. Indeed, being the custodians of the sacrifices gave the brahmins great authority, since correct performance of the sacrifices was considered essential to maintaining rita, the order of the universe.

Soma
Hallucinogen or Entheogen?

Soma is mentioned in ancient Indian texts as an energizing drink. It is also mentioned in Zoroastrian scripture (see Chapter 9), where it is called hoama. In the related ancient languages of India and Persia, the terms mean the same thing: something "pressed out" or expressed from the stalks of a plant.

In both the Indian and Persian traditions, soma/hoama is described as a plant and juice from a plant, as well as a god. In Indian texts, the juice is consumed by gods and by human beings, whom it makes feel like gods – perhaps a reference to what we today call a "religious experience."

The nature of the experience induced by consuming soma is difficult to determine. Some texts make it sound as if it produced visions or hallucinations: "We have drunk Soma and become immortal; we have attained the light, the gods discovered." (Rig Veda 9.48.3) In other texts it is described as having curative powers, and as something consumed before battle to give enhanced strength or endurance.

It is probable that the effect of soma varied with the strength of the product being used and the metabolism of the person using it, leading to a range of descriptions from mild stimulant to hallucinogen.

Today many scholars identify the source of soma as ephedra, a shrub that grows in North and South America, Europe, Africa, Central and South Asia. It is used as a stimulant and decongestant throughout these regions, where it is sometimes called medicinal and sometimes inspirational. Until it was banned by the U.S. Food and Drug Administration in 2004, ephedra was used in energy drinks marketed largely to college students, dieters, and athletes.

However, the use of drugs to facilitate spiritual experiences is not uncommon in the world's religions. In fact, it is so common that scholars have coined a word for it: **entheogen** – meaning, literally, something that generates "god within." Entheogens are described as psychoactive substances – substances that produce changes in consciousness, perception or awareness, cognition or thinking, mood, or behavior – that people interpret as metaphysical, spiritual, or even supernatural. Evidence of the use of peyote (a cactus that produces mescaline) for both medicinal and spiritual purposes by Native Americans has been documented from as early as the 4th century BCE. (It is still legal for a particular group who call themselves Native American Religion, although peyote is a controlled substance for others in the U.S. and Canada.) Ancient Greek and Mesopotamian myths refer to flowers – perhaps poppies – being consumed, as well as wine, and perhaps mushrooms – all of which can produce states of altered consciousness and are therefore potential entheogens. Quests for plants that give eternal youth or immortality, common in ancient stories, may have been variants on this theme, reflecting awareness that some substances at least make people feel immortal. Perhaps the tree that Adam and Eve were not supposed to eat from was an entheogen. Some scholars even argue about whether Jesus' healing miracles could be attributed to the use of psychoactive drugs.

For conducting and understanding the rituals, the brahmins used four kinds of composition dating from between 1500 and 600 BCE. Together they are called the Vedas, from the Sanskrit root *vid*, meaning "to know." (*Vid* is the source of our words "video," "vision," "wit," and "wise.") The Rig Veda consists of hymns to the gods; the Yajur and Sama Vedas are ritual formulas, and the Atharva Veda is mainly practical information regarding healing and other important tasks. The Vedas are traditionally ascribed to ancient "seers," called rishis, who "heard" or "perceived" them. That is, the knowledge they convey is not thought to be "revealed" in the way that Western scriptures are. Instead, the Rishis had extraordinary abilities to understand Reality, to "see" it as it truly is, and to convey that information in language.

The oldest of the four Vedas – the Rig – contains 1,028 hymns to various gods. Indra, the god of war and weather, is the most frequently praised, but there seems to be no hierarchy among the gods. Agni, the god of fire, is the second most often praised. Many of the deities are described in diverse ways. Soma is sometimes identified as the moon, for example, and sometimes as a sacred hallucinogenic beverage. The goddess Sarasvati is worshipped sometimes as a river and sometimes as the one who inspires people with noble thoughts. In later centuries, she would be the goddess of learning and the arts. Aditi is identified with light or the mind, and in some passages is called mother of the gods. Scholars see this diversity as evidence of the ancient origins of the tradition as well as of the multiple groups contributing to its development. Just as we saw with the Hebrew Bible (Chapter 6), not only do ancient traditions change over time, but different groups often have different names for a particular god, and varying ideas about that god's characteristics and "job description."

The four Vedas continue to be the most sacred scriptures in Hinduism. The highest praise you can give to a text is to call it the "the Fifth Veda." The brahmins say, in fact, that the vedas were not created but are eternal, not because they are of divine origin, as is said of the Bible and the Qur'an, but because the wisdom they convey is so profound and accurate a reflection of Reality.

However, the Vedas are not the only source of wisdom in the traditions that came to be called Hinduism. The Vedas were memorized and passed on orally by the brahmins for centuries. When the use of writing developed, the Vedas were written down, perhaps by 100 BCE. Around the same time, other forms of wisdom were developing – in particular, the Upanishads.

The Mystical Worldview of the Upanishads

The Upanishads are a series of treatises that are among the most influential in Hindu literature. Although Upanishads continued to be produced for perhaps a millennium and scholars are unsure of exactly how many there are (somewhere between 100 and 300), we know that the earliest was composed around 600 BCE, a time of intellectual and cultural questioning in India and elsewhere. In Greece, Western philosophy was beginning to develop. The period also produced Siddhartha Gautama, who began life in the Vedic tradition but then launched Buddhism. As we shall see, people like Gautama were unhappy with the emphasis on sacrifice in India and with the great power wielded by the brahmins.

The Upanishads do not reject the Vedas, but provide a radical new interpretation of them. That new interpretation not only downplays sacrifice and the gods, but presents significant teachings about the nature of the self, of knowledge, and of reality itself.

Presented in the form of conversations, many of the Upanishads focus on the search for a deeper truth than that reflected in the rituals of the brahmins. As the quote at the beginning of this chapter says, "Lead me from the unreal to the Real. Lead me from darkness unto Light."

At the core of the Upanishads is the idea that there is a profound unity to all existence, despite the apparent diversity we experience in our daily lives. The person seeking truth in the Mundaka Upanishad asks "What is it that, when it is known, everything else becomes known?" The Chandogya Upanishad tells of a brahmin father whose son came home from studying the Vedas in a forest school, proud of what he had learned. The father tells the boy that he must look beyond conventional religious knowledge. While it looks as if there are many things in the world, he says, there is really only one reality, one Existence or Being. And all things in the universe are this one ultimate Being. In the beginning, this one Being had the thought, "Let me grow forth." And so it projected the universe out of itself. Having projected everything out of itself, it is the stuff of which all things are made.

The essence of all things is the same, then; just as all rivers flow into one sea, so all the apparently separate things in our experience are really one. The name of this Ultimate Reality is Brahman. It is utterly simple and without beginning or end. It is what everything exists in, but itself it is uncreated and changeless.

> You are the fire,
> You are the sun,
> You are the air,
> You are the moon,
> You are the starry skies.
> You are Brahman Supreme:
> You are the waters – you,
> The creator of all….
> You are the dark butterfly,
> You are the green parrot with red eyes,
> You are the thundercloud, the seasons, the seas.
> Without beginning are you,
> Beyond time,
> Beyond space.
> (Shvetashvatara Upanishad IV-2-4)

The claim that everything is one is amazing enough but, as the dialogue above between father and son continues, the father adds something more astounding. He says, "That is you." This claim – in Sanskrit, *tat tvam asi* (from the Chandyoga Upanishad VI-8-7) – is considered one of the grand pronouncements of what will be called Vedanta ("the end of the Vedas"), the most important philosophical tradition in Hinduism. The idea follows naturally from the idea that all is one. If all is one, then there is no difference between the subject of experience and the object of experience. The Ultimate Reality Brahman is identical with Atman, consciousness, the self.

Mysticism and Monism

The idea that everything is ultimately one is not unique to India. Known as **monism** to scholars, this idea is found in religious traditions around the world, including Judaism, Christianity, and Islam. It is part of a worldview called **mysticism**. This worldview stems from experiences in which the ordinary distinctions between things fade away, and what is left is a powerful sense that All is One. Usually we think that there are many things spread out in space and in time. We commonly think that the mind is different from the body, and that the person who experiences something is different from what she experiences. But in mystical experience, time and space and the difference between subject and object disappear.

There are many ways to induce this experience of the oneness of everything. Meditation, along with special breathing techniques and other physical disciplines are sometimes used. Rhythmic chanting and music are some of the oldest techniques. Many mystics seem to take up music because it helps them get into a mood in which the ordinary boundaries between things dissolve.

Of course, it is perfectly possible to interpret the special experience of the oneness of all existence as the illusion, and the vast diversity of everyday experience as the reality. However, as William James pointed out (see Chapter 4), mystics typically experience cosmic unity with such intensity that it seems more real than ordinary experience. They feel they have experienced Truth.

The most common method for experiencing the oneness of Atman and Brahman, and realizing that consciousness is Ultimate Reality, is meditation. By quieting the noise that usually surrounds us, and emptying the mind of thoughts about this or that thing, it is possible to achieve a state of undisturbed consciousness in which we feel at one with Ultimate Reality. In Upanishadic terms, it is possible to experience the oneness of Atman and Brahman.

To express the oneness of the universe, Indians use the sound **Om**, *a-u-m*, in meditation and prayer. Om is said at the beginning and end of Hindu prayers. It is the most sacred sound in all Hindu traditions, and is written in temples, on doors and walls, and even on trucks. It is not considered a name as such, nor is it definable. Its verbal meaning is "to express loudly [in sound]," with the connotation that such expression is in praise. As we have seen with other terms for the Infinite, the term is best understood as reference to a reality that can be experienced, but not captured in language. The Mandukya Upanishad explains the unity of everything using this term:

Om is eternal Existence, Consciousness and Bliss. This entire universe, including our body, mind and senses, is its manifestation, extension and expansion. Past, present and future all are nothing but Om. This was true in the past, it is true in the present and will be true in the future. And whatever else exists beyond the three divisions of time, that also is indeed Om. What is the essence of Om? It is the eternal vibration of awareness.

The idea that Brahman, Ultimate Reality, is eternal and is the same as the Self implies that the Self is eternal. As the Katha Upanishad puts it,

The Self, whose symbol is Om, is the omniscient Lord. He is not born. He does not die. He is neither cause nor effect. The Ancient One is unborn, imperishable, eternal: though the body be destroyed, he is not killed.

This teaching is linked to two more new ideas in the Upanishads – reincarnation and karma – and it has deep implications for human life and happiness. Since the Self cannot be destroyed, what we call death is only the destruction of the body, which is a mere vehicle of the real Self. The Self survives, to be reborn in another body. What kind of body that is depends on its previous life. If the person lived a good life, then the Self will be reborn as a higher kind of human being. If the person lived a bad life, then the Self will be reborn into a lower state, as a person of lower social standing or perhaps even as an animal. All this happens automatically because of karma – as we saw in Chapter 2, the law of cause and effect that constitutes the natural justice of the universe. Good actions lead to good consequences and bad actions lead to bad consequences.

So, then, what constitutes good actions or a good life? And what happens when people manage to achieve it? Does the cycle of rebirths go on forever? The Upanishads teach that the ultimate goal of life is actually to escape or "be released from" samsara, the cycle of rebirths. This release from rebirth is called moksha, and the way to achieve it is to recognize the illusory nature of the material world and realize that one's true nature is indeed Brahman. To recognize one's true self (Atman) and its identity with Brahman, each person must become free of attachment to material things.

Classical Hinduism (3rd century BCE–7th century CE)

The profound wisdom expressed in the Upanishads has remained central to Hindu thought. However, on the level of practice, people were more concerned with how to deal with the struggles of daily life, while still moving toward correct awareness and detachment from the material world. And so examples of exemplary lives became widely popular. These examples are provided in the texts of the classical age of what we now call Hinduism. These texts reflect both ancient Vedic teachings about the gods and Upanishadic philosophy.

The major texts of this period were two great epics – the Ramayana and the Mahabharata, some stories about the gods called the Puranas, and moral and legal codes called the Laws of Manu.

THE RAMAYANA The first of the great epics was the Ramayana, about King Rama and his wife Sita. Ravana, the evil ten-headed king of Lanka, abducted Sita and tried to force her to

FIGURE 7.3 Arjuna and Krishna. © Frédéric Soltan/Corbis.

marry him. But Rama, with the help of Hanuman, a monkey descended from gods, rescued her with his monkey army. Rama ruled as an ideal king, with Sita as his ideal wife. This story became so popular that temples to Rama and Sita were built across India, and eventually Rama was said to be an incarnation of the great god Vishnu.

THE MAHABHARATA The second great Hindu epic is the Mahabharata. With 74,000 verses, it is the longest poem in the world. The story has been sung and danced and acted thousands of times. In the late 1980s, Indian television broadcast 94 episodes of the story, which drew huge audiences. When the series was shown on BBC television in the U.K., it drew 5,000,000 viewers, an audience unheard of for a program shown in the afternoon.

The Mahabharata revolves around a great (*maha*) struggle between two sets of cousins who were descended from King Bharata. The story favors the Pandava family, whom the other family, the Kauravas, try to cheat out of their share of the kingdom. The conflict leads to a war in which the Pandava warrior Arjuna is guided by his charioteer, Krishna, who is the god Vishnu in human form.

Before the fighting starts, Arjuna asks Krishna whether he should take part in a war that will slaughter many of his own relatives. Krishna answers that it is a duty to fight for what is right when there is no non-violent alternative, and that when one's motivation is altruistic (pure) rather than selfish the violence will not result in negative karma. So the negative effects of the violence will not attach themselves to his soul, dooming him to further rounds of reincarnation. The word for doing "what is right" and "one's duty" is thus the same: dharma. Arjuna and Krishna's discussion takes up 18 chapters of the Mahabharata. These

18 chapters are called the **Bhagavad Gita**. Combining an engaging story with philosophy and moral teaching, it is among the most beloved of Hindu scriptures.

As Krishna and Arjuna get into their conversation about the war, many other topics come up, such as the nature of the Self and the nature of the gods. Krishna reaffirms the eternity and indestructibility of the Self, and adds another new idea. He says that the Ultimate Reality underlying everything is a personal god who loves human beings and becomes human himself to help them. Krishna, an avatar (manifestation) of Vishnu, says

> I am the universal father,
> mother, granter of all, grandfather,
> object of knowledge, purifier,
> holy syllable om, threefold sacred lore.
>
> I am the way, sustainer, lord,
> witness, shelter, refuge, friend,
> source, dissolution, stability,
> treasure, and unchanging seed….
>
> When devoted men sacrifice
> to other deities with faith,
> they sacrifice to me, Arjuna,
> however aberrant the rites….
>
> The leaf or flower or fruit or water
> that he offers with devotion,
> I take from the man of self-restraint
> in response to his devotion.
>
> Whatever you do – what you take,
> what you offer, what you give,
> what penances you perform –
> do as an offering to me, Arjuna….
>
> Keep me in your mind and devotion,
> sacrifice to me, bow to me,
> discipline your self toward me,
> and you will reach me! (9:17–28)

In the Upanishads, as we saw, the Ultimate Reality is Brahman, which is not a person. However, in the Bhagavad Gita, Ultimate Reality is a person – the god Krishna – and not only is Krishna a person, but he appears to help Arjuna in his time of need. By implication, Krishna cares about all human beings and is willing to help them. Therefore, the Bhagavad Gita provides a new way to understand reality. Rather than focusing on Brahman, an esoteric metaphysical principle, the Gita focuses on a personal, loving god who befriends human beings and even becomes one himself. This idea of a loving God becoming human to help people is similar to the Christian teaching that God became a man in Jesus to redeem

Hatha Yoga

FIGURE 7.4 Woman bending backwards – hatha yoga.
Mehmet Dilsiz/Shutterstock Images.

Today in Western societies, when most people hear the word *yoga*, they think of **hatha yoga**, a discipline that combines bodily movements and postures with conscious breathing. This system was developed by Hindu yogis, holy men, as a way to prepare the body for long periods of meditation. It is part of jnana yoga, the yoga of knowledge, which fosters the realization that the Atman, the true Self, is identical with Brahman, Ultimate Reality. Hindus and non-Hindus who practice hatha yoga find that it has other benefits too, such as relaxation, reduction of stress, increased strength and flexibility, and better blood circulation.

In this passage from the Shvetashvatara Upanishad, translated by Max Müller (see Chapter 3), the physical discipline of hatha yoga is linked with meditation:

Holding his body steady with the head, neck and torso erect,
And causing the senses with the mind to enter the heart,
A wise man with the Brahma-boat will cross over
All the fear-bringing streams.
Compressing his breathings here in the body, and having his movements checked,
One should breathe through his nostrils with diminished breath.
Like that chariot yoked with vicious horses,
His mind the wise man should restrain undistractedly....
When the nature of the self, as with a lamp,
A practicer of Yoga beholds here the nature of Brahma, Unborn, steadfast, from
    every nature free –
By knowing God one is released from all fetters.

FIGURE 7.5 Statue of Sarasvati outside music college in Puttaparthi. Tim Gainey/Alamy.

the world, but according to the Hindu epics God manifests himself in many forms (has many avatars).

In classical Hinduism, as in Christianity, too, God not only loves human beings but wants devotion and love from them in return. This love of and devotion toward God is called **bhakti**, and it is one of three **margas** – "paths" or "ways of life" – described in the Bhagavad Gita. Each marga is also described as a **yoga**, a religious discipline. The way of devotion, bhakti yoga, gets the most attention in the Bhagavad Gita, and it became the most popular tradition in India, as it still is. When people surrender themselves to God in love, they drop their ordinary selfishness and live better lives. Indeed, the Bhagavad Gita says that such full loving devotion will make up for any bad karma. "Letting go all dharma, take refuge in me alone," Krishna says. "I shall deliver you from all sins; do not grieve." (18:66)

The second marga or way of life is jnana yoga, the way of knowledge. This consists largely of meditation and study of the scriptures. Like bhakti yoga, jnana yoga can counterbalance a person's bad karma. Just as fire turns wood to ashes, Krishna says, so the fire of knowledge destroys bad karma.

The third marga, karma yoga, is the way of action. It is based on not just any action, but unselfish action. One is acting not to gain a reward but simply to carry out one's dharma, one's duty. Different people have different dharmas based on their social status and their karma.

THE PURANAS The Puranas are stories about the gods, dating from 300 BCE–1000 CE, when Hinduism was spreading across India and incorporating the gods of many peoples. In the Puranas some of the older gods of the Vedas, such as Indra and Varuna, are ignored. Other older deities are given new roles. The goddess Sarasvati, for example, becomes the patron of learning and the arts.

Three deities that were unimportant in the Vedas become central in the Puranas, and in classical Hinduism – the gods Vishnu and Shiva, and the goddess Devi.

Vishnu is a god who works for righteousness. When dharma declines, he manifests himself to help the human race get back on track. One of the Puranas describes two dozen avatars of Vishnu, but ten is a more standard number. The most famous is Krishna, the charioteer of Arjuna in the Bhagavad Gita. Another is Rama in the Mahabaharta. The Buddha, founder of a tradition that split off from Hinduism, is a third avatar of Vishnu. In the future, Hindus say, Vishnu will appear again as Kalki, a Messiah-like figure who will destroy evil and restore moral order.

Most Hindus today, as we said, follow the path of devotion to a god, and many are devoted to Vishnu. They are called Vaishnavas.

The second major god in the Puranas and in classical Hinduism is Shiva, a god quite different from Vishnu. He has pairs of opposed features; he is creator and destroyer, he is helpful and threatening. There are three main images of Shiva. The first is as creative power. Here Shiva is represented by a lingam, a shaft that some scholars describe as an erect penis symbolizing the creative power of sex, set in a yoni, a term meaning the origin of life and represented as a vagina. Other scholars interpret the lingam as representing a sort of mini-temple.

Another image of Shiva is as Lord of the Dance. It is by dancing that Shiva creates the universe and later, when it is beyond repair, destroys it.

The third way Shiva is represented is as a wandering ascetic – someone who has renounced worldly possessions and pleasures – similar to today's sadhus, wandering holy men.

Hindus who are devoted mainly to Shiva are called Shaivites or Shaivas. Worshippers (or "devotees") of Shiva and worshippers of Vishnu can be distinguished by the designs painted on their foreheads.

Shaivites paint horizontal bands across their foreheads for ritual purposes, while Vaishnavites paint vertical lines on theirs.

Along with worship of Vishnu and Shiva, the other most popular form of devotion is to the Goddess, whose most universal name is Devi. While there are several names and

FIGURE 7.6 Shiva as Lord of the Dance.
© Paul Prescott/iStockphoto.

FIGURE 7.7 Shaivite with marks on
forehead. Stuart Forster/Alamy.

FIGURE 7.8 Vaishnavite with marks on forehead. © imagebroker.net/SuperStock.

descriptions of goddesses in the Puranas, for many Hindus they are all forms of one great Goddess. Some of the Puranas describe her as the wife of Shiva and as his **Shakti**, his power. Other texts treat her as the supreme divinity who created the universe, the ultimate mother. When she is portrayed as loving toward humans, the Goddess may be called **Parvati**. When she is seen as the destroyer of evil, she may be called **Kali**, a frightening figure who wears a necklace of human skulls. As a fighter, she is called **Durga**.

THE LAWS OF MANU   By 200 CE a set of legal and moral codes had been created that formalized traditional Indian social practices into sets of four: the Four Varnas (social classes), the Four Ends of Man, and the Four Stages of Life.

As we have seen, at the top of the Four Varnas are the brahmins, the elite priestly class who perform rituals and study the scriptures. Second are the kshatriyas, the warrior ruling class. Third are the vaishyas, merchants who also do farming and cowherding. The kshatriyas and the vaishyas may study the Vedas but not teach about them. The fourth varna is the shudras, the peasants. Unlike those above them, they are not allowed to study the Vedas or to build up wealth.

The varnas are not the same as the **castes** of Indian society, although the two systems are related. The varnas are scripturally validated; in fact, as we saw in Chapter 2, the Rig Veda describes how they were created through the sacrifice of the cosmic man, Purusha. From his

FIGURE 7.9 Dalits, Untouchables, at an anti-government rally, 2006. Raveendran/AFP/ Getty Images.

mouth came the brahmins, from his arms came the kshatriyas, from his thighs came the vaishyas, and from his feet came the shudras. The castes are called jati, and they are not religiously sanctioned. They reflect an individual's identification with a particular extended family and community, locale, and livelihood. Like the varnas, one is born into the jati, and mixing with those of other jati is traditionally prohibited. But unlike the varnas, the jati are receding into history as India modernizes, industrializes, and urbanizes. The caste system has actually been outlawed in modern India, although remnants of it survive.

Below all of these varnas and jati are dalits, the Untouchables. They are outside the caste system, outcastes. They must do the jobs that are too defiling for others to do, such as handling corpses, hauling garbage, and cleaning toilets. Most live in poverty. They are considered to be in a permanent state of impurity, so other Hindus are not supposed to touch them or eat with them. They must even drink from separate wells. Mahatma Gandhi, the great leader of modern India, called them harijans, children of God, and worked to eliminate the caste system which held them at the bottom of society. He made friends with Untouchables and ate with them. Nonetheless, the dalits – some 20% of the population – are still the poorest people in India.

The Laws of Manu thus authorize a strict social hierarchy. It is divided not only by social class but also by gender. Even women from the upper classes are considered servants of men. According to Manu, girls and women should not act on their own. "Nothing must be done independently by a girl, by a young woman, or by an old woman, even in her own house. As a girl, a female must submit to her father, as a young woman, to her husband, and when her

FIGURE 7.10 Carvings on the outside of Khajuraho temple.
© Prisma/SuperStock.

lord is dead, to her sons. A woman must never be independent." (*Manu* 5.137–148) Another rule is that wives owe their husbands total devotion. "Though he lacks virtue, and is unfaithful to his wife, and has not good qualities, a husband must be constantly worshipped as a god by a faithful wife." (*Manu* 5.154)

The Laws of Manu also describe the Four Ends of Man. These are the four main goals people pursue. The first is **kama** – pleasure. The second is **artha** – wealth, success, and power. Third is dharma – righteousness or duty. And the fourth is moksha – liberation from the cycle of death and rebirth. These four goals are not ranked; the Laws of Manu simply describe how different people follow different goals.

In Indian tradition, the pursuit of pleasure is not discouraged. One of the scriptures is the **Kama Sutra**, about kama, pleasure, and it gives advice about increasing sexual pleasure. Some Hindu temples, too, have statues of figures in various sexual positions – see Figure 7.10.

The last set of four in the Laws of Manu is the Four Stages of Life. These are presented not only from a male perspective, but from an upper-class male perspective. The first stage is that of Student, a time when young men are expected to pursue their studies full-time and not work. They are also expected to be celibate. The second stage is the Householder. Here the man marries and raises a family. Most people in traditional Indian culture have not gone beyond these two stages.

The third stage of life, that of the Forest Dweller, occurs at about the age when people retire today. Here the man turns over most of the duties of running the household to someone younger and spends more time in contemplative activities. The fourth stage involves a complete break with what has gone before. It is that of the **sannyasi**, or Renunciant. The man stops all work, gives away his possessions, and holds a funeral for the man he was. He moves to a retreat to pursue meditation and enlightenment full time.

Hinduism Today

In describing classical Hinduism, we have switched between the past tense and the present tense, mentioning events from two thousand years ago and then commenting on the beliefs and practices of Hindus today. That is because most of the basic ideas and practices found in the 7th century have continued to be represented in Hinduism in the present, in one form or another. Philosophers after this created various schools of Hindu thought, and reformers changed some practices, but most of the ideas and practices of classical Hinduism are alive and well somewhere in India today.

Rituals

A good way to get a feel for contemporary Hinduism is to look at its rituals. The general term for a Hindu ritual is **puja**, the act of showing reverence to a deity through prayers, songs, and offerings. Pujas are conducted both in the home and at temples.

Many homes have a room or part of a room set aside for worship, with pictures or statues of the family's special deity or deities. Worshippers welcome the deity as an honored guest, anoint it with ghee (clarified butter), and offer him or her flowers and food. They may also light oil lamps and burn incense.

Worship is also conducted in temples. An ideal temple is located near a body of water. At the center of the temple is a womb-house, where the god or goddess is enshrined. There are not as many organized group prayers in a Hindu temple as in a synagogue, a mosque, or a church. Instead most people come to the temple to see the god or goddess, and to be seen by them. This is called **darshana**.

When a Brahmin priest does conduct a formal ritual, he offers food or flowers to the deity and then gives some back to the people as a gift from the deity. Worshippers may even go to the temple kitchen to buy food that has been offered to the deity and is now a token of the deity's grace. This consecrated food is called **prasada**.

Temples are supported financially by donors. The most visited temple in India, Tirupati Balaji, draws thousands of visitors a day.

FIGURE 7.11 Students celebrating Holi. © Jayanta Shaw/Reuters/Corbis.

Besides rituals in the home and in temples, Hinduism has many seasonal festivals. **Holi**, for example, is a spring festival celebrated with bonfires and with people splashing colored powder and water on each other.

The birthdays of Krishna, Rama, and **Ganesha** are also celebrated.

As in other religions, too, there are rituals to mark important events in individuals' lives. After a child is born, there is a ceremony in which the father prays for the health and happiness of the child. There are also rituals for naming the child, for feeding the child its first solid food, and for the first cutting of its hair. Among the most important is a "rite of passage." At about age eight, a young brahmin boy is initiated into the study of the Vedas. The ceremony involves the chanting of a short **mantra** (sound or word or words that are considered effective in transforming reality, like a prayer in the monotheisms) and a day of begging. Then he is given a sacred thread to wear over his left shoulder, marking him as a brahmin.

Some groups have ceremonies to mark a girl's beginning of menstruation. She wears new clothing with flowers in her hair and is given special foods.

Weddings are major community events. There are many variations in the ceremonies, which can last from half an hour to five days. Traditionally, marriages are arranged by Hindu families. Parents try to match their offspring's mates in social class, age, and looks. When suitable possibilities are found, parents compare their horoscopes, to get compatible personality types and also to see that their horoscopes do not predict that they will have hardships at the same time in life. Today it is common for families to advertise their sons and daughters as eligible in newspapers and online. (To see what the process looks like, try http://www.bharatmatrimony.com.) All these rituals and precautions are good examples of how people's traditions provide rites of passage to mark the milestones in life, as

Mohandas Gandhi (d. 1948) on God, Truth, and Politics

FIGURE 7.12 Mohandas Gandhi.
Dinodia Photos/Getty Images.

Mohandas (Mahatma) Gandhi was the spiritual and political leader of India in its drive for political independence from Britain in the first half of the 20th century. The country officially calls him Father of the Nation, and he is also known simply as Bapu, Father. Gandhi's birthday, October 2, is a national holiday in India. He advocated non-violent civil disobedience to liberate India, an approach that inspired many other leaders, such as Martin Luther King Jr. in the U.S. Trained as a lawyer, Gandhi left many memorable writings and speeches.

What I want to achieve, – what I have been striving and pining to achieve these thirty years, – is self-realization, to see God face to face, to attain Moksha [freedom from birth and death].... All that I do by way of speaking and writing, and all my ventures in the political field, are directed to this same end.... The experiments I am about to relate are... spiritual, or rather moral; for the essence of religion is morality.

...I have given the chapters I propose to write the title of *The Story of My Experiments with Truth*. These will of course include experiments with non-violence, celibacy and other principles of conduct believed to be distinct from truth. But for me, truth is the sovereign principle, which includes numerous other principles. This truth is not only truthfulness in word, but truthfulness in thought also, and not only the relative truth of our conception, but the Absolute Truth, the Eternal Principle, that is God. There are innumerable definitions of God, because His manifestations are innumerable. They overwhelm me with wonder and awe and for a moment stun me. But I worship God as Truth only. I have not yet found Him, but I am seeking after Him…. Often in my progress I have had faint glimpses of the Absolute Truth, God, and daily the conviction is growing upon me that He alone is real and all else is unreal…. The instruments for the quest of truth are as simple as they are difficult…. The seeker after truth should be humbler than the dust. The world crushes the dust under its feet, but the seeker after truth should so humble himself that even the dust could crush him.

Gandhi 1957, Introduction

anthropologists such as Geertz have noted. They also show how they make sense of life by giving people ways to make their future more predictable and so controllable.

Funerals are, of course, the final rite of passage. After the death of a family member, the relatives prepare the body for cremation with ritual cleansing and dressing. Burning the corpse is seen as the ideal way to release the soul (sometimes called the "astral body"). Many believe that the soul will linger as long as the body is visible, so quick cremation is best. The body is carried to the cremation site as prayers are chanted to Yama, the god of death. At the site, the chief mourner, usually the eldest son, takes twigs of holy kusha grass from an ever-burning fire to the funeral pyre, the pile of wood on which the corpse rests. He walks around the pyre counterclockwise – because everything is backwards at the time of death – and then lights the fire. The dead person is now an offering to Agni, the fire. As in the most ancient Vedic times, the fire is seen as an offering to heaven.

When the corpse is almost completely burned, the chief mourner performs the "rite of the skull," using a bamboo stick to crack the skull, thus releasing the soul. After the cremation, the ashes are thrown into a river, ideally the Ganges, and the mourners walk away without looking back. Because corpses are impure, everyone takes a purifying bath after the funeral. The immediate family remains in a state of pollution for a set number of days (10, 11, or 13 in most places), after which close relatives gather for a ceremonial meal. During memorial services, *pindas* (rice balls) are offered to the spirit of the dead person. Some say that the *pindas* provide the dead with a symbolic transitional body.

Buddhism

In much the same way that Islam began as a reform movement within the monotheistic tradition, and Protestantism was a movement to reform Roman Catholicism, Buddhism grew out of Hinduism as a movement that rejected certain features of Vedic religion. Buddhism accepted three important Hindu beliefs: karma, the natural justice of the universe; samsara, the cycle of rebirth; and the goal of moksha, to escape from this cycle.

In Buddhism, the release from rebirth is known as **nirvana**. One who achieves this state is called "awakened." In fact, the title "Buddha" means "awakened."

However, Buddhism rejected two key aspects of Brahmanic teaching (the teaching of the Vedas). It denied that there is a changeless Ultimate Reality, Brahman, and it denied that there is such a thing as one's true "self," Atman.

In addition to his denial of Atman and Brahman, the Buddha also questioned the social structure of Hinduism, especially the dominance of the brahmins, and their complicated sacrificial rituals. The Buddha made no sacrifices, and did not even talk about the gods. His major concern was practical – the nature of suffering and how we can reduce it. The caste system, he said, was not religiously sanctioned, so he accepted people of all social classes as his followers.

Besides the things Buddhism accepted from Hinduism and those it rejected, Buddhism added some things of its own. First, it created a new form of religious social organization, the **sangha**, the community of monks or nuns. Buddhist monasteries were built across Asia, usually with the financial backing of governments. They were not just what in the West would be called religious centers; they were in effect community centers, providing education, banking services, and often free medical care, as well.

The way of life promoted by Buddhism also had some new emphases. Two central virtues were universal compassion, and non-violence.

History and Teachings of Buddhism

Buddhism began in a simple way. One person asked some basic questions about life, and worked out some new answers. That person was Siddhartha Gautama, a kshatriya prince from the border between today's India and Nepal who lived between around 550 and 450 BCE. The questions he asked were: What is suffering? and How should we deal with suffering?

According to tradition, before Siddhartha was born, it was predicted that he would be either a king or a religious figure. At birth, it looked as if he might be headed for religious greatness. (His very long ear lobes were a sign of wisdom and his golden skin indicated serenity.) But his father wanted the boy to follow in his footsteps, so he shielded him from all the problems in life – and, as we saw in Chapter 2, it is the problems of life that often lead people toward religion. So Siddhartha grew up in luxury, knowing nothing of suffering, sickness, or death. When he was 16, his parents arranged a marriage to his cousin, a princess, and he lived comfortably in the palace for years. But when he was in his late 20s, riding in a chariot away from the palace, he saw a man bent with old age. The chariot driver explained that this is what happens when people get old. Then Siddhartha saw a sick man, and his driver explained about illness. Lastly, he saw a group of people grieving in a funeral procession, which troubled him most of all. The charioteer explained that everyone eventually dies.

All these experiences caused the prince to think about all the suffering and disappointment in life. He yearned to understand suffering and how people might best respond to it. Then he saw a monk with a shaved head wearing a yellow robe. Though the man had given up the ordinary pleasures of life – tasty food, a comfortable home, a loving family – he looked happy and at peace. (These things Siddhartha saw – the old man, the sick person, the funeral procession, and the serene monk – are known as the Four Signs.) So Siddhartha decided to

FIGURE 7.13 Sculpture of the Buddha near starvation. Globuss Images/Alamy.

leave his comfortable palace and loving family to find a different way of life. He spent some time with teachers who showed him how to attain mystical states of consciousness, but this did not answer his questions about suffering. So he joined a group of five ascetics and followed traditional yogic paths toward enlightenment, including extreme self-denial. At one point, so the tradition says, he was down to eating a single grain of rice a day.

However, none of these efforts brought the understanding Siddhartha sought. After several years, tradition tells us that Siddhartha Gautama sat down beneath a tree and meditated until he figured out the key to release from suffering. He achieved the ability to see his own and other people's past lives, allowing him to contemplate the overall scheme of how people pass away and are reborn. Ultimately he came to understand what Buddhists call the **Four Noble Truths** about suffering. His mind was liberated; he understood suffering and how to overcome it. Now he was the Buddha; he was Awakened.

For seven weeks he enjoyed the peace of nirvana. According to tradition, he wondered whether he should even try to teach anyone else the profound understanding that had come to him. Then he walked to a deer park near Benares in northeast India, where he preached his first sermon to the five ascetics he had been with earlier. Buddhists call this sermon "The Turning of the Wheel of Dharma." Here "dharma" means the basic truths discovered by the Buddha, and the wheel became a symbol for it. The Four Noble Truths the Buddha had discovered became the foundation for Buddhism.

- The First Noble Truth is that human life is characterized by **dukkha**, the term for "suffering" in the Buddha's language, Pali. Life is full of conflict, unhappiness, and dissatisfaction.

- The Second Noble Truth is that suffering is caused by desire or attachment, to sensual pleasure, to power, to emotional or intellectual gratification, etc.

- The Third Noble truth is that human beings can be freed from suffering if they free themselves of desire or attachment. When they break their attachment to things, they can achieve nirvana, liberation.

- And the Fourth Noble Truth is that the way to nirvana is the **Noble Eightfold Path**: right views, right aspirations (hopes), right speech, right action, right way of living, right effort, right mindfulness, and right concentration.

This Eightfold Path, the path of moderation, is known as the "Middle Way."

Today when we think of nirvana, we may think of Kurt Cobain and the classic grunge rock band from Seattle, or else a state of bliss after death. However, the Buddha said that we can achieve nirvana in this life, and he thought of it as positive as well as negative. Negatively, it is the cessation of suffering and samsara, rebirth. The Sanskrit word *nirvana* is from the verb "to cool," as if blowing out the fires of passion that create bad karma and keep people in the cycle of suffering and rebirth. Positively, nirvana is bliss, in which the illusion of enduring ego has evaporated (or been "blown out"). It is release from selfishness – from "the wound I bear within me, which is my ego," as the French philosopher Gabriel Marcel (d. 1973) put it – into a life of joyous freedom.

The Buddha's sermon was so powerful, tradition tells us, that the five ascetics who heard it were immediately "awakened"; they became **arhats** – spiritual seekers who had successfully shed the burden of selfhood and achieved nirvana. They became the Buddha's first followers – the sangha, the community of monks.

When the group of monks grew to sixty, the Buddha sent them out to enlighten more people and bring them into the sangha. Thus he created the first missionaries. Initially, the monks traveled through the countryside, preaching as they went. They were allowed to take refuge during the three-month rainy season, in any shelter they could find. Gradually, these settlements became more permanent. Some became rather elaborate, especially when wealthy people donated land for the building of monasteries. In some places, whole tribes joined at the same time.

Late in his life, the Buddha allowed women to form a sangha; they are called nuns. According to tradition, the Buddha was reluctant to ordain women, predicting they would have a negative effect on the movement, although this may well be a reflection of others' misogynist misgivings.

FIGURE 7.14 The Great Stupa at Sanchi, Madhya Pradesh in India. © Hidekazu Nishibata/ SuperStock.

For 45 years, the Buddha traveled and preached. At age 80 he died of food poisoning. As his life was slipping away, one of his friends began crying. The Buddha said, "Do not weep. Have I not already told you that separation is inevitable from all near and dear to us? Whatever is born, produced, conditioned, contains within itself the nature of its own dissolution. It cannot be otherwise." (*Maha-parinibbana Sutta*, 35) His followers cremated his body and divided his ashes and bones to be enshrined in several **stupas** (Buddhist shrines).

Understanding the Four Noble Truths

While the Four Noble Truths may sound simple, they are based on some revolutionary ideas about human beings, their minds, and reality in general. We are unhappy, the Buddha said, because we crave things, people, power, etc. And this craving is based on two fundamental errors: belief in Brahman – a stable, changeless, Ultimate Reality, and belief in Atman – a "true self," which is really identical with Brahman. The Buddha not only denied a stable Ultimate Reality but also taught that nothing at all stays the same from moment to moment. This is known as the doctrine of impermanence (**anicca**). And it applies to the self as well as to things; there is no core identity of a person. This is known as the doctrine of "no-self" (**anatta** or **anatman**). What appears to be a stable "self," the Buddha said, is really

The Death of the Buddha

Then the Blessed One addressed the brothers, and said, "Behold now, brothers, I exhort you, saying, 'Decay is inherent in all component things! Work out your salvation with diligence!'" This was the last word of the Tathagata!...

Then the Blessed One, passing out of the state in which both sensations and ideas have ceased to be, entered the state between consciousness and unconsciousness. Passing out of the state between consciousness and unconsciousness, he entered the state of mind to which nothing at all is specially present. Passing out of the consciousness of no special object, he entered the state of mind to which the infinity of thought is the only thing present. Passing out of the mere consciousness of the infinity of thought, he entered the state of mind to which the infinity of space is alone present. Passing out of the mere consciousness of the infinity of space, he entered the fourth stage of deep meditation.... Then he passed out of the last stage of deep meditation, and immediately he died.

When the Blessed One died, those of the brothers who were not yet free from the passions, some stretched out their arms and wept. Others fell headfirst on the ground, rolling around in anguish at the thought, "Too soon has the Blessed One died! Too soon has the Happy One passed away from existence. Too soon has the Light gone out in the world!"

But those brothers who were free from the passions bore their grief collected and composed at the thought, "All component things are impermanent! How is it possible that [they would not pass away]?" (*Maha-parinibbana Sutta* 6.10–14).

a constantly changing bundle of the five **skandhas** (physical form, sensation, perception, mental formations, and consciousness).

After the time of the Buddha, some of his followers got into complicated philosophical debates about the nature of mind and reality. However, the Buddha himself did not engage in deep philosophical explanations. Instead, he said that his teaching was therapy; he was like a doctor prescribing for an illness. The "illness" was attachment to the idea of a self. When people insisted on explanations for his novel approach, the Buddha usually offered parables. He said, for example, that insisting on having explanations for his therapeutic teachings was like a person who is trapped in a burning building but refuses to leave until she finds out who started the fire, when, and how; or like a person who has been shot with a poisoned arrow but refuses to remove the arrow until he finds out who shot it and of what the poison consists. Again, he stressed that life is characterized by suffering, and his Middle Way was a prescription for ending the suffering.

Another famous parable is attributed to a monk named Nagasena, who was trying to answer the questions of a curious king. Think of a particular chariot, Nagasena said. It is made up of wheels, an axle, the yoke, etc. No single part of the chariot constitutes the chariot itself; all the parts are replaceable. However, even if you replace the wheels, the axle, the yoke, and all the other parts, you will still think of it as the same chariot. In the same way, even though our physical cells and our mental and emotional states change constantly and entirely over a lifetime, we still think of ourselves as somehow the same.

Many people within and outside Buddhism have asked how the doctrine of *anatman* ("no-self") can be reconciled with karma and rebirth. If there is no self, no enduring substance, then what is it that gets reborn? Why should a person be suffering today for what an earlier person did? Again, the Buddha offered a comparison rather than an explanation. He described a flame being transferred from one candle to another. Is the flame on the second candle the same flame as on the first, or that on the third the same as on the second? The answer, he implied, is of no importance. What is important is that the current flame is there, and it was caused by the earlier flame. Similarly, when we die, our desires and attachments ignite new desires and attachments in those who are born after us. In this sense we are "reborn."

The Ethics of "Awakening"

Many people also ask about the ethical implications of Buddhist teaching. If life is all about suffering and selves are not real, then why should we care what happens to people? From a Buddhist perspective, the illusory nature of the self explains empathy. It explains why we suffer when others suffer. If we were radically separate entities, then why would we feel other beings' pain? Because we are all part of the same reality, it is inevitable that we are affected by what happens to other people. As we awaken, the illusory isolation of self from other people ends and, we realize – as Will Smith put it in a "declaration of interdependence" at the Live 8 conference on July 4, 2005 – that "We are all in this together."

In other words, the end of the illusion of the self is the end of selfishness. It is reflected in the Buddhist **unlimited virtues**. The first is loving-kindness, friendliness to all people and animals. The second is compassion, resonating with the sufferings of other people and animals, and taking action to help them. Third is sympathetic joy, feeling happy instead of envious when others do well. And last is even-temperedness – keeping your cool, not being upset when things go badly for you and not being self-centered when they go well.

Buddhists also stress the ancient Vedic notion of non-injury, **ahimsa**. However, unlike the teaching of the Mahabharata, which allows for violence in some circumstances, Buddhism rejects violence and includes abstaining from taking life as the first of its Five Precepts – along with rejection of theft, sexual misconduct, lying, and the consumption of intoxicants.

The Core of All Buddhist Traditions

The Buddha appointed no successor. Instead, he said that his teaching – the dharma – would be his successor. So after he died, the arhats decided they needed to establish exactly what he had taught. They all gathered, and called upon his assistant Ananda, who had memorized every sermon the Buddha had preached over his 45-year career. According to tradition, they did this annually in order to preserve the Buddha's teachings.

The Three Jewels

Early on, people who wanted to follow the Buddhist way were encouraged to pledge themselves to the **Triratna**, the **Three Jewels**, or the **Three Refuges** – "I take refuge in the Buddha, the Dharma, and the Sangha." Although Buddhism developed diverse expressions, the Triratna remains the core of all of them.

- *"I take refuge in the Buddha."* The starting point for all forms of Buddhism is the "awakening" experience of the Buddha. All Buddhists want to "wake up" to see the true nature of reality, which is a liberating experience. Because this experience is central, all the traditions venerate or even worship the Buddha or other Buddha-figures. All Buddhist countries celebrate the Buddha's birthday, the day of his awakening, the day he achieved nirvana. Venerating the Buddha may take the form of meditating on what he taught. Or, like Hindu worship, it can be offering food, flowers, or incense to a statue of the Buddha or to his relics preserved at a stupa. One simple popular ritual is to pour water into a vessel and chant some words of the Buddha. This consecrates the water, which then people may drink or use to bless themselves.

- *"I take refuge in the dharma."* In Hinduism dharma was conceived as duty, the law. In Buddhism, it means teachings of the Buddha.

- *"I take refuge in the sangha."* The sangha is the community of monks and nuns. This form of social organization is found in all Buddhist movements. It was missionary monks who brought Buddhism to the various parts of Asia and beyond.

Originally, as we saw, members of the sangha were itinerant, living on handouts from people. But then, as the sanghas became settled monasteries and convents, eighteen variants of the monastic code developed. However, there were general patterns among them, including democratic governance. Sanghas established near cities or villages set up a reciprocal relationship with the laypeople. The laypeople gave them material goods such as food and clothing. This kind of donation, called dana, earned them good karma, merit toward a higher rebirth. The monks and nuns, in return, provided advice, education, prayers, and the opportunity to earn merit; and conducted important rituals for the community, especially funerals. This relationship with the community remains important today.

While ordinary laypeople provided food and basic necessities for the monks, it was rich donors and kings who gave them land and money to build monasteries. The growth of Buddhism across Asia was supported by rulers who commissioned the building of monasteries, temples, and shrines. The monks showed their appreciation for government

FIGURE 7.15 Buddhist laypeople putting food into the bowls of monks. © imagebroker.net/SuperStock.

support by conducting public rituals to insure the prosperity of the ruler and the state. An especially generous king might be hailed by Buddhists as a **bodhisattva**, a future Buddha. Even today, in Japan, Thailand, and Nepal, monks chant so that the ruler may have a long life. In Sri Lanka before the modern period, the king had the title of *sangha-raja*, Ruler of the Sangha.

In the eyes of early Buddhists, the ideal ruler was Ashoka, who ruled over most of the Indian subcontinent from 270 to 230 BCE. After he converted to Buddhism, he tried to build an empire based on Buddhist virtues, helping to spread the religion across India and beyond, to Sri Lanka, Myanmar (Burma), and Thailand.

The Development of the Three Main Traditions

Like any religious tradition, Buddhism changed over time. As a missionary movement – the world's first – it spread from northern India where it started, south, north, and east. As it spread, its followers developed different rituals and different interpretations of what the Buddha had taught. Indeed, on his deathbed the Buddha said that some of his rules would become unnecessary, but there was no agreement within the community about just which rules those might be. So by the early centuries of the common era, Buddhism had separated into two distinct groups, often called "vehicles." The more conservative tradition claimed that it preserved all the Buddha's original teaching. It is known as Theravada, but is sometimes pejoratively called Hinayana or "Lesser Vehicle." It is flourishing today in

Sri Lanka, Myanmar, Thailand, Cambodia, and Laos. The other form, which started in India but then spread to China, Mongolia, Korea, Japan, Taiwan, Vietnam, and Singapore, is called Mahayana, the "Greater Vehicle." Mahayana became the dominant kind of Buddhism in China, Korea, and Japan. It made some changes to Buddha's original message, and it is the most popular kind of Buddhism today. A third tradition, **Vajrayana**, developed in the 6–7th century in India, and East and Southeast Asia. The version of this tradition that is best known is that of Tibet, because the Dalai Lama is its leader.

THERAVADA (HINAYANA)   Theravada is the oldest school of Buddhist thought and practice, and is generally considered to be most like the Buddha's own community. It stresses the Pali canon of sacred writings, the **Tripitaka** or the "Three Baskets" of discourses, which Theravadans believe contains precisely the Buddha's original teachings. The first basket, the Vinaya, contains rules governing monks' and nuns' behavior. The others consist of ethical discourses, accounts of the Buddha's teachings, and the Abidhama or scholastic interpretations of the Buddha's teachings. In particular, Theravada Buddhism stresses the importance of strict adherence to the Vinaya, and careful reasoning and analysis of each individual's experience in the path toward enlightenment or insight. This path of reasoning and analysis must be based on understanding of the first three of the Noble Truths, and disciplined practice of the fourth – the Eightfold Path.

MAHAYANA   Mahayana Buddhism developed starting in the 1st or 2nd century BCE. Mahayanists developed their own texts, which tell of a second and third "turning of the wheel of dharma," both attributed to the Buddha. According to Mahayana, the Buddha gave these teachings only to select disciples, which explains why these teachings came to the community relatively late. These teachings, known as the Perfection of Wisdom teachings and the Mind-Only teachings, are considered supplements to the Buddha's original sermons.

Mahayana Buddhism reflects the diverse influences of the many communities where it became popular. The most obvious difference between Theravada Buddhism and this new movement is that Mahayanists believe that awakening can be facilitated by the spiritual power of bodhisattvas – "future buddhas" or awakened beings who are dedicated to becoming like the Buddha and helping others become awakened as well. Mahayana encourages all people to work toward bodhisattva status and to help others get there.

Both Theravada and Mahayana emphasize the Buddha's past lives, and accept the Hindu teaching that the cosmos goes through four stages – it is created, abides, dissolves, and lies dormant, and then the whole cycle begins again. However, while Theravada teaches that there is only one Buddha per cycle (or world system), Mahayana allows for multiple buddhas at the same time. (Both Theravada and Mahayana think of the Buddha – or, in the case of Mahayana, buddhas – as beginning their careers as bodhisattvas.)

The Lotus Sutra, one of the first Buddhist scriptures to use the term "Mahayana," speaks of bodhisattvas, as well as "solitary" (or "private") buddhas – people who become awakened but who then die and are never heard of again. It also speaks of arhats – the highest spiritual level for monks in the Theravada tradition. The Mahayana thinkers accused the Theravada

FIGURE 7.16 Statue of the Bodhisattva Kannon with blue sky. © Prisma/SuperStock.

monks of selfishly pursuing the arhat ideal, stressing their own personal awakening and nirvana, and ignoring the Buddha's emphasis on loving-kindness and compassion.

Mahayana Buddhism also stresses diverse practices for the achievement of nirvana. Any technique – chanting, devotional ritual, even folk practices – may be effective. In some Mahayana sects, the route to awakening is chanting the name of a special Buddha, other than Siddhartha Gautama. Others stress **prajna** (wisdom or intellectual awakening), moral action, or devotions.

One of the most venerated of the bodhisattvas is **Avalokitesvara**, the Buddha of Compassion, whose mercy for humans is captured in one of Buddhism's most popular mantras, "Om mani padme Hum," "O, the jewel in the lotus." Like other buddhas and bodhisattvas, Avalokitesvara exists in his own heavenly realm, where he will bring those who have faith and pray to him. In China, Avalokitesvara became female, and she was called

Kuan-yin. In Japan, she is known as **Kannon**, Mother of Mercy, with many arms stretched out to her devotees. She is often called the "Virgin Mary of East Asia" – comparing her to the mother of Jesus – because of the many temples dedicated to her, pilgrimages in her honor, and claims of visions of her. In Kyoto, the old capital of Japan, there is a temple with 3,000 different images of Kannon.

One path to awakening in Mahayana Buddhism is philosophical. The greatest thinker in this tradition was Nagarjuna (c. 150–250 CE). Following the reasoning of the Buddha, he taught that everything in the world of ordinary perception is ultimately unreal. According to his "Doctrine of Emptiness," ordinary experience is "void." Even nirvana is "void" or empty; it is characterized by a lack of self-existence. Moreover, since the world is unreal, language about it is not ultimately reliable. One of his best-known teachings is the Two Truths, which distinguishes between conventional, everyday truth and ultimate truth. Our ordinary experience can be considered more or less true, in that it helps us get on with our lives, but the ultimate truth is that there is really nothing to the world or to language.

Nagarjuna influenced a later movement called Dhyana (meditation) in India, Chan in China, and **Zen** in Japan, which not only teaches the Doctrine of Emptiness but questions words, concepts, rational thinking, and logic. Chan/Zen emphasizes meditation and sudden awakening, and is still a popular form of Buddhism today. This tradition is famous for its koans – questions that send the mind on a "wild goose chase" to show the unreliability of conceptual thinking. The most famous koan is "What is the sound of one hand clapping?" (We shall talk more about Chan/Zen in Chapter 8.)

Another form of Mahayana that is still popular is "Pure Land" Buddhism. Like many versions of Christianity, it emphasizes simple faith as the key to salvation. According to tradition, Pure Land Buddhism began with a monk, Dharmakara, who vowed to establish a Happy Land in a heavenly realm if he achieved nirvana. He did reach nirvana, and became the Buddha of Unlimited Light – **Amitabha** in Sanskrit, **Amida** in Japanese. He sits in his Pure Land heavenly realm – the land of Sukhavati ("The Land of Bliss"), helping people reach salvation by escaping from the sufferings of life. Among the ways to do this is to call the name of this Buddha at the moment of death, which will allow the person to be reborn in the Pure Land. Here the emphasis has shifted from becoming awakened to reaching a paradise. Some versions of Pure Land Buddhism add that, once in the Pure Land, the person will be coached by Amida Buddha himself in order to achieve awakening. (In Chapter 8 we shall say more about this tradition.)

VAJRAYANA Sometimes called the "Diamond Vehicle," Vajrayana Buddhism began within Mahayana Buddhism in the 7th century, and split off from other Mahayana sects in the 8th century. From Hinduism it got yoga practices, including some practices known as tantric. Tantric practices are based on scriptures known as tantras that present Shakti – divine feminine power – as the most important deity, along with her consort Shiva. Some tantric practices deliberately break moral rules against sex and drinking alcohol. Vajrayana Buddhism was given a mysterious air by its association with the strict guidance of a **guru** (spiritual teacher) and by secret ceremonies and secret teaching, so sometimes it is called Esoteric Buddhism or Tantric Buddhism. However, the main feature that distinguishes

The Dalai Lama and Religious Tolerance

FIGURE 7.17 Tenzin Gyatso, the 14th Dalai Lama, is the best known representative of Vajrayana Buddhism. Mike Flokis/Getty Images.

When I was a boy in Tibet, I felt that my own Buddhist religion must be the best – and that other faiths were somehow inferior. Now I see how naïve I was, and how dangerous the extremes of religious intolerance can be today.

…Granted, every religion has a sense of exclusivity as part of its core identity. Even so, I believe there is genuine potential for mutual understanding….

An early eye-opener for me was my meeting with the Trappist monk Thomas Merton in India shortly before his untimely death in 1968. Merton told me he could be perfectly faithful to Christianity, yet learn in depth from other religions like Buddhism….

A main point in my discussion with Merton was how central compassion was to the message of both Christianity and Buddhism. In my readings of the New Testament, I find myself inspired by Jesus' acts of compassion. His miracle of the loaves and fishes, his healing and his teaching are all motivated by the desire to relieve suffering.

…The focus on compassion that Merton and I observed in our two religions strikes me as a strong unifying thread among all the major faiths….

Take Judaism, for instance. I… have learned how the Talmud and the Bible repeat the theme of compassion, as in the passage in Leviticus that admonishes, "Love your neighbor as yourself."

> In my many encounters with Hindu scholars in India, I've come to see the centrality of selfless compassion in Hinduism too – as expressed, for instance, in the *Bhagavad Gita*, which praises those who "delight in the welfare of all beings."
>
> ...Compassion is equally important in Islam – and recognizing that has become crucial in the years since Sept. 11.
>
> "Many Faiths, One Truth." Op Ed in *New York Times*, May 24, 2010

Vajrayana from other forms of Mahayana Buddhism is its "deity yoga," through which the spiritual seeker may achieve nirvana in a single lifetime, rather than taking the "three countless eons" required by other Mahayana paths. Deity yoga involves visualizing oneself as a buddha, through specific rituals and complex meditation.

We shall continue to discuss Buddhism in the next chapter on China, but here we can note that, if Buddhism had not been transported to East Asia and elsewhere, it would probably have gone extinct, because in India itself it had died out by the 12th century as a result of successive invasions by Huns and Muslims, and the rise of popular Hinduism.

Buddhism Today

European colonization of Asia had a negative impact on Buddhism. Colonial powers often demanded that governments withdraw their support for Buddhist institutions, and some even destroyed monasteries.

The Communist takeover of Asian countries further hurt Buddhism. China, Mongolia, Vietnam, and North Korea launched campaigns to get rid of monks, calling them parasites on society and accusing them of superstition.

Nonetheless, Buddhism has survived and today is the fourth largest religious tradition in the world, with about 350,000,000 worldwide. Over 98% of Buddhists live in Asia. Mahayana Buddhists outnumber Theravada by a ratio of two to one. There are perhaps 700,000 Buddhist monks and nuns in the world today. In all Theravada countries except Sri Lanka, virtually every young man spends at least one year as a monk. There are far more monks than nuns, but there are strong lineages of Buddhist nuns in Taiwan and South Korea.

Today in most monasteries, begging is largely symbolic, as arrangements have been made with lay people for regular donations of food and necessary goods.

Most Buddhist communities have at least one stupa (shrine with relics of the Buddha or another important Buddhist personage), as well as stupas for ashes of important monks.

In the West, Buddhism has proven fascinating to intellectuals, beginning in the 1800s. Western intellectuals have often described Buddhists as rationalists who reject ritual and push social reform. The meditation techniques have been seen as ancient authentic practice compatible with science. Zen Buddhism became popular in the West after World War II. In the U.S. today, half a million people identify themselves as Buddhist. In the U.K. about 150,000 say they are Buddhist; in Europe, 3 million do, mostly in Russia.

Rituals

Two rituals established early on have always been central to Buddhism. First is the veneration of the Buddha, or in Mahayana, a Bodhisattva. This is done by showing respect for the figure, as by offering gifts, and by meditating on what that figure did. The second ritual is the interchange between monks and laypeople. Monks represent a higher level of spiritual merit, which they can share with laypeople. In return laypeople give the monks gifts such as food, robes, and blankets. In traditional monasteries, monks were not allowed to make or prepare their own food; it was only through the kindness of laypeople that they got to eat.

Another popular ritual that began early in Buddhism is making a pilgrimage to a holy site, such as a stupa.

Other rituals that have evolved are tied to the calendar. As noted, the Buddha's birthday is celebrated, as well as the day of his awakening and his passing into final Nirvana with the death of his physical body. In early Buddhism, and still in Theravada countries, services are held in temples four times each month, at the four main phases of the moon. There may be meditation exercises, flowers offered to the Buddha, and scriptures recited. In some places Buddhists celebrate the New Year and the harvest by carrying statues of the Buddha through the streets in procession, visiting Buddhist sanctuaries, and even having dramatic performances of episodes from the life of the Buddha.

As in most religions, too, there are rites of passage – rituals to mark important life changes. The most important are the two rites for initiation into the sangha, the religious community. In the first, the person renounces secular life and accepts the monastic life of a novice (beginner). In the second, which may occur years later, the person is fully consecrated as a monk. When the two rituals are combined, the postulant (person becoming a monk) typically shaves his head and beard and puts on the yellow robe of a monk. He bows to the abbot and sits with legs crossed and hands folded, saying three times the formula of triple refuge: "I take refuge in the Buddha, I take refuge in the dharma, I take refuge in the sangha." He renounces secular life and accepts monastic life. Then the abbot consecrates him as a monk.

In many parts of Asia, funerals are the special province of Buddhists, even for people who are not religious or observant as Buddhists. Funerals typically revolve around a cremation, inherited from Hinduism, although in places where firewood is scarce the corpse may be buried. Buddhists generally think that a person's thoughts at the moment of death are important and determine their next life, so religious texts may be read to a dying person, or to a corpse, since the belief is that something of consciousness lingers around the body for three days. Mourners carefully dispose of the corpse, as in Hinduism and for the same reason – to make sure the dead person does not become a hungry ghost or a demon that will bother the living. Mourners may make donations and transfer the merit from themselves to the dead person to improve their lot when they are next reincarnated.

Conclusion: Religious Studies and Indian Traditions

At the end of Chapter 6, we noted that Religious Studies has had significant impact on the Western monotheisms. This is not surprising, given that Religious Studies developed in European and American culture. What about the impact of Religious Studies on Indian traditions?

Many scholars believe that the field of Religious Studies has had an enormous impact on the traditions of India and Asia more generally. Some scholars argue, in fact, that Religious Studies actually transformed the diverse traditions of Asia into Hinduism and Buddhism. By assuming that religion is universal and everywhere recognizable by a fixed set of criteria (even though there is no agreement about just what those criteria are), early scholars of religion imposed on Indian traditions a uniformity that did not exist. University of Michigan historian Tomoku Masuzawa titles her 2005 book accordingly *The Invention of the World Religions*. We shall return to this discussion in Chapter 10.

As in the case of Islam, some efforts to apply the tools of Religious Studies to Indian traditions have met with strong resistance. A 2001 edition of Paul Courtright's *Ganesha: Lord of Obstacles, Lord of Beginnings* featured a picture of the god naked on the cover. This was considered insulting, but it was the scholar's highly Freudian analysis of the god's relationship with his parents that ignited outrage. The Indian edition was ultimately withdrawn and the publishers issued an apology for any offense it had caused. In 2003 University of Chicago scholar Wendy Doniger was pelted with an egg while lecturing at the University of London. Doniger has published a number of texts employing Freudian analysis of Indian gods. Doniger attributes such reactions to a right-wing politicization of Indian traditions, particularly in the late 20th century.

Whether Western scholars of religion "invented" Hinduism and Buddhism or not, many people today readily identify themselves as Hindus or Buddhists, and both traditions (or sets of traditions) remain diverse and flexible. The Buddha himself offered his teachings and techniques not as the absolute truth but as helpful suggestions for improving people's lives. If they work for you, he said, follow them. If they don't work, try something else. This practical attitude became especially prominent as Buddhism crossed the Himalayan mountains and became part of the culture of China, as we shall see in Chapter 8.

DISCUSSION QUESTIONS

1. What are the similarities and differences between Indian views on moksha and nirvana and Western notions of salvation?

2. What are the major differences between Indian and Western notions of good and evil?

3. How do Indian notions of justice compare with Western views of morality?

4. Do you see any correlation between the polytheism of Indian traditions and religious tolerance in general?

5. Does the "impurity" associated with the dalits, the Untouchables, in India fit Mary Douglas's explanation?

6. How would Marx describe the Laws of Manu?

7. The Buddha did not leave written instructions for his followers. How did this affect the subsequent history of Buddhism? Do you see any parallels here with other religions, such as Christianity?

8. The Buddha emphasized that everything changes. Is there anything about you that is exactly the same as on the day you were born? Is there anything about you that is exactly the same as yesterday?

9. For the Buddha, the unhappiness in life comes from our desires, our attachments. What would an advertising executive say about this? What do you think about it?

10. We suggested some similarities between the idea of a bodhisattva and the Christian understanding of Jesus. Can you think of any more similarities? Can you think of differences?

REFERENCES

Paul B. Courtright, *Ganesha: Lord of Obstacles, Lord of Beginnings*. Oxford: Oxford University Press, 2001.

Eknath Easwaran, translator, *The Bhagavad Gita* (Classics of Indian Spirituality), 2nd ed. Tomales, CA: Nilgiri, 2007.

Mohandas Gandhi, *An Autobiography: The Story of My Experiments with Truth*. Boston: Beacon, 1957.

Tenzin Gyatso, "Many Faiths, One Truth," *New York Times*, May 24, 2010. http://www.nytimes.com/2010/05/25/opinion/25gyatso.html.

Tomoku Masuzawa, *The Invention of the World Religions*. Chicago: University of Chicago Press, 2005.

Sister Vajira and Francis Story, translators, *The Maha-parinibbana Sutta* (revised edition). Kandy: Buddhist Publications Society, 1998.

FURTHER READING

Karen Armstrong, *The Great Transformation: The Beginnings of Our Religious Traditions*. New York: Knopf, 2006.

Bikkhu Bodhi and the Dalai Lama, *In the Buddha's Words: An Anthology of Discourses from the Pali Canon (Teachings of the Buddha)*. Somerville, MA: Wisdom, 2005.

Wendy Doniger, *Hindu Myths: A Source Book Translated from the Sanskrit*. Harmondsworth: Penguin, 2004.

Eknath Easwaran, translator, *The Upanishads* (Classics of Indian Spirituality), 2nd ed. Tomales, CA: Nilgiri, 2007.

Diana Eck, *Darsan: Seeing the Divine Image in India*. New York: Columbia University Press, 1998.

S. N. Eisenstadt, *The Origins and Diversity of the Axial Age*. Albany, NY: State University of New York, 1986.

Harry Falk, "Soma I and II," *Bulletin of the School of Oriental and African Studies*, University of London, 52, No. 1 (1989), 77–90.

Gavin Flood, *An Introduction to Hinduism*. Cambridge: Cambridge University Press, 1996.

Karl Jaspers, *Way to Wisdom: An Introduction to Philosophy*. New Haven, CT: Yale University Press, 1951.

Walter Ong, *Orality and Literacy: The Technologizing of the Word*, 2nd ed. New York: Routledge, 2002.

Rodney Stark, *Discovering God: A New Look at the Origins of the Great Religions*. New York: HarperOne, 2007.

D. T. Suzuki, *An Introduction to Zen Buddhism*. New York: Grove, 1994.

BALANCING AND BLENDING
Confucianism, Taoism, and Buddhism in China

"Nothing happens next. This is it."

FIGURE 8.1 © Gahan Wilson 1980/The New Yorker Collection/www.cartoonbank.com.

The Religion Toolkit: A Complete Guide to Religious Studies, First Edition. John Morreall and Tamara Sonn.
© 2012 John Morreall and Tamara Sonn. Published 2012 by Blackwell Publishing Ltd.

Overview

The dominant element of Chinese traditions is the Tao (or Dao), the "way" of the universe.

- Chinese traditions view the universe and the place of human beings in it as one great system in which many parts work together and balance one another.

- If humans fit into this natural system, their lives go well. If they struggle against it or try to dominate it, they suffer.

- The balance of the Tao is represented in the symbols of the *yin* and *yang*, which are complementary opposites.

- The Chinese tradition that focuses on the Tao is called Taoism, developed in a collection of analects (wise sayings) attributed to 6th-century BCE (Axial Age) teacher Lao Tzu.

Chinese traditions reflect concern with practical ways to achieve harmony and balance.

- One reflection of concern for harmony and balance is emphasis on respect for history, particularly respect for the ways of the ancestors.

- Chinese concern with practical ways to achieve balance and harmony, and emphasis on the ways of the ancestors, were developed into a way of life attributed to 6th-century-BCE (Axial Age) teacher Confucius (Kung Fu Tzu), and known as Confucianism.

The Tao, Yin and Yang

The History of Chinese Religious Thought
  The Shang Period
    (18th–11th centuries BCE)
  The Zhou Period
    (11th–3rd centuries BCE)

Confucius (551–479 BCE)

Taoism

Buddhism in China
  Pure Land Buddhism
  Chan (Zen) Buddhism

Chinese Folk Traditions

Rituals in Chinese Traditions
  Weddings
  Funerals

Chinese Traditions Today

Conclusion: Religious Studies and the Traditions of China

FIGURE 8.2 Help one another, for we are all in the same boat – old Chinese saying.

Buddhist teaching entered China as early as the 1st century CE.

- Chinese traditions strongly influenced Buddhist teachings, so Chinese Buddhism has characteristics distinct from Buddhism in other areas.
- Under the influence of Chinese traditions, Buddhism developed into a number of schools of thought and practices, including Chan (which would become Zen in Japan) and Pure Land Buddhism.

Like Western monotheisms, Chinese traditions hold that there is an afterlife.

- Unlike Western traditions, the purpose of afterlife in Chinese traditions is not to be rewarded or punished but to assist the living.
- Unlike Indian traditions, Chinese traditions do not teach reincarnation.

Like Indian traditions, Chinese traditions have more than one god.

- Also like Indian traditions, Chinese traditions do not require belief in a god.
- Unlike Indian traditions, Chinese traditions posit no single God underlying all reality.

The Tao, Yin and Yang

Many religions have myths about how their group came to be in their homeland. The Hebrew Bible tells how Abraham was called by "the god of our fathers" to move from Ur to the land of Canaan (see Chapter 6), and how Moses brought the people of Israel back to Canaan from Egypt. However, the people of China have no such myth, perhaps because they did not migrate to China from anywhere else; they have always lived there. (Again, as we saw in Chapter 2, scholars use the term "myth" not to mean "something false" but to refer to an explanation, usually in story form, of something important to a particular group, such as how the world was created or how the group came to exist.) As far back as 4,000 BCE, there were villages along the Yellow River, where the ancestors of today's Chinese people were growing crops and raising pigs. The sense of permanence in Chinese culture is reflected in the strong identification with the land and with history. This sense of permanence has created great stability in Chinese religious traditions over three millennia. The list of gods to whom the last emperor of China sacrificed in 1907 is identical to the list of gods in a record from 1100 BCE (except for the name of Confucius, who lived long after 1100 BCE).

FIGURE 8.3 Part of a giant traditional Chinese landscape painting: A Trip to Hills and Lakes in Spring by Chen Minglou. http://commons.wikimedia.org/wiki/File:A part of Giant Traditional Chinese Painting6.jpg.

Traditional Chinese society consisted mostly of farmers who lived at a subsistence level. In traditional Chinese thought, the way to make sure that the crops do well and the village flourishes is to have people live in harmony with nature – the seasons, the rain, and the sun. Similar to the traditions of Native Americans, Chinese traditions have reflected awareness that if people do not fit into the natural order of things, they will not last long. Therefore, while modern capitalist society emphasizes progress and development, traditional Chinese culture emphasizes balance and harmony. Rather than expectations of increased annual growth or profit, traditional Chinese societies, like traditional agricultural societies everywhere, looked forward to a harvest that provided enough for everyone to eat for another year.

Chinese traditions view the universe and the place of human beings in it holistically, that is, as a whole. There is one great system in which many parts work together and balance one another. In contrast to the Western worldview in which humans are the culmination of all Creation, in the Chinese worldview human beings are an integral – but not dominant – part of the whole. If humans fit into this natural system, their lives go well. If they struggle against it or try to dominate it, they suffer. The traditional word for this system is Tao (sometimes written Dao, because that is how it is pronounced), which can be translated as "the Way" or as "Nature." The overall perspective is represented in the Chinese painting in Figure 8.3, where people and buildings are shown, but they do not dominate the natural world.

The Chinese emphasis on harmony and balance is reflected in the Taoist worldview, where all things are viewed as either *yin* or *yang*. **Yin and yang** are opposites, but not opposites in conflict with each other. Instead, they complement or complete each other. Indeed, they make each other possible.

FIGURE 8.4 Yin–yang.

YIN	YANG
Cold	Hot
Wet	Dry
Dark	Bright
Earth	Heaven
Female	Male
Autumn	Spring
Valley	Mountain
West	East
Dragon	Tiger

There could not be a mountain without a valley. There could be no "East" without "West." How could we identify "up" if we did not know "down," or "dark" without "light," or "young" without "old"? Neither one of the complementary pairs is good or bad. They are not even, in the strictest sense, absolute opposites. Each member of each pair contains an element of its complement within it. There is no absolute "cold" or "hot," for example; there is always a bit of warmth in cold, and vice versa; and just as morning becomes night, night becomes morning. What is good is both elements in each pair balancing each other in dynamic tension. What is bad is an imbalance between them. The symbol for this dynamic balance of complementary opposites is shown in Figure 8.4.

The concern with balance and order in the world extends to society, as well. People must live in harmony not only with nature, but also with each other. They must work together for the common good. Farmers need to get along with their neighbors. Village leaders and the emperor have to treat people fairly. The Chinese emphasis on the common good contrasts with the emphasis on the wellbeing of the individual that is so common in Western traditions. Rather than showing primary concern with individual salvation, Chinese tradition demonstrates overwhelming concern with the prosperity of the community.

The holistic worldview and emphasis on the common good are evident in the focus in Chinese traditions on issues that matter in the lives of ordinary people. In Christianity, theologians have constructed complex theories about the Trinity and about the human soul. We saw the claim in Hinduism that ordinary experience is *maya*, illusion, and that what is really real is Brahman, the infinite and unchanging ground of all being. However,

Chinese traditions focus less on abstract theoretical issues and more on how people should treat their family and their neighbors, and how they can live long, healthy lives.

This practicality shows, for example, in the orientation toward life after death in Chinese traditions. The highest good is not said to be eternal life in heaven. It is living a long, healthy, prosperous life with a loving family, in a just, peaceful society. The Chinese do believe in life after death, but the deceased ancestors are said to be concerned with their living relatives, dispensing advice and favors, rather than simply abiding in bliss.

The History of Chinese Religious Thought

In previous chapters we have written of "The History and Teachings" of the monotheisms (Western religious traditions: Judaism, Christianity, and Islam) and Indian religious traditions. We must change our language slightly for our treatment of Chinese traditions. As we mentioned in Chapter 1, many languages do not have words that mean what the English word "religion" means. We noted that the Hebrew and Arabic *din* gets translated as "religion" even though its root meaning differs from that term's root meaning. What English speakers call "religions" are called "teachings" in Chinese. In the 16th century, Chinese religious thought was identified as **San-chiao**: the "three teachings" of Confucianism, Taoism, and Buddhism. Since each of these "teachings" deals with things that Western traditions classify as religious, Western thinkers often see the "three teachings" as religions. So in order to avoid redundancy (as in "The History and Teachings of The Three Teachings"), we shall describe the development of the teachings historically.

The Shang Period (18th–11th centuries BCE)

Most histories of China begin with the Shang. They lived in what is now Henan Province in Northeastern China, where a king ruled over 200–300 clans. Their supreme god, governing everything, was Lord (**Di**) or Lord-on-high (**Shang-di**). Di ruled over a court of nature gods representing the sun, moon, wind, rain, rivers, and other natural forces. When people wanted favors, they prayed not to this high god but to the nature gods, asking them to intercede with Di to bring rain, for example, or avert a plague or other natural disaster.

Early Chinese culture also involved the veneration of ancestors, especially male ancestors. In one ritual, people put food and wine into special bronze containers for the ancestors, asking them for guidance and protection.

The most important rituals at this time were conducted by the king. As in many religious traditions, Shang rituals had to be performed correctly in order to be effective. If the king did the rituals properly, it was said, this would insure the harmony of people with Heaven and Earth. If there was a flood, famine or other disaster, this meant that the king had not performed the rituals properly.

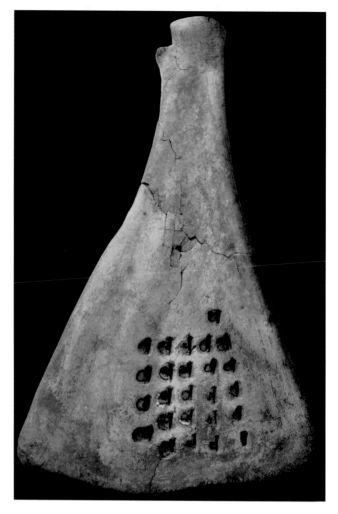

FIGURE 8.5 An oracle bone with writing on it. AKG Images/Erich Lessing.

Just as in ancient Egypt, the importance of kings during the Shang period is reflected in the way they were buried. The king's body was adorned with jade ornaments and surrounded with precious objects. When the funeral party arrived at the burial site, hundreds of servants, along with the horses that had pulled the hearse, were sacrificed and buried with the king, so that they would continue to assist him in the afterlife.

Much of what we know about the people of the Shang period comes from what they wrote on **oracle bones**. These were shoulder blades of oxen and shells of turtles that were believed to reveal the will of the gods or ancestors. The bone or shell was heated until it cracked. Then skilled **diviners** – people believed to be endowed with special powers to perceive truths hidden from ordinary people – interpreted the cracks to figure out what the gods or ancestors wanted to communicate. Like other forms of divination, oracle bones were also used to answer practical questions – about the weather, marriage, health, war, or the sex of unborn children. Over 150,000 oracle bones had been discovered, often by farmers in their fields, by the 19th century. Many of the people who used them wrote their questions on the bones, along with the answers that the gods or ancestors gave.

Here are some inscriptions on oracle bones:

Will Di send down drought upon us?

It has not rained [for a long time]. Is Di harming this city [at Anyang]; does Di not approve [of our actions]? The king did the divination saying, "It is Di who is harming the city; [Di] does not approve."

Shall we pray for harvest to Yue Peak with a burnt offering of three sheep and three pigs and the decapitation of three oxen?

Is it Father Yi who is hurting the king's tooth?

Should we perhaps pray for a child to High Grandmother Ping?

If the king issues a great order to the multitudes saying, "Cultivate the fields," shall we receive a harvest?

Lopez 1996, 46–51

The Zhou Period (11th–3rd centuries BCE)

After more than six centuries, the Shang rulers were overthrown by the Zhou people, a group of tribes from the western part of China. Shang-di, Lord-on-high, remained as the supreme god, but the Zhou people began to refer to him as Tien, "Heaven."

The way the Zhou rulers explained their history was that they had been given a mandate by Heaven to take over the government when the Shang became corrupt. Heaven is not just a power that can help human beings, they said. It is a moral power that supports good governments and opposes corrupt ones. The good ruler's relation to Heaven is like that of a dutiful son to his father. The ruler even came to be called the Son of Heaven. So over time Tien was thought of in less personal terms than Shang-di had been. The Zhou also emphasized morality more than the Shang had. They were especially concerned with justice and good government.

In the last three centuries of the Zhou Dynasty the central government collapsed and local warlords began fighting with each other. Floods and famines added to people's distress. This is known as the Period of the Warring States. Naturally, people began to ask what had gone wrong, and they came up with many answers. Why were the old ways no longer effective in maintaining harmony? Had the rituals been inappropriate? Was Heaven displeased? People looked to respected thinkers to explain. From these thinkers came the great religious traditions of Confucianism and Taoism. Their answers differ from each other, as we shall see, but in a yin–yang way; they do not contradict but instead complement each other. Confucianism and Taoism became counterbalancing traditions.

The Axial Age and the Evolution of Religions

As we saw in Chapters 6 and 7, similar revolutionary changes were occurring at the same time in monotheistic thought in the Middle East and in Indian thought. So profound are the shifts in Greek, Judaic, Indian, and Chinese thought during the period when the Upanishads were composed that the German philosopher Karl Jaspers (d. 1969) coined a term for the period, which he estimates to be roughly 800–200 BCE: the **Axial Age**.

Extraordinary events are crowded into this period. In China lived Confucius and Lao [Tzu]… all the trends in Chinese philosophy arose…. In India it was the age of the Upanishads and of the Buddha; as in China, all philosophical trends, including skepticism and materialism, sophistry and nihilism, were developed. In Iran Zarathustra put forward his challenging conception of the cosmic process as a struggle between good and evil [see Chapter 9]; in Palestine prophets arose: Elijah, Isaiah, Jeremiah, Deutero-Isaiah [Chapters 40–66 of the Book of Isaiah]; Greece produced Homer, the philosophers Parmenides, Heraclitus, Plato, the tragic poets, Thucydides and Archimedes. All the vast development of which these names are a mere intimation took place in those few centuries, independently and almost simultaneously in China, India and the West…. (Jaspers 1951, 135)

Jaspers believes the "axial" age was the pivot point between whatever was going on in the olden days and the basic way we operate as human beings today. He thinks that this later way of operating is characterized by concern with the meaning of life, the nature of good and evil, and the purpose of suffering, and an awareness that the answers to these questions are the same for all human beings.

Jaspers is more concerned with the characteristics of the religious and philosophical thought that developed during the Axial Age than with its causes, though he does link it to social turmoil caused by political struggles. Some scholars link it to the introduction of coinage during this period. The ability to exchange land and herds, for example, for small pieces of metal made possible the amassing of unprecedented wealth, a development which could certainly have upset the status quo and led to political struggles. More recent discussions of the causes of the Axial Age have focused on the development of literacy, which facilitated the development of abstract thought. It may have been associated as well with the evolution of human consciousness, which gave rise to awareness of suffering and death and concern with both the self and others. But whatever the cause of the shifts, there is clearly a tendency toward abstract thought and concern with major questions of morality and metaphysics sweeping many cultures, as the Upanishads demonstrate.

Confucius (551–479 BCE)

Unlike some religious leaders, Confucius (Kung Fu Tzu, or Master Kung) lived an undramatic life, had few new ideas, and did not claim to be starting a new religious tradition. He said little about anything supernatural. Occasionally he mentioned Heaven, but he saw it as part of the order of the world rather than as something beyond the world. Nonetheless, Confucius is by far the most influential religious thinker in China's long history. His birthday, September 28th, is widely observed. In 121 CE Emperor Wu created an imperial university that was based only on Confucian texts. And from then until the 20th century, applicants for government jobs had to take qualifying exams in Confucian thought.

The Five Confucian Classics

I Ching, The Book of Changes. This work describes the universe as a great system in which the forces of yin and yang are in dynamic balance. It also presents methods of divination – techniques to see more deeply into the world and to foretell future events. According to the *I Ching*, the ideal nobleman should emulate the pattern of dynamic tension in the universe by striving for "unity of man and Heaven."

The Book of Poetry. Like Western poetry, Chinese poetry celebrates human emotions. *The Book of Poetry* celebrates the emotions of all kinds of people from all social levels, individuals as well as groups. Many of the verses emphasize the importance of people's responding to and cooperating with each other.

The Book of Rites. Also emphasizing the theme of cooperation, this book describes the four occupations of scholar, farmer, craftsperson, and merchant. In the ideal state, each person respects and trusts others, and all people serve the common good they share.

The Book of History. This book presents a political vision of the world in which the ideal way to govern is through moral persuasion and moral education. The model ruler, like the legendary Three Emperors of old – Yao, Shun, and Yū – lives a virtuous life himself and inspires the people to do likewise. Ideally, this kind of government motivates people to live in social harmony without forcing them to do anything and without punishing them.

The Spring and Autumn Annals. In this historical record of the state of Lu, where Confucius grew up, a major theme is the need for people to be aware of their own history and to carry on its best traditions. It evaluates political events from the 8th to the 5th century BCE, making moral judgments about leaders and condemning murder and illegal seizures of power.

Confucius spent his early life in government service, but later turned to teaching. He was well prepared, having been educated in poetry and history, and trained in the Six Arts of classical Chinese education – music, archery, charioteering, calligraphy, arithmetic, and ritual. His success as a teacher, and the success of his students in their careers, convinced him that education was essential to human fulfillment. It was not simply job training, but preparation for a happy, moral life.

Another interesting contrast between Confucius and many other religious leaders is that he did not write new books. Instead, he edited old ones and compiled them into a canon (set of official texts) called The **Five Classics**:

I Ching, The Book of Changes (a book of divination)
The Book of Poetry
The Book of Rites
The Book of History
The Spring and Autumn Annals.

In 175 CE, these Five Classics compiled by Confucius were carved on large stone tablets and displayed in the capital as China's official sacred scriptures, which they have remained ever since.

After his death, the followers of Confucius wrote four more books that became part of the canon:

The Analects
The Great Learning
The Mean
The Book of Mencius.

The Analects presents the teachings of Confucius in twenty chapters, with titles such as "Studying," "The Practice of Government," and "Living in Brotherliness." Chapter 10 gives some details about Confucius' daily activities. A good part of this book is conversations between Confucius and his followers. In one of them, Confucius talks with his students about their hopes and dreams. Student Zi Lu says that his dream is to share beautiful carriages and expensive leather coats with his friends. Confucius said that his dream is a world in which old people can spend their later years in peace and happiness, people can trust one another as they do their close friends, and all children are loved and given a good education.

The Great Learning stresses the importance of moral and spiritual cultivation for the good ruler. Ancient leaders who wanted their kingdoms to be virtuous "first regulated their families. Wishing to regulate their families, they first cultivated their own person. Wishing to cultivate their person, they first put their hearts in order."

"*The Mean*" refers to the middle point between extremes. This book focuses on being psychologically balanced so that the various parts of the mind are in harmony. "When there are no stirrings of pleasure, anger, sorrow, or joy, the mind is in a state of equilibrium. When those feelings have been stirred, and they act properly, there is a state of harmony. This equilibrium is the great root from which all human actions grow, and this harmony is the universal path which they all should pursue."

The Book of Mencius is a record of conversations between Mencius and his followers. Mencius, or Meng Tzu, is the second most important thinker in the Confucian tradition. Like Confucius, he taught that human nature is fundamentally good. "The tendency of man's nature to goodness is like the tendency of water to flow downwards. All have this tendency to good, just as all water flows downwards." (Ebrey 1993, 22–24)

Recalling that Confucius rose to prominence in the wake of the Period of Warring States, it is not surprising that the works of Confucius contain an explanation of what had gone wrong during that period, and prescriptions for how to assure that such chaos never breaks out again. The problem was, he said, that people had thrown aside the traditional rules that ensure that society functions harmoniously. Rulers had become selfish and greedy, and they no longer modeled themselves on the emperors of old in governing fairly and wisely.

The *jun-zi*, the ideal person, Confucius said, is a scholar steeped in tradition, who serves society unselfishly. His chief virtue is **jen** (often written **ren**, because that is how it is pronounced), humaneness. The way to be humane is to practice **li**, which is living morally, showing good manners, and engaging in ritual performances – on musical instruments, in sacrifices, and in the veneration of ancestors.

In the *Analects* the term *jen* appears over 100 times, and it is explained in different ways. When a student asks what *jen* is, Confucius answers, "Love others." Later Mencius extended this definition to "Love others as you do your own relatives, and love all creatures as you do human beings." When a student asks how *jen* can be achieved, Confucius talks about five virtues: dignity, lenience, honesty, industriousness, and kindness.

Confucius saw these virtues as developing from five basic relationships. The primary one, on which the others are based, is father and son. The others are ruler and subject, older brother and younger brother, husband and wife, and friend and friend.

The ideal son shows **hsaio**, filial piety, toward his parents. He puts their needs and wishes first. When his father dies, he continues to show his respect. In traditional China, a son mourned his father for three years. Similarly, people living under an emperor will put aside their own desires and defer to the ruler, who is ruling not for his own benefit, but to serve the common good. Carrying out the duties of all of these roles should be motivated by *jen*, humaneness.

Devotion to the gods is also modeled on *hsaio*, filial piety. In the Han period (206 BCE–220 CE), when Confucianism dominated China, the emperor became the chief priest (religious authority). As the "Son of Heaven," he performed sacrifices to the ancestors and worshiped Heaven and Earth as his cosmic parents.

Confucius taught that all human beings are naturally good and that, if they are given a proper education, they will develop their *jen*, their natural humaneness. When societies go astray, as in the Period of the Warring States, it is because they have poor role models and do not teach their citizens the right ways to act.

The influence of Confucius on Chinese society was so great that within a few centuries of his death, he was revered almost as a god – an eternal being who can help those of us who are mortals. Temples were built to Confucius, and all two thousand counties in China still have them. In 1908 the government of China declared that Confucius is coequal with Heaven and Earth.

Taoism

Around the time of Confucius, another group of people were trying to figure out what had gone wrong in Chinese society, leading to the Period of Warring States. Focusing more on individual attitudes than on social balance, they developed what would be called Taoism. Like Confucius, they offered ways for human beings to fit into the Tao – the "way" of Nature, but instead of his emphasis on government and civic virtues this group recommended withdrawal from society. For the founders of Taoism, the Confucian approach to life was too artificial and complicated. What people really needed was to harmonize with the Tao, to "act naturally," without rational calculation and effort. They needed to stop trying so hard, and simply go with the flow of the Tao. For the Taoists, the main virtue was not *jen*, humaneness, but **wu-wei**, letting things happen on their own. *Wu-wei* is often described as creative inaction, or just simplicity.

The most important text in the Taoist tradition is the **Tao Te Ching** (*Daodejing*). It is attributed to Lao Tzu, but this is not a person's name; it is a description that means

FIGURE 8.6 Lao Tzu, riding his legendary "green" buffalo, Chinese, 18th century. Bibliothèque Nationale, Paris, France/Archives Charmet/The Bridgeman Art Library.

"old master." Scholars assume that the Tao Te Ching is a compilation of the work of more than one person.

The heart of Taoist teaching can be seen in the following principles from the *Tao Te Ching*:

- The Tao underlies everything. All events occur within the Tao.
- The things and qualities that emerge from the Tao are opposites – *yin* and *yang* – that complement each other and work together. "Opposition is the source of all growth." (Tao Te Ching, 6)
- The Tao does not exert itself. All events are within it, so there is nothing outside it for the Tao to act *on*. "The Tao never acts, yet it activates everything." (Tao Te Ching, 37)
- What happens in accordance with the Tao is good. "Whatever is natural is good." (Tao Te Ching, 50)
- Human beings are part of the Tao, and so find their happiness by living in accordance with the Tao. Indeed, "Whoever acts naturally is the Tao itself acting." (Tao Te Ching, 23)
- "The Tao is already as good as it can be." (Tao Te Ching, 29)
- "The Tao's way is to produce good without evil." (Tao Te Ching, 81)
- "The Tao cannot be improved upon. He who tries to redesign it, spoils it." (Tao Te Ching, 29)

This worldview is obviously optimistic and trusting of the natural world. To be happy, all people have to do is accept the natural order of things, instead of trying to change them, by creating complex governments and rules, for example. If we think of the Tao as a river in which we are floating, then we should let the current carry us along, rather than trying to swim upstream. "Do nothing, and nothing will be left undone," Lao Tzu said. (Tao Te Ching, 48)

The second most influential figure in Taoism is Zhuang Tzu ("Master Zhuang," 369–286 BCE), who was even more opposed to governments and rules than Lao Tzu was. Whereas the *Tao Te Ching* was addressed to rulers, Zhuang Tzu distrusts all rulers and government. He celebrates the value of *wu-wei*:

> [*Wu-wei*] makes a person the lord of all fame; *wu-wei* serves him as the treasury of all plans; *wu-wei* fits him for the burden of all offices; *wu-wei* makes him the lord of all wisdom.

In Zhuang Tzu's writing there is an appealing – and often challenging – playfulness and lack of solemnity that shows considerable imagination. In a famous passage, he tells how he woke from dreaming that he was a butterfly. Was that Zhuang Tzu dreaming he was a butterfly, he asks, or perhaps it was a butterfly dreaming he was Zhuang Tzu?

Some of the more imaginative parts of Zhuang Tzu's writing were taken literally by his readers. He writes, for example, about flying supermen who dine on air and feast on dew, who are immune to heat and cold, and who live forever. Instead of reading these passages as imaginative descriptions of people so practiced in the art of *wu-wei* that they became one with the Tao, some schools of Taoism understood them to be describing "The Immortals," and set out to discover how they could literally live forever.

As teaching about how to live in harmony with the universe, Taoism is loosely organized, with no central authority. So it allows for creativity and breadth of expression, developing many kinds of belief and practice – including divination techniques, acupuncture, several martial arts, and **feng-shui**, an approach to design based on channeling the natural energies of "wind" and "water."

Some schools of Taoist thought, as we said, sought immortality. Some thought they could achieve it through meditation, breathing exercises, fasting, and specific sexual practices. Others tried alchemy, making elixirs from gold and mercury. Gold was prized because it does not rust or decay, and solutions containing mercury can preserve living tissue. In 1972, archaeologists in China discovered the body of a middle-aged woman from the second century BCE, which had been immersed in a solution containing mercury sulfide. Its condition was nearly perfect, like the corpse of someone dead only a few weeks. These mercury-based concoctions, unfortunately, are highly toxic. Seven emperors died from drinking them to attain immortality.

Faced with the diversity of interests found in Taoist thought, some Western scholars have attempted to distinguish between religious and non-religious aspects of Taoism. It is perhaps more instructive to students of religion to simply recognize that the distinction between "religion" and other aspects of life is not universal. "Religious" Taoism and other aspects of Taoist thought and practice (sometimes called "philosophical Taoism") served to balance Confucianism's ruler-focused way of life with a nature-focused approach to life.

Buddhism in China

Around the same time that the teachings of Confucius and Lao Tzu were being offered as correctives to the decline in stability in China, another thinker was addressing similar questions in India. As we saw in Chapter 7, Siddhartha Gautama, the Buddha, advocated a life of simplicity, moderation, and compassion as a path to enlightenment or "awakening." (Although early scholars of Buddhism used the term "enlightenment," contemporary scholars consider the term "awakening" to be more accurate. We use the terms interchangeably.) However, his teachings were not confined to India. Buddhist missionaries spread the teachings of "the Middle Way" far and wide, and they actually became most popular outside of India.

Buddhist monks from India reached China via the "Silk Road" (the ancient trading route from Rome to western China) in the 1st or 2nd century CE. By that time, Buddha's teachings had undergone a number of interpretations and had developed into diverse practices. In a clear example of how religious teachings change to adapt to new cultures, early Chinese Buddhists, influenced by the Taoist quest for immortality, did not teach the Buddha's idea of *anatman*, "no-self," but instead taught that humans had an indestructible soul. So in Chinese Buddhism *nirvana* changed from meaning "awakening" by transcending the self, to meaning living fully as an individual, totally unaffected by anything or anyone else. Chinese Buddhists also taught rebirth – the idea described in Chapters 2 and 7 that individuals are

FIGURE 8.7 A painting of Confucius, Lao Tzu, and the Buddha together by Kano Masonobu, 1480. AKG Images/Ullstein Bild.

reborn into a number of lifetimes. In fact, the idea circulated widely that Lao Tzu, the founder of Taoism, had been reborn in India as the Buddha. This idea had the practical benefit of allowing emperors to worship Lao Tzu and the Buddha together.

Chinese Buddhism, then, was from the start distinctly Chinese, and was blended with Taoist and Confucian traditions.

Buddhism was especially popular in cities, where it received the patronage of emperors and aristocrats. People in the upper classes paid for the building of Buddhist temples and for the translation of Buddhist scriptures into Chinese.

At first, some Confucian scholars complained that Buddhism clashed with Chinese culture. Its monasteries with celibate monks undermined the Chinese emphasis on the family, and Buddhism did not emphasize service to the state as Confucianism did. They also pointed out that the gods and goddesses in Buddhism were foreign. These complaints fell mostly on deaf ears, however, because at the time, the Han Dynasty (206 BCE–220 CE), which supported Confucianism, was losing its power, and people were open to new ideas. After the Han Dynasty fell, Buddhism spread widely across China, and then into Korea by the 4th century CE. From there it spread to Japan by the 6th century, and within a century it had become Japan's state religion.

In China, when the Sui Dynasty (581–618) came to power, Buddhism became their official religion. In the next dynasty, the T'ang (618–907), the government expanded monasteries and supported pilgrimages to India.

Toward the end of the T'ang Dynasty, however, Emperor Wu-Tsung turned against Buddhism. In 845 he launched a major wave of persecutions. A quarter million monks and nuns were forced to return to life as laypeople, and 4,600 temples and 40,000 shrines were destroyed. After that, Buddhism was never as robust again in China. Yet it did survive, blending even more with the Taoist and Confucian traditions around it.

As Buddhism spread across East Asia, the two most important traditions were **Pure Land Buddhism** and Chan Buddhism (called Zen in Japan), and these are still the dominant forms of Buddhism in East Asia today.

Pure Land Buddhism

As we saw in Chapter 7, "Pure Land" is a group of schools in Mahayana Buddhism. They teach that, because we are living in a degenerate time, it is difficult to achieve nirvana through meditation. Instead of trying to reach "awakening" by our own efforts, we need to rely on "other power." Specifically, we need to ask the help of Amitabha Buddha, who in Japan is called Amida Buddha. Amitabha was originally a monk who vowed to save all beings, and the great merit he achieved created the Pure Land, a paradise where awakening into buddha-hood is assured. One of his vows was that he would grant rebirth in his Pure Land to those who recite his name, especially at the moment of death.

The difference between early Buddhism and Pure Land Buddhism is something like the difference between Catholicism and Protestantism in Christianity. Like Catholicism, early Buddhism taught that one had to work toward salvation; effort counted. But like Luther and Calvin, Pure Land Buddhists taught that people are too degenerate to work toward salvation themselves. Instead, they must rely on a savior to do the work. In Pure Land Buddhism, this is Amida Buddha, and in Protestantism it is Jesus. Protestants believe that only through faith in Jesus as Lord and Savior will they reach paradise. So too, Pure Land Buddhists believe that only by putting their faith in Amida Buddha will they reach paradise.

Because this movement did not require difficult meditation or study, it was especially popular among the common people. In some versions of Pure Land Buddhism, all that was necessary for salvation was saying the name of the Amida Buddha once.

Chan (Zen) Buddhism

The idea that people could leave it to a savior Buddha to bring them to nirvana was not accepted by everyone in China. By about 600 CE a school called *Chan* was forming. *Chan* is a Chinese translation of the Sanskrit word for meditation. This school emphasized that the

Buddha had taught that we achieve awakening through our own meditation; no one else can do it for us. Further, the Chan school rejected the idea of putting off awakening until the next life. They emphasized awakening in this life.

Meditating was the traditional Buddhist technique for reaching awakening, of course, but Chan Buddhists said that enlightenment should come suddenly and without great effort. Instead of studying scriptures and putting students through difficult meditation exercises in a gradual process of awakening, Chan masters developed quick, direct means to bring them to basic truths.

According to Chan tradition, the movement started in India when, instead of delivering a discourse on the Middle Way, the Buddha sat in silence, holding a flower in his hand. The students seemed confused about why the Buddha did not speak – except for one, who smiled knowingly. The Buddha handed him the flower; his smile had shown that he understood that there are no words for enlightenment. He was, in fact, already enlightened. After this, the secret of the smile was passed down through a succession of masters, until in the early 5th century CE Bodhidharma brought the Chan tradition to China. From there it went to Korea and then to Japan, where it was called Zen, from the Japanese *zazen*, meaning seated meditation.

In Zen Buddhism, meditation is not limited to sitting quietly. Any activity that is done "mindfully " – with full attention to what you are doing – can be meditation: archery, the martial arts, the tea ceremony, arranging flowers, making a garden, writing poetry, doing calligraphy, and painting are all good candidates for Zen mindful activity. Whatever you do, do it spontaneously, naturally, and with full attention. As the Zen saying goes, "Before enlightenment, chop wood, carry water. After enlightenment, chop wood, carry water." The spontaneous kind of awakening taught in Zen appealed especially to people attracted to the Taoist idea of *wu-wei* (achieving something through "creative inaction") and those who were suspicious of rational systems such as Confucianism. In Zen, logic and rational thinking are thought to get in the way of enlightenment. They are attempts to capture or master the world, and so they foster attachment to things, which Buddhism rejects.

Understanding through words and logic is inferior, according to Zen teaching, in at least three ways. First, it puts words and concepts between us and reality, while Zen seeks direct experience. Second, words and concepts are static, while reality is constantly changing. Third, conceptual thinking works by making distinctions, while reality is essentially a unity.

Our minds automatically form concepts and through them try to freeze, divide, and control what we experience. So we need to constantly remind ourselves that concepts are only tools and do not provide a direct connection with reality. To make this clear, Zen uses exercises such as **koans** to "break up" our natural reliance on conceptual thought. A koan is a question given to a student that has no rational answer. "What is the sound of one hand clapping?" "What did your face look like before your parents were born?" When students realize the futility of thinking logically about such questions, they relax, let go of conceptual thinking, and are open to awakening.

The purpose of Zen meditation is to go beyond words and concepts, even beyond subject and object, to direct experience of Ultimate Reality. To help students transcend conceptual thinking and logic, some Zen masters have said or done intentionally irrational things. When an ancient master known as Tozan was asked "What is the Buddha?" for example, he

Humor in Zen

FIGURE 8.8 Meditating frog, painting by Sengai. Idemitsu Museum of Arts.

The derailing of logical thought in Zen often strikes people as funny. Humor, psychologists tell us, is a reaction to incongruity – to something that violates our concepts and expectations. So humor is prized in Zen, and Zen masters may even sound like standup comedians.

A favorite Zen story is about the old master who lay dying. Closest to his bed were the oldest monks, and next to them were others in descending order of seniority. The senior monk leaned over and the master whispered, "Tell them Truth is like a river." The senior monk whispered the message to the next in line and told him to pass it on down the line, until it reached the youngest monk, who did not understand it. "What does he mean – Truth is *like a river*?" the young monk whispered to the one next to him. The question worked its way back up the line to the senior monk, who put it to the master. The master answered, "All right – Truth is *not* like a river."

With their emphasis on direct experience and spontaneity, Zen masters had little use for all the scriptures and commentaries on them in traditional Buddhism. If to reach nirvana we need to be non-attached, they said, then we should not be attached to doctrines. We should not even be attached to the Buddha himself. And so Zen has a lot of iconoclastic humor, that is, humor showing irreverence for the sacred. Master Sengai drew the picture in Figure 8.8 of a meditating frog with a big grin. His inscription on the picture is "If by sitting in meditation, one becomes a Buddha…." The implied punch line is "Then all frogs are Buddhas."

According to a beloved Zen story, the master Tanka visited a temple where deep snow had covered up the monks' supply of firewood. Feeling cold, he took one of the wooden images of the Buddha down from the altar, broke it up, and burned it for warmth.

Pushing this iconoclasm to the limit, the Zen master Tokusan said, "The Buddha is a dried piece of barbarian dung, and sainthood is only an empty name." There is even a Zen saying, "If you meet the Buddha on the road, kill him."

answered, "Three pounds of flax." Master Rinzai would often answer questions with "Kwatz" – which has no more meaning in Chinese than it does in English. Some masters have even responded to questions by slapping students or twisting their noses.

Chinese Folk Traditions

Long before the rise of Confucianism, Taoism, and Buddhism, people in China had developed strong attachments to ancestral gods, and many of the ancient folk traditions are still alive and well in China. They are part of Chinese "lived religion" (see Chapter 6) and are

Gods: Multi-Taskers or Otiose

Many gods have multiple tasks or functions. Often the relationship between gods' diverse roles is obvious. The Indian god Agni is both the god of fire and the messenger god – because human messages to the gods often come in the form of sacrifices, and the most efficient way to get the sacrifice to the gods is to burn it. The smoke becomes the vehicle of the offering. The Greek god Hermes is also a messenger, and the inventor of fire. With wings on his feet, he can fly from the abode of the gods to humans' earthly realm with ease. And his fire is the communicator of humans' messages to gods – again, in the form of sacrifices or burnt offerings.

The biblical and Qur'anic story of the trouble between Adam and Eve's two sons may actually allude to such a god-function. Both sons offered gifts to God, but the smoke carrying Cain's (Qabil's) gift drifted sideways – appearing to be rejected by Heaven – while Abel's (Habil's) smoke went straight up.

If there was such a god in ancient Mesopotamia, its name has been lost to history. In contrast to Western traditions, where the devotion to the one God required the demotion of earlier gods, Indian and Chinese traditions allow for multiple gods to coexist. In some cases the older gods remain prominent; in others the older gods recede in importance though they remain respected. Scholars have a term for such gods: *deus otiosus* – an extra, unnecessary, or idle god. The term *deus otiosus* is attributed to the Western rationalist movement called Deism in 17th- to 18th-century Europe to designate a god who may have created the world but is no longer involved in its workings. Eliade (see Chapter 4) uses it this way, noting that such gods may have been "closer" to humans in pre-history. Some scholars use the term more generically to refer to gods who became defunct when newer gods took over their functions or when society no longer needed their services. In Greek religions, for example, Uranus is replaced by his grandson Zeus and becomes "otiose," and in India the Vedic Indra recedes into the background as Shiva and Vishnu become more dominant.

blended with Confucianism, Taoism, and Buddhism. Just as children who grow up speaking two languages need not distinguish them, the Chinese can participate in all these traditions without thinking of them as "different religions," or even different anythings. As outsiders, *we* may say, "That wedding you went to today was Taoist, the funeral for your grandfather was Buddhist, and the harvest festival planned for next week is a folk tradition." But the people participating in these rituals need not make any such distinctions.

A good example of a folk religious tradition is the popular cult of the **Tu-Di-Gong**. (The "Di" in this name reflects its ancient Chinese origin; recall that Di was the Lord on High in the ancient Shang period.) This is a god who watches over a particular place – a town, a village, or even a building. Like a police officer walking his beat, the Tu-Di-Gong provides protection for the residents of that place. People can turn to him with requests about public or private matters, anything that calls for divine assistance.

For matters in the home, there is **Tsao Chun**, the kitchen god. His picture hangs on the wall above the stove, from where he watches over the family. Farmers pray to specific gods of farming, and pregnant women pray to goddesses of childbirth. As is common in folk traditions, each place, each profession, and each realm of life has deities (or saints) who can help.

One of the most popular of the ancient deities is Kuan Kung, originally a great general who came to be known as the god of war, and so was a patron of soldiers. But gradually his popularity expanded and so did his job description. In China today Kuan Kung is known as a god of healing, a god of wealth, and a god to invoke when finalizing a business contract. It is common to keep a statue of him facing the entrance of a home or in a place of business.

Rituals in Chinese Traditions

There is great variety across China in religious rituals, which come from Taoism, Confucianism, Buddhism, and folk traditions, but certain festivals are common everywhere. The longest and most important holiday is the celebration of the New Year, which begins with the new moon on the first day of the lunar year and ends with the full moon fifteen days later. On the last day is the Lantern Festival, when lanterns are lit and children carry lanterns in parades. As in many cultures, the new year is seen as a time to reestablish family unity and put aside bad feelings.

In preparation for New Year's festivities, people thoroughly clean their houses to sweep away traces of bad fortune and make way for good fortune. On windows and doors they place red paper decorations with popular themes of happiness, wealth, and longevity. One week before the New Year, the family goes to the kitchen, takes down the picture of Tsao Chun, the kitchen god, and puts honey on his mouth to make him happy. Then they send him on his way to the Jade Emperor, to report on what the family has been doing all year. They do this by burning his picture.

On New Year's Eve, there is a family feast with such foods as pork, duck, chicken, and sweets. The spirits of the ancestors are welcomed, bringing all the generations together. Early on New Year's morning, children wish their parents a healthy and happy new year, and the parents give them red envelopes containing money. Later there is lots of light and noise, as torches, lanterns, bonfires and firecrackers are lit to chase away the *kuei*, evil spirits.

Traditional New Year's celebrations included a ceremony to honor Heaven and Earth, the gods of the household, and the family ancestors. The family also put up a new picture of Tsao Chun, the kitchen god, to watch over them for another year.

Another popular festival is **Ch'ing Ming**, a day for remembering the ancestors. It is celebrated on the third day of the third month. Families visit the graves of dead relatives, offer sacrifices, and clean up or repair the grave, if necessary.

Like other cultures, the Chinese have rituals to mark rites of passage such as marriage and death.

Weddings

While ceremonies vary, the main functions of traditional Chinese weddings are to join the two people and the two families, and to ensure many descendants. Common themes are reverence for parents and ancestors, fertility, wealth, and the incorporation of the bride into her husband's family. To make sure that everything goes well, the day of the wedding is carefully chosen according to astrological signs. The color red, symbolic of love, joy, and prosperity, is everywhere in Chinese wedding rituals – it's the color of the bridal gown, the invitations, the gift boxes, and many of the decorations.

One tradition in preparation for the wedding is to have the bride-to-be withdraw from her ordinary routine and live in a separate part of the house with her best friends. This gives the young woman time to symbolically mourn the loss of her friends and family. The groom prepares by installing the new bridal bed on the day before the wedding. With the bed in place, children are invited onto the bed as an omen of fertility. Sometimes the bed is scattered with red dates, oranges, and other fruits, also as an omen of fertility.

On the morning of his wedding day, the groom is symbolically dressed by his parents. He then goes to the bride's house on the way to the place of the wedding, which may be his home. A child may accompany the groom as an omen of his future family, and firecrackers, drums, and gongs may announce the procession. He brings gifts of cash for his bride's friends, so that they will "let her go." The bride and groom then leave for the wedding ceremony together.

That ceremony is simple. The couple bow three times to Heaven and Earth, to their ancestors, and to Tsao-Chun, the kitchen god. Tea is then presented to the groom's parents, generally with two lotus seeds or two red dates in the cup. Lastly, the couple bow to each other, completing the ceremony.

Funerals

We have mentioned that ancestor worship has been important in China for thousands of years. We have also emphasized the practicality of the Chinese – their concern with the everyday things needed for a happy life. Both this practicality and the worship of ancestors show in the rituals that follow death. At a Chinese funeral, clothing, towels, money, even a toothbrush may be placed in the coffin. This shows how the mourners think of the next world – as very similar to this one. Often, rather than putting such things in the casket, they burn paper or cardboard replicas of them. This sends these necessities to the next world to get the dead person off to a good start. Today, even replicas of cell phones and computers

FIGURE 8.9 Traditional Chinese wedding. © Chao-Yang Chan/ Alamy.

are burned at funerals. If for some reason the family fails to conduct funeral rituals properly, on the other hand, this can bring misfortune on the family.

At the wake, the family gathers around the coffin. Children and daughters-in-law wear black to indicate that they grieve the most. Grandchildren wear blue and great-grandchildren light blue. Sons-in-law, who are thought of as outsiders, wear brighter colors such as white. The eldest son sits at the left shoulder of his dead parent and the widow or widower at the right. Food is placed in front of the coffin as an offering to the dead person. At night a monk may chant verses from Buddhist or Taoist scripture to help smooth the person's passage to the next world.

Chinese cemeteries are usually located on hillsides, since this is thought to improve feng-shui. Having a grave that is high on the hill is better still. When the coffin is taken from the hearse and lowered into the ground, everyone present must turn and look away.

After the burial, all clothes worn by the mourners are burned in order to avoid the bad luck associated with death. The family sets up a home altar to remember the person. Usually

FIGURE 8.10 Mao Zedong. © Bettmann/Corbis.

it features a picture of the person, and regular offerings of food, wine, or money are made to provide for the person's needs in the afterlife. Statues representing servants may also be placed near the altar. After 49 days, altars are usually taken down. This custom comes from the Mahayana Buddhist belief that the dead undergo judgment for 49 days before being reborn. After this the dead person is worshipped along with the rest of the family's ancestors. To keep their memory alive, their name and dates are inscribed on special wooden tablets, in which they are thought to dwell. These tablets are kept in a shrine at home and in the clan's ancestral temple. The standard period of mourning is 100 days; formerly, it was up to three years.

Chinese Traditions Today

The description of Chinese religious traditions that we have been giving does not take into account the huge cultural changes in China over the last 60 years. The most important was the new Communist government of Mao Zedong (1893–1976) that started in 1949. The

Communism and Religious Freedom in China

When Mao Zedong (d. 1976) came to power in 1949 and established the People's Republic of China, his government systematically suppressed religions for over two decades. He was especially hostile to the "old thought" of Confucianism, which he saw as the governing ideology of China before the Communist Revolution. Since the death of Mao in 1976, the government has been more tolerant toward traditional religion. However, the United States Commission on International Religious Freedom (USCIRF) lists China as a "Country of Particular Concern" in its 2010 Annual Report due to the country's restrictive legal framework regarding religions. According to China's National Regulations on Religious Affairs (NRRA), the state protects all "normal" religious activity, requiring religious groups to register with the state in order to determine whether they are to be protected. The law, passed in 2005 and updated two years later, lists Buddhist monasteries, Taoist temples, mosques and churches as examples of protected institutions, and mentions that in order to qualify for this protection a group must be "independent" and "self-governing." Any group that fails to register with the state, or that fails to meet the criteria of normalcy, independence, and self-governance in the eyes of the state, is subject to fines, confiscation of property, intimidation, and prosecution. USCIRF notes that Tibetan Buddhists and Uighur Muslims in particular have been subjected to harassment, as well as those Catholics and Protestant groups that refuse to submit to state regulation, and the new religious movement Falun Gong, which has been officially banned since 1999.

People's Republic of China accepted Karl Marx's (see Chapter 3) hostile assessment of religion and declared itself to be atheist. It systematically suppressed all religious traditions for decades. The last ten years of his rule were notoriously harmful to religions. As the government admits, "The 'cultural revolution' (1966 to 1976) had a disastrous effect on all aspects of the society in China, including religion." (http://www.china.org.cn) So under Communism, generations of Chinese grew up knowing little about Confucianism, Buddhism, or Taoism. As a result, the number of people who call themselves religious has declined to about 8%, the lowest rate in the world.

Despite this decline, the three big traditions, along with smaller organized traditions and folk traditions, did not die out in China. According to the Chinese government's count, there are still "over 100 million followers of various faiths," and the 1993 edition of *The Atlas of Religion* estimated the number of atheists in China at only 10–14%. Today Buddhism has the most adherents, followed by Taoism. There are also 18 million Muslims, 10 million Protestants, and 4 million Catholics, in a population of 1.35 billion. Since the death of Mao Zedong in 1976, the government has been more tolerant toward religions. It has even seen practical value in the way religions such as Buddhism help to build "the Harmonious Society." But it accepts only five traditions – Buddhism, Taoism, Islam, Protestantism, and Catholicism – and it requires them to register with the government. Practicing any other tradition is illegal. The government has branded one new religious movement, Falun Gong, an "evil cult" and has imprisoned and tortured thousands of its members.

Conclusion: Religious Studies and the Traditions of China

We saw in Chapter 7 that a number of scholars of religion question the use of the term "religion" outside its original Western – and particularly Christian – settings. They believe that using the term runs the risk of distorting the relative importance of various phenomena grouped under the "religion" rubric and missing some important phenomena that do not happen to fit into Western notions of "religion." We have noted throughout this chapter that Chinese traditions have more in common with each other than with their counterparts – in particular, Buddhism – practiced in other cultures. Indeed, although the study of religion identifies Taoism as a distinct tradition, we have pointed out that the notion of Tao is characteristically Chinese and is evident across the ideological divides in Chinese traditions. This raises again the question of the adequacy of our terminology as we attempt to understand not only other traditions, but our own as well. We will return to this discussion in Chapter 10. Before that, however, we will look at a smaller question: What qualifies a tradition as a "world religion"?

DISCUSSION QUESTIONS

1. Should Confucianism be counted as a religion?

2. Should Taoism be counted as a religion?

3. We have emphasized how the Chinese have a practical attitude toward religion, as in blending Confucianism, Taoism, Buddhism, and folk traditions. In traditional Chinese culture, most people were agricultural peasants living in rural areas. But now China is shifting to a manufacturing economy, with hundreds of millions of people moving into cities to work in factories. How do you think this might affect religion in China?

4. How would Emile Durkheim view the traditional Chinese emphasis on ancestors?

5. Because of overpopulation, China has in recent decades tried to restrict families to a single child. What impact might this have on religious traditions in China?

6. Can you think of any Western religious traditions that have ideas like those in Taoism?

7. Zen Buddhism has a tradition of irreverent humor. Do you know of humor in other religious traditions? How is it like and unlike the humor in Zen?

8. In addition to beliefs and practices from Confucianism, Taoism, and Buddhism, the Chinese have many folk traditions. Can you think of folk traditions in a Western

religious tradition – things that are not part of the official teachings and practices but grew up alongside the "official" religion?

9. Do some research on the new religious movements in China that have been suppressed by the government, such as Falun Gong. Why is the government so opposed to them?

REFERENCES

Patricia Buckley Ebrey, *Chinese Civilization: A Sourcebook*. New York: Free Press, 2nd ed., 1993.

Karl Jaspers, *Way to Wisdom: An Introduction to Philosophy*. New Haven, CT: Yale University Press, 1951.

Lao Tzu, Stephen Mitchell, translator, *Tao Te Ching: A New English Version*. New York: Harper Perennial, 2006.

Donald S. Lopez, editor, *Religions of China in Practice*. Princeton, NJ: Princeton University Press, 1996.

"The Present Conditions of Religion in China," http://www.china.org.cn/e-white/Freedom/f-1.htm.

FURTHER READING

Daniel A. Bell, *China's New Confucianism: Politics and Everyday Life in a Changing Society*. Princeton, NJ: Princeton University Press, 2010.

Jonathan Chamberlain, *Chinese Gods: An Introduction to Chinese Folk Religions*. Hong Kong: Blacksmith, 3rd ed., 2010.

Annping Chin, *The Authentic Confucius: A Life of Thought and Politics*. New York: Scribner, 2007.

Jacques Gernet, Franciscus Verellen, translator, *Buddhism in Chinese Society*. New York: Columbia University Press, 1998.

Deborah Sommer, *Chinese Religion: An Anthology of Sources*. New York: Oxford University Press, 1995.

ZOROASTRIANISM, SHINTO, BAHA'I, SCIENTOLOGY, WICCA, AND SENECA TRADITIONS

What Makes a "World Religion"?

FIGURE 9.1 © Chon Day 1993/The New Yorker Collection/
www.cartoonbank.com.

The Religion Toolkit: A Complete Guide to Religious Studies, First Edition. John Morreall and Tamara Sonn.
© 2012 John Morreall and Tamara Sonn. Published 2012 by Blackwell Publishing Ltd.

9

The earth is but one country, and humankind its citizens.

BAHA ULLAH, FOUNDER OF BAHA'I

Overview

Judaism, Christianity, Islam, Hinduism, Buddhism, Taoism, and Confucianism are generally called "world religions," but this designation is questionable since it is not based on a set of features they share. For example:

- Judaism is ancient and influenced many later traditions, but it is followed by only a tiny fraction of the world's population, while Zoroastrianism is older than Judaism and also influenced later traditions.

- Judaism, Christianity, and Islam are found throughout the world, but so is Baha'i; and Confucianism and Taoism are not international traditions, and they call themselves "teachings" rather than religions.

- Shinto is a national tradition, but its practitioners sometimes say it is a religion and sometimes say it is not a religion.

Such issues lead scholars to try to be more inclusive in their survey of religious traditions. In this chapter we shall survey six more traditions, pointing out key characteristics that may help us understand the phenomenon of religion.

- Zoroastrianism is the ancient tradition of Persia. It is monotheistic and scholars believe that its teachings about the purpose of life, the coming of a savior, and the afterlife influenced Judaism, Christianity, and Islam.

What Makes a "World Religion"?

Zoroastrianism
  History and Teachings of Zoroastrianism
  Zoroastrian Rituals

Shinto
  History and Teachings of Shinto
  Shinto Rituals

Baha'i
  History and Teachings of Baha'i
  Baha'i Rituals

Scientology
  History and Teachings of Scientology
  Scientology Practices
  Scientology Rituals

Wicca
  History and Teachings of Wicca
  Wiccan Rituals

The Traditions of the Seneca
  History and Teachings of the Seneca
  Seneca Rituals

Conclusion: To Be or Not to Be a Religion?

- Shinto, the ancient tradition of Japan, is so closely related to the rulers of Japan that it is often designated simply a national tradition rather than a religion, even though it involves belief in spiritual beings and rituals focusing on personal and family matters rather than political issues.
- Baha'i is less than two centuries old and accepts all other religions as valid.
- Scientology was invented by one man as a kind of psychotherapy; then he began calling it a religion.
- Wicca was developed in the 1950s to resurrect the "nature religions" of the British Isles before the arrival of Christianity.
- The Seneca, a Native American tribe, had no word or concept "religion," though other people often talk about their "beliefs" and "religious rituals."

After surveying these traditions, we shall return to the issue of defining religion, noting the political and legal implications of the designation.

What Makes a "World Religion"?

In the last three chapters, we have explored seven major traditions that are alive and well. This is far from a complete examination of the 10,000 traditions identified by The *World Christian Encyclopedia* as today's religions, not to mention the thousands that have gone extinct. We chose Judaism, Christianity, Islam, Hinduism, Buddhism, Confucianism, and Taoism because they are commonly called "world religions" – the "Big Seven" – in Religious Studies textbooks. But what makes them count as "world" religions? Is it because they are followed by huge numbers of people? This is not true of Judaism. Judaism is included because it is foundational to two traditions that are followed by large numbers of people. But if this is enough to be counted a "world religion," then Zoroastrianism should count too, because of its enormous influence – in the perspective of Religious Studies – on Judaism, Christianity, and Islam. But Zoroastrianism is not called a world religion. Is a "world religion" one that it is followed by people in diverse regions around the world? This does not apply to Confucianism and Taoism, for example, but they are among the Big Seven.

In fact, the inclusion of the seven traditions in the standard listing of "world religions" is somewhat arbitrary. It grew out of the early efforts by European scholars to understand the phenomenon of religion, which we discussed in Chapter 3. As we saw, it took some effort for Western Christian scholars to recognize non-Christian traditions as religions at all, rather than as mere "superstition," "magic," "heresy," or even the dreaded "paganism." The phrase "world religions" came into use when the first Parliament of the World's Religions was held in Chicago, during the time of the 1893 world's fair (the World Columbian Exposition), but representation at the Parliament was neither systematic nor comprehensive.

In light of such criticism, many universities have changed their "World Religions" courses to courses focused on specific traditions, such as Chinese traditions or Islamic Studies. Over the past several decades, scholars have thought more carefully about other categories as well, and have tried to treat all religious traditions with equal respect. Some have rejected the

What Is a Pagan?

FIGURE 9.2 Wiccan Beltane Fire Festival, Edinburgh, spring 2008.

Jeff J. Mitchell/Getty Images.

People who grew up in a monotheistic tradition often hear non-monotheists referred to as "pagans." Dictionary definitions of the term range from "non-believer" to "polytheist" – someone who believes in more than one god. The photo above, from *National Geographic*, depicts what it calls a "pagan fire fest," actually a Wiccan Beltane celebration of spring in 2008.

The term "pagan" is avoided by scholars of religion because of its negative connotations. The term comes from a Latin root that means someone from the countryside rather than from the city. The connotation goes beyond today's adjective "country" – referring to someone who is unsophisticated and lacks polish, someone with the characteristics valorized in "country" music in the U.S. (See Gretchen Wilson, "Redneck Woman" and Hank "Bocephus" Williams Jr., "A Country Boy Can Survive.") Reflecting the correlation between religion and politics throughout history, a pagan was someone not involved in the central government's urban religious organization and therefore was considered untrustworthy and a potential threat. So the Latin *paganus* refers to someone both uncivilized (literally: not living in settled/urban society) and uncouth (literally: not known to anyone in our group; outlandish – meaning from "outside our land" and therefore strange, foreign). A pagan was someone who did not recognize the religion of the city – the religion that legitimized the central government. This is why a pagan was a potential traitor, just like anyone else who failed to recognize the principles that legitimate the government.

"church–sect–cult" taxonomy that we mentioned in Chapter 1, seeing the term "church" as reflecting a unique (i.e., not universal) Christian paradigm, and "cult" as unnecessarily prejudicial. "New Religious Movements" (NRMs) is a phrase introduced by American scholar J. Gordon Melton (b. 1942) in the 1970s and adopted by many scholars in place of "cult." As well, many universities have introduced the study of African Traditional Religions (ATRs) into the curriculum, along with other "indigenous religions" of colonized areas – such as Native American Religions.

In this chapter, we shall briefly examine six traditions that do not get counted as "world religions." Two of them are ancient, one being international because of its profound influence on the monotheisms (Zoroastrianism), and the other being found only in Japan (Shinto). We shall also look at two new religions (Baha'i and Scientology), and one that defies categorization as ancient or new (a modern version of an ancient tradition – Wicca). We shall then consider the traditional culture of the Seneca, an indigenous people of what is now New York State. Having surveyed these diverse traditions, we should have a broader understanding that will help us as we return to the question of defining religion.

Zoroastrianism

History and Teachings of Zoroastrianism

Before Islam came to Iran (formerly called Persia) in the 7th century, Zoroastrianism was the major religion there. It probably began in the 9th or 10th century BCE, but it appears in historical records only in the 6th century BCE. Founded by the prophet Zoroaster, it was the state religion of several Persian empires. Iran today lies between India to the East and what the ancient Greeks called Mesopotamia to the West. Scholars of religion are therefore not surprised to find that Zoroastrianism has much in common with both Hinduism and the Western monotheistic traditions. Many of the core beliefs of Christians, Jews and Muslims have earlier counterparts in Zoroastrian tradition. According to Mary Boyce (2001,1), "Zoroastrianism is the oldest of the revealed world-religions, and it has probably had more influence on mankind, directly and indirectly, than any other single faith." Ideas in Western monotheism about the cosmic struggle between good and evil, the coming of a savior who will ultimately vanquish evil, a final judgment, and life after death are examples.

As we saw in Chapter 2, according to Zoroastrian teaching, the single eternal and transcendent god, Ahura Mazda, created a beautiful and orderly universe. Evil is represented by Angra Mainyu, also known as Ahriman, an evil spirit independent of the great creator Ahura Mazda. All of history is characterized by the conflict between good and evil, but in the end Ahura Mazda will triumph over all evil.

Zoroastrianism teaches that human beings participate in the maintenance of a well ordered universe by thinking, speaking, and acting well. Prefiguring the biblical teaching, Zoroastrianism teaches that at the end of time, a savior – a **Saoshyant** ("one who brings benefit") – will renew the world, restoring its perfect order. The Saoshyant, according to tradition, will be born of a virgin – a characteristic that was later stressed in Christian and Islamic teachings about Jesus. Dead people will be resurrected and they, along with the people still living at that time, will be judged. From a History of Religions perspective (see Chapter 4), this appears to be a forerunner of biblical teachings about the Last Judgment.

The details of the final judgment vary slightly in different Zoroastrian traditions. According to some versions, judgment will be by ordeal. People will have to walk through a river of molten stone. To those whose thoughts, words, and deeds were pure, the river will feel like cool milk. Those who contributed to disorder through dishonest thoughts, words, or deeds will, of course, burn. According to another version, people will have to cross a very narrow bridge suspended above fires of molten rock. Those whose thoughts, words, and deeds were pure will be guided easily across the bridge by the luminous reflection of their souls. This reflection will be in the form of a pure – or "virginal" – angelic figure, a daena, standing in paradise at the end of the bridge.

Scholars have coined a technical term for a "guide for the soul" – **psychopomp** – because such figures are found in a number of traditions around the world. The psychopomp role can be played by ancestors, for example, as they are in some African traditions, or angels, as in some folk traditions of Judaism, Christianity, and Islam. In the modern Persian language, the term for the daena is *din*, which, as we saw in Chapter 1, is used for the English term "religion" – so that religion becomes the "guide for the soul." The Persian term is also related to the Sanskrit *dharma*, which, as we saw in Chapter 7, can be translated as law or duty – also appropriate "guides for the soul."

Interestingly, scholars see the Zoroastrian daena as a possible source for the traditional Islamic teaching of the houris. As we saw in Chapter 6, houris are mentioned in the Qur'an as "pure companions" for those who make it to heaven. But in Islamic traditional literature (hadiths), they are described as voluptuous heavenly virgins awaiting righteous men. It goes without saying that these traditions have been passed on by males, some of whom have determined that there will be precisely 72 such beauties awaiting them. Why 72? The Muslim traditionists do not explain. But in a fascinating coincidence, the special belt – kushti (or kusti) – that Zoroastrians wear for prayer is made of 72 perfectly white wool threads. These 72 threads represent the 72 chapters of Zoroastrian scripture (Yasna, the main collection and the ritual recitation of scripture). Kushti means "pathfinder," again indicating a connection with the notion of daena as a psychopomp. The Zoroastrian undershirt worn during prayer is called a shudreh (or sedreh), "good" or "righteous path." And in another fascinating coincidence, some scholars relate the term shudreh to the Sanskrit *shudra*. As we saw in Chapter 7, in Hindu teaching the shudras are the lowest varna. But the root meaning of the term in Sanskrit is "color of the soul," which seems to tie in with the notion of the daena as a luminous reflection of one's conscience.

Also like Abrahamic traditions, Zoroastrian scripture was revealed to the human race through a prophet, in this case Zoroaster. The holy volume is called the Avesta. It includes the **Gathas**, hymns attributed to Zoroaster, as well as later writings, totaling twenty-one books.

Other aspects of Zoroastrian teaching about spiritual beings are complex and have evolved over time. For example, Ahura Mazda's communication with humans comes through a number of Entities or Attributes, called the Bounteous Immortals. In Zoroaster's writings, these Immortals are sometimes presented as abstract concepts and other times described as if they are persons. In one version of the theology, Ahura Mazda had rival twin sons, Spenta Mainyu (Bounteous Spirit) and Angra Mainyu (Destructive Spirit). The first

Freddie Mercury, Famous Zoroastrian

FIGURE 9.3 Freddie Mercury.
© Hulton-Deutsch Collection/Corbis.

Freddie Mercury (d. 1991), lead singer of the British band Queen, was born Farookh Bulsara to Indian parents who were Parsees. He grew up in Mumbai and was initiated into Zoroastrianism at age 8 in the ancient ceremony called Mayjote. After a bath of purification, during which a priest chanted prayers, young Freddie stood before one of the eternal fires and repeated the prayers of acceptance into Zoroastrianism. Then he was given his *shudreh*, a shirt made of white muslin symbolizing innocence and purity. Around his waist the priest tied the kushti, a cord made of pure white lamb's wool symbolizing service to humanity. The kushti was wrapped around him three times to remind the young boy of the three aspects of Ahura Mazda – creator, preserver, and rebuilder of the world. Finally, the boy was showered with rice, rose petals, coconut, and pomegranate and dressed in his new clothes.

In Mumbai, Freddie attended St. Peter's boarding school, where he learned Western classical music along with Indian music. There he and four schoolmates formed the rock band The Hectics, in which he played piano. When he was 18, Freddie's family moved to Britain, where he attended Ealing College of Art in London. Later he played in several bands, most famously Queen, which he formed with Brian May, Roger Taylor, and John Deacon. Freddie wrote most of their hit songs, including *Bohemian Rhapsody* and *We Are the Champions*. When Mercury died in 1991, his funeral was conducted by Zoroastrian priests in the ancient Avestan language.

chose good, and so is associated with truth, justice, and life. The Destructive Spirit, Angra Mainyu, chose evil and so destruction, injustice, and death. In Zoroaster's telling, these forces are under the ultimate control of Ahura Mazda. However, after Zoroaster was gone, some of these forces were re-described by later generations as gods themselves. In some interpretations, Ahura Mazda was identified as the god of good and Angra Mainyu as the god of evil, calling into question the monotheism of Zoroastrianism.

In the 7th century, when Arabs brought Islam to Persia, many Persians converted to the new religion. In the 8th–10th centuries, Zoroastrianism was suppressed in Persia, so many of its members emigrated east to India, settling in the Gujarat and Maraharashtra states, especially around Mumbai. There they were called "Parsees," that is, Persians. Most Parsees were farmers until the British colonized India in the 18th century. They flourished under the British, adopting British customs and dress. By the 19th century, the Parsees were well known in Indian society for their education, generosity, and success in business.

Today there are fewer than 200,000 Zoroastrians worldwide, mainly in Iran and India. Famous Zoroastrians include the orchestra conductor Zubin Mehta, the rock musician Freddie Mercury of the band Queen, and the Tata family, who are car manufacturers in India. While Zoroastrianism discourages marriage with outsiders, many Zoroastrians in modern times have intermarried. Women are encouraged to join the professions, too, so they tend to have fewer children than their neighbors. Intermarriage and the low birth rate have contributed to the decline in the number of Zoroastrians.

Zoroastrian Rituals

The energy of Ahura Mazda, the creator, is represented by fire, the sun, and light in general. (This is why General Electric used "Mazda" as a brand name for light bulbs from 1909 to 1945.) Zoroastrians pray in front of a fire or a source of light. Rituals center around fire, keeping it lit, and feeding the fire five times a day.

The centrality of fire in Zoroastrian ritual has misled some into believing that Zoroastrians are "fire-worshipers." They do not worship fire. Instead, fire represents Ahura Mazda and it is seen as a purifying element. Zoroastrian worship services are carried out in a "fire temple" – a building that houses an urn with a fire and a source of water. The fire is in a small central room with no other source of light. The fire is maintained by a priest, the only person allowed to enter the special room. The priest conducts the Yasna service, the recitation of Avestas in their entirety. At the end of the recitation, the priest makes an offering "to the water" of a mixture of hoama twigs (see Chapter 7), pomegranate, and milk, for symbolic purification.

The most important Zoroastrian holiday is the beginning of the new year, **Norūz**, believed to have been founded by Zoroaster. It is celebrated on the first day of the vernal (Spring) equinox, around March 21. Even after Zoroastrianism was marginalized by Islam in Iran, Norūz remained a popular holiday, as it is still throughout regions influenced by Persia. It remains a holiday in many parts of Central Asia, India, Afghanistan, and Kashmir, though generally without religious significance for non-Zoroastrians, and is celebrated by Baha'is and some Muslims as a religious holiday, too.

Similar to Jewish practice associated with Passover, Zoroastrians prepare for Norūz with a thorough housecleaning. As well, on the last Tuesday evening of the year is the

FIGURE 9.4 A Zoroastrian priest starts a fire as part of Sadeh, the ancient feast celebrating the creation of fire. © Eye Ubiquitous/SuperStock.

"Festival of the Fire." People build fires outside and jump over them. In the secular celebrations of Norūz, people think of this as marking the transition from the old year to the new year. The religious meaning is expressed in a prayer in which people consign their fears, weakness, and suffering to the fire for purification, exchanging them for courage, strength, and health in the new year.

It is also common for people to precede the holiday with prayers at the family cemetery. Reflecting the folk belief that the ancestors' spirits visit at this time, children traditionally put on "ghost" costumes and go from house to house to get sweets.

On new year's day itself, people put on new clothes and begin a 12-day period of visiting family members and friends, where they are served sherbet, pastries, and dried fruits and nuts. A special table is set for Norūz, the "Seven S's" (*haft sin*) table, with flowers and seven items beginning with the letter "s." These items symbolize good things for the new year: rebirth, wealth, love, beauty, health, and patience.

Zoroastrians share with Hindus a concern for purity. This is perhaps most evident in their unique funerary practice. According to Zoroastrian rules of purity, a corpse is utterly impure – the ultimate pollutant. Only specially ordained "pollutant caretakers" – nasellars – can handle them safely. The nasellar takes the corpse to a dakhma – a circular tower with an inclined plane on top (known in English as "towers of silence"), where it is exposed to the elements (and birds of prey) until all that is left are bones. Once the bones are thoroughly dried out, they are put in a pit at the center of the tower where they gradually disintegrate and disappear into the soil, eventually to be washed to sea.

Shinto

History and Teachings of Shinto

As we saw, many of Zoroastrians' foundational beliefs are shared by other monotheists throughout the world, and the secular celebration of the new year in the spring is popular in diverse cultures. Shinto, by contrast, is an ancient tradition grounded in one place and one culture, Japan. It flourished in Japan long before the Chinese traditions of Confucianism and Buddhism arrived, and has continued to reflect Japanese culture and values throughout the ages.

Shinto has no founder, no inerrant doctrines, and no scriptures that are considered sacred, as if they were revealed by a god. The oldest written record of its teachings and practices dates from the 8th century. Known as the **Kojiki** ("Records of Ancient Matters"), this text includes a story describing the creation of Japan. The gods commissioned the creation of a new, perfect land. After some missteps, the eight islands of Japan were created. The missteps had to do with attempts to defy the laws of nature – which in the story included the priority of males over females. According to the story, when the man and woman commissioned by the gods to create this beautiful place began their project, the woman greeted the man first – and nothing happened. Then they tried again, but with the man speaking first; this time things went much more smoothly.

As we have seen (in Chapters 5 and 7, for example), explanations for the subservient status of women are not unusual in religious traditions. They reflect the rise in the social status of warriors as human beings made the transition from hunter-gatherer to agrarian lifestyles and warriors were needed to protect the newly settled land on which people's livelihood depended. With the ascendancy of warriors came the domination of males over females – particularly in their control of female sexuality, as warriors sought to make sure that their offspring alone benefited from the fruits of their labor. However, Shinto is not one of the traditions known for inequality between males and females. The emphasis in the Kojiki is less on social or moral teachings than on the rise of the imperial family who commissioned the text. The second oldest text, the **Nihon Shoki** ("Continuing Chronicles of Japan"), also from the 8th century, focuses even more intently on formalizing the imperial government. These early sources demonstrate that, from the beginning, Shinto has been a strictly Japanese tradition and reflects a fundamental orientation toward nature.

Shinto is not the only tradition that has influenced Japan. We saw in Chapter 8 that Buddhism came to Japan from Korea in the 6th century, and Confucianism not long thereafter. Many Shinto shrines were built on the grounds of Buddhist temples and evidence from the earliest written records of Shinto show signs of Buddhist influence. Starting around 1600, religious scholars in Japan emphasized the unity of Shinto and Confucian teachings in such things as the virtues of filial piety, sincerity and loyalty, and the need for emperors to show wisdom, benevolence, and courage. Still, Shinto remains the indigenous tradition of Japan.

The word *Shinto* comes from the Chinese *Shēntao*, which means "the way of **kami**." In a general sense, kami means divine or supernatural power – "the force" or power of the universe, which is considered sacred in all its manifestations. In a narrower sense, kami

Kamikaze: the First Suicide Bombers?

FIGURE 9.5 *Kami kaze* – "the wind of the kami" or "divine wind."

Most people think of Kamikaze as the deadly attacks by Japanese planes, full of explosives, against Allied sites during World War II. That is indeed the name given to these suicide attacks. The name actually comes from the Japanese *kami*, for god, and *kaze*, wind. It is the name given to the giant storms that protected the Japanese from invading Mongol fleets in the 13th century. The practice of crashing planes into targets began with the use of planes for war. When a plane was damaged or on the verge of being captured, pilots were instructed to use them as weapons – a more honorable course of action. Interestingly, the Japanese were not the only ones instructed to do so. American pilots were told to do the same thing.

refers to various gods and spirits. Some kami are associated with specific natural forces such as wind (*kami kaze*) and waves, and some with natural elements such as rocks and mountains – good examples of what scholars call animism (see Chapter 5). Some kami are associated with more abstract powers such as growth and healing – good examples of anthropomorphism (see Chapter 5). Some are imagined in more human form – including heroic figures of the past and ancestors, and some are considered guardians who protect specific places or clans. Unlike many traditions we have discussed, where deities are in competition with one another, Shinto kami are said to cooperate with each other and with people. They reflect a harmonious natural order. Moreover, because they are guardians of people, establishing good relationships with them brings general prosperity.

Proper relationships with the kami are characteristically maintained through veneration at shrines – both public shrines and private shrines in homes. In contrast to traditions that are based on belief or faith, such as Christianity, and those based on following moral laws, such as Judaism and Islam, Shinto is based on ritual practice – specifically veneration of kami at shrines. This does not mean, however, that Shinto is devoid of moral teachings. In Shinto, bad deeds – such as lying, stealing, and murder – show extreme disrespect and therefore are described as impure. Shrines, as the abode of kami, are pure, and other places are made pure through ceremonies conducted by priests. New buildings, for example, and even cars are commonly purified by priestly rituals.

Schematizing the vast diversity of Shinto, scholars distinguish several kinds of Shinto practice, including folk Shinto, state or shrine Shinto, and sect Shinto. Folk Shinto is the oldest and least systematized form of Shinto practice. It is a rural phenomenon, grounded in agricultural tradition. Consistent with its oral roots, folk Shinto has a remarkable array of practices and reflects a good deal of syncretism (mixing of elements from a range of sources). Folk Shinto centers on the veneration of small roadside images and on agricultural rites associated with planting and harvest. However, it also includes divination and healing practices (shamanism; see Chapter 5), and spirit possession (see Chapter 2).

State Shinto dates from the earliest written records of Shinto, the Kojiki, which describe the ascendancy of the leaders of a clan who lived near the city of Nara, whose kami was the sun goddess **Amaterasu**. (Many countries identify periods in their history by the name of the ruler or dynasty, such as Britain's "Victorian Era" or the Chinese "Ming Dynasty." But Japan's classical history is commonly divided into periods identified by the name of the region or capital of the ruling family – reflecting the importance of place in Japanese thought. So the period during which the Kojiki was produced is called the Nara period, 710–794 CE.) The ruling clan were described as descendants of Amaterasu, and she was considered the most important kami of all. This clan was therefore recognized as the Japanese imperial household and became the center of the Japanese nation. The Kojiki explains that Amaterasu herself bequeathed to them the **Three Sacred Treasures** in Shinto – the mirror, sword, and jewel, which represent wisdom, valor, and wealth or generosity, respectively.

Under this union of Shinto with the state, the government supported thousands of shrines and provided offerings to the kami. By around 900 CE there were 3,000 shrines throughout Japan receiving state offerings. As the strength of the central government declined, however, state Shinto declined along with it. After 1300, the government supported far fewer shrines and offerings. Nevertheless, the Three Sacred Treasures remain symbols of the imperial authority to this day (even though their precise locations are not known with certainty and no one but the emperor and priests of the imperial household are allowed to see them). Clearly demonstrating the fusion of religious authority and political power, the word for "government" in Japanese is *matsuri-goto*, which means "affairs of religious festivals," and the Japanese emperor remains today the symbolic head of state as well as the highest authority in Shinto.

"Shrine Shinto" refers to the common practice centered on visits to any of the thousands of shrines spread across the length and breadth of Japan. People go to shrines and express their respect for the kami on special occasions, and to ask for protection and assistance with specific undertakings. As well, major public celebrations, such as seasonal festivals, are marked by visits to shrines.

"Sect Shinto" is a term devised in the 19th century for practices not conducted at state-maintained shrines but in private halls instead. Sect Shinto is often described as a more spiritually oriented practice than the nationalist state Shinto. Scholars currently identify 13 groups practicing "Sect Shintoism." They include groups concerned with purification, healing, and devotion to a specific kami such as that of the sun or Mount Fuji (the highest peak in Japan). Some of these groups are considered "new" – dating from only the last century.

Shinto Rituals

The most common Shinto ritual is worship at the family shrine – the kamidana. A kamidana is a "kami home" where the family kami lives. The kamidana is usually on a high shelf and contains a special object called a shintai – which can be a mirror, a stone, or any of a wide

FIGURE 9.6 A Shinto shrine with a torii gate. © JTB Photo/SuperStock.

variety of other things that are considered suitable places for the kami to abide. (Kamidana are also commonly found in Japanese martial arts studios called dojos.) Kamidana ritual is simple. It begins with washing the hands and involves prayers and gifts of food and flowers to the kami in the shintai.

Public Shinto shrines are identifiable by their distinctive gates – torii. Torii are constructed of two upright members and two lintels, the upper one longer than the first lintel and curved. Torii are often unpainted, but if they are painted, it is in bright reddish-orange (vermillion). Shrines may have more than one such gate. Some have many, since it is common for people to donate torii in gratitude for blessings. Crossing through a torii symbolizes entry into sacred space, the domicile of the shrine's kami.

People go to shrines for special occasions, entering through the torii into the public worship and offering halls. There is another room that only the priest can enter, except for special occasions. This is the room housing the shintai.

Rituals at shrines vary but commonly include bowing to show respect before entering the shrine. People also remove their shoes, again to show respect. Many shrines have basins with ladles so that worshipers may wash their hands, mouth, and feet. Some shrines have bells, which people ring before praying. After prayer people bow again and put their hands together in a clapping motion before completing a final bow.

Japanese weddings are traditionally performed at Shinto shrines. In the most traditional form, the bride is covered in white make-up and wears a white kimono to symbolize that she is a virgin. Her hat is decorated with good luck charms, and she may also wear a hood symbolizing deference to her new mother-in-law. The groom wears a black kimono. The priest purifies the couple and the guests. The couple exchange vows, and then they, their family, and close friends drink cups of sake (an alcoholic drink brewed from rice) to symbolize their union. Traditionally the bride and groom take nine sips of sake. After this, the bride changes into a red kimono (and then into other fancy kimonos or dresses as well) and a festive reception begins.

A great variety of other practices are associated with Shinto, including kagura, ritual dance accompanied by music and believed to protect the souls of the newly departed and to please the ancestor kami. Practices associated with assuring good fortune are also common in Shinto. People can buy (or make an offering in return for) a special amulet for protection, or for a prediction about their future. But many of these practices are a result of Shinto's interaction with other traditions (primarily Buddhist) and are considered folk practices.

Baha'i

History and Teachings of Baha'i

The identity of Shinto and the state in Japan was reinforced in the modern period, beginning with the Meiji Restoration in 1868. The power of the imperial family, whose ascendancy was described in the Kojiki and Nihon Shoki, had declined in the Middle Ages, and feudal warlords (shoguns) had taken control of various regions. In 1868, the shoguns ceded authority to Mitsuhito, descendent of the imperial family, who was acknowledged as the Emperor Meiji, "the enlightened emperor." The motto of the government officials was "Shinto ceremonies and political affairs are one and the same." During this period of modernization in Japan, the government set up a Bureau of Shrines, Shinto holidays were declared national holidays, and the emperor was revered as the symbol of the nation itself. It would be hard to find a better example of Durkheim's theory that "God is society, writ large" (see Chapter 4). So intense was the identification of Shinto and the state that, following Japan's defeat in World War II, the American occupation forces "disestablished" Shinto as the state religion and forced the emperor to declare that he was human (rather than a kami).

In contrast to this identification of Shinto with the Japanese state, Baha'i is a religion that forbids political involvement. The Baha'i religion was founded in the mid-1800s by a Persian nobleman who took the name Baha Ullah ("glory of God"). He was born a Shi'a Muslim. His followers said that he was the latest of a series of prophets that includes Abraham, Zoroaster, Krishna, Moses, the Buddha, Jesus, and Muhammad. Baha Ullah wrote over 100 works, which his followers believe to be divinely inspired. Today there are over six million Baha'is around the world, representing over 2,100 ethnic, racial, and tribal groups. Their scriptures have been translated into over 800 languages.

Membership is open to everyone who accepts the teachings of Baha Ullah. There are no initiation rituals, clergy, sacraments, or worship rituals. Baha'is are governed locally by an elected assembly. There are also national assemblies, and they come together periodically to elect the Universal House of Justice, which is the supreme administrative, legislative, and judicial body for Baha'is.

The essential message of Baha Ullah is unity and peace. The three basic teachings in Baha'i are the unity of God – Allah in Baha'i texts, the unity of religion, and the unity of the human race. The concept of God is the familiar monotheistic one of an eternal, transcendent creator who is omniscient, almighty, and the source of all revelation.

God has sent messengers since ancient times, Baha Ullah taught. Their messages may sound different, because each was adapted to a specific time and place, but the essential revelation in all of them is one. Thus all the world's religions are valid. Some social rules, such as dietary restrictions, may be specific to one culture at a particular time, but general principles, such as charity and being a good neighbor, hold for all people for all time.

All human beings have a "rational soul," and so can recognize God as their creator. All have a responsibility to recognize the sovereignty of God and the message of his prophets. Through worship and obedience, prayer and serving others, they become closer to God. At death, the soul passes into the next world, is judged, and proceeds with the spiritual development it began in its earthly life. Heaven and Hell are spiritual states of the soul's nearness or distance from God.

The teachings of Baha Ullah include discourses on spiritual growth, and Baha'is are encouraged to meditate on them. Baha Ullah describes stages of spiritual development, beginning with the desire to grow closer to God. One must follow her inclination toward God as a lover is drawn to a loved one. Through patience and perseverance, the seeker will begin to understand the mysteries of life and see God in all creation. Losing all traces of ego, successful seekers will be unaffected by either good or bad fortune, and will abide in ecstatic wonder at the glory of God.

On the social level, Baha'is believe that, because the human race is one and its members are equal, sexism, racism, nationalism, and social classes are obstacles to human development. The time has come, Baha Ullah taught, for all peoples to unite into a peaceful and integrated global society. "The earth is but one country, and humankind its citizens," he wrote.

The unity of humankind is well reflected in Baha'i itself. Although its members come from over 2,100 ethnic groups, there are no factions or sects. Even the process of electing local and national assemblies involves no parties, nominations, or campaigning for office.

For a global society to flourish, Baha Ullah said, it must be based on moral principles. They include the elimination of all prejudice, equality between the sexes, the elimination of extremes of poverty and wealth, universal education, the harmony of science and religion, a sustainable balance between nature and technology, and the establishment of a world government.

These goals are obviously similar to those of the United Nations, and many Baha'is work in cooperation with the United Nations. Indeed, taking citizenship responsibilities seriously is a major Baha'i value. Baha'is are required to obey the laws of their country of residence and participate in elections. However, they are not allowed to join political parties, run for office, or accept political appointments. Partisan political involvement is considered a violation of the Baha'i ethic of working for social unity.

Jazz Tuesdays at the Baha'i Center, New York City

FIGURE 9.7 Dizzy Gillespie. © Craig Lovell/ Corbis.

Dizzy Gillespie (d. 1993) was one of the greatest jazz trumpeters of all time. His early years reflected the stereotypical jazz life: amazing music interrupted by drugs, alcohol, and violence. He was also irreverent. In 1964 he ran for president. He promised that if he were elected, the White House would be renamed "The Blues House," and his cabinet would be composed of Duke Ellington, Secretary of State; Miles Davis, Director of the CIA; Max Roach, Secretary of Defense; Charles Mingus, Secretary of Peace; Ray Charles, Librarian of Congress; Louis Armstrong, Secretary of Agriculture; Mary Lou Williams, Ambassador to the Vatican; Thelonious Monk, Traveling Ambassador; and Malcolm X, Attorney General. He said his running mate would be Phyllis Diller.

Four years later, Gillespie became a Baha'i. In his memoirs he writes that becoming a Baha'i changed his life. He became a teacher and mentor to young artists.

The Baha'i Center in New York City honors Mr. Gillespie's work, holding jazz concerts every Tuesday. He is now known as the "Beebop Baha'i."

Baha'i Rituals

Like Zoroastrianism, Baha'i teaches that we have a duty to live in the world and improve it. Useful work is a form of worship. Baha'is are required to pray daily and abstain from alcohol and non-medical drugs, gambling and extra-marital sex. They also observe an annual sunrise-to-sunset fast from March 2 to March 20, the final month of the Baha'i calendar, followed by the celebration of the new year on Norūz.

The Baha'i calendar consists of 19 months of 19 days each. The calendar is fixed in accordance with the Gregorian calendar, so four extra days are inserted to make 365. (During the Gregorian "leap year," five days are added.) These "intercalary" days are inserted

FIGURE 9.8 Baha'i temple in Wilmette, Illinois, in the U.S. © Corbis/SuperStock.

just before the month of fasting. Known as Ayyam-i Ha, the "days of H" (which is a symbol of God), they are the occasion for festive meals, family visits, and gift-giving.

Baha'is' greatest celebration is the 12-day Ridvan Festival. It begins on April 21 of the Gregorian calendar, and commemorates the announcement of Baha Ullah as prophet. The first, ninth, and twelfth days are the holiest, and are marked with communal prayers. Other holy days include the declaration of the Bab, the forerunner of the Baha Ullah (May 23), the ascension of Baha Ullah to heaven (May 29), the martyrdom of the Bab (July 9), the birth of the Bab (November 12), the Day of the Covenant (November 26), and the ascension of Baha Ullah's son Abdul Baha to heaven (November 28).

Baha'is have established a number of houses of worship around the world. Currently, there are seven: one each in Wilmette, Illinois, in the U.S.; Kampala, Uganda; Sydney, Australia; Frankfurt, Germany; Panama City, Panama; Tiapapata, Samoa; and Delhi, India. The first one was built in Ashgabat, Turkmenistan, but was confiscated by the Soviet government in 1938, damaged by an earthquake in 1948, and destroyed in 1963. One is under construction in Santiago, Chile. The Baha'i houses of worship are constructed with nine sides so that they seem circular. They have no altars or decoration other than the words of Baha'i scripture in exquisite calligraphy. They are surrounded by beautiful gardens and are meant to serve their communities. They are open to all people. No rituals or sermons are conducted in them, only prayer and meditation.

Marriage is a solemn undertaking in Baha'i, an institution that brings great happiness and spiritual development to the spouses, and creates the essential foundation for society – the

PART II USING THE TOOLS: SURVEYING WORLD RELIGIONS

family. The ceremony itself is simple, consisting of vows to abide by the will of God, made by the bride and groom to each other and witnessed by two people.

Scientology

History and Teachings of Scientology

Although Baha'i is a "new" religion established in the modern age, it is not considered an NRM (New Religious Movement) because of its ancient origins. Baha'i is to Islam as Islam is to Judaism and Christianity, and Christianity is to Judaism. Its roots are in what it calls earlier "dispensations" of the one religion, brought by successive "manifestations" (messengers) of the one God. Scientology, on the other hand, is definitely a new movement, although, as we shall see, there is some dispute as to whether or not it counts as "religious."

Scientology was founded by L. Ron Hubbard (1911–1986) – an American writer specializing in adventure and fantasy stories. In 1937, Hubbard started developing a worldview based on dualism. "Life is composed of two things," he wrote, "the material universe and an X-factor… that can evidently organize and mobilize the material universe." This "X-factor" is similar to traditional ideas of spirit and soul. In 1950 Hubbard published *Dianetics: The Modern Science of Mental Health*, in which he presented a kind of psychotherapy for dealing with harmful emotions such as irrational fears. He invented the term *Dianetics* for the study of "what the soul is doing to the body."

Dianetics is the most popular self-help book of all time, selling over 21 million copies, but it was met with concern by mental health professionals. The American Psychological Association issued a warning in September of 1950 for professionals to avoid "the techniques 'peculiar' to a new approach to mental health called Dianetics," noting that they were not based on empirical evidence. Soon after its publication, Hubbard began shaping the ideas in this book into a new religion that he called "Scientology." This term had been coined earlier in the 20th century to refer to either religious devotion to science or the study of science as a phenomenon. Hubbard used this in a new way to mean "the study of knowledge or truth." In 1952 he published *Scientology, a Religious Philosophy*, and the next year he founded three churches in Camden, New Jersey – the "Church of Scientology," the "Church of American Science," and the "Church of Spiritual Engineering." The movement spread quickly in the English-speaking world.

The core idea in Scientology is that a person is neither a body nor a mind, but an immortal spiritual being. Sometimes Hubbard used the word "soul" to refer to the spiritual essence of a human being. But "soul" means many different things to many different people, so Hubbard devised a new term, **thetan**, from the Greek letter *theta*, a traditional symbol for thought and life. The thetan, he said, is what a person really is. It is "that which is aware of being aware," in his words. According to Scientology, each thetan has existed for billions of years, is naturally good, and has been reincarnated in countless bodies in a process Hubbard called **assumption**.

Scientology teaches that human beings operate on the basis of eight "dynamics" (or impulses) of survival. The first is the urge for personal survival. The second is the urge to

Celebrities in Scientology

From its beginning, Scientology has vigorously recruited celebrities to join the religion and promote it in the media. In 1955 L. Ron Hubbard started "Project Celebrity" to get Scientologists to convert actors and musicians. The Church of Scientology operates special Celebrity Centers in Los Angeles, Paris, and Nashville. According to religion scholar Hugh B. Urban, Scientology has a natural appeal for many celebrities because it celebrates the individual person (as an immortal spiritual thetan), and it valorizes the celebrity lifestyle of wealth and fame. Among the best known celebrity Scientologists are actors Tom Cruise, Katie Holmes, John Travolta, Kirstie Alley, Jason Lee, and Nancy Cartwright (the voice of Bart Simpson), and musical artists Lisa Marie Presley, Beck, and Edgar Winter.

survive through one's family and children. The third is for group survival, as in a corporation or a nation. The fourth is to survive as the human race. And the last four dynamics are the urges to survive through other living things, the physical universe, the spiritual universe, and Supreme Being.

The moral teachings of Scientology are based on these dynamics. Adopting what philosophers call a utilitarian ethic, Scientology teaches that good actions are those that benefit the greatest number of these dynamics and harm the fewest. As **Utilitarianism** would say, good actions are those that bring "the greatest good for the greatest number of people."

Besides helping individuals within the church, Scientologists engage in many kinds of humanitarian aid, and social service programs such as the Narconon anti-drug program and the Criminon prison rehabilitation program.

Scientology Practices

According to Scientology, people develop mental problems because they do not understand themselves and the nature of human life. The goal of Scientology, similar to that of Hinduism and Buddhism, is to help people understand their true nature (bring "enlightenment" or "awakening") and thus achieve happiness. Scientology distinguishes between two parts of the mind. The first is the "analytical mind," which is rational and self-aware. It is similar to what Sigmund Freud called the conscious mind. Mental problems typically originate in the other part, the "reactive mind," which is like what Freud called the unconscious mind. The reactive mind stores mental images called **engrams** from past negative experiences. These engrams are not readily available to the analytical mind, but they cause mental problems when the person has an experience similar to a past negative experience. Just as Freud taught (see Chapter 3), if someone has a negative experience in childhood with her father, for example, she may experience problems in adulthood with male authority figures. It is such past negative experiences that cause our fears, negative thoughts, and irrational behavior, according to Scientology (and Freud). And because of reincarnation, we carry engrams of our bad experiences from life to life. (This part would have been rejected by Freud, who did not believe in reincarnation.) So the most damaging things in our reactive mind may be from our previous lives. As engrams accumulate in the reactive mind, people move further and further away from their true identity as thetans and so from happiness.

FIGURE 9.9 The Hubbard Professional Mark Super VII E-Meter. Photo by Salimfadhley, http://en.wikipedia.org/wiki/File:Scientology_e_meter_blue.jpg.

The main religious practice in Scientology is a form of therapy called "**auditing**." It is designed to help people reach self-awareness, overcome mental problems, and achieve higher states of consciousness. A counselor called an "auditor" uses a device called an electro-psychometer – E-meter for short – to measure mental activity in subjects and detect troubled areas. The auditor asks them questions and gives directions to help them understand themselves and their problems. Traumatic memories are brought into consciousness. Once people understand themselves and their past experiences, they can begin to correct their problems.

The goal is for people to gradually free themselves of their engrams and realize that they are immortal spiritual thetans. Those who study Scientology materials and go through sessions of auditing advance from a status of "Preclear" to "Clear" and then to "Operating Thetan." The ultimate goal of the religion is to "clear the planet" – to clear all people of their engrams.

Scientology also has several kinds of training to teach people deeper understandings of the nature of life and human beings. For example, according to Hubbard, the thetan can leave the body and exist on its own. Once free of the body, the thetan can "see without eyes, hear without ears, and realize its true nature as an immortal spirit." Scientology offers ways to achieve this **exteriorization**, although it does not make this information public. But overall, Scientology training and auditing are designed to bring people to a higher state of spiritual existence in which they are free from dependence on the material world. Scientologists therefore call the set of auditing and training procedures "The Bridge to Total Freedom."

Scientology Rituals

Scientology places far more emphasis on its therapeutic practices than on its rituals. Its auditors are therefore more important than its rituals. Nevertheless, Scientology does ordain ministers to conduct important ceremonies for life events such as weddings and funerals. Such ceremonies are simple in Scientology. At weddings, the couple pledge fidelity, marriage being part of the second dynamic – the urge to survive through procreation. Funerals reflect Scientologists' belief that physical life is relatively unimportant, and that the real person – the thetan – is immortal. As well, Scientologists may gather at weekly Friday meetings to discuss members' activities during the week and any concerns they may have.

Wicca

History and Teachings of Wicca

"Wicca" is the modern name for witchcraft, in particular the ancient nature-based witchcraft found in the British Isles and France before Christianity arrived. It is sometimes called simply "The Craft" or "The Old Religion." There are a number of strains of modern witchcraft, some referred to as **neopagan** (a modern religious movement that traces its roots to pre-Christian European religion). Because of their newness and lack of institutional development, as well as a tendency toward privacy in order to avoid widespread prejudice, there is relatively little scholarly work available on "The Craft." The best known of the movements that call themselves Wicca are those associated with British Traditional Wicca (BTW) – especially Gardnerian and Alexandrian Wicca. Both trace themselves to Gerald Gardner (d. 1964). Gardner said that he had been initiated into a traditional **coven** of witches in 1939 in the New Forest region of England, and that they were the inheritors of the ancient traditions of Britain. In 1949 Gardner wrote a novel about medieval witchcraft called *High Magic's Aid*. Then in 1951 he published *Witchcraft Today*, which describes the rituals and traditions of the coven he belonged to.

Covens of witches that have followed Gardner are headed by a High Priestess, and worship the **Lady** and the **Lord**. The Lady, or the Goddess, is also called the Great Mother and the Triple Goddess. She is a fertility deity and is associated with the earth and the moon, and with three phases of women's lives: maidenhood, motherhood, and old age. The Lord is also called the **Horned God**. Represented as a man with a goat's head with huge horns, he is lord of the hunt and death. He is associated with the sun, and rules over the **Summerland**, an after-death paradise. The Lady and the Lord complement each another, much like male and female forms of Shiva in Hinduism. Some Wiccans consider them aspects of a single god, some consider them the only two gods, some consider them one or two among many gods, and some consider them symbolic of the cosmic life force. What scholars call the "ontological" status of gods – whether or not they really exist – is not considered important in Wicca. But Wiccans do believe that the cosmic forces – or the Goddess and the God – become incarnate (take human form) in the priestess and priest during Wiccan rituals.

The Horned God is also the lord of **magick**, which is the ability to cause change at will. The spelling was devised by Aleister Crowley (d. 1947), British occult writer and practitioner, to distinguish this power from the illusions known in popular entertainment as "magic." Magick is not illusory, Wiccans believe. Instead, it is the ability to master the great unseen ("occult") power of the cosmos through sheer force of will, and command it to do one's bidding – a skill achieved by very few practitioners. (Aleister Crowley is not considered a representative of Wicca, but he did influence Gerald Gardner, with whom he worked at the end of his life, and many people involved in contemporary pop culture, such as comic book writer Alan Moore, horror writer extraordinaire Clive Barker, and musician Ozzy Osbourne.)

There is no rigid doctrine or set of rituals in Wicca. People are free to believe as they like and engage in whatever rituals they find satisfying. Many groups add to the Lady and the Lord divinities from Celtic, Greek, or other traditions. Some worship Diana, goddess of the moon from Greek and Roman religions, or Brigit, the Celtic goddess of fire, poetry, healing, and childbirth. Beyond the Goddess and the God, Gerald Gardner said, there is a Prime Mover, also called "The One," who is unknowable and so not of concern.

Though there are no doctrines in Wicca, five beliefs are common. First, the divine is imminent in the world, not outside it. Second, humans can interact with the divine easily. Third, the divine is both female and male. Fourth, after death, people are reincarnated. And fifth, the natural world is a system of forces that balance each other, which is similar to the ideas of Taoism (see Chapter 6).

As long as people do not interfere with the happiness of others, they are free to do what they want. Pleasure, especially sex, is good. A central moral principle is called the **Wiccan Rede** ("advice"): "An [as long as] it harm none, do what you will." This is derived from Aleister Crowley's motto, "Do what ye will." Scholars see predecessors to this sentiment all the way back to the Christian thinker Augustine, who interpreted the Gospel of John as a call to "love and do what you will." In Wiccan teaching, it is meant to empower individuals to trust their inner moral sense.

FIGURE 9.10 Calling the elements (earth, air, fire, water, and aether) – part of a Wiccan ritual of handfasting (marriage). Paul Gapper/www.worldreligions.co.uk.

Wicca also teaches the **Rule of Three** (or **Law of Threefold Return** or Law of Return). Reflecting what Gerald Gardner called "the joke of witchcraft" known only to witches – that "she will get three times what she gave," this rule has been compared to the Golden Rule of Christianity as well as to the karmic law of reciprocity.

Wiccan Rituals

Unlike most of the traditions we have surveyed, Wicca has no churches or temples. As we have seen, churches and temples are places considered "sacred." As one enters them, one passes into "sacred space" from space that is not sacred (**profane**). However, in Wicca, all of nature is considered sacred. Not surprisingly, then, Wiccan rituals are held *au natural* – in more ways than one. They are held outdoors, and often the participants are "skyclad" – in the buff, bare-naked – although, again, in keeping with Wiccan respect for individual preference, this is not a requirement.

Wiccan rituals involve the casting of spells or "workings." In Roman Catholicism, sacraments are ritual actions performed by priests who are believed to effect real changes through those rituals. Thus, the priest can really change bread and wine into the body and blood of Jesus, and can really confer "absolution" – divine forgiveness for sins, provided everything has been done just right. In Wiccan workings, the priestess can channel the power of the cosmos to effect healing or protection or a number of other physical changes requested by the petitioner. However, spells should be cast for good only, such as for love and wisdom. And no magick, even for good, should be performed on anyone without their consent. Casting love spells, for example, to make someone fall in love without her consent would interfere with her autonomy.

Rituals typically begin with summoning the powers of the four points of the compass and the five basic "elements" – earth, air, fire, water, and "aether," which is considered the cosmic force that underlies all of nature. Wiccan orientation toward these five points is reflected in the symbol of the tradition, the **pentagram**. Ritual objects include knives

FIGURE 9.11 The Wiccan pentagram.

Three Wiccan Spells
Love Spell

Take three cords or strings of pleasing pastel colors – perhaps pink, red, and green – and braid them tightly together. Firmly tie a knot near one end of the braid, thinking of your need for love.

Next, tie another knot, and another, until you have tied seven knots. Wear or carry the cord with you until you find your love.

After that, keep the cord in a safe place, or give it to one of the elements by burning and scattering the ashes in the ocean or in a stream.

Fertility Spell

During your most fertile time (usually two days before, during and after ovulation), light nine white candles in your bedroom. Place them around your bed. Sit or stand nude with your partner facing the North and repeat the following:

With one mind, we call to thee.
With one heart, we long for thee
Childe of Earth, Wind, Fire & Sea,
Into our lives, we welcome thee.

Turn to the East, then South, then West, repeating this incantation each time you do so. Proceed as nature requires. Repeat this spell each of the five nights before intercourse.

Job Spell

Begin on Sunday. Light a gold- or yellow-colored candle and say the following spell:

A good job awaits me, I know
For thy brilliant light scans and searches a place for me.
A good job awaits me, for thy goodness is great
My faith in thee is complete, a good job waits for me.

Speak this spell three times. Perform this ritual every day until employment is found. Instead of "good job," maybe it would help to personalize it and change the words to "record deal," or something else that appeals to you.

(an "athame" or a "boline," symbolizing male creativity), a chalice or cup (symbolizing female creativity), a stick ("besome"), the pentacle (symbolizing the five powers), and a wand, a cauldron, candles, and other objects of symbolic value.

The Wiccan calendar – the "Wheel of the Year" – is punctuated with celebrations called **Sabbats**, which are holidays tied to the seasons of the year. British Traditional Wicca celebrates eight Sabbats. The four "greater Sabbats" correspond to ancient European seasonal festivals. The fall festival is called **Samhain** (the Celtic word for "Summer's End"), which Christians celebrate as Halloween or "All Hallows Evening." In ancient Celtic and Wiccan tradition, this is the night when spirits of the departed intermingle with the living. Wiccans mark this Sabbat by inviting the ancestral spirits to join in a celebration in which they express respect for all creatures, living and dead, especially relatives and friends. While Samhain is a dark Sabbat, its opposite is **Beltane**, the celebration of spring, sometimes called May Day or the Fire Festival. At the halfway point between the spring equinox and summer solstice, this Sabbat is celebrated with bonfires and maypole dancing, and may involve symbolic or ritual sex (known as the Great Rite) performed by the priestess and priest. **Imbolc** (or Candlemas) is celebrated at the first signs of spring, and **Lughnasadh** (or **Lammas**) is a harvest festival. The four lesser Sabbats – the summer and winter solstice and the spring and fall equinox – may also be celebrated, as may be each full moon and new moon.

Like other religions, Wicca also celebrates initiation into the group and major life events (rites of passage). Some Wicca traditions recognize graduated levels of initiation, from a simple member to someone who can found an independent coven.

The Wicca marriage ceremony is called a **handfasting**: in it the couple promise to stay together for two years, five years, "as long as love lasts," or whatever period of time they are comfortable with.

When a child is born, there is a ritual like baptism called **wiccaning**, in which the baby is presented to the Goddess and the God for protection. Respecting children's autonomy, the parents say that they may later choose not to follow Wicca.

The Traditions of the Seneca

History and Teachings of the Seneca

The five religions we have considered so far in this chapter raise not only the question of what a "world religion" is, but also the question of whether there is some essence shared by all religions. The last "religion" we shall look at – that of the Seneca, a native American tribe – raises even more questions.

The Seneca were the largest tribe in the Iroquois Confederacy. Also called the "Six Nations," this alliance included the Oneida, Mohawk, Onondaga, Cayuga, and Tuscarora tribes. They lived in what is now New York State. As the westernmost tribe in the group, the Seneca were the "Keepers of the Western Door." Today an estimated 25,000–40,000 Seneca live on reservations in New York State, in Canada, and in Oklahoma.

As oral cultures, the Six Nations did not have a written constitution. What united them was The Great Binding Law received by the spiritual leader Deganawida (Great Peacemaker), who was helped by the Mohawk leader Hiawatha. Some ideas from this Law were admired by the founders of the U.S. and incorporated into their Constitution. One version of the Law began with the words "We, the people, to form a union" – the very words used for the U.S. Constitution. In 1988, the U.S. Congress passed Concurrent Resolution 331 to recognize the influence of the Six Nations constitution on the foundational documents of the U.S.

FIGURE 9.12 Dancers from the Allegany and Cattaraugus Reservations of the Seneca Nation of Indians perform at St. Bonaventure University's first Native American Heritage Celebration in 2008. Photo Tom Donahue.

The Seneca lived in **longhouses**, wood-framed structures covered in elm bark, up to 100 feet in length, which housed up to 60 people. They had a matrilineal social structure, that is, membership in the group was passed on through the mothers. Men hunted and served as tribal chiefs, making trade agreements and conducting wars, but women were in charge of farming and property. They owned the land and the homes, and they chose the men who served on tribal councils. While today people live in houses and the longhouse is used mainly for tribal meetings and ceremonies, the position of women in tribal society remains strong and both group identity and property ownership are passed on through mothers.

If we were to travel back in time four centuries to a Seneca village and ask someone there, "What is your religion?" not only could that question not be answered – it could hardly be translated. As we saw in Chapter 5, one feature of oral cultures is that they do not distinguish "religion" from "politics" or "culture." Seneca beliefs, customs, and rituals that others might call "religious" were continuous with Seneca storytelling, art, music, politics, agriculture, medicine, history, etc. There was no separate part of of life called "religion."

Like other North American native traditions, too, and like oral cultures around the world, the Seneca showed animism and anthropomorphism in the way they described the world around them. That is, they tended to see everything as alive, and they tended to think of living things as like human beings. For example, they called their most important crops – corn, beans, and squash – "The Three Sisters." The sun was "Elder Brother" and the thunder "Grandfather." When they visited the huge waterfall called "Nee-ah-gah-rah"(Niagara),

Patriarchy and Matriarchy

Since the early days of modernity, scholars have analyzed the nature and origins of male dominance in human society. It is clearly reflected in historical religions, particularly those that developed in settled societies and have written records. Official interpretations of the biblical and Qur'anic stories of Adam and Eve are often used to explain that women are weaker than men, both physically and morally, and therefore need to be protected and controlled by men. Male dominance is also institutionalized in most religions. It is only in recent years that women have been eligible for positions of authority in most religious groups.

However, some scholars have wondered if patriarchy is indeed dictated by nature or a function of specific socioeconomic developments in history. Among the earliest to question male control of females was Friedrich Engels (d. 1895), Karl Marx's collaborator. Engels saw patriarchy as a result of the dominant position gained by warriors when human beings made the transition from the nomadic life of hunters and shepherds to the settled life of farmers whose land and crops were the source of survival and therefore widely coveted.

Many contemporary scholars believe that patriarchy is not an essential part of life but something that simply developed and has been kept in place by institutions. Gerda Lerner (b. 1920) describes organized religions as the institutionalization of patriarchy in her landmark *The Creation of Patriarchy* (1987). Some scholars see male dominance as having outlived its usefulness. Correlated with the prevalence of military approaches to conflict, patriarchy should be replaced with more reasonable and balanced approaches to social organization, before the human race eradicates itself in a militarist frenzy. Andrew Bard Schmookler expresses this view in his groundbreaking *Parable of the Tribes* (1984/1995).

Other scholars have recommended the replacement of male dominance with female dominance – **matriarchy**. Some have even imagined an ancient time when women ruled the world and life was full of peace and harmony. However, anthropologist Cynthia Eller disputes this notion in her *The Myth of Matriarchal Prehistory: Why an Invented Past Won't Give Women a Future* (2001). There is general agreement among scholars that non-patriarchal societies are not dominated by women (and therefore are not matri*archal*); rather, they are matrilineal (meaning that lineage or property are passed on through mothers) or matrilocal (meaning that upon marriage a couple becomes part of the bride's extended family rather than the groom's).

meaning Thundering Waters, they heard its roar as the voice of the Spirit of the Waters. In addition to the spirits in such natural forces, animals, and plants, the Seneca also believed in a personal god, sometimes called the Great Spirit or Great Mystery, who created the world, taught people how to live, and watches over all creation.

Chief Red Jacket's Response to Christian Missionaries

FIGURE 9.13 Portrait of Red Jacket by John Lee Mathies, oil on canvas, 1828. Memorial Art Gallery of the University of Rochester, lent by the estate of John W. Brown.

In 1822, Red Jacket, Chief of the Seneca, called a council in Batavia, New York. Here are some of his comments there about the attempts of Christian missionaries to convert the native tribes:

> When the Great Good Spirit made the world, he put in it the trees of the forests, the birds of the air, all kinds of animals, and fishes that live in the waters. To all these he gave their respective shapes, colors, natures, actions, etc.... Those are all fixed, you see, and are immovable. They cannot change colour, nature or their actions or customs. He also at the same time made the White Man, the Red Man, and the Black Man. To the White Man he gave one way to worship him and certain customs; to the Red Man another, and his customs and way to live; and to the Black Man others still. Now I say we can't change our religion or custom, because they are fixed by the Great Good Spirit, and if we attempt to do it, we shall offend our Great Spirit and he will punish us for it.

> From the rising to the setting sun examine all the different tribes of Indians, and see in what a condition you find them. I have travelled far. I have been from the Atlantic to the shores of the Pacific, and I know the habits, customs and situation of almost every tribe and nation of Indians. And I say that it is a fact, that whenever you find a tribe of Indians that have been Christianized and have changed their custom or habit, which the Great Good Spirit gave them, you will see that they are a poor, worthless, lying, ragged, miserable and degraded set of beings.... I say, therefore, that the Great Spirit will not suffer his Red Children to change their religion or custom.... It is not because the White Men love the Indians that they want to make them Christians, it is because they want to cheat them out of their property. The Black Coats [missionaries] that they send among us with honey on their tongue, have always proved themselves to be dishonest; they are an ignorant, idle set of creatures, incapable of getting a living amongst their White brethren, and are therefore sent amongst us to get a living. They bring along with them a worthless set of White Men who steal our horses and seduce our Squaws.

Although the Great Spirit of the Seneca is similar to the God of the Bible, the Europeans who came to North America often treated the indigenous peoples (Native Americans or "Indians") as "heathens" (people from the "heath" –lands covered with shrubs that were uncultivated, in the literal sense of not being farmed) and their beliefs and rituals as "paganism" (see p. 277). The Iroquois tribes had a ritual of sacrificing a maiden to Nee-ah-gah-rah, for example. They put her in a white canoe decorated with flowers and fruit and pushed it over the falls. European missionaries condemned this sacrifice as barbaric and tried to replace such traditions with Christian beliefs and rituals. However, some of the native people asked the missionaries about the death of Jesus on the cross, which Catholics reenact – indeed "celebrate" – in the Sacrifice of the Mass. Wasn't that killing meant to please God, they asked. And if that sacrifice of a young man was good, then why is our sacrifice of a young woman bad?

Seneca Rituals

Unlike traditions with writing, Seneca traditions were passed down orally. They are expressed mostly in stories and rituals, not in doctrines or "teachings." If we assume the categories used in Christianity, we can talk about "Seneca beliefs," but this is not the way the Seneca traditionally talked about what they thought and did. They understand the world to be controlled by many spirits, the greatest being the Creator that Chief Red Jacket called the "Great Good Spirit." However, this understanding of the world is not called "belief" as distinguished from "knowledge" – something that can be proven. Instead, as in many traditions, Seneca understandings of the world are better thought of as a worldview.

The lives of the Seneca historically depended on the crops they grew and the animals they hunted, and so they were attuned to the four seasons. Each year they had six major festivals in which they thanked the Great Spirit for the plants and animals they ate, and asked the Great Spirit for continued blessings:

- Midwinter or New Year's Festival, lasting nine days, in January or February.
- Thanks-to-the-Maple Festival, late February or March. As the sap began to rise in maple trees, they gave thanks to the Great Spirit for the gift of the maple, and to the maple itself for yielding its sweet sap.
- Corn Planting Festival, in early May or June. As the seeds of the vegetables were planted, they invited the Great Spirit to bless them. They also asked "Our Grandfathers the Thunders" to bring rain on the crops, and "Our Elder Brother the Sun" to not burn the young plants as they emerge from the ground.
- Strawberry Festival in June. This was a "first-fruits" ritual thanking the Great Spirit for the earliest crop of the season.
- Green Corn Festival, lasting four days, in late August or September. The Seneca thanked the Great Spirit that the crops had ripened.
- Harvest Festival in October. As the corn was picked, dried, and stored for winter, the Seneca thanked the Great Spirit for another year's harvest.

The Midwinter Festival is still very popular. Its format varies from tribe to tribe, but all have the same essential components. The general theme of the festival is to honor the Great Spirit, thank him for the blessings of the past year, and ask him to bless the people with another fruitful year. On the first day, there is a public naming of the babies that have been born since the last Green Corn Festival. The second day begins with the Big Heads, two men dressed in bearskin coats and masks made of cornhusks, waking people up and announcing that the new year has begun. The Big Heads call the people to the council house (the building where special tribal meetings are held) or the longhouse to reveal their dreams, and warn that if they do not come they will be obsessed by the desires that caused the dream. On the third day, called Ashes Stirring, small groups of people visit the houses in the village to stir the ashes in the hearth as a symbol of thanks for the blessings of the previous year. Then they return to the council house or longhouse to sing songs of thanksgiving.

The fourth day is for rituals of the special medicine societies, such as the **False Face Society**, the Buffalo Society, and the Otter Society. They perform healing rituals for sick people. On the fifth day, the main ritual used to be the burning of a spotless white dog as a sacrifice to the Creator. Earlier it had been strangled (no blood could be shed) and its body, decorated with beads and ribbons, had been hung on a wooden statue of the Creator. Today a white basket is substituted for the dog. After the sacrifice, a Thanksgiving Dance is performed.

The Origin of the False Face Society

There are many tellings of the origin of the healing powers of the medicine men of the False Face Society. According to one short version:

The Spirit Medicine Man, a man blessed with healing powers in response to his love of living things, met a stranger and they had a contest… [to see] who could move a mountain. The stranger made the mountain quake. The Medicine Man said that the stranger did indeed have skills, but not enough to move a mountain. The Spirit Medicine Man moved the mountain, but so suddenly, it hit the stranger and left him disfigured. The Spirit Medicine Man healed him and taught him the ways of medicine. The stranger became a very famous healer knows as "Old Broken Nose." (http://www.support-native-american-art.com/iroquois-masks.html)

Six Nation traditions explain that the stranger then went to live in the forest. Masks made in his image summon his power when needed. Those initiated into the Society go to the forest to be inspired by Old Broken Nose's spirit, whereupon they carve a mask from a nearby tree. The masks, representing Old Broken Nose, are considered sacred and are not supposed to be photographed or sold for profit.

The sixth day features several activities. Some people play the Sacred Bowl Game, which symbolizes the struggle between the Good Twin and the Evil Twin as the world was created. Others go house to house asking for food. The medicine societies perform dances for sick people. Then come the Husk Faces – men dressed as women with masks made of braided cornhusks. They explain that they are a group of supernatural farmers from the western rim of the earth, where they must quickly return after they do the Women's Dance to honor the "Three Sisters" – corn, beans, and squash.

On the seventh day there are some public thanksgiving rituals, and on the eighth day people sing songs of thanksgiving. The whole festival concludes on the ninth day, when new council-house leaders are inaugurated and the Great Feather Dance is performed one last time.

Of particular interest is the Dream Sharing Ritual. As we said in Chapter 5, oral cultures often think of dreams as channels of information, even divine revelations. The Seneca have a sophisticated belief that dreams reveal something hidden within the dreamer's mind. Their idea is like that of Sigmund Freud, who said that dreams express desires that we ordinarily repress. For the Seneca, what people dream about is important to them and must be understood. In some cases, actions depicted in dreams should be carried out after they wake up. If they dream about making a journey or holding a feast, for example, then the next day they should try to make the trip or arrange the feast. However, the implications of other dreams are not so evident and need interpreting. Dreams must be discussed ("shared"). They may reveal emotional problems or disorders that need healing. This is the task of the False Face Society. Once the dreams have been interpreted, the False Face medicine men can perform a curing ritual.

What these and other Seneca beliefs, practices, and rituals reveal is a culture in which what we call "religion" is thoroughly entwined with other aspects of life. As we said, some of these activities seem to clearly count as "religious" – prayers of thanksgiving to the Creator, for example. But what about the healing practices, and those associated with tribal governance? The scholars who developed Religious Studies (see Chapters 3 and 4) would consider these "secular" activities, because they lived in societies that distinguish between "spiritual" and "mundane" spheres of life. Does the fact that Native American traditions reflect a holistic approach to life in which the distinction between spiritual and mundane is meaningless mean that they have no religion? Or does it mean that everything is religion? Or does it mean that the category "religion" needs work?

Conclusion: To Be or Not to Be a Religion?

Other aspects of Native American religious traditions raise still more questions – particularly legal ones. We saw in Chapter 7 that some Native American traditions involve the use of peyote, a substance controlled by the U.S. Government. The people following this set of traditions organized themselves into a "church" – the Native American Church – and are officially exempt from the criminal penalties imposed by federal law for the use of peyote.

Federal recognition of a tradition has other advantages, as well. A group that organizes itself officially and collects money from its members will inevitably be noticed by tax collectors. In the U.S., religions enjoy "tax-exempt" status; they do not have to pay taxes once they demonstrate to the government's satisfaction that they are not involved in the business of making money for the sake of profit. In some countries, religions receive support from the government, for their schools, for example, if they convince the government that they are legitimate. So whether or not a group is recognized as a religion by the government has important financial implications, as well.

Scientology has faced serious identity challenges in this regard. It has convinced some governments that it is a religion – Australia and Spain, for example. However, it is not recognized as a religion in Canada, Germany, France, or Israel. England recognizes it as a non-profit organization, but not as a religion. The U.S. has categorized it as a charitable organization – but that was only in 1993, after a lengthy legal battle with the Internal Revenue Service.

Wicca's identity challenges are somewhat different. It is the focus of a great deal of prejudice. The prejudice is partly a function of allegations of Satan worship and sexual impropriety, but the dynamics of European history are also at play. Christianity, as a monotheistic tradition, the dominant tradition of Europe, considers non-Christian traditions not only wrong theologically but misguided morally. And as a **proselytizing** religion (one devoted to converting people), Christianity sometimes forcibly suppressed non-Christian traditions, demonizing the traditions it sought to replace. This was the case as the Christianized Roman Empire (see Chapter 6) asserted control over Europe. The history of European anti-Semitism, culminating in the horrors of the **Shoah (Holocaust)**, is the most egregious example of this pattern.

Seen in this light, the charges leveled against "witchcraft" – considered by its practitioners to be part of Europe's indigenous religions – by Christians are understandable. From around 1450 to 1700, thousands of people in Europe and British-colonized North America were tried as witches. Many were convicted and executed by burning. Britain had a Witchcraft Act from 1735 to 1951. Under that law, women accused of practicing witchcraft were imprisoned as recently as 1944.

While there is still prejudice against Wicca in the U.S., it is officially recognized as a religion, as a result of a 1986 court case. Herbert Daniel Dettmer was a convicted criminal, incarcerated in the state of Virginia. He wanted to practice his religion, in accordance with the right accorded him by the First Amendment of the U.S. Constitution. But he was a Wiccan, and his ritual involved the presence of the atheme (or boline) – the ritual knife, and prisoners are not allowed to have knives. Mr. Dettmer sued the Department of Corrections for violating his constitutional right to practice his religion. The Department of Corrections based its argument not on the issue of the knife itself, but on the issue of whether or not Wicca was really a religion. The court rejected their argument about Wicca, recognizing Wicca as a religion. (The case was appealed, and the court ruled again that the prisoner had a right to practice Wicca, a religion. However, it did not let him have his knife, since that prohibition had nothing to do with religion.)

Further official acceptance of Wicca came in 2007, when the U.S. government allowed military veterans to have the Wiccan pentagram carved on their gravestones.

The legal struggles of movements such as Scientology and Wicca reflect a larger ongoing struggle to understand the phenomenon of religion. Scholars' categories for making sense of religious phenomena, and relating them to other social and cultural phenomena, are not carved in stone but are still evolving. Hopefully, as we think more carefully and universally about human life, we shall better understand religion and its roles. In the next chapter we shall look at several issues that should help in this effort.

DISCUSSION QUESTIONS

1. Is there a difference between Western ideas about gods and Japanese ideas about kami?

2. Is the Baha'i goal of a single world government a realistic one?

3. What arguments could you give that Scientology *should* be classified as a religion? What arguments could you give that it *should not* be classified as a religion?

4. What arguments could you give that Shinto *should* be classified as a religion? What arguments could you give that it *should not* be classified as a religion?

5. In what ways are the ethics of Wicca like traditional Jewish, Christian, and Islamic ethics? In what ways are they different?

6. How are Wiccan spells like and unlike prayers in the monotheistic traditions?

7. What might E. B. Tylor say about the worldview of the Seneca?

8. What might Sigmund Freud say about the Seneca's ideas about dreams?

REFERENCES

Mary Boyce, *Zoroastrians: Their Religious Beliefs and Practices*. London: Routledge, 2nd ed., 2001.

Cynthia Eller, *The Myth of Matriarchal Prehistory: Why an Invented Past Won't Give Women a Future*. Boston: Beacon, 2001.

L. Ron Hubbard, *Dianetics: The Modern Science of Mental Health*. Los Angeles, CA: Bridge, 2002.

Gerda Lerner, *The Creation of Patriarchy*. New York: Oxford University Press, 1987.

Andrew Bard Schmookler, *Parable of the Tribes*. Albany, NY: SUNY Press, 1984/1995.

FURTHER READING

Kenneth E. Bowers, *God Speaks Again: An Introduction to the Baha'i Faith*. Wilmette, IL: Baha'i Publishing, 2004.

Vine Deloria Jr., Leslie Marmon Silk, and George E. Tinker, *God Is Red: A Native View of Religion*. Golden, CO: Fulcrum, 30th anniversary ed., 2003.

Michael Howard, *Modern Wicca: From Gerald Gardner to the Present*. Woodbury, MN: Llewellyn, 2010.

L. Ron Hubbard, *Scientology: The Fundamentals of Thought*. Los Angeles, CA: Bridge, 2007.

James R. Lewis, editor, *Scientology*. New York: Oxford University Press, 2009.

C. Scott Littleton, *Shinto: Origins, Rituals, Festivals, Spirits, Sacred Places*. New York: Oxford University Press, 2002.

Moojan Momen, *The Baha'i Faith: A Beginner's Guide*. London: Oneworld, 2007.

John G. Neihardt, *Black Elk Speaks: Being the Life Story of a Holy Man of the Oglala Sioux*. Albany, NY: SUNY Press, annotated ed., 2008.

Stephen T. Newcomb, *Pagans in the Promised Land*. Golden, CO: Fulcrum, 2008.

S.A. Nigosian, *The Zoroastrian Faith: Tradition and Modern Research*. Montreal: McGill-Queen's University Press, 1993.

Sarah M. Pike, *New Age and Neopagan Religions in America*. New York: Columbia University Press, 2006.

Motohisa Yamakage, *The Essence of Shinto: Japan's Spiritual Heart*. Tokyo: Kodansha, 2007.

CLOSING QUESTIONS

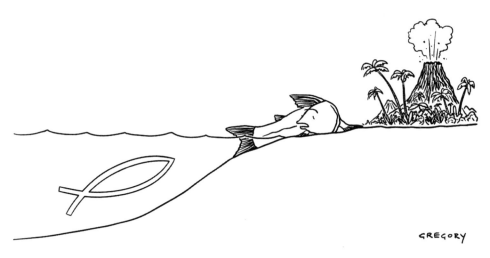

"*I guess this is where we part ways.*"

FIGURE 10.1

The Religion Toolkit: A Complete Guide to Religious Studies, First Edition. John Morreall and Tamara Sonn.
© 2012 John Morreall and Tamara Sonn. Published 2012 by Blackwell Publishing Ltd.

A religion old or new, that stressed the magnificence of the universe as revealed by modern science, might be able to draw forth reserves of reverence and awe hardly tapped by the conventional faiths. Sooner or later, such a religion will emerge.

CARL SAGAN

10

Overview

Religious Studies today embraces many topics, fields, and academic disciplines. We can get some appreciation for what scholars in Religious Studies are doing now by looking at old questions still being debated, and at new questions.

- On the question of whether religion can be defined, most scholars say no; there are no necessary and sufficient conditions for applying the term "religion."

- On the issue of whether the secularization thesis is valid, scholars such as Peter Berger have argued that it has proven false. The case for "desecularization" is usually based on the growth of Islam and of certain kinds of Protestantism in the U.S. Europe, however, appears to have become mostly secularized.

- Both the issue of defining religion and the issue of secularization seem to be based on the problematic distinction between parts of life that are religious and parts that are not religious.

Turning to newer questions, we look at issues in the medical sciences.

- Studies of the correlation between people's reported religiosity and their physical health show mostly positive correlations.

- Studies of the correlation between religiosity and mental health are mostly positive. People who belong to

Can We Define Religion?

Secularization?
Contemporary Atheist Views
Contemporary Opposition to
Secularization Theory
Religion Revisited

Other Issues
The Range of Research Areas in the
American Academy of Religion
Medical Science and Religion

Conclusion: Another Surprise?

religious groups generally report higher levels of satisfaction with their marriages and their lives overall. Negative correlations occur with lesbians and gay men who belong to religions that condemn homosexuality.

- Studies of the possible effects of prayer on patients' recovery from heart surgery are mixed.
- Studies of the brain during mystical experience show that the feeling that all reality is one is correlated with reduced levels of activity in the parts of the brain responsible for making the distinction between self and other.

In this final chapter, we are going to present some of what Religious Studies scholars are doing today. To do this, we shall start with two old questions that are still being debated: "Can religion be defined?" and "Is the Secularization Thesis correct?" Then we shall turn to some newer questions from the medical sciences.

Can We Define Religion?

Walter Ong, the scholar of literature we met in Chapter 5, has shown that the categories with which people classify things are based at least as much on the people doing the classifying as on the things being classified. Classification is not as easy as *Sesame Street* made it look with their little song

> Three of these things belong together.
> Three of these things are kind of the same.
> Can you guess which one of these doesn't belong here?
> Now it's time to play our game.

On the TV screen would be, for example, a pair of pliers, a hammer, a saw, and a piece of wood. From a *Sesame Street* perspective, the piece of wood is the odd one out; and the other three belong together, because they are tools. However, a woodworker doing this exercise might well say that the hammer, saw, and wood go together, while the pliers do not belong in the group, because pliers are not used on wood.

What about the category "religion"? What are the phenomena that should be grouped under it, and what things do not belong in it? We have seen throughout this book that "religion" is controversial among scholars. It is not a well-defined term. Scholars do not agree on any essential features for religion. It has no "necessary and sufficient" conditions, as philosophers say; there is nothing that absolutely has to be there for people to agree that something is religion, and there is nothing that people agree is sufficient to qualify something as religion.

The 19th- to 20th-century German theologian Ernst Troeltsch defined religion this way: "Everywhere the basic reality of religion is the same: an underivable, purely positive, again and again experienced contact with the Deity." (Troeltsch 1991, 79) This definition is based on the conviction that religion is a universal phenomenon, and that it is contact with a god. However, we have seen that many scholars would dispute this definition, saying that it does not fit such traditions as early Buddhism and Confucianism.

Even definitions that are less grounded in Western monotheism, such as E. B. Tylor's, seem inadequate. As we saw in Chapter 3, Tylor defined religion as "the belief in spiritual beings." But what if someone believes in ghosts – and only in ghosts? Is this what we mean by religion? And, again, traditions that are often called religions, such as early Buddhism and Confucianism, do not seem to require belief in spiritual beings.

We have also seen that some scholars insist that religion is *sui generis* – that nothing else can do what religion does. However, other scholars argue that religion is reducible to a form of social organization (Durkheim), a psychological condition (Freud), or an ideology to control the masses (Marx). Still other scholars, such as Geertz and Douglas, take a broader approach, looking at religion as a collection of phenomena fulfilling a variety of personal needs and social functions.

Because of disagreements such as these over how we might define religion, some scholars present theories of religion that do not include definitions. Ninian Smart, whom we mentioned in Chapter 2, has an approach that many find useful. He identifies and discusses seven features that are found in many of the traditions we call religions. These are doctrine, myth, ethics, ritual, experiences, institutions, and material culture. Smart does not claim that something must have all seven features to be called a religion, nor does he say that only religions have these features. Indeed, he often talks about "worldviews" rather than "religions" when discussing these features. He does think, however, that we can understand religions (and other ideologies such as Maoism in China) better if we look for these features.

Another popular way to handle the problems above is to avoid the term "religion" and use "tradition" instead, as we have often done in this book. But does a shift in terminology from "religion" to "tradition" solve our problems? In particular, does it clarify what people are talking about when they talk about religions? Consider the controversy over secularization theory.

Secularization?

Contemporary Atheist Views

In the last few years, a number of atheists have written books arguing that religion is an unfortunate holdover from an earlier time, and that people should get over it. Some argue, as did thinkers such as Marx and Freud, that religion should simply be replaced by modern science. Science is based on rational belief in what is verifiable; its teachings should be favored over unverifiable religious teachings. Some argue as well that not only is religion based on unverifiable claims, but it supports morally objectionable attitudes and behavior, such as sexism, racial prejudice, and the persecution of nonbelievers. The best known of these authors today are Daniel Dennett, Sam Harris, Richard Dawkins, and Christopher Hitchens.

In *Breaking the Spell: Religion as a Natural Phenomenon*, philosopher Daniel Dennett argues that religion evolved among early humans because it had some benefits that helped them survive and reproduce. One is that it gave them some reassurance and feelings of control in a dangerous world. However, religions, especially fundamentalist ones, have also had harmful effects, he says, one of which is that they interfere with understanding the world in a rational way, as science does. Like Freud, Dennett argues that religion is based on wishful thinking. Religious traditions keep people ignorant of the true nature of the world, they valorize blind obedience, and they perpetuate irrational, harmful behavior. Dennett argues that religions need to engage in careful self-examination to protect future generations from the ignorance and primitive behavior they have so often fostered in the past.

Sam Harris wrote *The End of Faith* when he was a graduate student. He followed that book with the short *Letter to a Christian Nation*. In both, Harris argues that religion arose at a primitive stage of history in which people had little idea of how the world worked and what was good for them. In the barbaric ancient world, for example, people sometimes sacrificed their own children, believing that would please the gods, as God's commanding Abraham to sacrifice his son illustrates. The Christian belief that the torture and murder of Jesus by the Romans pleased God and "paid the debt for" Adam's sin, Harris says, is a "direct and undisguised inheritance of the scapegoating barbarism that has plagued bewildered people throughout history." (Harris 2007) Today, according to Harris, we need to overcome such harmful beliefs by thinking rationally and scientifically. Doing this requires that we stop valorizing faith, which is believing in something for which you do not have good evidence. Harris points out that the 19 hijackers who flew the planes into the World Trade Center and the Pentagon on September 11, 2001 did so out of deep religious faith. The world can no longer afford this kind of thinking or behavior, he says.

The third atheist who argues that religion is incompatible with science and rationality is Richard Dawkins, a prominent geneticist. His intention in writing *The God Delusion*, he says, was to raise people's consciousness with four messages:

1. Atheists can be happy, moral, and intellectually fulfilled.
2. Atheists should be proud because atheism is evidence of a healthy, independent mind.
3. Evolution and other scientific theories are superior to a "God hypothesis" in explaining the cosmos and the origin of living things.
4. Children should not be labelled by their parents' religions. Calling a young girl or boy a "Catholic child" or "Muslim child" makes no more sense than calling someone a "Marxist" child.

Although many people consider religion beneficial because it fosters morality, Dawkins argues that we do not need religion to be good. He gives a Darwinian explanation of morality: altruistic genes were selected in evolution because they had survival value for groups of people. With altruism comes our natural human empathy for others. The Ten Commandments did not create our reluctance to hurt other people without good reason. They simply put a religious stamp of approval on the reluctance we already had.

When Dawkins assesses the effects of religion on society, he sees mostly harm. Religion undermines science, he says, and encourages fanaticism and bigotry against other groups and against minorities such as homosexuals. He considers the indoctrination of young children into religions by parents and teachers to be a form of child abuse.

Christopher Hitchens argues in similar ways. In the U.S., his book is titled *God Is Not Great: How Religion Poisons Everything*. In the U.K. it has the less provocative subtitle *The Case against Religion*. From the start, this book has a negative, angry tone. Religion, according to Hitchens, is "violent, irrational, intolerant, allied to racism and tribalism and bigotry, invested in ignorance and hostile to free inquiry, contemptuous of women and coercive toward children." Like Dawkins, Hitchens considers religious education a form of child abuse.

Contemporary Opposition to Secularization Theory

Critics of religion such as Dennett, Harris, Dawkins, and Hitchens say that religion *should* fade away, but this raises the question: *Is* it fading away? This question has been debated since the mid-1800s. As we saw in Chapters 3 and 4, a number of scholars proposed what was later called secularization theory (or the secularization thesis). It predicts that, as societies become more modern and scientific, the importance of religious belief and ritual in people's lives will decline. In the 1960s many scholars thought that by the year 2000 Western cultures would be thoroughly secular, and institutional religion would have little influence on people's lives.

A thoroughly secularized society would be one in which few people would think of the world as controlled by supernatural agents, and few would engage in worship. The natural world described by science would be thought of as existing on its own and operating according to scientific laws. Knowledge, values, and social norms would be based only on natural or scientific principles. Social status would not be linked to religious belief or practice. Changes such as these were even celebrated as an ideal by Harvey Cox of Harvard Divinity School in his best-selling book *The Secular City* (1965/1990). For Cox, God would not disappear, nor would religion. People would just develop more sophisticated understandings of God, and express them through civil, cooperative behavior – rather than expecting miraculous manifestations of divine power and insisting that everyone believe as they do.

As we saw in Chapter 3, a number of scholars today reject the secularization thesis. Peter L. Berger, for example, says the theory was all wrong, using as evidence what is commonly called the resurgence of religion today. As Berger puts it, "The world today is as furiously religious as it ever was." (Berger 1999, 2) Why? Because people have begun to realize that human existence without "transcendence" is just unbearable.

The rejection of secularization theory is based on the increasingly public profile of religion, particularly in many Muslim-majority countries and in the U.S. However, a closer look reveals that the issues are not all that clear.

Resurgent Islam

The "resurgence" of Islam is probably the paradigm case of religious resurgence in the contemporary world. As we saw in Chapter 6, the modern period of Islam has been characterized by efforts to recover from years of European domination and to revitalize Islamic life. The term "renaissance" (*nahda*) was introduced in the 19th century to characterize the desired Islamic cultural resurgence.

The combination of economic and political challenges facing Muslim societies made life very complex. Countries from Morocco to Malaysia were under various forms and degrees of foreign control. The countries enforcing this control – France, Britain, Italy, Russia, and Holland – were competing with one another for economic advantage, and none of them wanted to lose the game. They employed diverse tactics to maintain strategic advantage, sometimes co-opting local leaders, sometimes imposing direct control, sometimes pitting one local faction against another, and so on. So it was not a simple task for people spread over this huge quadrant of the world and living in vastly different circumstances to devise effective ways to liberate themselves. World Wars I and II in the 20th century did not make things any easier.

Not surprisingly, efforts at recovery and reform took a number of forms. We noted in Chapter 6 that early 20th century reformers tended to be secularist, seeking independence and development based on models adopted from Western Europe. By the mid-20th century, many of the foreign powers had been evicted. However, efforts to organize independent states with European-style laws and political structures had produced few measurable gains for the majority of people. As in many parts of the formerly colonized world – such as Latin America and Africa – Soviet-inspired socialist models then enjoyed brief popularity. Like Che Guevara, leaders from North Africa to Southeast Asia could be seen wearing military fatigues and smoking cigars, discussing "the revolution" against capitalism.

However, neither the early Western-European-model leaders nor the socialists were effective in delivering on their promises. Countries gradually evicted their European overlords, but often at enormous expense. Petro-dollars were pouring into some countries – those with the smallest populations overall. But foreign domination, revolution, and war left many countries devastated economically and socially.

Nor did the early Western-European-model leaders and the socialists represent the majority of people. At the grassroots level, people continued to struggle with the daily needs of life. Making a living, finding suitable mates, nurturing and educating children, creating a secure and satisfying social environment – these needs are similar around the world, but they were not being met by the post-colonial leaders in the capitals.

This is the environment in which observers see a resurgence of Islam. Local Muslim leaders got attention and became popular because they addressed the needs of people at the grassroots level. They spoke of daily struggles in terms people understood. Language drawn from their Islamic heritage was both familiar and comforting. It assured people that there is hope, and it encouraged them to "get up, stand up, stand up for your rights," as Bob Marley put it. (He was not Muslim but his message brought comfort and encouragement to people in postcolonial conditions similar to those of Muslims.)

Resurgent Islam is evidenced in dress in many places. Whereas 40–50 years ago "Western" dress was widely popular, over the past few decades people have chosen to express their identities in modern versions of traditional styles. In some areas, of course, women are forced to cover themselves completely; there is little choice about it. However, many Muslim women throughout the world have chosen to wear headscarves to assert their Muslim identity. For men there is no such universal symbol of Muslim identity.

But more important than the symbols are the choices people are making about the role of Islam in their lives. And there is clear evidence that Muslims increasingly identify with their religion. A recent Gallup Poll of the Muslim World surveyed attitudes in 40 Muslim-majority countries between 2001 and 2006, interviewing over 1.3 million people from across the social and economic spectrum. Its results were published in *Who Speaks for Islam? What a Billion Muslims Really Think* (2008) by John Esposito and Dalia Mogahed. According to the data, an extraordinarily high percentage of Muslims – over 90% in many Muslim countries – feel that religion is important in their daily lives.

Resurgent Religion in the U.S.?

Gallup polls of Americans' religious identity since the mid-20th century reveal that overall levels of religiosity have remained pretty constant, with at least 94% of Americans reporting that they "believe in God or a universal spirit," and over 60% identifying themselves as members of a church, synagogue, mosque, or other religious group. In a 1997 survey asking people whether religion was important in their lives, 53% of Americans said "very important." In another survey in 2002, 52% of Americans said that they prayed every day, with another 18% reckoning "several times a week."

While religion has remained relatively important to Americans over the last 60 years, a closer look reveals that there have been some major changes. Some kinds of religion have increased in popularity. Between 1960 and 2000, membership in the Evangelical Free Church of America increased by over 630%, the Pentecostal Assemblies of the World increased by 1,000%, and the Church of God in Christ increased by 1,300%.

This kind of growth, however, has not occurred in the large older mainline Protestant churches. The United Methodist Church lost 20% of its membership between 1960 and 2000; the Episcopal Church lost 27%.

FIGURE 10.2 A megachurch service, Katedral Mesias, Jakarta. © Enny Nuraheni/Reuters/Corbis.

Among the most spectacular instances of religious resurgence in the U.S. today are Evangelical Protestant churches and non-denominational churches that stress "positive psychology" – especially the **megachurches**. Megachurches are generally defined as congregations that draw more than 2,000 people per week to their services, and have a charismatic senior minister and many social and outreach ministries. Megachurches attract large numbers through the use of modern media and technology, such as jumbotronic TV screens and state-of-the-art sound systems. In many ways, the services are designed to be like the performances of rock bands; indeed, many megachurches feature bands playing Christian rock music.

According to Scott Thumma and Dave Travis, in *Beyond Megachurch Myths: What We Can Learn From America's Largest Churches* (2007), the U.S. had just 50 megachurches in 1970 and now has over 1,300. In 2005, California led with 178 megachurches, followed by Texas with 157 and Florida with 85. Nine out of ten megachurches doubled in membership between 2002 and 2007. In 2007 the average megachurch income was $6.5 million. Altogether, American megachurches now have incomes totaling $8.5 billion. The biggest of them is Lakewood Church in Houston, Texas, headed by Pastor Joel Osteen. Weekly attendance averages 45,000 and Lakewood's budget is $70 million. Besides the 7 million people watching on television in the U.S., services are broadcast to more than 100 other countries. To hold all the people, Lakewood Church leased the former Compaq Center, where the Houston Rockets basketball team used to play, from the city of Houston in 2004, paying $13 million in cash for the first 30 years' rent. Then they spent another $95 million to make the 650,000-square-foot building feel more comfortable. There is wall-to-wall carpeting, a waterfall at each end of the huge stage, and three jumbotronic screens, the largest 32 feet by 18 feet. The second-largest megachurch is also in Houston – five miles from Lakewood Church. It is Second Baptist Church. With 24,000 people coming each week to its "21st Century Worship Center," it boasts fitness centers, bookstores, a café, a K-12 school, and free automotive repair work for single mothers.

At the same time as megachurches have been growing by the week, however, the number of people self-identifying as Catholics has remained relatively constant over the past half-century. The proportion of Roman Catholics has been steady at about 25% of the U.S. population, but this is mainly because of immigration, largely from Latin America. The number of Latina and Latino Catholics in the U.S. has doubled since 1960. Today almost 40% of American Catholics are Latina/Latino, and some observers predict that that proportion of Catholics will increase.

What do these changes among American Catholics mean? There is clear evidence that "being Catholic" today can mean something quite different from what it meant 50 years ago. Until the 1960s, allegiance to the pope was a hallmark of being an American Catholic. In 1860, when the revolutionary forces forming the new nation of Italy took away the Papal States from Pope Pius IX, Catholics across the U.S. protested; hundreds even went to Italy as soldiers to get back the pope's land. Today, by contrast, a majority of American Catholics reject the pope's position on one or more major issues.

This split with the Vatican started in 1968 when Pope Paul VI issued his encyclical (a letter addressed to the church hierarchy expressing the pope's position on a significant issue) *Humanae Vitae* (*Of Human Life*). For five years a papal commission had been reevaluating the church's ban on contraception. That group of theologians, doctors, and other experts then recommended that the ban be dropped. But in his encyclical, the pope reaffirmed the traditional position that contraception was inherently immoral and a mortal (grave or serious) sin. When the encyclical was issued, millions of ordinary Catholics were disheartened and hundreds of priests and theologians protested. Opposition to the pope's ban on contraception has grown stronger over the last four decades, to the point that now over 90% of American Catholics reject it.

This opposition to papal authority carries over to other issues on which the pope has taken a firm stand, such as abortion. More than half of American Catholics believe a woman can have an abortion and remain a good Catholic. Sixty-five percent reject the church law forbidding Catholics from getting a divorce and remarrying. To accommodate the thousands of Catholics wanting to divorce and remarry, the church has made it much easier to obtain an annulment (a declaration that a marriage was invalid). In 1968 it granted 338 annulments; now it grants over 50,000 a year.

The traditional rules that only men can be priests and that they may not be married are also questioned by American Catholics: 60% favor the ordination of women, and 70% say that priests should be allowed to marry. An estimated 20% of American priests, in fact, have gotten married.

Seventy-seven percent of American Catholics now believe that being a good Catholic does not require attending Mass on Sundays, something that was unthinkable fifty years ago; failure to attend Sunday Mass is a mortal sin in Catholic teaching.

As well, many of the theological doctrines that traditionally defined Catholicism have been given up by many Catholics born since 1960. One is the idea that the bread and wine consecrated at Mass are "transubstantiated" by the priest into the actual body and blood of Jesus. According to a recent *New York Times* poll, 70% of American Catholics age 18 to 44 believe the consecrated bread and wine are merely a "symbolic reminder" of Jesus.

In this atmosphere of breaking away from the rules and teachings of the institutional church, the number of young men and women becoming priests and nuns has fallen precipitously. In 1960 there were 41,000 Catholic seminarians in the U.S.; in 2000 there were 3,400. Fifteen percent of American Catholic churches are without a priest, and bishops regularly recruit priests from Africa or India to make up for the shortage of native-born priests. The number of sisters teaching in Catholic schools has declined by 94% since 1965. The Christian Brothers, a religious order of teachers, had 912 seminarians in 1965; in 2000 it had 7. As thousands of Catholic elementary schools and half of Catholic high schools have closed, the traditional education that generated loyalty to the pope and the institutional church has become available to fewer and fewer students.

While the total number of Catholics has kept pace with the U.S. population, then, there seems to have been a gradual secularization among American Catholics. Tens of millions have simply quit the church. While 31% of the U.S. population were raised Catholic, only 24% describe themselves as Catholics now. The vast majority of ex-Catholics have not joined another denomination. And the majority of those who still call themselves Catholic have become "cafeteria Catholics," as their critics call them. They pick and choose the beliefs, rituals, and rules that they agree with, and reject those they do not agree with. They may have their children baptized, get married in a Catholic church, and have a funeral in the

Catholic Church. But they do not attend weekly Mass, they use contraception, they divorce and remarry, and they feel no need to accept what the pope says.

Secularization in Europe

If the American examples constitute a kind of religious resurgence, it seems to be a different kind from that we described among Muslims. Grouping both examples under a rubric such as "desecularization" obfuscates the different roles religion seems to be playing in the lives of Americans – particularly Christians – and Muslims worldwide. Further, the desecularization that Berger talks about does not seem to have occurred in Europe, at least among non-Muslim Europeans.

Few scholars dispute that secularization has indeed proceeded as predicted in Europe. In a 1997 survey asking people whether religion was important in their lives, only 16% of Britons, 14% of French, and 13% of Germans reported that religion is "very important" in their lives. By most accounts, Sweden is now the most secular country in the world. Traditionally, it had a state Lutheran church to which Swedes belonged by default. But starting in the late 1800s, there was a push for separation of church and state, which was put into law in 2000. Today about 85% of Swedes are still members of the Church of Sweden, but in polls 95% of them say that they "seldom or never" participate in public worship. The Church of Sweden estimates that fewer than 2% of its members attend church regularly. The vast majority of Swedes are baptized, married, and buried by the Church, but they have little further involvement with the church. Only 15% of Swedes claim belief in a personal God; only 19% believe in life after death. This level of belief is much lower than that of the most non-believing group in the U.S. – scientists – who have a 40% rate of belief in both God and life after death. In Sweden, church leaders generally do not express opinions on public policy, nor do Swedish politicians invoke the name of God in speeches, as is common among U.S. politicians.

Britain, with a national church similar to Sweden's, falls between Sweden and the United States in its level of secularization. Between 1979 and 2005, half of all British Christians stopped going to church on Sunday; now on a typical Sunday fewer than 10% of Britons attend church. Fewer than half of Britons claim to believe in God. Though 72% of the population told the 2001 Census that they were Christian, 66% have no connection to any church.

This kind of decline in the importance of religion in people's daily lives in Europe is addressed in the book *The Desecularization of the World*. However, it is dismissed there as "The Exception That Proves the Rule." This is the title of a chapter in the book written by sociologist Grace Davie, who says, "In a world characterized by religious resurgence rather than increasing secularization, Western Europe bucks the trend." It is "something of a ghost at the feast." She argues that, while the data clearly seem to confirm the predictions of secularization theory, maybe it is not that Europeans "are so much *less* religious than citizens of other part of the world, as *differently* religious." (Berger et al. 1999, 65) However, she concedes that this argument is a bit of a stretch. She concludes, "An ignorance of even the most basic understandings of Christian teaching is the norm in modern Europe, especially among young people; it is not a reassuring attribute." (83)

Other scholars take the decline in importance of religion in Europe at face value. It is the topic of recent research by sociologist Phil Zuckerman. In his *Society without God: What the*

Least Religious Nations Can Tell Us about Contentment (2010), he presents it as a positive development. He acknowledges people's claims about religious resurgence elsewhere.

> The world seems more religious than ever these days. Across the Middle East, fervent forms of Islam are growing more popular and more politically active. Muslim nations that were somewhat secularized 40 years ago… are now teeming with fundamentalism. In Turkey and Egypt, increasing numbers of women are turning to the veil as an overt manifestation of reinvigorated religious commitment. But it isn't just in the Muslim world that religion is thriving. From Brazil to El Salvador, Protestant Evangelicalism is spreading with great success, instilling a spirited, holy zeal throughout Latin America. Pentacostalism is proliferating, too… and not only throughout Latin American, but in Africa and even China. In the Philippines, tens of thousands of people are committing themselves to new religious movements such as El Shaddai, with its powerful theology of prosperity. And many nations of the former Soviet Union, which had atheism imposed upon them for decades, have emerged from the Communist era with their faith not only intact, but strong and vibrant. Even in Canada, a nation hardly known for its religious vitality, there is evidence of a spiritual and religious renaissance. To quote a leading sociologist of religion, Peter Berger, "most of the world is bubbling with religious passions." (1)

Zuckerman then goes on to describe the refreshing contrast of Denmark and Sweden – "clean and green Scandinavia," as he calls them – "an earthly heaven for secular folk." "They may be few and far between," he says, "but there are indeed some significant corners of the world today, however atypical, where worship of God and church attendance are minimal." (2) Contrary to Berger, he argues that "society without God is not only possible, but can be quite civil and pleasant." (4)

Religion Revisited

What can we conclude based on these portrayals of Muslims, various kinds of American Christians, the British, generic Europeans and, in particular, Scandinavian Protestants? Was the secularization thesis all wrong and the importance of religion is increasing, even in modern industrialized societies? Or was the secularization thesis correct, and religion is decreasing in importance, especially in modern industrialized societies? The data show that the importance of religion is increasing in some places and not in others, and what makes the difference is not necessarily whether the place is modern and industrialized. But what good is the theory if it does not explain why its predictions sometimes hold true and sometimes do not?

Perhaps the problem with the theory lies in its vocabulary. Maybe leaving the term "religion" undefined is not really such a good idea. Maybe leaving it vague – or substituting the even vaguer "tradition" for it – does not avoid the problem of imposing a Christian paradigm on everyone. Maybe it does the opposite. Maybe it masks the assumption that "religion" is a universal phenomenon.

We have noted that many languages do not have a word that means what "religion" means in English. Some scholars have argued that this is unimportant. Some are worried about a reversion to the ethnocentrism of early Religious Studies scholars who dismissed non-Christians as pagans or heathens (see Chapter 3). They point out that the fact that people may have no direct linguistic equivalent for "religion" does not mean that they do not have values and morals and ethics and orderly lives. This is why so many scholars use "tradition" instead of "religion" in an effort to be non-judgmental and inclusive.

However, other contemporary scholars believe that usage obfuscates a deeper problem. Whether we use "religion" or "tradition," we are still referring – if only vaguely – to a set of features that somehow resemble what we recognize in our own societies as "religion." Note that the evidence for religious resurgence in the U.S. is based primarily on Christian communities. And note in the above quotations that sociologist Davie seems to associate "basic understanding of… teaching" – in this case, Christian – with religiosity, and Zuckerman seems to equate "belief in God" and "church attendance" with religion. It is this category "religion" – with its implied distinction between "religious" and "non-religious" parts of life – that causes problems.

Durkheim (Chapter 4) – a giant in the field of Religious Studies – believes that religion deals "naturally and fundamentally" with what he calls the sphere of the sacred. (1999, 218) This sphere is reflected in belief and ritual. Further, Durkheim claims that the "profane" everyday world is utterly distinct, alien, and even hostile to the sphere of the sacred. While not all scholars of religion subscribe to Durkheim's characterization of the relationship between the sacred and the profane, the existence of these two spheres is assumed in the use of the term "religion." In order to identify something as religious, it has to be possible to distinguish it from things that are not religious.

Because of issues such as these, some scholars dispute the suitability of using the category "religion" outside of Christianity, where it originated. University of Chicago scholar Jonathan Z. Smith has reached legendary status, partly for his claim that "there is no data for religion. Religion is solely the creation of the scholar's study. It is created for the scholar's analytic purposes by his imaginative acts of comparison and generalization. Religion has no independent existence apart from the academy." (Smith 1982, xi)

Smith enjoys making provocative claims, but his point is important. He is warning students and scholars of religion that we may be so influenced by our own paradigms that we try to impose them on others. And this paradigm – the distinction between spheres of the world that pertain to religion and those that do not – is one specific to Christian history. It is even possible to identify how that split developed in Christian-dominated European history. It began with the bifurcation of law into political matters and spiritual matters (or profane matters and sacred matters), after a long struggle between two centers of power – kings and popes – who were competing for complete control.

As we saw in Chapter 6, the pope seemed to gain the upper hand when he claimed the right to crown the emperor (800). But this was followed by a period during which the kings' power surged, allowing them to appoint and depose popes. In the 11th century, the church reasserted its independence, claiming the right to appoint bishops, which the kings had claimed for themselves, since they paid their salaries. Historian Hans Kohn points out that this was the background for the church's declaration in 1302 that there is only one power, and it is not the king. (Kohn 1961) The announcement in question – called *Unam Sanctam*, "one holy," insisted that there is only one church, the pope is the head of it, and belonging to it is absolutely essential for salvation, since the church alone can grant forgiveness for sins. That is, the pope holds the "plentitude of power." Anyone who resists the power of the pope is resisting the law of God. *Unam Sanctam* acknowledges that there are two "swords" – one spiritual and one temporal (or worldly or secular). However, the temporal is subordinate to the spiritual. "Both, therefore, are in the power of the Church, that is to say, the spiritual and the material sword, but the former is to be administered by the Church [and] the latter for the Church; the former in the hands of the priest; the latter by the hands of kings and soldiers, but at the will and sufferance of the priest." (www.fordham.edu/halsall/source/b8-unam.html)

Despite this claim of absolute papal authority, various regions had already claimed independent authority from the church and established bases for autonomous monarchies in England and France, for example. And what would prove to be a critical distinction between spiritual and civil crimes had already been established, when Pope Innocent III (d. 1216) had asserted exclusive right to absolve sins and issue dispensations – allowing kings to deal with less serious "crimes" and their earthly punishments. *Unam Sanctam* could not turn back the tide of decentralization.

It took several more centuries of struggle between popes and kings to complete the separation of "sacred" from "secular" spheres. As we saw in Chapter 6, the early European states held complete power, according to the Augsburg formula: Whoever is in charge politically is also in charge religiously.

Looking at the struggle to separate life into sacred and profane spheres historically, it can be argued that the distinction is not "natural" or essential at all. It can be seen as a reflection of specific European struggles for power. Indeed, it can be argued that what appears to be the West's secular law is simply the most recent interpretation of Christian ethics. Philosopher John Rawls implies as much, identifying the Christian heritage of modern European notions of justice. (Rawls 1993)

This historical background to the division of life into sacred and profane spheres does not make it any less real. For people who have grown up with this distinction, it seems as real as anything else. Nor does it mean that the distinction does not exist outside of Christian dominated cultures. In fact, thanks to colonization, English has become a universal language, and some of its paradigms are deeply embedded in it. As people around the world learn English, they absorb its paradigms. However, note that in the Gallup Poll of the Muslim World, the term used in the question about the importance of religion in people's lives was *din*. As we saw, this term technically means "judgment" – as in "day of" or "court of" – in both Arabic and Hebrew, and is closely related to the term "justice" (just as "judgment" and "justice" are related in English). How are we to determine if people answering the poll heard the question as "Does judgment/justice play an important role in your daily life?" or as "Do belief and worship play an important role in your daily life?" There is a big difference.

Therefore, paying attention to the biases of our vocabulary is critical to Religious Studies. Jonathan Smith offers another analogy in this regard. He says that using our own models of religion to study others' is like focusing on our maps instead of the territories we are trying to navigate. (Smith 1993) We focus on our own descriptions of people rather than letting the people describe themselves. What he means is that using the term "religion" to characterize what other people do potentially distorts our understanding of what they do. It prompts us to look for things such as gods and sacred texts, prophets and organizations (including "churches," denominations, and sects) – in places where they do not exist. As we saw, many traditions operate without one or more of the elements designated as "religious" by Western scholars. And it prompts us to look for a distinction between what is sacred and what is not – a distinction that may well not be recognized by others.

Another danger is that insisting on using "religion" as a category may lead us to overlook important elements in another tradition – simply because they are not important elements in the Western Christian paradigm. Honoring ancestors, for example, is central to many traditions. But it is not a part of the Christian paradigm of "religion." So honoring ancestors can be dismissed as superstition, or misunderstood as "worship," or even overlooked altogether – along with the wisdom, values, and worldview associated with it.

University of Alabama scholar Russell McCutcheon thinks the category "religion" is particularly problematic when we use it to explain world events. (McCutcheon 1997) We may decide, for example, that it is religious ideology that is motivating certain political actions when, in fact, it could be something quite different. For example, the United States has formulated a single rationale for its wars in Afghanistan and Iraq, its military strikes in Pakistan and Yemen, and its support for Israel's military campaigns in Lebanon and Gaza. That category or paradigm is: The Global War on Terror (GWOT). And the terror that is the target of the global war is identified as motivated by radical Islam, or "Islamo-fascism" – a term coined recently, and popularized by Western journalists such as Christopher Hitchens. The problem with this terminology is that it lumps together the diverse motivations of those being targeted. It focuses attention on what is typically included in the Western religious paradigm – such as ideology – and away from factors not typically accounted for in that paradigm – such as political and economic grievances, the desire for self-determination and good governance, and an end to foreign intervention. Without understanding the reasons various people are fighting, it is difficult to devise strategies that might be effective in getting them to stop fighting.

Other Issues

The Range of Research Areas in the American Academy of Religion

Thankfully, not all Religious Studies scholars spend their time arguing about what religion is, or whether it is growing or declining. The range of issues in which they are interested goes way beyond these questions. Religious Studies scholars have professional organizations that meet regularly to discuss common interests. The largest of these is the American Academy of Religion (AAR), one of the oldest professional organizations in the country. With thousands of members, its annual meetings last for several days and involve hundreds of lectures and discussions concerning a mind-boggling array of topics. AAR is divided into a number of program units in which people may work with like-minded scholars on their specific research areas. A list of the program units will give an idea of the range of topics that come under "Religious Studies."

Sections
Arts, Literature, and Religion
Buddhism
Christian Systematic Theology
Comparative Studies in Religion
Ethics
History of Christianity
North American Religions
Philosophy of Religion
Religion and Politics
Religion and the Social Sciences
Religion in South Asia
Study of Islam
Study of Judaism
Teaching Religion
Theology and Religious Reflection
Women and Religion

Groups
African Religions
Afro-American Religious History
Anthropology of Religion
Asian North American Religion, Culture, and Society
Augustine and Augustinianisms
Bible in Racial, Ethnic, and Indigenous Communities
Bible, Theology, and Postmodernity
Bioethics and Religion
Black Theology
Bonhoeffer: Theology and Social Analysis
Buddhist Critical-Constructive Reflection
Buddhist Philosophy
Chinese Religions
Christian Spirituality
Comparative Religious Ethics
Comparative Studies in Hinduisms and Judaisms
Comparative Theology
Confucian Traditions
Contemporary Islam
Contemporary Pagan Studies
Critical Theory and Discourses on Religion
Cultural History of the Study of Religion

Daoist Studies
Eastern Orthodox Studies
Ecclesiological Investigations
Evangelical Theology
Feminist Theory and Religious Reflection
Gay Men and Religion
Hinduism
Indigenous Religious Traditions
Islamic Mysticism
Japanese Religions
Kierkegaard, Religion, and Culture
Korean Religions
Latina/o Religion, Culture, and Society
Law, Religion, and Culture
Lesbian-Feminist Issues and Religion
Men, Masculinities, and Religions
Mysticism
Native Traditions in the Americas
New Religious Movements
Nineteenth Century Theology
Platonism and Neoplatonism
Practical Theology
Pragmatism and Empiricism in American Religious Thought
Psychology, Culture, and Religion
Qur'an
Reformed Theology and History
Religion and Disability Studies
Religion and Ecology
Religion and Popular Culture
Religion in Latin America and the Caribbean
Religion, Film, and Visual Culture
Religion, Holocaust, and Genocide
Religion, Media, and Culture
Religions, Medicines, and Healings
Religions, Social Conflict, and Peace
Ritual Studies
Roman Catholic Studies
Sacred Space in Asia
Schleiermacher
Science, Technology, and Religion
Scriptural Reasoning
Tantric Studies
Theology and Continental Philosophy
Tibetan and Himalayan Religion

Tillich: Issues in Theology, Religion, and Culture
Wesleyan Studies
Western Esotericism
Womanist Approaches to Religion and Society
World Christianity

Seminars
Christian Zionism in Comparative Perspective
Comparative Philosophy and Religion
Religion and the Literary in Tibet
Religion in the American West
Religion, Food, and Eating
Religions in Chinese and Indian Cultures: a Comparative Perspective

Consultations
African Diaspora Religions
Animals and Religion
Body and Religion
Buddhism in the West
Childhood Studies and Religion
Christianity and Academia
Cognitive Science of Religion
Death, Dying, and Beyond
International Development and Religion
Jain Studies
Latina/o Critical and Comparative Studies
Liberal Theologies
Liberation Theologies
Martin Luther and Global Lutheran Traditions
Middle Eastern Christianity
Mormon Studies
Music and Religion
North American Hinduism
Open and Relational Theologies
Pentecostal-Charismatic Movements
Queer Theory and LGBT Studies in Religion
Religion and Cities
Religion and Colonialism
Religion and Humanism
Religion and Migration
Religion and Sexuality
Religion Education in Public Schools: International Perspectives
Religion in Europe
Religion in Europe and the Mediterranean World, 500–1650 CE
Religion in Southeast Asia

Religion, Memory, History
Religious Conversions
Ricoeur
Scriptural/Contextual Ethics
Sex, Gender, and Sexuality in Premodern Christianity
Sikh Studies
Sociology of Religion
Space, Place, and Religious Meaning
Theology and the Political
Theology of Martin Luther King Jr.
Transformative Scholarship and Pedagogy
Transhumanism and Religion
Women of Color and Scholarship, Teaching, and Activism
Yoga in Theory and Practice
Yogacara Studies

Even if we wrote just a few sentences about each of the topics above, we would go over the word-limit for this book – and probably leave you dizzy. So that is not a good way to give you an impression of the kinds of things Religious Studies does today. Instead of trying to describe the whole forest, then, we are going to focus on a few trees. Here we shall look at issues of the life-and-death kind that, as we saw in Chapter 2, have always been of concern to human beings. These are in what we now call the medical sciences.

Medical Science and Religion

As we have seen, some religions make specific claims about health. The first medical license in Europe was issued by the Catholic Church in the 12th century, and if the doctor was excommunicated from the Church he forfeited the license. In the Church of Jesus Christ of Latter Day Saints (Mormons), the promotion of good health is found in the scripture *Word of Wisdom*. It restricts the consumption of wine, liquor, meat, and tobacco.

Around the world, people pray for their own health and that of their relatives and friends. They pray that mothers will bear healthy children and be healthy themselves. They pray for people who are about to have surgery, and for the recovery of those who are sick. In Western society, "faith healers" such as televangelist Benny Hinn claim to heal people on the spot, in front of the TV audience.

Many people have claimed that they were miraculously cured after they prayed or someone prayed for them. In the Catholic tradition, such cures are the usual grounds for declaring a person to be a saint. Someone with an illness prays to a holy person who has died, asking him or her to intercede with God on their behalf. If the person is cured, this is considered evidence that the dead person is enjoying eternal reward in heaven. In the process of determining whether or not someone deserves sainthood, the Church requires investigation by physicians to make sure that the cure cannot be attributed to natural causes.

One of the most famous places for miraculous cures is Lourdes, France, where a peasant girl named Bernadette reported that she had several visions of the Virgin Mary in 1858. She

FIGURE 10.3 Pilgrims visiting the grotto at Lourdes, France. Mike Blenkinsop/Alamy.

was told by Mary to scratch the ground there, and when she did, a spring gushed forth. The water is said to have miraculous properties, and millions of pilgrims visit the site each year, including many sick and disabled people praying to be cured.

Religion and Physical Health

Since the 1960s there have been scientific studies on the connection between religion and health. Two guiding questions have been whether belonging to a religious community makes people healthier physically or mentally, and whether prayer for sick people has an effect on their recovery. Most of the research has been done with Christians, with the standard criterion for religiousness being church attendance.

A major impetus for the recent study of religion and health has been the new understanding in medicine of the psychological and social factors involved in health and illness. This area is called **psychoneuroimmunology**. *Psycho-* is from the Greek word for mind, *-neuro-* refers to the nervous system, and immunology is the study of the immune system. Getting sick is not just a matter of being exposed to germs. Our bodies are exposed to billions of bacteria and viruses every day, but this does not automatically cause illness. Crucial to whether we get sick or not is our immune system. The activity of our immune systems, in turn, is influenced by our thoughts and emotions. So what we think and feel influences our ability to resist infections, and thus stay healthy.

A major suppressor of the immune system is the pattern of emotions we call stress. When bad things happen and we have no way of coping with them, we react with negative emotions such as fear, anger, and sadness, which reduce the activity of our immune systems, making us more susceptible to illness. Things that reduce stress, enhance the immune system, and thus equip us to fight off infections include exercise, laughter, and feeling close to other people. When one spouse in an older couple dies, the other one sometimes dies not long after that. The traditional way to describe this is to say that the widow or widower "died of a broken heart." The new medical explanation is that the death of their spouse caused them great stress, which suppressed their immune system, making them susceptible to the disease that killed them.

Among the ways we get to feel close to other people is through religion, and so religion can enhance our immune systems. People who make good friends at their synagogue, temple, mosque, or church may thereby reduce the stress in their lives, boost their immune systems, and thus stay healthier.

There are other ways in which religions influence people's thoughts and emotions, too, and so affect immune system activity and health. As we saw in Chapter 2, religion provides people with a worldview – a way to understand their experience, a purpose in life, and ways to react to events both good and bad. Religions explain suffering and death, and they offer hope and compensation, such as life after death. When people suffer, they may be encouraged to identify with the suffering of other people or to think of it as a test of their faith. This way, their pain does not seem pointless. When someone dies, religious people often say that they are "in a better place now" or "with God." Such comforting thoughts allow people to cope with whatever happens, and in this way religion can reduce stress and boost the immune system.

The research into the effects of religion on health consists mostly of two kinds of study. The first are correlational studies. Researchers ask large groups of people about how religious they are, typically by asking how often they attend religious services or pray. Then they record basic facts about the subjects' physical and mental health. Lastly, they correlate the degree of religiousness with those health factors.

The second kind of study consists of experiments in which people are exposed to different conditions, and then their health after this is correlated with those conditions. This kind of experimental research is in its infancy. It is done almost exclusively with just two controlled variables – meditation and prayers for sick people.

Hundreds of correlational studies have been done linking people's degree of religiousness with various health factors. Most show a positive correlation between religiousness and both physical and mental health, but some show negative correlations. A large number of studies have shown that religious people live longer and that they rate themselves as happier. There are also smaller numbers of studies that show a correlation between religiousness and

- lower blood pressure
- lower incidence of heart disease, emphysema, and cirrhosis
- lower incidence of suicide
- lower anxiety in heart-transplant patients
- reduced pain in cancer patients
- decreased disability in elderly people in nursing homes.

Religion and Mental Health

Until quite recently, the relation between religions and mental health was not a happy one. The idea of mental illness is barely a century old. In earlier times, people who acted in strange ways and who could not get along with others were not thought of as ill. Instead they were thought to be possessed by demons, or to be witches. And so they were often mistreated, even put to death.

When Sigmund Freud developed some of our modern ideas about mental illness and mental health a century ago, furthermore, he had negative views about religion, as we saw in Chapter 3. Indeed, he called religion the "universal obsessional neurosis of mankind." So psychiatrists trained in the Freudian tradition often viewed religion as itself a kind of mental illness. Psychotherapists who came after Freud, too, were often hostile to religion. Albert Ellis, founder of Rational Emotive Behavior Therapy, thought of religion as based on irrational thinking and emotional imbalance. And even when therapists did not consider a patient's religion to be part of the problem, they usually ignored it in treating them.

In the last few decades, psychotherapists have begun to appreciate the importance of religion in people's lives, and to include it in their treatment. In 2006 the Mental Health Foundation in the U.K. produced a review of the literature on the impact of religion and spirituality on mental health. In 2008 the California Institute for Mental Health established the California Mental Health and Spirituality Initiative to promote the "inclusion of spirituality as a potential resource in mental health recovery and wellness." There is even a journal called *Mental Health, Religion and Culture*.

The studies of the relation of religion to mental health have found mostly positive correlations, as we said earlier. Overall there is strong evidence that highly religious people tend to have higher levels of well-being, self-esteem, and satisfaction with their lives and their marriages. There is also a strong positive correlation between religious involvement and some skills for coping with troubling life events. Religions, for example, often draw attention away from the body and toward the non-physical aspects of a person; this can help people with physical disabilities.

While some religious beliefs and practices have been associated with these mental health benefits, not all are. Some studies have found correlations between "negative coping styles" in certain religions and increased stress, depression, and suicide. A lesbian or a gay man growing up in a religious community that condemns homosexuality, for example, might experience considerable shame, guilt and anxiety. They may be less well-adjusted and less mentally healthy precisely because of their religion.

Most researchers who study the relation between religion and health are cautious to avoid the word "cause." If they have found that people who attend church often have good coping skills, for example, they do not conclude that going to church often *causes* good coping skills. This is because when A and B vary together, it is not necessarily because A causes B. Maybe B causes A. Or maybe both A and B are caused by some third factor, C. Perhaps people who already have good coping skills are somehow attracted to religion. Or perhaps there is some personality factor that causes people to *both* have good coping skills *and* be inclined to religion. The correlation by itself does not tell us which of these possibilities is the case.

Another caution is needed here. While it is true that people who attend religious services often are better at coping with life's problems, it need not be anything religious that accounts for this coping. Human beings are a social species. To be happy and to cope with problems, they need to be with others, to care about others, and to feel that others care about them. Belonging to a religious community can fulfill these needs, but so can belonging to other groups – a club, a musical group, a labor union, a bunch of friends. In the correlational studies showing that churchgoers have better coping skills, maybe the non-religious people they were being compared with did not belong to any community that could support them in times of trouble. The same caution is needed in assessing any other correlational study.

Does Prayer Work?

Another issue now being studied is whether praying for sick people helps them recover. At Harvard University Medical School, the Religion, Health, and Healing Initiative was established in 2000 to study healing and religion. Researchers at Harvard and elsewhere have tried to determine whether patients who have people praying for them get better at a higher rate than people who are not prayed for. Most experiments involve "third-party" prayers – prayers by people unknown to the patients.

Two studies have found that third-party prayers are followed by medical benefits, but two other studies found no benefits. The largest study, done in 2006 and called STEP (Study of the Therapeutic Effects of Intercessory Prayer), was conducted with 1,806 people undergoing coronary bypass surgery at six hospitals around the U.S. The STEP study was paid for by the John Templeton Foundation, which supports research on science and religion. Among those participating were Catholics, Jews, Protestants, and people with no religion. They were divided into three groups. One group received no prayers. The second group were prayed for after being told that they may or may not be prayed for. And the third group was prayed for after being told that people would pray for them.

The prayers came from three Christian groups – two Catholic, and one Protestant. Those praying were given the first name and last initial of each patient, and they said a standard prayer "for successful surgery with a quick, healthy recovery and no complications."

After the surgery, there were complications in 59% of those who were prayed for. Only 51% of those who received no prayers had complications, and 52% of those who received prayers but did not know it. Deaths during the month after surgery were similar in the three groups. The big question researchers had, of course, is why the patients who knew that people were praying for them did not do as well after surgery as those who were prayed for without their knowing, or those who were not prayed for at all. Dr. Charles Bethea, a principal investigator, said that the patients' knowledge that they were being prayed for "might have induced a form of performance anxiety or made them feel doubtful about their outcome." The Rev. Dean Marek, director of chaplain services at the Mayo Clinic, said that perhaps patients who knew they were prayed for "thought they were home free and discounted the traumatic effect that surgery has upon the body, so were ill-prepared for it."

Brain Science and Mystical Experience: Neurotheology

The last question we shall consider that illustrates the overlap between Religious Studies and the medical sciences is: What happens in the brain when people have religious experiences? In Chapter 4 we mentioned that a century ago William James popularized the

The John Templeton Foundation

Scientific research into religion requires funding, and one organization that provides it is the John Templeton Foundation, which gives away about $70 million a year in research grants and program funding. Sir John Templeton (1912–2008), an investor and philanthropist, created the foundation in 1987 to serve

> as a philanthropic catalyst for discoveries relating to the Big Questions of human purpose and ultimate reality. We support research on subjects ranging from complexity, evolution, and infinity to creativity, forgiveness, love, and free will. We encourage civil, informed dialogue among scientists, philosophers, and theologians and between such experts and the public at large, for the purposes of definitional clarity and new insights. Our vision is derived from the late Sir John Templeton's optimism about the possibility of acquiring "new spiritual information" and from his commitment to rigorous scientific research and related scholarship. The Foundation's motto, "How little we know, how eager to learn," exemplifies our support for open-minded inquiry and our hope for advancing human progress through breakthrough discoveries. (http://www.templeton.org/who-we-are/about-the-foundation/mission)

The Foundation funds many high-level scientific research projects, using peer evaluation, and it holds international competitions to which university researchers apply. Each year the foundation gives the Templeton Prize to "a living person who has made exceptional contributions to affirming life's spiritual dimension." Francisco Ayala, an evolutionary biologist and geneticist at the University of California, Irvine, won the 2010 Prize, worth about $1.5 million, for his books and talks arguing that there is no essential contradiction between religious faith and belief in science.

term *religious experience* in his book *The Varieties of Religious Experience*. We also sketched his analysis of mystical experiences. Since James, people have used the phrase "religious experience" in many ways. Sometimes it means a personal encounter with God, understood as a direct perception laden with emotions. Other times, religious experience simply means thinking about an ordinary experience in a religious way. Someone looking at the stars filling the summer sky, for example, might suddenly think of the vastness of creation. Because of the ambiguity of the term, we are not going to talk about "religious experience" here, but about a specific kind – mystical experience.

Mystical experience is described as a special psychological state in which people feel the unity of all that exists. Reality is experienced not as many things spread out in space and over time. Reality is One.

When people describe mystical experiences, they often talk about how immediate and comprehensive the feelings are. They go beyond a simple intellectual experience. Mystical experience feels like a direct awareness that brings complete certainty. As one person described it, "I felt a deep and profound sense of connection to everything, recognizing that there never was a true separation at all."

Another person went into more detail:

> There was a feeling of energy centered within me … going out to infinite space and returning…. There was a relaxing of the dualistic mind, and an intense feeling of love. I felt a profound letting go of the boundaries around me, and a connection with some kind of energy and state of being that had a quality of clarity, transparency and joy. ("Religion and the Brain," *Newsweek* 2001)

After Sophy Burnham visited Machu Picchu in South America, here is how she described one of her experiences there, in her 1999 book *The Ecstatic Journey*:

> I could hear the singing of the planets, and wave after wave of light washed over me. But … I was the light as well … I no longer existed as a separate I … I saw into the structure of the universe. I had the impression of knowing beyond knowledge and being given glimpses into ALL. (Burnham quoted in *Newsweek* 2001)

As we have seen, mystical experience is not specific to any particular tradition. It is represented in varying degrees in the Western monotheisms, and is a feature of many indigenous traditions around the world. However, it is perhaps most prevalent in Indian traditions. We saw in Chapter 7 how the *Upanishads* present a worldview based on cosmic unity. Here is how the *Chandogya Upanishad* expresses it:

> As the rivers flowing east and west
> Merge in the sea and become one with it,
> Forgetting they were ever separate rivers,
> So do all creatures lose their separateness
> When they merge at last into pure Being.

When people began analyzing mystical experiences and their religious implications, the data were generally limited to people's reports of their experiences. Such reports seemed hard to study scientifically. However, in the 1980s brain scientists began using new technologies such as MRI (magnetic resonance imaging) to study what is going on in the brain during mystical experiences, meditation and prayer. This kind of research, done at places such as Columbia University's Center for the Study of Science and Religion, is often called "neurotheology."

One neuroscientist who has studied these patterns is James Austin, who got into this research because of a mystical experience he had in 1982. On a Sunday morning he was in a London railway station waiting for a train that would take him to a Buddhist retreat. He glanced away from the tracks toward the river Thames and saw nothing unusual: the grimy station, a few dingy buildings, the gray sky. But then, unexpectedly, he had a feeling utterly

Mystics in India

FIGURE 10.4 A mystic in India. Around the World in a Viewfinder/Alamy.

Hinduism has the oldest tradition of mystical experience. As we saw in Chapter 7, this tradition began with the *Upanishads*, in which it is said that all reality is ultimately Brahman, and that Brahman is identical with Atman, the self. In Hinduism, the way to achieve an awareness of these ultimate truths is to meditate. Here an Indian mystic cultivates his ability to meditate by assuming positions of hatha yoga.

unlike any he had experienced before. His ordinary sense of being an individual different from the world around him evaporated. He was no longer a subject experiencing objects separate from each other and separate from him. Instead, as he described it, he saw things "as they really are." Losing the ordinary sense of "I, me, mine,"

> time was not present... I had a sense of eternity. My old yearnings, loathings, fear of death and insinuations of selfhood vanished. I had been graced by a comprehension of the ultimate nature of things....

Austin's experience in the railway station led him to ask questions about mystical experience and to do extensive research on brain events underlying it. He presents this research in his 844-page book *Zen and the Brain* (1988).

As a neuroscientist, Austin reasoned this way: In mystical experiences of whatever religious tradition, several features of ordinary psychological awareness are reduced or missing altogether. These include a sense of time, self-consciousness, and fear. If these experiences are suppressed, then certain brain circuits are probably suppressed. So Austin measured brain activity in people undergoing mystical experiences to see which parts of the brain were quiet. These turned out to be

- the frontal lobes and temporal lobes, which mark time and generate self-awareness
- the parietal lobe, which orients us in space and marks the distinction between self and not-self
- the amygdala, which monitors the environment for threats and registers fear.

When these three areas go quiet, Austin concluded, "what we think of as our 'higher' functions of selfhood appear to be 'deleted from consciousness'" and we feel unified with all that is.

Two more neuroscientists studying mystical experience are Eugene D'Aquili and Andrew Newberg, working at the University of Pennsylvania. In 1999 they published *The Mystical Mind: Probing the Biology of Religious Experience*, and then in 2001, the book *Why God Won't Go Away*. In the mystical experiences they studied, a bundle of neurons in the superior parietal lobe, toward the top and back of the brain, went quiet. This region, called the "orientation association area," processes information about space and time, and the orientation of the body in space. It determines where the body ends and the rest of the world begins. Specifically, the left orientation area creates the sensation of a physically limited body. The right orientation area creates the sense of the physical space in which the body exists.

Both the left orientation area and the right orientation area require sensory input – from the eyes and ears, for example – to do their calculations. So when a person blocks out visual and sound perceptions in mystical experience or in meditation, the left orientation area may not be able to distinguish between the self and the rest of the world. As a result, the brain tends "to perceive the self as endless and intimately interwoven with everyone and everything." Similarly, Newberg says, when the right orientation area, the part responsible for creating the sense of space, is deprived of sensory input, it defaults to a feeling of infinite space.

Although neuroscientists have just begun studying what happens in the brain during mystical experience, they have established a few basics. In a mystical experience, the brain is in an unusual state. The areas of the brain that normally provide a sense of space and time, and that mark the person as separate from what they are experiencing, are inactive. So the person feels that reality is not spread out over space and time, and they are not distinct from everything else. Reality is one.

Having seen that mystical experience is correlated with certain events in the brain, however, we should add that nothing in this research shows that those experiences exist "only" in the brain, or that what is experienced in mystical experience is not true. After all, all our ordinary perceptions – seeing a mountain, hearing thunder, feeling the coldness of ice – are correlated with certain events in the brain. But this does not mean that mountains or thunder or ice are "only" in the brain, with no independent reality. Neurology helps explain mystical experience and other kinds of religious experience, but it need not explain them away. In the end, as Newberg says, "There is no way to determine whether the neurological changes associated with spiritual experience mean that the brain is causing those experiences… or is instead perceiving a spiritual reality." (*Newsweek* 2001)

Conclusion: Another Surprise?

We began this book with a little advice: If you want to study religion, be prepared for surprises. Throughout our discussions of various religions and diverse theories of religion, we have been challenging many common assumptions and paradigms, including the word "religion" itself. If you have read this far, then you are probably the kind of person who is up to such challenges. So we have one last challenge for you. Look back over the list above, of things studied by scholars in the American Academy of Religion, and try to think of some area of human life that would be off-limits to Religious Studies. Not medicine, as we just saw. And not philosophy, psychology, sociology, anthropology, economics, geology, history, literature, art, or music.

Maybe the biggest surprise in studying religion is that we are still unable to define just what it is we are studying. Or, to put it another way, it seems that there is no aspect of life left out of the study of religion – because there is no aspect of life left out of the myriad traditions throughout the world that are identified as religious. Maybe oral cultures like that of the Seneca are on the right track when they do not coin a word for "religion" because every dimension of life potentially has the specialness that Western cultures are trying to isolate with that term.

However, for all the diversity of phenomena examined in Religious Studies, there are perhaps a few generalizations that can be drawn. We close with a list drawn up by a friend of ours, an Anglican priest with a Dutch-English-Indian family background, familiar with Hindu, Baptist, Mennonite, Unitarian, and Roman Catholic traditions, who currently serves a multicultural Episcopalian congregation and as a part-time chaplain at a small, formerly Catholic liberal arts school.

1. Religions are not the same, nor are they completely different.
2. Religious traditions have as much diversity within them as they do between them.
3. Most religions are not single traditions, but multiple traditions.
4. Traditions include – but are not limited to – rituals, myth-making, moral teaching, and organizational systems.
5. Traditions mingle and change according to context.
6. Holy texts are largely unrelated to popular practice.
7. We often misunderstand other people's traditions, as well as our own.

8. Religious conflict is often a result of political conflict.

9. Few people know all the rules of their traditions, and few follow all the rules they do know.

10. We often ignore the bad parts of our traditions, and sometimes ignore the good parts of other traditions.

DISCUSSION QUESTIONS

1. Check Ninian Smart's 1974 book on Maoism in China, *Mao*. In what ways could Maoism be considered a religion?

2. Would we lose anything if we completely stopped talking about "religions" and just talked about "worldviews," "traditions," and "cultures"? Would we gain anything?

3. Read one of Sam Harris's books – either *The End of Faith*, or the shorter *Letter to a Christian Nation*. Which of Harris' arguments seem reasonable to you, and which unreasonable?

4. Choose a country other than the U.S., the U.K. and Sweden. Find out what types of religion are rising or falling there. How might these changes be explained?

5. How might Durkheim or Weber explain the phenomenon of "cafeteria Catholics"?

6. Are there any ways in which religion might promote physical or mental health that have not been mentioned in this chapter?

7. Find some more descriptions of mystical experiences. Do they fit the pattern described in this chapter?

REFERENCES

James Austin, *Zen and the Brain*. Cambridge, MA: MIT Press, 1988.

Peter L. Berger, Jonathan Sacks, David Martin, Tu Weiming, George Weigel, Grace Davie, and Abd Allah Ahmad Naim, editors, *The Desecularization of the World: Resurgent Religion and World Politics*. Grand Rapids, MI: Eerdmans, 1999.

Sophie Burnham, *The Ecstatic Journey: Walking the Mystical Path in Everyday Life*. New York: Wellspring–Ballantine, 1999.

Harvey Cox, *The Secular City: Secularization and Urbanization in Theological Perspective*. New York: Collier, 25th anniversary ed., 1990.

Eugene D'Aquili and Andrew Newberg, *The Mystical Mind: Probing the Biology of Religious Experience*. Minneapolis, MN: Fortress, 1999.

Eugene D'Aquili and Andrew Newberg, *Why God Won't Go Away. Brain Science and the Biology of Belief*. New York: Ballantine, 2001.

Richard Dawkins, *The God Delusion*. New York: Houghton Mifflin, 2006.

Daniel Dennett, *Breaking the Spell: Religion as a Natural Phenomenon*. New York: Viking, 2006.

Emile Durkheim, "From Elementary Forms of the Religious Life," in *Theory and Method in the Study of Religion*, Carl Olson, editor. Belmont, CA: Wadsworth–Thomson, 2003.

John L. Esposito and Dalia Mogahed, *Who Speaks for Islam? What a Billion Muslims Really Think*. Washington, DC: Gallup, 2008.

Sam Harris, *The End of Faith: Religion, Terror, and the Future of Reason*. New York: Norton, 2004.

Sam Harris, *Letter to a Christian Nation*. New York: Knopf Doubleday, 2008.

Sam Harris, "The Sacrifice of Reason," *Washington Post/Newsweek*, August 31, 2007. http://newsweek.washingtonpost.com/onfaith/panelists/sam_harris/2007/08/the_sacrifice_of_reason.html.

Hans Kohn, *The Idea of Nationalism*. New York: Macmillan, 1961.

Russell T. McCutcheon, *Manufacturing Religion*. New York: Oxford University Press, 1997.

John Rawls, *Political Liberalism*. New York: Columbia University, 1993.

Red Jacket, "Speech [Communicated] 1822." http://www.buffalonian.com/history/articles/1801-50/1822-redjacketspeach.html.

"Religion and the Brain," *Newsweek*, May 7, 2001.

Ninian Smart, *Mao*. London: Fontana, 1974.

Jonathan Z. Smith, *Imaging Religion: From Babylon to Jonestown*. Chicago: University of Chicago Press, 1982.

Jonathan Z. Smith, *Map Is Not Territory: Studies in the History of Religions*. Chicago: University of Chicago, 1993.

Scott Thumma and Dave Travis, *Beyond Megachurch Myths: What We Can Learn From America's Largest Churches*. San Francisco: Jossey-Bass, 2007.

Ernst Troeltsch, James Luther Adams and Walter F. Bense, translators, *Religion in History*. Philadelphia: Fortress Press, 1991.

Phil Zuckerman, *Society without God: What the Least Religious Nations Can Tell Us about Contentment*. New York: New York University Press, 2010.

FURTHER READING

Talal Asad, *Genealogies of Religion*. Baltimore, MD: Johns Hopkins University Press, 1993.

Daniel Dubuisson, W. Sayers, translator, *The Western Construction of Religion: Myths, Knowledge, and Ideology*. Baltimore, MD: Johns Hopkins University Press, 2003.

Timothy Fitzgerald, *The Ideology of Religious Studies*. New York: Oxford University Press, 2000.

Chester Gillis, *Roman Catholicism in America*. New York: Columbia University Press, 2000.

Tomoku Masuzawa, *The Invention of World Religions: Or, How European Universalism Was Preserved in the Language of Pluralism*. Chicago: University of Chicago Press, 2005.

G. A. Oddie, *Imagined Hinduism: British Protestant Missionary Constructions of Hinduism, 1793–1900*. New Delhi: Sage, 2006.

Ninian Smart, *Worldviews: Crosscultural Explorations of Human Belief*. Englewood Cliffs, NJ: Prentice Hall, 3rd ed., 1999.

Rodney Stark, "Secularization, R.I.P. – Rest in Peace," *Sociology of Religion*, 60, No. 3 (Fall 1999), 249–273.

GLOSSARY

Abbasids Islamic caliphate ruling from Baghdad from 750 to 1258

Abrahamic religions traditions such as Judaism, Christianity, and Islam, which all trace themselves to Abraham

Aditi early Hindu goddess identified with the light or the mind, sometimes called the mother of the gods

Agni early Hindu god of fire

ahimsa in Hinduism and Buddhism, the moral principle of non-violence

Ahura Mazda the single, eternal, transcendent god in Zoroastrianism

Allah Arabic word for God

Amaterasu a sun goddess in Shinto

Amida Buddha (Amhitabha) the Buddha who promises salvation in a heaven called the Pure Land

anatta (anatman) the Buddhist teaching that there is no stable self in a person

Angra Mainyu an evil spirit in Zoroastrianism, also known as Ahriman

anicca in Buddhism, the impermanence of everything

animism the tendency to perceive everything that moves as alive and having a soul

anthropomorphism the human tendency to see non-human things and processes as like humans

apocalypse literally, "revelation," often applied to the events at the end of the world as revealed in the New Testament book of Revelation

apostles in Christianity, the twelve closest male followers of Jesus

a priori philosophical term for what is known without having to observe anything

archetypes Carl Jung's term for ideas that are found in the collective unconscious mind of the whole human race

arhat in Buddhism, a highly accomplished spiritual seeker

Arjuna hero of the Hindu epic *Mahabharata*

ark in Judaism, the ornamented cabinet in a synagogue or temple containing the Torah scroll

artha in Hinduism, wealth, success, and power

Aryans literally, the "Noble Ones," a term applied to themselves by the warrior tribes who invaded northwest India and Pakistan around 2000–1500 BCE

ascetic a person who renounces worldly possessions and pleasures

asha the principle of order and truth in Zoroastrianism

Ashura in Islam, a day of fasting and mourning on the tenth day of the new year

assumption in Scientology, the reincarnation of a thetan into a new body

atman in Hinduism, the consciousness or self

auditing in Scientology, a form of therapy to help people reach self-awareness, overcome mental problems, and achieve higher states of consciousness

Avalokitesvara the Buddha of Compassion

avatar a manifestation of a god as a human or a god: Rama and Krishna, for example, are avatars of Vishnu

Avesta the scriptures of Zoroastrianism

Axial Age Karl Jaspers' term for the period 800–200 BCE

BCE "before the Common Era," a term replacing BC, "before Christ"

Babylon the southern part of ancient Mesopotamia (present day Iraq)

Babylonian Captivity the period in the mid-6th century BCE when the Israelites were held captive in Babylon

Bar Mitzvah/Bat Mitzvah Jewish rituals marking the transition from boyhood to manhood/girlhood to womanhood

Beltane Wiccan spring festival

Bhagavad Gita eighteen chapters from the Hindu epic Mahabharata that explore philosophical and moral issues

bhakti in Hinduism, love of and devotion to a god or goddess

Bismallah in Islam, the preface to prayers, "In the name of God the most merciful and compassionate"

bodhisattva in Buddhism, a person who forgoes nirvana to be reborn and help other people

bracketing in phenomenology, setting aside questions about what is real or true in order to simply examine how things appear

Brahma a creator god in Hinduism

Brahman in Hinduism, Ultimate Reality, which is beyond the gods

brahmin in Hinduism, a member of the priestly class

bris Jewish ritual of circumcision

Buddha literally, "awakened one," first applied as a title to Siddhartha Gautama

CE "common era," a term replacing AD, "in the year of Our Lord"

canon an official list of writings considered authentic or important

castes in India, a system of social classes, also called jati

Ch'ing Ming in China, a special day for remembering the dead

chuppah the canopy under which the couple stand at a Jewish wedding

Church Fathers influential thinkers in the early centuries of Christianity, also called Doctors of the Church

Comparative Religions the branch of Religious Studies that compares and contrasts the ways several religions deal with a certain topic, such as war or salvation

Constitution of Medina the set of rules established by Muhammad in Medina to govern his new community

cosmology a description of the structure of the universe

coven a community of witches

dalits in India, the lowest social class, also called the Untouchables

dana in Buddhism, a lay person's donation of food, clothing, or other goods to monks or nuns

darshana in Hinduism, seeing and being seen by a god or goddess in a temple

Dead Sea Scrolls ancient documents discovered in caves near the Dead Sea in the 1940s that included versions of what are now books of the Bible

deity a god, a supernatural person

desecularization the process of becoming less secular, more religious

Devi a Hindu goddess

dharma in Hinduism, righteousness or duty; in Buddhism, the teaching of the Buddha

Di (Shang-di) supreme deity in ancient China

diaspora the dispersing of people from their homeland

din Arabic word in the Qur'an for the core of the monotheistic tradition shared by Judaism, Christianity, and Islam

disciple a follower or student of a religious leader

divination rituals used to determine hidden information such as what will happen in the future

Divine Command Ethics a way of understanding morality in which an action is right if God commands it, and wrong if God forbids it

diviner a person who engages in divination

divine right kingship the belief that a king has power because God wills it

druj in Zoroastrianism, chaos, disorder

dualism belief that a human being is composed of two things: an immaterial soul/mind and a material body

dukkha Buddhist term for suffering or unsatisfactoriness

Durga literally, "Invincible"; a warrior Hindu goddess

ecumenical council in Roman Catholicism, a meeting of bishops from around the world

Eid al-Adha Islamic feast celebrating Abraham's willingness to sacrifice his son to God

engrams in Scientology, stored mental images from past experiences

entheogen a drug such as peyote that induces "spiritual" experiences

Enuma Elish ancient Babylonian creation epic

Epistles in Christianity, the letters of Paul and others that became part of the Bible

eschaton the "last thing," the end of the world

Essenes group of Jews in the early centuries CE who withdrew from society to live in monastic communities

exclusivism belief that there is only one true religion

exteriorization in Scientology, the thetan's leaving the body and existing independently

False Face Society group of men within the Seneca who perform rituals of healing

feng-shui in China, an approach to design based on channeling the natural energies of "wind" and "water"

Five Classics the set of official texts in Confucianism

folk religion beliefs and practices that are not officially part of the religion but are not in conflict with it

Four Noble Truths in Buddhism, the basic beliefs about suffering and how to overcome it

fundamentalist a word popularized in 1920 for a Christian who believes "the fundamentals," now also applied to other traditions to mean a person who interprets scripture and doctrine literally and rejects modern trends within the tradition

Ganesha Hindu god, the Remover of Obstacles, who has the head of an elephant

Gathas hymns believed to have been composed by Zoroaster

Gemara in Judaism, the part of the Talmud that is the rabbis' commentaries on the Mishnah

ghee in Hindu rituals, clarified butter offered as a sacrifice to the deities

gospel literally "good news," an account of the life and sayings of Jesus Christ

Great Schism in Christianity, the splitting of the Greek Orthodox Church from the Roman Catholic Church in 1054

guru a religious or spiritual teacher

hadith in Islam, a report of the words and deeds of Prophet Muhammad

halal in Islam, "permitted" or "lawful" kinds of meat that may be eaten

handfasting Wiccan marriage ceremony with promise to stay together for a specified period of time

Hanukkah annual Jewish celebration of the victory of Jews rebelling against their Assyrian overlords in the second century BCE

haram in Islam, forbidden kinds of meat that may not be eaten

harijans literally "children of God," Mahatma Gandhi's term for the dalits, the untouchables

Hasidism in Judaism, a movement begun in the 18th century that emphasizes the emotional side of religion, and centers around a leader who has a simple pious love of God

Haskelah the European Enlightenment within Jewish culture

hatha yoga in Hinduism, a discipline combining bodily movements and postures with conscious breathing

Hebrew Bible the sacred scripture of Judaism, called the Old Testament by Christians

hermeneutic a method of interpreting documents

Hijra the migration of Muhammad and his followers from Medina to Mecca

History of Religions the branch of Religious Studies that examines traditions as they have developed over time

Holi a spring festival in Hinduism

holy sacred, special in a supernatural way

Horned God the main male deity in Wicca, also called The Lord

houris in Islam, the "pure companions" for those who go to heaven

hsaio Chinese term for filial piety, respect and love for one's parents

Imbolc (Candlemas) Wiccan festival in early spring

Indra early Hindu god of war and storms

indulgence in Roman Catholicism, a church-granted reduction in the time a person has to spend in Purgatory after death

inerrant without error, often said of scriptures

Islamism 20th-century movement that politicizes Islam

jati in India, a system of social classes, also called castes

jen (ren) in Confucianism, the virtue of humaneness

jihad in Islam, effort or struggle to do the will of God, which may take the form of military action

jnana yoga in Hinduism, the discipline of meditating and studying the scriptures

Kaaba cubically shaped building in Mecca in the direction of which Muslims pray

Kabbala tradition of mysticism in medieval Judaism

Kali Hindu goddess who is frightening and wears a necklace of human skulls

Kalki in Hinduism, an avatar (manifestation) of the god Vishnu who will destroy evil and restore moral order

kama in Hinduism, pleasure

Kama Sutra Hindu scripture about pleasure

kami in Shinto, gods, spirits, or supernatural powers

Kannon the Mother of Mercy, female Japanese goddess comparable to Avalokitesvara

karma in Hinduism and Buddhism, the natural justice of the universe, in which good actions bring good effects and bad actions bring bad effects

karma yoga in Hinduism, the discipline of unselfish action

khalifah in the Qur'an, human steward of earth

koan a verbal exercise in Zen Buddhism used to shake reliance on conceptual, rational thought

Kojiki "Records of ancient matters," the oldest written record of Shinto teachings and practices, from the 8th century CE

kosher in Judaism, things that are acceptable as foods

Krishna in Hinduism, a god who is an avatar (manifestation) of Vishnu

the Lady the main female divinity in Wicca, also called the Great Mother and the Triple Goddess

Law of Threefold Return (Rule of Three) Wiccan principle that what people do comes back to them three times

li in Confucianism, living morally, showing good manners, and engaging in rituals

lingam in Hinduism, a sculpture resembling an erect penis, one of the images of Shiva

lived religion Wilfred Cantwell Smith's term for popular religious belief and practices that may differ from official or orthodox religion

logical positivism school of philosophy that emphasizes clear thought and language, and links the meaning of statements to the ways they can be verified

longhouses wooden structures, up to 100 feet long, in which the Seneca traditionally lived

the Lord the main male deity in Wicca, also called the Horned God

Lughnasadh (Lammas) Wiccan harvest festival

magic practices such as casting spells that are believed to yield results in ways outside those understood by science

magick in Wicca, the ability to command the unseen powers in nature to achieve one's goals

Mahdi in Islam, the Messiah who will appear at the end of the world

mantra in Hinduism, a sound or phrase thought to be effective in transforming reality

Manu, Laws of in Hinduism, a scripture that gives rules governing the four varnas (social classes) and women

maqasid in Islam, the goals of Sharia (Islamic law)

Marduk a god described in the Enuma Elish who killed his grandmother Tiamat and made the world out of her body

marga in Hinduism, a path, a way of life

martyr someone who dies for a religion or a principle

Masorti literally, "traditional," the term used outside the U.S. for a kind of Judaism started in the early 20th century, called Conservative Judaism in the U.S.

matriarchy rule by mother-figures

maya Hindu term for "illusory," said of ordinary sense perception

megachurch Protestant congregations that draw more than 2,000 people per week to their services, and have a charismatic senior pastor and many social and outreach ministries

Mesopotamia literally, "between the rivers" (Tigris and Euphrates); ancient land now called Iraq

Messiah literally, "the Anointed One:" In the first century CE, the Messiah was a hoped-for king who would liberate the people of Israel from their oppressors

mikvah in Judaism, a ritual bath

minyan in Judaism, the minimum number of men – ten – required to hold a public ritual

Mishnah Jewish law code written about 200 CE

mitzvah, plural mitzvot in Judaism, a commandment from God

moksha in Hinduism, enlightenment which involves liberation from the cycle of rebirth

monasticism withdrawal from ordinary social life to devote oneself to spiritual development

monism the belief that everything is one, or is one kind of stuff

monogamy marriage to a single spouse

monotheism belief in only one God

mosque a Muslim place of worship

mysticism worldview that sees all reality as essentially unified, allowing humans to be one with the divine

myth a story that explains something, especially the origin of something

Navaratri Hindu Festival of Nine Nights

Neolithic Revolution the transition from a hunter-gatherer way of life to agriculture, which began in the Middle East around 12,000 BCE

Neopaganism modern religious movement that traces its roots to pre-Christian European religion

New Testament the 27 books that Christians added to the Old Testament to form the Christian Bible

Nicene Creed official statement of Christian beliefs written at the Council of Nicea in 325

Nihon Shoki "Continuing Chronicles of Japan," a Shinto text

Ninety-Five Theses the list of Martin Luther's complaints about the Roman Catholic Church

nirvana in Buddhism, a blissful state achieved by awakening and being released from the cycle of rebirth

Noble Eightfold Path in Buddhism, the way to achieve nirvana

Norūz the holiday of the New Year in Zoroastrianism

noumenon in the philosophy of Immanuel Kant, a thing in itself, apart from anyone's knowledge of it

numinous Rudolf Otto's word for the way the Holy is experienced as both frightening and fascinating

Old Testament name given by Christians to the books Jews call the Hebrew Bible

Om in Hinduism, the sacred sound that represents Ultimate Reality

oracle bones in ancient China, shoulder blades of oxen and turtle shells used in divination – to reveal the will of the gods and ancestors

Orthodox in Judaism, the group that represents the oldest beliefs, laws, and traditions; in Christianity, the group that began in Greece in the first century and split from the Roman Catholic Church in 1054

orthodoxy "correct belief" within a tradition

Paleolithic (Old Stone Age) the time before people grew food crops, before about 12,000 BCE

parable a story told to teach a lesson

Parvati Hindu goddess who is loving toward humans

patriarchy rule by a father-figure such as a king or pope

pentagram five-pointed star symbolizing Wicca

Pharisees group of Jews in the early centuries CE who believed in the resurrection of the dead and the coming Messiah

phenomenology the study of phenomena, the study of how things appear to us

phenomenon in the philosophy of Immanuel Kant, the way something appears to someone

pilgrimage travel to a place of special religious significance

Pillars of Islam the five basic principles of Islam

pluralism belief that many religious traditions are legitimate

pope in Roman Catholicism, the bishop of Rome, who leads the Church

popular religion religious practices that are widespread though they may not be based on official doctrine

prajna in Buddhism, wisdom or intellectual awakening

prasada in Hinduism, food that has been offered to a deity and is now a token of that deity's grace

predestination in Christianity, the belief that from all eternity God knew whom he would choose to save, and knew who would be damned

presbyter in Christianity, an elder or leader of a church

priest a religious authority who mediates between humans and the divine

Problem of Evil a philosophical puzzle that asks how an all-good, all-powerful God could permit all the evil found in the world

profane worldly, ordinary, the opposite of sacred

prophet a human being who speaks on behalf of God

proselytize to try to convert people to a religion

Protestant Ethic term coined by Max Weber for a European worldview that values career success, hard work, self-control, self-denial, and thrift

Protestant Reformation the movement begun by Martin Luther in 1517 to reform the Roman Catholic Church

Psalm a sacred song or poem used in worship

psychoneuroimmunology branch of medical science that studies the relations between the mind, the brain and nervous system, and the immune system

psychopomp "guide for the soul" who escorts the dead to the next world

puja in Hinduism, a ritual of worship for a deity

Puranas in Hinduism, stories about the gods composed in the Classical Period (3rd century BCE–7th century CE)

Pure Land Buddhism a group of schools based on the promise of Amitabha (Amida) Buddha to bring everyone who asks him to a paradise where buddha-hood is assured

purgatory in Christianity, a temporary state of suffering endured by the dead whose sins keep them from being fully reconciled to God

Qur'an the sacred scripture of Islam

rabbi in Judaism, a religious teacher

Ramadan the ninth month of the Muslim calendar, during which Muslims refrain from food, drink, smoking, and sexual activity from sunrise to sunset

Ramayana Hindu epic about Rama, an avatar (manifestation) of the god Vishnu

Rashidun in Islam, the "rightly guided" successors to Prophet Muhammad as leaders of the Islamic community

reincarnation belief that after death people are born again in new bodies

Religionswissenschaft Max Müller's term for Religious Studies

religious naturalism the tendency to de-emphasize anything supernatural in religion and to treat ethical values and spirituality as a natural part of human life

Rig Veda an important ancient Hindu scripture

rishis in Hinduism, the ancient seers who composed the Vedas

rita in Hinduism, the order of the universe

rite of passage a ritual to mark a person's transition from one stage of life to another, such as from childhood to adulthood

ritual an act or series of acts regularly repeated in a set manner

Roman Catholic Church the largest Christian denomination, led by the Pope

Rosh Hashanah in Judaism, the feast of the New Year, held in the fall

Sabbat any of several Wiccan holidays tied to the seasons of the year

Sabbath in Judaism and Christianity, the holy day of the week: Saturday in Judaism, Sunday in Christianity

sacrament in Christianity, a special ritual believed to have been instituted by Jesus

sacred special in a supernatural way

sacrifice the offering of something of value to a deity

sacrilege an action that shows disrespect for something sacred

Sadducees important group of Jews in the first century who did not hold such beliefs as the resurrection of the dead

sadhu in Hinduism, a wandering holy man

Samhain Wiccan fall festival

samsara in Hinduism and Buddhism, the cycle of rebirths

San-chiao Chinese term for the "Three Teachings" of Confucianism, Taoism, and Buddhism

sangha in Buddhism, the community of monks and/or nuns

sannyasi in Hinduism, a renunciant, a person at the last stage of life who pursues meditation and enlightenment full-time

Saoshyant in Zorastrianism, a savior who will renew the world and bring perfect order

Sarasvati Hindu goddess of knowledge, music, and the arts

scripture sacred writings such as the Bible, the Qur'an, and the Hindu Vedas

secularization thesis the claim that as societies become modern and industrialized they become less religious

Seder in Judaism, the special dinner at Passover

sexism discrimination against people because of their sex

Shahada Arabic term for "bearing witness" that refers to the vow "I bear witness that there is no god but God and Muhammad is the messenger of God"

shaman an intermediary between the human world and the world of spirits, who gains access to special knowledge and who can solve problems in the community such as sickness

Sharia Islamic law

Shaiva (Shaivite) a follower of the Hindu god Shiva

Shakti in Hinduism, "power," applied to a goddess

she'ol Hebrew word for "the pit," "the grave," the hole in the earth in which a person is buried

Shi'i Islam the form of Islam dominant in Iran and southern Iraq: it claims about 15% of the world's Muslims

Shiva a major multifaceted god in Hinduism, commonly known as both destroyer and transformer

Shoah Hebrew word for the Jewish Holocaust

sitting shivah in Judaism, the week-long period of mourning

skandhas in Buddhism, the five phenomena that make up a human being

social construction of reality Peter Berger's term for the way people's concepts are influenced by their social context

soma in ancient Hinduism, a sacred beverage with stimulant and perhaps hallucinogenic properties

stupa a Buddhist shrine

sufi a Muslim mystic

Sukkot in Judaism, the Feast of Tabernacles, the harvest festival

Summerland in Wicca, the after-death paradise

Sunna in Islam, the example set by Muhammad to guide Muslims, as found in the hadith reports

Sunni Islam the dominant form of Islam, with about 85% of the world's Muslims

synagogue in Judaism, an assembly of people, or the building in which they meet

Synoptic Gospels the Gospels of Matthew, Mark, and Luke

Talmud in Judaism, a central text that records rabbis' discussions of Jewish law, ethics, and other aspects of Jewish life

Tao (Dao) in Chinese thought, the inherently orderly working of the universe; sometimes translated as "the Way"

Tao Te Ching (Daodejing) the most important text in Taoism, attributed to Lao Tzu

tawhid in Islam, the principle that there is only one God and that God is one rather than three persons

Teleological Argument an argument for the existence of God based on the order and apparent design in the universe; also called the Argument from Design

theodicy an explanation of how God can be just even with all the evil in the world

theosis in Orthodox Christianity, becoming like God and unified with God

thetan in Scientology, the spirit or soul of a person

Three Sacred Treasures in Shinto, the mirror, sword, and jewel, representing wisdom, valor, and wealth or generosity

Tiamat a goddess in ancient Babylon, representing disorder and evil

Torah one of the most essential words in Judaism, with several meanings: in a narrow sense, Torah is the first five books of the Bible; broadly, Torah includes the Bible and the Talmud

tradition a group's beliefs and practices insofar as they are associated with that group's ultimate concerns, values, and ideas about the meaning of life

Trinity in Christianity, the three persons who together are God

Tripitaka in Buddhism, the "Three Baskets" of writings thought to contain the Buddha's original teachings

Triratna, the Three Jewels, the Three Refuges in Buddhism, the phrase "I take refuge in the Buddha, the Dharma, and the Sangha"

Tsao Chun in China, a kitchen god

Tu-Di-Gong in China, a god who watches over a particular place

Twelvers a branch of Shi'a Muslims who accept the legitimacy of twelve generations of Imams, ending in the 9th century

Umayyads Islamic caliphate that ruled from 661 to 750 from Damascus

unlimited virtues in Buddhism, loving-kindness, compassion, sympathetic joy, and even-temperedness

Upanishads Hindu philosophical texts that reflect on humans and their place in the universe

Utilitarianism an ethical system in which good actions are those that bring the greatest happiness to the greatest number of people

Vaishnava (Vaishnavite) a follower of the Hindu god Vishnu

Vajrayana (Diamond Vehicle) a form of Buddhism that involves visualizing oneself as a Buddha

varnas the four social classes in traditional Indian culture: the Brahmanas (priests, teachers, and intellectuals); the Kshatriyas (warriors, police, and administrators); the Vaishyas (farmers, merchants, and business people); and the Shudras (artisans and workers)

Vishnu one of the major gods in Hinduism, the preserver and protector of the world

wiccaning the Wiccan ritual comparable to infant baptism in Christianity

Wiccan Rede a basic moral principle in Wicca: "An ye harm none, do what ye will"

witch a human being with supernatural powers derived from secret knowledge of nature

wu-wei the main virtue in Taoism – letting things happen on their own

yeshiva a Jewish school

yin and yang Chinese terms for complementary opposites such as cold and hot, wet and dry

yoga in Hinduism, a religious discipline

Yom Kippur in Judaism, the Day of Atonement, at which people are penitent for their sins

yoni in Hinduism, a sculpture resembling a vagina, symbolizing the origin of life

Yoruba a West African group who came to the Americas as slaves and developed the traditions of Santeria and Vodou

Zealots Jewish group in the first century CE who fought against the Romans in Palestine

Zen a form of Buddhism that emphasizes meditation and sudden awakening, and that questions the value of words, concepts, and rational thinking; known as Chan in China

INDEX

Abbasids   xix, 176–177
Abraham   xvi, 20, 35–36, 83, 125–126,
    129–135, 151, 153, 167–168, 170,
    248, 287, 312
Aditi   213
agency-detection system   109–110
Agni   213, 232, 265
ahimsa   235, 338
Ahura Mazda   20, 278–281
Allah   xix, 134, 167, 175, 196
Amaterasu   285
American Academy of Religion   309,
    322–326
Amida Buddha (Amhitabha)   240, 262
anatta (anatman)   233
ancestors   32, 247, 251–253, 257,
    266–267, 269, 279, 282, 284, 322
Angra Mainyu   20, 278–279, 281
anicca   233
anima   59–61
animism   59–61, 105–106, 108–109, 117,
    122, 284, 299
Anselm of Canterbury   85, 161, 163
anthropomorphism   48, 50, 105–106,
    108–109, 127, 184, 199
anti-Semitism   175, 305
apartheid   194–195
apocalypse   28, 134, 152, 157
Apocalypse of John (Revelation)   28, 157
Apostles   156–157, 166
Aquinas, Thomas   51–52, 56, 161
archetypes   98–99
argument from design, see teleological
    argument
arhat   239
Aristotle   48–51, 60, 143, 177
Arius of Alexandria   158
Arjuna   217–218, 221
ark   149, 190
artha   225
Aryans   211
asceticism   221
asha   20, 27, 36–37
Asherah   55, 131–133

Ashoka   xvii, 237
Ashura   182
assumption   291
astrology   30
atheism   51–52, 81, 95, 148, 208, 312, 319
atman   214–216, 219, 230, 233, 333
atonement   85–87, 150, 163
Attis   64
auditing   293
Augustine of Hippo   10, 19, 97, 160–161,
    165, 295
Austin, James   332
Avalokitesvara   239
avatar   210, 218, 221, 338, 340
Avestas   7, 27, 281
awakening, see enlightenment
Axial Age   254
Ayala, Francisco   331
Aztecs   12

Baal   55, 131–132
Babylon   38, 130, 134, 137
Babylonian Captivity   134, 137
Baha'i   276, 287–291
Baha Ullah   275, 287–288, 290
Bali   90
baptism   39, 156, 158, 166, 298
bar mitzvah/bat mitzvah   149
Barong   91
Beatitudes   153–154
Bellah, Robert   79, 95–96, 101
Beltane   277, 298
Berger, Peter   94–95, 150, 309, 313, 319
Bhagavad Gita   xvii, 220, 221, 242
bhakti   220–221
Big Bang Theory   88
Bismallah   180–181
Bodhisattva   237–239, 243
Bodin, Jean   39
bracketing   82, 95
Brahma   209, 219
Brahman   209, 214–216, 218–219, 230,
    233, 250, 333
Brahmin   33, 252–253

brain   109, 310, 330–335
bris   149
Buddha   6–7, 26, 21, 230–240, 242, 254,
    260–264
Buddhism   208–209, 229–243, 260–265
Bultmann, Rudolf   184, 192
Burnham, Sophy   332

calendars   107
Calvin, John   xx, 73, 86–87, 61, 63, 165
Campbell, Joseph   77, 84, 99
Canaan   xvi, 128–130, 133, 248
canon   128, 158, 238, 256
capitalism   47, 65–66, 72–74, 314
cargo cult   63
castes   223–224, 230
Chan Buddhism, see Zen Buddhism
Charlemagne   xix, 39, 55, 176
Chauvet Cave   37
Ch'ing Ming   267
Christianity   151–167
chuppah   150
church   4, 72
Church Fathers   137
Church, Forrest   18
Church of England   55, 165, 193
civil religion   95–96
Comanche   21
Communism   270
Comparative Religions   7
Confucianism   255–257
Confucius   xvi, 8, 248, 254–258, 260–261
Conservative (Masorti) Judaism   148, 151
Constantine   xviii, 50–51, 157–160
Constitution of Medina   175
contraception   317–318
Corn King   62, 64
cosmology   143, 186, 189
coven   194
Cox, Harvey   313
Craig, William Lane   87–89
creation myth   31–32
Crossan, John Dominic   186–187,
    191–192

Crowley, Aleister   294
cult   4, 266, 271, 278
Cybelé   64

Dalai Lama   xx, xxi, 238, 241
dalits   224
Dana   236
D'Aquili, Eugene   334
darshana   226
Darwin, Charles   65, 105, 189
David, king of Israel   xvi, 130, 134, 151
Dawkins, Richard   311–312
Dead Sea Scrolls   136, 184
death   17–18, 22–26, 60–61, 106,
      111–116, 120, 150–151, 161, 163,
      173, 216, 229, 234, 240, 251,
      267–268, 288, 294–295, 328
demythologizing scripture   185
Denmark   319
Dennett, Daniel   311–313
denomination   4
desecularization   95, 318
Devi   221
dharma   6, 217, 221, 225, 232, 235,
      243, 279
Di (Shang-di)   251, 253, 266
Dianetics   291
diaspora   136
din   6, 131, 167–168, 170, 251, 279, 321
divination   30, 252–253, 255–256, 260,
      285, 339
Divine Command Ethics   36, 144
divine right kingship   39
dogmatic theology   51, 70
Douglas, Mary   101, 145, 181
Dream Sharing Ritual   304
druj   27, 36
dualism   61, 291
dukkha   232
Durga   210, 223
Durkheim, Emile   71–72, 75, 79, 83, 117,
      142, 311, 320

Easter   9, 64
Eastern Orthodox churches   xix, 160, 163
Ecclesiastes   22, 128
ecumenical council   xviii, 192
ecumenical movement   166
Eid al-Adha   84, 181
Einstein, Albert   41
Eliade, Mircea   78, 83–85, 100–101, 106,
      188, 265
Electro-psychometer   293
Ellis, Albert   329
engrams   292–293
enlightenment (awakening)   208, 226,
      238, 260, 263, 292

Enlightenment   85, 99, 141–145, 147–148
entheogen   212
Enuma Elish   27
epistemology   143
Epistles   155, 158
Esack, Farid   194–196
eschaton   28
Essenes   135–136
essentialism   77–78, 83, 100–101, 106
Evil, Problem of   17–19
exclusivism   7
exteriorization   293
Ezra   134

False Face Society   303–304
falsifiability   81
Falun Gong   270–271
Feminist Theology   196–203
feng-shui   260
fertility goddess   106, 113, 118, 131
Five Classics   xvii, 256
Flew, Antony   81
folk religion   162
Four Noble Truths   231–233
Four Stages of Life   223, 226
Fox sisters   23
Frazer, James   61–62, 64–65, 109
Frederick the Great   74
Freud, Sigmund   45–46, 68–70, 79,
      83, 96, 98–100, 112, 244, 292, 304,
      311–312, 329
functionalism   72, 100–101
fundamentalism   29, 189–191, 311, 319

Gandhi, Mohandas (Mahatma)   xxi, 224,
      228–229
Ganesha   7–8, 227
Gardner, Gerald   294–296
Gathas   279
Geertz, Clifford   89–91
Gemara   xviii, 137
Genesis   10, 27, 31, 53, 128–129, 133,
      138, 145, 189–190, 197
genetic (historical) theory   100
ghee   211, 226
ghost   23, 60–61, 100, 105, 243, 311
Gillespie, Dizzy   289
God, goodness of   17–19, 81–82
God, names of   133–134
God, proofs for the existence of   51–52,
      87–89, 161
goddess, fertility, see fertility goddess
Gospel   xvii, 28, 135, 151, 54, 56–58, 184,
      187, 194, 200
Great Schism   xix, 163
guru   240
Gutierrez, Gustavo   192–194

hadith   169, 203, 279
Haiti   20
halal   145, 181
Hammurabi   38
handfasting   298
Hanukkah   135, 149, 150
haram   145
harijans   224
Harris, Sam   311–312
Hasidism   141
Haskelah   142, 147
hatha yoga   219, 333
Hawking, Stephen   88
health   97, 162, 211, 251, 282, 291, 309,
      327–330
Hebrew Bible   10, 20, 24–25, 27–28, 31,
      35–36, 53–54, 67, 92–93, 112, 120,
      126–135, 137, 144, 153, 155, 167,
      184, 192
Hephaestus   119–120
hermeneutic   203
Hick, John   85–87
hierophany   84
hijra   xviii, 174
Hinayana, see Theravada
Hinduism   208–229
hiraba   35
historical (higher) criticism   54–55
historical (genetic) theory   100
historicism   202
History of Religions   7, 84, 100, 126, 279
Hitchens, Christopher   311, 313, 322
Hobbes, Thomas   30
Holi   227
Horned God   294
houris   173, 279
hsaio   257
Hsun Tzu   30
Hubbard, L. Ron   291–293
Humanae Vitae   316–317
Hume, David   80, 88
hunter-gatherers   107, 115–116,
      118, 283
Husserl, Edmund   82, 95

Ibn Khaldun   177, 179
Ibn Taymiyya   179
Imbolc (Candlemas)   298
immune system   353–354
Indra   213, 221, 265
indulgence   165
Indus Valley civilization   xi, xvi, 211
illusion   69–70, 75, 232, 235, 250
Irenaeus   19
Iroquois Confederacy   298
Islam   167–183
Islamism   180

James, William 96–98, 215, 330–331
jati 224
Jefferson, Thomas 74
jen (ren) 257
Jesus of Nazareth xvii, 10, 24, 36, 50, 54,
  64, 85–87, 98, 136, 140, 151–159,
  161–167, 170, 184, 186–188,
  190–192, 194, 198, 200, 212, 218,
  241, 262, 287, 312
Jesus Seminar 187
jihad 171, 173, 202
jnana yoga 219, 221
Job 47–48
John Templeton Foundation 330–331
Jones, Rev. Jim 12
Joshua 128, 130
Judaism 126–151
Jung, Carl 98–100

Kaaba xix, 175, 181–182
Kabbala 141
Kali 120, 223
Kalki 221
Kama Sutra 22
kami 283–287
kamikaze 284
Kannon 239–240
Kant, Immanuel 80
Kaplan, Mordechai 148
karma 36–37, 207, 216–217, 220–221,
  229, 232, 235–236
karma yoga 221
kashrut (kosher) 145
khalifah 168–169
koan 240, 263
Koestler, Arthur 18, 27
Kojiki 283, 285
kosher 145, 148, 181
Krishna 7, 210, 217–218, 220–221,
  227, 287
Kuan Kung 266

The Lady 294
Lao Tzu xvi, 258–261
Lascaux, France 107–108
Law of Threefold Return (Rule of
  Three) 296
leaders, ideal types of 72
Left Behind 29
Leibniz, Gottfried 19
Lerner, Gerda 300
Leviticus 11, 53, 93, 128–129,
  145, 153, 241
li 257
Liberation Theology 192–193, 196, 198
lingam 221
lived religion 162, 265

logical positivism 81
longhouses 299, 303
The Lord 294
Lourdes, France 326–327
Lughnasadh (Lammas) 298
Luther, Martin xx, 140, 161, 163–167,
  201, 262

magic 6, 46, 61–65
magick 294, 296
Mahabharata xvii, 221
Mahayana xviii–xix, 238–240
Mahdi 183
Maimonides, Moses 140–141
mantra 227, 239
Manu, Laws of xvii, 34, 216, 223–226
Mao Zedong xxi, 269–270
maqasid 174
Marduk 27
marga 220–221
Marx, Karl 65–68, 83, 100, 311
Mary, mother of Jesus xviii, 10, 64,
  98, 162–163, 170, 187, 200, 240,
  326–327
Masorti, see Conservative Judaism
matriarchy 300
maya 250
McCutcheon, Russell 322
Mecca xviii–xix, 41, 170, 172, 174–175,
  181–182
megachurch 315–316
Mehta, Zubin 281
Mencius xvii, 30, 256–257
Mendelssohn, Moses 147
Mercury, Freddie 280–281
Mesopotamia xx, 10, 27, 118, 120,
  132, 212
Messiah 134–136, 141, 150–152, 154,
  170, 183, 194, 200, 221
mikvah 156
minyan 134
Mishnah xvii, xviii, 137–138, 140
mitzvah (plural mitzvot) 138, 145, 153
Mohenjo-daro 211
moksha 216, 225, 228–229
monasticism 135, 166, 236, 243
monism 215
monogamy 203
monotheism 24, 62, 69–70, 84, 140, 146,
  159, 167, 171, 183, 208, 278, 281
Mosaic Law 129, 135, 137, 141, 146
Moses xvi, 53–54, 69, 129–131, 133,
  135, 137, 141, 146, 151, 184, 188,
  194, 199, 287
mosque 206–207
Muhammad xviii–xix, 168–171, 174–175
Müller, Max 5, 57–58

Museum of Creation 190–191
mystical experience 97, 215–216, 331–335
mysticism 183, 215
myth 31–32, 41, 84, 119, 188, 248,
  311, 335

Nagarjuna xvii, 240
Navaratri 201–210
Neandertals 113
Neolithic Revolution 118–121
Neopaganism 294
neurotheology 330–335
New Religious Movements 278, 319
New Testament xviii, 11, 126–127, 155,
  158, 184–186, 197
Newberg, Andrew 334–335
Nicene Creed xviii, 51, 158
Nietzsche, Friedrich 66
Nihon Shoki 283
Ninety-Five Theses 164
nirvana 230, 232, 239–240, 242–243,
  260, 262, 264
Noble Eightfold Path 232
Norūz 281–2
numinous 83
Nun Bun 110

Old Testament 10, 20, 24–25, 27–28, 31,
  35–36, 53–54, 67, 92–93, 112, 120,
  126–135, 137, 144, 153, 155,
  167, 184
Om 215–216, 218
oracle bones 252–253
oral cultures 59, 115–119, 143, 285,
  298–299, 304, 335
Original Sin 19–20, 68, 70, 73, 85, 161,
  163, 165–166
Orthodox churches xix, 160, 163–164,
  166, 193
Orthodox Judaism 126, 141, 148–149,
  196, 198
Otto, Rudolf 82–83, 101

pagan 276–277, 302, 320
Paleolithic era (Old Stone Age) 37,
  113–115
Paley, William 87–88
parable 152–153, 234
Parsees 20, 280–281
Parvati 223
patriarchy 118–119, 196, 201, 300
Paul VI, Pope 316–317
pentagram 296, 305
Pharaoh 186
Pharisees 135, 137
phenomenology 82–85
philosophy 47–52, 80–82, 85–89, 99–100

pilgrimage   40–41, 162, 181, 240, 243, 262
Pillars of Islam   180–181
Pius IX, Pope   39, 316
Plaskow, Judith   198–199
Plato   48, 161, 177
pluralism   7, 175, 268
pope   xviii–xix, 39, 160, 163, 165–167, 198, 316–318, 321
popular religion   162
prajna   239
prasada   226
predestination   165
presbyter   158
printing press   52
Problem of Evil   18–19, 51
profane   71, 84, 122, 296, 320–321
Protestant Ethic   72–74
Protestant Reformation   xx, 55, 73, 140, 164, 201
Psalms   128–133
psychoneuroimmunology   327
psychopomp   279
Ptolemy   143
puja   226
Puranas   xvii, 216, 221, 223
Pure Land Buddhism   xviii–xix, 240, 262
Purgatory   165–166
purity (impurity)   34, 91–94, 136, 146, 153, 156, 181, 224, 280, 282
Purusha   33–34, 249–250

Qur'an   xix, 126–127, 167–174, 178, 194, 196, 202–203, 279

Ramadan   181
Ramayana   xvii, 210, 216–217
Rangda the witch   90–91
Rashidun   176
Rawls, John   321
Reconstructionist Judaism   148–151
Red Jacket   301–302
reductionism   79, 83–84, 100
Reform Judaism   142, 144–148, 150
reincarnation   26, 61, 209, 216, 293
Religionswissenschaft   5, 57, 58
religious experience   41, 82–83, 96–97, 212, 331, 335
religious naturalism   148
resurgent Islam   313–314
resurgence of religion   313–316
resurrection   24–25, 135, 146, 158, 186–187
Revelation (Apocalypse of John)   xvii, 28–29
Rig Veda   33, 58, 213
rishis   213
rita   36, 211

rites of passage   117, 159, 227, 229, 243, 267, 298
Robertson, Pat   20
Rochefoucauld, François de La   22
Roman Catholic Church   xxi, 39, 56, 73, 160, 163–167, 189, 192, 196, 296, 316
Romulus and Remus   188
Rosh Hashanah   150
Ruether, Rosemary Radford   199–201
Rumi   179, 183

Sabbat   297–298
Sabbath   10, 138, 148–149, 153, 180
sacrament   73, 166, 396
sacred, as opposed to worldly, secular, or profane   5, 71, 78, 84–85, 122, 321–322
Sadducees   135–136
sadhu   221
Sagan, Carl   309
Samaritans   132, 153
Samhain   298
samsara   216, 229, 232
San-chiao   251
sangha   230, 232, 236, 243
sannyasi   226
Sanskrit   57–58, 211
Santeria   30, 37
Saoshyant   278
Sarasvati   210, 213, 220–221
Schleiermacher, Friedrich   82
Schmookler, Andrew Bard   300
Schneerson, Rebbe Menachem   141–142
Scientology   4, 291–294
Scopes "Monkey Trial"   190
Second Temple   134, 136–137
sect   3–4, 278
secularization   72, 74, 95–96, 311–322
Seder   84, 149–150
Seneca (American tribe)   298–304, 335
Seneca (philosopher)   45
Sengai   264
sexism   198–200, 288, 311
Shahada   171, 180
shaman   37, 66, 114, 116
Shang Period   xvi, 251–253
Sharia   174
Shaiva (Shaivite)   221–222
Shakti   223, 240
she'ol   24
Shi'i Islam   39, 169, 182
Shinto   7, 283–287
Shiva   209, 221–223, 240
Shoah   305
Siddhartha Gautama   xvi, 213, 230–231, 260

Sinai   129, 137, 151
sitting shivah   150
skandhas   234
slavery   11, 198
Smart, Ninian   41, 311
Smith, Jonathan Z.   12, 320
Smith, Wilfred Cantwell   13–14, 162
Smith, William Robertson   54–55
Socrates   48
soma   211–213
"The Sorcerer"   114–115
source criticism   52–54
spells   62, 111, 296–297
Spinoza, Baruch   53–54
Spiritualism   23
Stanton, Elizabeth Cady   196–198
Stark, Rodney   74
Stupa   233, 236, 242–243
Sufism   179, 183
Sukkot   150
Summerland   294
Sunna   169
Sunni Islam   169, 182–183
Sweden   318–319
sympathetic magic   62
Synoptic Gospels   184

Talmud   xviii, 135, 137, 139–140, 142, 147, 241
Tanka   264
Tao (Dao), Taoism   258–260
Tao Te Ching (Daodejing)   258–259
taqwa   178–179
tawhid   197
teleological argument   87
terrorism   35, 173, 180
theodicy   19–22, 132
theology   47–52, 85, 140, 161, 163, 192–203
theory   79, 99–101
theosis   163
Theravada (Hinayana)   xvii–xx, 237–238, 242–243
thetan   291–294
Thirty Years War   xx, 56
Three Sacred Treasures   285
Tiamat   27
Tillich, Paul   41
Tokusan   264
Torah   xvii, 127–135, 135, 137, 141, 148–149, 167, 170, 199
torii gate   286
totemism   71
Trinity   159, 170–171, 197
Tripitaka   238
Triratna, the Three Jewels, the Three Refuges   236

Troeltsch, Ernst   310
Tsao Chun   266–267
Tu-Ti-Gong   266
Tutu, Desmond   3
Twelvers   183
Tylor, Edward Burnett   58–61, 99–100, 108–109, 311

Umayyads   xix, 176–177
Unam Sanctam   321
unconscious   69, 79, 98–99, 292
unlimited virtues   235
Untouchables   224
Upanishads   xvi, 7, 213–216, 332–333
Upper Paleolithic era   106, 113–115
Utilitarianism   292

Vaishnava (Vaishnavite)   221, 223
Vajrayana (Diamond Vehicle)   xviii, 238, 240–242
varnas   34, 223, 279
Vedanta   214

Vedas   xvi, 58, 211, 213–214
Venus of Willendorf   113
verifiability   81–82
Vishnu   7, 209–210, 217–218, 221, 265
Vodou   30
Voltaire   17, 74

Wadud, Amina   201–203
Weber, Max   72–74
Wellhausen, Julius   54, 184
Westphalia formula   56
Whirling Dervishes   178, 183
Wicca   294–298, 305
wiccaning   298
Wiccan Rede   295
witch   90–91, 111
Woolston, Thomas   74
world religion   276
wu-wei   258–260, 263

Xenophanes   48–50

Yahweh   xvi, 55, 97, 120, 131, 135
Yellow River valley   120, 248
yeshiva   137
yin and yang   250
yoga   219–221, 240, 242, 333
Yom Kippur   150, 182
yoni   221
Yoruba   30, 37

zakat   181
Zealots   136
Zen Buddhism   xviii–xix, xxi, 240, 243, 262–264, 334
Zeus   58, 119–120, 135, 188, 265
Zhou Period   xvi, 253
Zhuang Tzu   xvii, 259–260
Zohar   141
Zoroaster   278–279, 281, 287
Zoroastrianism   7, 20, 24–25, 27, 36, 173, 212, 278–282
Zuckerman, Phil   319–320